Pg

2 Init Pg 109

84   Where is OSTCBPrioTbl initializ ⬦

82   C CONSTRUCT .. != OR-EQUAL?

97   Can An ISR (which must be in Assembler) call a C-function?

109   When would OSTCBList ever = ∅?

85   Where is OSPrioCur established? in OSStart, Pg 102

92   implications of "tAsk may not be pending when ISR posts..."

85   Details of context switch ... OSCtxSw().

102✓   Details of OSStartHighRdy() - Pg 198

141   It SAYS OS.EVENT.SEM. DOES IT MEAN OS.EVENT-TYPE.SEM?

149   "..# of times an event can be signalled" - what does this mean?

✱ 151   If EventType <> Sem, why doesn't the function return immediately?

✱ 151   Reverse the order of those two tests.

✱ 148   Possible way to "Un-Suspend" a Task inadvertently?

✱ 152   If no tasks are waiting when semaphore is posted, EVENT COUNTER IS INCREMENTED. WHY? HOW USED?

✱ 153   In checking the Event type, why return ∅ if there is an error?

✱ 182   Typo? OSMemFreeList should be pmem?

198/203   why is call to OSTaskSwHook() necessary?

109   OSStartHighRdy() - ? This function is not called from anywhere else? i.e. It is only used here?

58   - Task synchronization questions

OS-CPU.H   76,114
OS-CPU_A.ASM   102   OS_CPU_C.C   110,107

OS-CORE.C   88,103,99

OS-CONFIG.H   82,99

OS-CFG.H _____   77,82,116,130,99,134,144

uCOS-II.H   81,150,117

OS-TASK.C   105,109
OS-TIME.C _____ 133

MicroC/OS-II

The Real-Time Kernel

Jean J. Labrosse

OSTASKStkInit( )   107

CMP Books
Lawrence, Kansas 66046

Assembler Routines:
  Tick ISR   96
  ANY ISR   91

Context Switching Code   80
  OSCtxSw( )   85 & OSIntCtxSw( ) 95
? OSIntEnter( ) } 91 & 94
? OSIntExit( ) }

MACROS   OS-TASK-SW( )   85
  OS_ENTER_CRITICAL } 76
  OS-EXIT-CRITICAL }

CMP Books
CMP Media, Inc.
1601 West 23rd Street, Suite 200
Lawrence, KS 66046
USA
www.cmpbooks.com

Acquisitions Editor:	Berney Williams
Managing Editor:	Michelle Dowdy
Copyeditor:	Rita Sooby
Cover Art Design:	Robert Ward

Distributed in the U.S. and Canada by:
Publishers Group West
1700 Fourth Street
Berkeley, CA 94710
1-800-788-3123
www.pgw.com

ISBN: 0-87930-543-6

R&D Developer Series

RRD #4 02/01

Table of Contents

•

To my loving and caring wife, Manon, and to our two lovely children James and Sabrina

Preface

My first book, *μC/OS, The Real-Time Kernel*, is now six years old, and the publisher has sold well over 15,000 copies around the world. When I was asked to do a second edition, I thought it would be a fairly straightforward task — a few corrections here and there, clarify a few concepts, add a function or two to the kernel, and so on. If you have a copy of the first edition, you will notice that *μC/OS-II, The Real-Time Kernel* is, in fact, a major revision. For some strange reason, I wasn't satisfied with minor corrections. Also, when my publisher told me that, this time, the book would be in hard cover, I really wanted to give you your moneys' worth. In all, I added more than 200 new pages and rewrote the majority of the pages I did keep. I added a porting guide to help you migrate μC/OS-II to the processor of your choice, and I added a chapter that will guide you through a μC/OS to μC/OS-II upgrade.

The code for μC/OS-II is basically the same as that of μC/OS, but it contains a number of new and useful features, has better commenting, and should be easier to port to processor architectures. μC/OS-II offers all the features provided in μC/OS as well as the following new features.

- A fixed-sized block memory manager.

- A service that allows a task to suspend its execution for a certain amount of time (specified in hours, minutes, seconds, and milliseconds).

- User-definable callout functions that are invoked when

    - a task is created,

    - a task is deleted,

    - a context switch is performed, or

    - a clock tick occurs.

- A new task create function that provides additional features.

- Stack checking.

- A function that returns the version of μC/OS-II.

μC/OS-II Goals

Probably the most important goal I had for μC/OS-II was to make it backward compatible with μC/OS (at least from an application's standpoint). A μC/OS port might need to be modified to work with μC/OS-II, but the application code should require only minor changes (if any). Also, because μC/OS-II is based on the same core as µC/OS, it is just as reliable. I added conditional compilation to allow you to further reduce the amount of RAM (data space) needed by µC/OS-II. This is especially useful when you have resource-limited products. I also added the features described in the previous section and cleaned up the code.

In the book, I wanted to clarify some of the concepts described in the first edition and to provide additional explanations about how µC/OS-II works. I had numerous requests to write a chapter on how to port µC/OS, so Chapter 8, Porting µC/OS-II, has been included in this book.

Intended Audience

This book is intended for embedded systems programmers, consultants, and students interested in real-time operating systems. µC/OS-II is a high-performance, deterministic, real-time kernel and can be embedded in commercial products (see , Licensing & the µC/OS-II Web Site). Instead of writing your own kernel, you should consider µC/OS-II. You will find, as I did, that writing a kernel is not as easy as it first looks.

I'm assuming that you know C and have a minimum knowledge of assembly language. You should also understand microprocessor architectures.

What You Need to Use µC/OS-II

The code supplied with this book assumes that you will be using an AT-compatible PC (80386 minimum) running under DOS 4.x or higher. The code was compiled with Borland International's C++ V3.1. You should have about 5Mb of free disk space on you hard drive. I compiled and executed the sample code provided in this book in a DOS window under Windows 95.

To use µC/OS-II on a different target processor, you need to port it to that processor or obtain a previously written port from the µC/OS-II official Web site at `http://www.uCOS-II.com`. You also need appropriate software development tools, such as an ANSI C compiler, an assembler, a linker/locator, and some way of debugging your application.

The µC/OS Story

Many years ago, I designed a product based on an Intel 80C188 at Dynalco Controls, and I needed a real-time kernel. I had been using a well-known kernel (I'll call it kernel A) in my work for a previous employer, but it was too expensive for the application I was designing. I found a lower cost kernel ($1,000 at the time), I'll call it kernel B, and started the design. I spent about two months trying to get a couple of very simple tasks to run. I was calling the vendor almost on a daily basis for help to make it work. The vendor claimed that kernel B was written in C; however, I had to initialize every single object using assembly language code. Although the vendor was very patient, I decided that I had had enough. The product was falling behind schedule, and I really didn't want to spend my time debugging this low-cost kernel. It turns out that I was one of the vendor's first customers, and the kernel really was not fully tested and debugged.

To get back on track, I decided to go back and use kernel A. The cost was about $5,000 for five development seats, and I had to pay a per-usage fee of about $200 for each unit that was shipped. This was a lot of money at the time, but it bought some peace of mind. I got the kernel up and running in about two days. Three months into the project, one of my engineers discovered what looked like a bug in the kernel. I sent the code to the vendor, and sure enough, the bug was confirmed as being in the kernel. The vendor provided a 90-day warranty, but that had expired, so in order to get support, I had to pay an additional $500 per year for maintenance. I argued with the salesperson for a few months that they should fix the bug since I was actually doing them a favor. They wouldn't budge. Finally, I gave in and bought the maintenance contract, and the vendor fixed the bug six months later. Yes, six months later! I was furious and, most importantly, late delivering the product. In all, it took close to a year to get the product to work reliably with kernel A. I must admit, however, that I have had no problems with it since.

As this was going on, I naively thought that it couldn't be that difficult to write a kernel. All it needs to do is save and restore processor registers. That's when I decided to try to write my own kernel (part time, nights and weekends). It took me about a year to get the kernel to work as well, and in some ways better, than kernel A. I didn't want to start a company and sell it because there were already about 50 kernels out there, so why have another one?

Then I thought of writing a paper for a magazine. First I went to *C User's Journal* (CUJ) because the kernel was written in C. I had heard CUJ was offering $100 per published page when other magazines were only paying $75 per page. My paper had 70 or so pages, so that would be nice compensation for all the time I spent working on my kernel. Unfortunately, the article was rejected for two reasons. First, the article was too long, and the magazine didn't want to publish a series. Second, they didn't want "another kernel article."

I decided to turn to *Embedded Systems Programming* (ESP) magazine because my kernel was designed for embedded systems. I contacted the editor of ESP (Mr. Tyler Sperry) and told him that I had a kernel I wanted to publish in his magazine. I got the same response from Tyler that I did from CUJ: "Not another kernel article?" I told him that this kernel was different — it was preemptive, it was comparable to many commercial kernels, and the source code could be posted on the ESP BBS (Bulletin Board Service). I was calling Tyler two or three times a week, basically begging him to publish my article. He finally gave in, probably because he was tired of my calls. My article was edited down from 70 pages to about 30 pages and was published in two consecutive months (May and June 1992). The article was probably the most popular article in 1992. ESP had over 500 downloads of the code from the BBS in the first month. Tyler may have feared for his life because kernel vendors were upset that he published a kernel in his magazine. I guess that these vendors must have recognized the quality and capabilities of μC/OS (called μCOS then). The article was really the first that exposed the internal workings of a real-time kernel, so some of the secrets were out.

About the time the article came out in ESP, I got a call from Dr. Bernard (Berney) Williams at CMP Books, CMP Media, Inc. (publisher of CUJ) six months after the initial contact with CUJ. He had left a message with my wife and told her that he was interested in the article. I called him back and said, "Don't you think you are a little bit late with this? The article is being published in ESP." Berney said, "No, No, you don't understand. Because the article is so long, I want to make a book out of it." Initially, Berney simply wanted to publish what I had (as is), so the book would only have 80 pages or so. I told him that if I was going to write a book, I wanted to do it right. I then spent about six months adding content to what is now known as the first edition. In all, the book published at about 250 pages. I changed the name from μCOS to μC/OS because ESP readers had been calling it "mucus," which didn't sound too healthy. Come to think of it, maybe it was a kernel vendor that first came up with the name. Anyway, *μC/OS, The Real-Time Kernel* was born. Sales were somewhat slow to start. Berney and I had projected about 4,000 to 5,000 copies would be sold in the life of the book, but at the rate it was selling, I thought we'd be lucky if it sold 2,000 copies. Berney insisted that these things take time to get known, so he continued advertising in CUJ for about a year.

A month or so before the book came out, I went to my first Embedded Systems Conference (ESC) in Santa Clara, California (September 1992). I met Tyler Sperry for the first time, and I showed him a copy of the first draft of my book. He very quickly glanced at it and asked if I would like to speak at the next

Embedded Systems Conference in Atlanta. Not knowing any better, I said I would and asked him what I should talk about. He suggested "Using Small Real-Time Kernels." On the trip back from California, I was thinking, "What did I get myself into? I've never spoken in front of a bunch of people before. What if I make a fool of myself? What if what I speak about is common knowledge? People pay good money to attend this conference." For the next six months, I prepared my lecture. At the conference, I had more than 70 attendees. In the first twenty minutes I must have lost one pound of sweat. After my lecture, about 15 people or so came up to me to say that they were very pleased with the lecture and liked my book. I was invited back to the conference but could not attend the one in Santa Clara that year (1993). I was able to attend the next conference in Boston (1994), and I have been a regular speaker at ESC ever since. For the past couple of years, I've been on the conference Advisory Committee. I now do at least three lectures at every conference and each has an average attendance of between 200 and 300 people. My lectures are almost always ranked among the top 10% at the conference.

To date, well over 15,000 copies of *µC/OS, The Real-Time Kernel* have been sold around the world. I have received and answered well over 1,000 e-mails from many countries. In 1995, *µC/OS, The Real-Time Kernel* was translated into Japanese and published in Japan in a magazine called *Interface*. µC/OS has been ported to, among others, the following processors.

Analog Devices AD21xx
Advanced Risc Machines ARM6, ARM7
Hitachi 64180, H8/3xx, SH series
Intel 80x86 (Real and PM), Pentium, Pentium II, 8051, 8052, MCS-251, 80196, 8096
Mitsubishi M16 and M32
Motorola PowerPC, 68K, CPU32, CPU32+, 68HC11, 68HC16
Philips XA
Siemens 80C166 and TriCore
Texas instruments TMS320
Zilog Z-80 and Z-180

In 1994 I decided to write a second book: *Embedded Systems Building Blocks, Complete and Ready-to-Use Modules in C* (ESBB). For some reason, ESBB has not been as popular as µC/OS, although it contains much valuable information not found anywhere else. I always thought that it would be an ideal book for people just starting in the embedded world.

In 1998 I opened the official µC/OS WEB site www.uCOS-II.com. I intend this site to contain ports, application notes, links, answers to frequently asked questions (FAQs), upgrades for both µC/OS and µC/OS-II, and more. All I need is time!

Back in 1992, I never imagined that writing an article would change my life as it has. I met a lot of very interesting people and made a number of good friends in the process. I still answer every single e-mail that I receive. I believe that if you take the time to write me, I owe you a response. I hope you enjoy this book.

Acknowledgments

First and foremost, I would like to thank my wife for her support, encouragement, understanding, and especially patience. Manon must have heard the words, "Just one more week!" about a dozen times while I was writing this book. I would also like to thank my children James (age 8) and Sabrina (age 4) for putting up with the long hours I had to spend in front of the computer. I hope one day they will understand.

I would also like to thank Mr. Niall Murphy for carefully reviewing most of the chapters and providing me with valuable feedback. Special thanks to Mr. Alain Chebrou and Mr. Bob Paddock for passing the code for μC/OS-II through a fine tooth comb.

I would like to thank all the fine people at CMP Books for their help in making this book a reality and for putting up with my insistence on having things done my way.

Finally, I would like to thank all the people who have purchased *μC/OS, The Real-Time Kernel* as well as *Embedded Systems Building Blocks*. In doing so, they have encouraged me to pursue this interesting past-time.

Introduction

This book describes the design and implementation of μC/OS-II (pronounced "Micro C O S 2"), which stands for *MicroController Operating System Version 2*. μC/OS-II is based on *μC/OS, The Real-Time Kernel* that was first published in 1992. Thousands of people around the world are using μC/OS in all kinds of applications, such as cameras, medical instruments, musical instruments, engine controls, network adapters, highway telephone call boxes, ATM machines, industrial robots, and more. Numerous colleges and universities also have used μC/OS to teach students about real-time systems.

μC/OS-II is upward compatible with μC/OS V1.11 but provides many improvements, such as the addition of a fixed-sized memory manager; user-definable callouts on task creation, task deletion, task switch, and system tick; TCB extensions support; stack checking; and much more. I also added comments to just about every function, and I made μC/OS-II much easier to port to different processors. The source code in μC/OS was placed in two files. Because μC/OS-II contains many new features and functions, I decided to split μC/OS-II into a few source files to make the code easier to maintain.

If you currently have an application that runs with μC/OS, it should run virtually unchanged with μC/OS-II. All of the services (i.e., function calls) provided by μC/OS have been preserved. You may, however, have to change include files and product build files to "point" to the new filenames.

This book contains all the source code for μC/OS-II and a port for the Intel 80x86 processor running in *real mode* and for the *large model*. The code was developed on a PC running the Microsoft Windows 95 operating system. Examples run in a DOS-compatible box under the Windows 95 environment. Development was done using the Borland International C/C++ compiler V3.1. Although μC/OS-II was developed and tested on a PC, μC/OS-II was actually targeted for embedded systems and can be ported easily to many different processor architectures.

µC/OS-II Features

Source Code   As I mentioned previously, this book contains all the source code for µC/OS-II. I went to a lot of effort to provide you with a high-quality product. You may not agree with some of the style constructs that I use, but you should agree that the code is both clean and very consistent. Many commercial real-time kernels are provided in source form. I challenge you to find any such code that is as neat, consistent, well commented, and well organized as that in µC/OS-II. Also, I believe that simply giving you the source code is not enough. You need to know how the code works and how the different pieces fit together. You will find that type of information in this book. The organization of a real-time kernel is not always apparent when staring at many source files and thousands of lines of code.

Portable   Most of µC/OS-II is written in highly portable ANSI C, with target microprocessor-specific code written in assembly language. Assembly language is kept to a minimum to make µC/OS-II easy to port to other processors. Like µC/OS, µC/OS-II can be ported to a large number of microprocessors as long as the microprocessor provides a stack pointer and the CPU registers can be pushed onto and popped from the stack. Also, the C compiler should provide either in-line assembly or language extensions that allow you to enable and disable interrupts from C. µC/OS-II can run on most 8-, 16-, 32-, or even 64-bit microprocessors or microcontrollers and DSPs.

All the ports that currently exist for µC/OS can be converted to µC/OS-II in about an hour. Also, because µC/OS-II is upward compatible with µC/OS, your µC/OS applications should run on µC/OS-II with few or no changes. Check for the availability of ports on the µC/OS-II Web site at www.uCOS-II.com.

ROMable   µC/OS-II was designed for embedded applications. This means that if you have the proper tool chain (i.e., C compiler, assembler, and linker/locator), you can embed µC/OS-II as part of a product.

Scalable   I designed µC/OS-II so that you can use only the services you need in your application. This means that a product can use just a few µC/OS-II services, while another product can have the full set of features. This allows you to reduce the amount of memory (both RAM and ROM) needed by µC/OS-II on a per-product basis. Scalability is accomplished with the use of conditional compilation. Simply specify (through #define constants) which features you need for your application or product. I did everything I could to reduce both the code and data space required by µC/OS-II.

Preemptive   µC/OS-II is a fully preemptive real-time kernel. This means that µC/OS-II always runs the highest priority task that is ready. Most commercial kernels are preemptive, and µC/OS-II is comparable in performance with many of them.

Multitasking   µC/OS-II can manage up to 64 tasks; however, the current version of the software reserves eight of these tasks for system use. This leaves your application up to 56 tasks. Each task has a unique priority assigned to it, which means that µC/OS-II cannot do round-robin scheduling. There are thus 64 priority levels.

Deterministic   Execution time of all µC/OS-II functions and services are deterministic. This means that you can always know how much time µC/OS-II will take to execute a function or a service. Furthermore, except for one service, execution time of all µC/OS-II services do not depend on the number of tasks running in your application.

Task Stacks   Each task requires its own stack; however, μC/OS-II allows each task to have a different stack size. This allows you to reduce the amount of RAM needed in your application. With μC/OS-II's stack-checking feature, you can determine exactly how much stack space each task actually requires.

Services   μC/OS-II provides a number of system services, such as mailboxes, queues, semaphores, fixed-sized memory partitions, time-related functions, and so on.

Interrupt Management   Interrupts can suspend the execution of a task. If a higher priority task is awakened as a result of the interrupt, the highest priority task will run as soon as all nested interrupts complete. Interrupts can be nested up to 255 levels deep.

Robust and Reliable   μC/OS-II is based on μC/OS, which has been used in hundreds of commercial applications since 1992. μC/OS-II uses the same core and most of the same functions as μC/OS yet offers more features.

Figures, Listings, and Tables Convention

You will notice that when I reference a specific element in a figure, I use the letter "F" followed by the figure number. The number in parenthesis following the figure number represents a specific element in the figure that I am trying to bring your attention to. F1.2(3) thus means look at the item numbered "3" in Figure 1.2.

Listings and tables work exactly the same way except that a listing starts with the letter "L" and a table with the letter "T".

Source Code Conventions

All μC/OS-II objects (functions, variables, #define constants, and macros) start with OS, indicating that they are related to the Operating System. Functions are found in alphabetical order in all the source code files. This allows you to locate any function quickly.

You will find that the coding style I use is very consistent. I have been using the K&R style for many years; however, I have added some of my own enhancements to make the code (I believe) easier to read and maintain. Indention is always four spaces, Tabs are never used, at least one space appears on each side of an operator, comments are always to the right of code, and comment blocks are used to describe functions.

Table 1 provides the acronyms, abbreviations, and mnemonics (AAMs) used in this book. I combine some of these AAMs to make up function, variable, and #define names in a hierarchical way. For example, the function OSMboxCreate() reads like this: the function is part of the operating system (OS), it is related to the mailbox services (Mbox), and the operation performed is to Create a mailbox. All services that have similar operation share the same name. For example, OSSemCreate() and OSMboxCreate() perform the same operation, but on their respective objects (i.e., semaphore and mailbox, respectively).

Table 1 *Acronyms, abbreviations, and mnemonics used in*
this book.

Acronym, Abbreviation, or Mnemonic	Meaning
Addr	Address
Blk	Block
Chk	Check
Clr	Clear
Cnt	Count
CPU	Central Processing Unit
Ctr	Counter
Ctx	Context
Cur	Current
Del	Delete
Dly	Delay
Err	Error
Ext	Extension
FP	Floating Point
Grp	Group
HMSM	Hours Minutes Seconds Milliseconds
ID	Identifier
Init	Initialize
Int	Interrupt
ISR	Interrupt Service Routine
Max	Maximum
Mbox	Mailbox
Mem	Memory
Msg	Message
N	Number of
Opt	Option
OS	Operating System
Ovf	Overflow
Prio	Priority
Ptr	Pointer
Q	Queue
Rdy	Ready
Req	Request
Sched	Scheduler

Table 1 Acronyms, abbreviations, and mnemonics used in this book. (Continued)

Acronym, Abbreviation, or Mnemonic	Meaning
Sem	Semaphore
Stat	Status or statistic
Stk	Stack
Sw	Switch
Sys	System
Tbl	Table
TCB	Task Control Block
TO	Timeout

Chapter Contents

Chapter 1, Sample Code   This chapter is designed to allow you to experiment with and use µC/OS-II immediately. The chapter starts by showing you how to install the distribution diskette and describes the directories created. I then explain some of the coding conventions used. Before getting into the description of the examples, I describe the code used to access some of the services provided on a PC.

Chapter 2, Real-Time Systems Concepts   Here, I introduce you to some real-time systems concepts such as foreground/background systems, critical sections, resources, multitasking, context switching, scheduling, reentrancy, task priorities, mutual exclusion, semaphores, intertask communications, interrupts, and more.

Chapter 3, Kernel Structure   This chapter introduces you to µC/OS-II and its internal structure. You will learn about tasks, task states, and task control blocks; how µC/OS-II implements a ready list, task scheduling, and the idle task; how to determine CPU usage; how µC/OS-II handles interrupts; how to initialize and start µC/OS-II; and more.

Chapter 4, Task Management   This chapter describes µC/OS-II services that create a task, delete a task, check the size of a task's stack, change a task's priority, suspend and resume a task, and get information about a task.

Chapter 5, Time Management   This chapter describes how µC/OS-II can suspend a task's execution until some user-specified time expires, how such a task can be resumed, and how to get and set the current value of a 32-bit tick counter.

Chapter 6, Intertask Communication and Synchronization   This chapter describes µC/OS-II services that allow tasks and ISRs (Interrupt Service Routines) to communicate with one another and share resources. You will learn how semaphores, message mailboxes, and message queues are implemented.

Chapter 7, Memory Management   This chapter describes the µC/OS-II dynamic memory allocation feature using fixed-sized memory blocks.

Chapter 8, Porting μC/OS-II   This chapter describes in general terms what needs to be done to adapt μC/OS-II to different processor architectures.

Chapter 9, 80x86 Large Model Port   This chapter describes how μC/OS-II was ported to the Intel/AMD 80x86 processor architecture running in real mode and for the large model. Code and data space memory usage is provided as well as execution times for each of the functions.

Chapter 10, Upgrading from μC/OS to μC/OS-II   This chapter describes how easy it is to migrate a port done for μC/OS to μC/OS-II.

Chapter 11, Reference Manual   This chapter describes each of the functions (i.e., services) provided by μC/OS-II from an application developer's standpoint. Each function contains a brief description, its prototype, the name of the file where the function is found, a description of the function arguments and the return value, special notes, and examples.

Chapter 12, Configuration Manual   This chapter describes each of the #define constants used to configure μC/OS-II for your application. Configuring μC/OS-II allows you to use only the services required by your application. This gives you the flexibility to reduce the μC/OS-II memory footprint (code and data space).

Appendix A, Example Source Code   Fully commented source code for the examples and PC services (see Chapter 1) is provided in this appendix and consists of 11 files.

Appendix B, μC/OS-II Microprocessor-Independent Source Code   The source code for the portion of μC/OS-II that is not dependent on any specific processor is provided in this appendix and consists of nine files.

Appendix C, 80x86 Real-Mode, Large Model Source Code   The source code for the 80x86 processor-dependent functions is found in this appendix and consist of three files.

Appendix D, TO and HPLISTC   This appendix presents two DOS utilities: TO and HPLISTC. I use TO to move quickly between MS-DOS directories without having to type the CD (change directory) command. HPLISTC prints C source code in compressed mode (i.e., 17 cpi) and allows you to specify page breaks. The printout is assumed to be to a Hewlett Packard (HP) Laserjet type of printer.

Appendix E, Bibliography   This section provides a bibliography of reference material that you may find useful if you are interested in getting further information about embedded real-time systems.

Appendix F, Licensing   This section describes the licensing policy for distributing μC/OS-II in source and object form.

μC/OS-II Web Site

To provide better support to you, I created the μC/OS-II Web site (www.uCOS-II.com). You can obtain information about

- news on μC/OS and μC/OS-II,
- upgrades,
- bug fixes,
- availability of ports,
- answers to frequently asked questions (FAQs),
- application notes,
- books,
- classes,
- links to other Web sites, and more.

Sample Code

This chapter provides three examples on how to use μC/OS-II. I decided to include this chapter early in the book so you could start using μC/OS-II as soon as possible. Before getting into the examples, however, I will describe some of the conventions I use throughout this book.

The sample code was compiled using the Borland International C/C++ compiler V3.1 and options were selected to generate code for an Intel/AMD 80186 processor (large memory model). The code was actually run and tested on a 300MHz Intel Pentium II PC, which can be viewed as a superfast 80186 processor (at least for my purposes). I chose a PC as my target system for a number of reasons. First and foremost, it's a lot easier to test code on a PC than on any other embedded environment (i.e., evaluation board, emulator, etc.): there are no EPROMs to burn and no downloads to EPROM emulators, CPU emulators, etc. You simply compile, link, and run. Second, the 80186 object code (real mode, large model) generated using the Borland C/C++ compiler is compatible with all 80x86 derivative processors from Intel, AMD, or Cyrix.

1.00   Installing μC/OS-II

This book includes a companion diskette in DOS format containing all the source code discussed. It is assumed that you have a DOS or Windows 95 computer system running on an 80x86, Pentium, or Pentium II processor. You will need less than 5Mb free disk space to install μC/OS-II and its source files on your system.

Before starting the installation, make a backup copy of the companion diskette. To install the code, follow these steps:

1. Load DOS (or open a DOS box in Windows 95) and specify C: as the default drive
2. Insert the companion diskette in drive A:
3. Enter A:INSTALL [*drive*]

Note that [*drive*] is an optional drive letter indicating the destination disk on which the source code provided in this book will be installed. If you do not specify a drive, the source code will install on the current drive.

INSTALL.BAT is a DOS batch file found in the root directory of the companion diskette. It creates the directory \SOFTWARE on the specified destination drive then changes directory to \SOFTWARE and copies the file uCOS-II.EXE from A: to this directory. INSTALL.BAT then executes uCOS-II.EXE, which creates all other directories under \SOFTWARE and transfers all source and executable files provided in this book. Upon completion, INSTALL.BAT deletes uCOS-II.EXE and changes the directory to \SOFTWARE\uCOS-II\EX1_x86L, where the first example code is found.

Make sure you read the READ.ME file on the companion diskette for last minute changes and notes. Once INSTALL.BAT has completed, your destination drive will contain the following subdirectories.

\SOFTWARE The main directory from the root where all software-related files are placed.

\SOFTWARE\BLOCKS The main directory where all building blocks are located. With µC/OS-II, I include a building block that handles PC-related functions used by the example code (see \SOFT-WARE\BLOCKS\PC).

\SOFTWARE\HPLISTC This directory contains the files for the HPLISTC utility (see Appendix D, HPLISTC and TO). The source file is HPLISTC.C and is found in the \SOFTWARE\HPLISTC\SOURCE directory. The DOS executable file (HPLISTC.EXE) is found in the \SOFTWARE\HPLISTC\EXE directory.

\SOFTWARE\TO This directory contains the files for the TO utility (see Appendix D, HPLISTC and TO). The source file is TO.C, found in the \SOFTWARE\TO\SOURCE directory. The DOS executable file (TO.EXE) is in the \SOFTWARE\TO\EXE directory. Note that TO requires a file called TO.TBL, which must reside on your root directory. An example of TO.TBL is also found in the \SOFT-WARE\TO\EXE directory. You need to move TO.TBL to the root directory to use TO.EXE.

\SOFTWARE\uCOS-II The main directory where all µC/OS-II files are located.

\SOFTWARE\uCOS-II\EX1_x86L This directory contains the source code for Example 1 (see section 1.07, Example 1), which is intended to run under DOS (or a DOS window under Windows 95).

\SOFTWARE\uCOS-II\EX2_x86L This directory contains the source code for Example 2 (see section 1.08, Example 2), which is intended to run under DOS (or a DOS window under Windows 95).

\SOFTWARE\uCOS-II\EX3_x86L This directory contains the source code for Example 3 (see section 1.09, Example 3), which is intended to run under DOS (or a DOS window under Windows 95).

\SOFTWARE\uCOS-II\Ix86L This directory contains the source code for the processor-dependent code (a.k.a. the port) of µC/OS-II for an 80x86 real-mode, large model processor.

\SOFTWARE\uCOS-II\SOURCE This directory contains the source code for the processor-independent portion of µC/OS-II. This code is fully portable to other processor architectures.

1

1.01 `INCLUDES.H`

You will notice that every `.C` file in this book contains the following declaration:

```
#include "includes.h"
```

`INCLUDES.H` allows every `.C` file in your project to be written without concern about which header file is actually included. In other words, `INCLUDES.H` is a master include file. The only drawback is that `INCLUDES.H` includes header files that are not pertinent to some of the `.C` files being compiled. This means that each file will require extra time to compile. This inconvenience is offset by code portability. There is an `INCLUDES.H` for every example provided in this book; that is, you will find a different copy of `INCLUDES.H` in `\SOFTWARE\uCOS-II\EX1_x86L`, `\SOFTWARE\uCOS-II\EX2_x86L`, and `\SOFTWARE\uCOS-II\EX3_x86L`. You can certainly edit `INCLUDES.H` to add your own header files.

1.02 *Compiler-Independent Data Types*

Because different microprocessors have different word lengths, the port of µC/OS-II includes a series of type definitions that ensures portability (see `\SOFTWARE\uCOS-II\Ix86L\OS_CPU.H` for the 80x86 real mode, large model). Specifically, µC/OS-II code never makes use of C's `short`, `int`, and `long` data types because they are inherently nonportable. Instead, I defined integer data types that are both portable and intuitive, as shown in Listing 1.1. Also, for convenience, I have included floating-point data types even though µC/OS-II doesn't make use of floating-point numbers.

Listing 1.1   *Portable data types.*

```
typedef unsigned char    BOOLEAN;
typedef unsigned char    INT8U;
typedef signed   char    INT8S;
typedef unsigned int     INT16U;
typedef signed   int     INT16S;
typedef unsigned long    INT32U;
typedef signed   long    INT32S;
typedef float            FP32;
typedef double           FP64;


#define BYTE             INT8S
#define UBYTE            INT8U
#define WORD             INT16S
#define UWORD            INT16U
#define LONG             INT32S
#define ULONG            INT32U
```

The INT16U data type, for example, always represents a 16-bit unsigned integer. µC/OS-II and your application code can now assume that the range of values for variables declared with this type is from 0 to 65,535. A µC/OS-II port to a 32-bit processor could mean that an INT16U would be declared as an unsigned short instead of an unsigned int. Where µC/OS-II is concerned, however, it still deals with an INT16U. Listing 1.1 provides the declarations for the 80x86 and the Borland C/C++ compiler as an example.

For backward compatibility with µC/OS, I also defined the data types BYTE, WORD, and LONG (and their unsigned variations). This allows you to migrate µC/OS code to µC/OS-II without changing all instances of the old data types to the new data types. I decided to make this transition and break away from the old-style data types because I believe that this new scheme makes more sense and is more obvious. To some people a WORD may mean a 32-bit value, whereas I originally intended it to mean a 16-bit value. The new data types should eliminate such confusion.

1.03 Global Variables

Following is a technique that I use to declare global variables. As you know, a global variable must be allocated storage space in RAM and must be referenced by other modules using the C keyword extern. Therefore, declarations must be placed in both the .C and .H files. This duplication of declarations, however, can lead to mistakes. The technique described in this section requires only a single declaration in the header file but is a little tricky to understand. However, once you know how this technique works, you will apply it mechanically.

The following declaration in Listing 1.2 appears in all .H files that define global variables.

Listing 1.2   Defining global macros.

```
#ifdef    xxx_GLOBALS
#define   xxx_EXT
#else
#define   xxx_EXT extern
#endif
```

Each variable to be declared global is prefixed with xxx_EXT in the .H file. xxx represents a prefix identifying the module name. The module's .C file contains the following declaration:

```
#define   xxx_GLOBALS
#include "includes.h"
```

When the compiler processes the .C file, it forces xxx_EXT (found in the corresponding .H file) to nothing (because xxx_GLOBALS is defined), so each global variable is allocated storage space. When the compiler processes the other .C files, xxx_GLOBALS is not defined, and xxx_EXT is set to extern, allowing you to reference the global variable. To illustrate the concept, look at uCOS_II.H, which contains the following declarations:

1

```
#ifdef    OS_GLOBALS
#define   OS_EXT
#else
#define   OS_EXT extern
#endif


OS_EXT  INT32U      OSIdleCtr;
OS_EXT  INT32U      OSIdleCtrRun;
OS_EXT  INT32U      OSIdleCtrMax;
```

and uCOS_II.C, which contains the following declarations:

```
#define  OS_GLOBALS
#include "includes.h"
```

When the compiler processes uCOS_II.C, it makes the header file (uCOS_II.H), as shown below because OS_EXT is set to nothing.

```
INT32U      OSIdleCtr;
INT32U      OSIdleCtrRun;
INT32U      OSIdleCtrMax;
```

The compiler is thus told to allocate storage for these variables. When the compiler processes any other .C file, the header file (uCOS_II.H) is as shown below because OS_GLOBALS is not defined, so OS_EXT is set to extern.

```
extern INT32U      OSIdleCtr;
extern INT32U      OSIdleCtrRun;
extern INT32U      OSIdleCtrMax;
```

In this case, no storage is allocated, and any .C file can access these variables. The nice thing about this technique is that the declaration for the variables is done in only one file, the .H file.

1.04 *OS_ENTER_CRITICAL() and OS_EXIT_CRITICAL()*

Throughout the source code provided in this book, you will see calls to the macros OS_ENTER_ CRITICAL() and OS_EXIT_CRITICAL(). OS_ENTER_CRITICAL() disables interrupts and OS_ EXIT_CRITICAL enables interrupts. Disabling and enabling interrupts is done to protect critical sections of code. These macros are obviously processor specific and are different for each processor. They are found in OS_CPU.H Listing 1.3 shows the declarations of these macros for the 80x86 processor. Section9.03.02 ( )discusses why there are two ways of declaring these macros.

Listing 1.3   Macros to access critical sections.

```
#define   OS_CRITICAL_METHOD      2


#if       OS_CRITICAL_METHOD == 1
#define   OS_ENTER_CRITICAL()   asm   CLI
#define   OS_EXIT_CRITICAL()    asm   STI
#endif


#if       OS_CRITICAL_METHOD == 2
#define   OS_ENTER_CRITICAL()   asm {PUSHF; CLI}
#define   OS_EXIT_CRITICAL()    asm   POPF
#endif
```

Your application code can make use of these macros as long as you realize that they are used to disable and enable interrupts. Disabling interrupts obviously affects interrupt latency, so be careful. You can also protect critical sections using semaphores.

1.05 PC-Based Services

The files PC.C and PC.H (in \SOFTWARE\BLOCKS\PC\SOURCE) contain PC-compatible services that I use throughout the examples. Unlike the first version of µC/OS-II (i.e., µC/OS), I decided to encapsulate these functions (as they should have been) to avoid redefining them in every example and to allow you to adapt the code to a different compiler easily. PC.C basically contains character-based display, elapsed time measurement, and miscellaneous services. All functions start with the prefix PC_.

1.05.01   Character-Based Display

The display functions perform direct writes to video RAM for performance reasons. On a VGA monitor, video memory starts at absolute memory location 0x000B8000 (or using segment:offset notation, B800:0000). You can use this code on a monochrome monitor by changing the #define constant DISP_BASE from 0xB800 to 0xB000.

The display functions in PC.C are used to write ASCII (and special) characters anywhere on the screen using *x* and *y* coordinates. A PC's display can hold up to 2,000 characters organized as 25 rows (*y*) by 80 columns (*x*). Each character requires two bytes to display. The first byte is the character that you want to display, and the second byte is an attribute that determines the foreground/background color combination of the character. The foreground color is specified in the lower four bits of the attribute, and the background color appears in bits 4 to 6. Finally, the most significant bit determines whether the character blinks (1) or not (0). Use the #define constants declared in PC.H (FGND means foreground and BGND is background). PC.C contains the following four functions:

PC_DispClrScr()	Clear the screen
PC_DispClrLine()	Clear a single row (or line)
PC_DispChar()	Display a single ASCII character anywhere on the screen
PC_DispStr()	Display an ASCII string anywhere on the screen

1.05.02   Elapsed Time Measurement

The elapsed time measurement functions are used to determine how much time a function takes to execute. Time measurement is performed by using the PC's 82C54 timer number 2. Make a time measurement by wrapping code with the functions `PC_ElapsedStart()` and `PC_ElapsedStop()`. However, before you can use these two functions, you need to call the function `PC_ElapsedInit()`, which basically computes the overhead associated with the other two functions. This way, the execution time returned by `PC_ElapsedStop()` consists exclusively of the code you are measuring. Note that none of these functions are reentrant, so you must be careful that you do not invoke them from multiple tasks at the same time. The example in Listing 1.4 shows how to measure the execution time of `PC_DispChar()`. Note that time is in microseconds (µs).

Listing 1.4   Measuring code execution time.

```
INT16U time;


PC_ElapsedInit();

.

.

PC_ElapsedStart();
PC_DispChar(40, 24, 'A', DISP_FGND_WHITE);
time = PC_ElapsedStop();
```

1.05.03   Miscellaneous

A µC/OS-II application looks just like any other DOS application. In other words, you compile and link your code just as you would a single-threaded application running under DOS. The `.EXE` file that you create is loaded and executed by DOS, and execution of your application starts from `main()`. Because µC/OS-II performs multitasking and creates a stack for each task, the single-threaded DOS environment must be stored in case your application quits µC/OS-II and returns to DOS. Saving the DOS environment is done by calling `PC_DOSSaveReturn()`. When your application needs to return to DOS (and exit µC/OS-II), simply call `PC_DOSReturn()`. `PC.C` makes use of the ANSI C `setjmp()` and `longjmp()` functions to save and restore the DOS environment, respectively. These functions are provided by the Borland C/C++ compiler library and should be available on most other compilers.

You should note that either a crashed application or invoking `exit(0)` without using `PC_DOSReturn()` can leave DOS in a corrupted state. This may lead DOS or the DOS window within Windows 95 to crash.

`PC_GetDateTime()` obtains the PC's current date and time and formats this information into an ASCII string. The format is MM-DD-YY HH:MM:SS, and you will need at least 19 characters (including the `NUL` character) to hold this string. `PC_GetDateTime()` uses the Borland C/C++ library functions `gettime()` and `getdate()`, which should have their equivalents on other DOS compilers.

`PC_GetKey()` checks to see if a key was pressed and, if so, obtains that key and returns it to the caller. `PC_GetKey()` uses the Borland C/C++ library functions `kbhit()` and `getch()`, which also have their equivalents on other DOS compilers.

`PC_SetTickRate()` allows you to change the tick rate for µC/OS-II by specifying the desired frequency. Under DOS, a tick occurs 18.20648 times per second, or every 54.925ms. This is because the counter of the 82C54 chip wasn't initialized and the default value of 65,535 took effect. Had the chip been initialized with a divide by 59,659, the tick rate would have been a very nice 20.000Hz! I decided to change the tick rate to something more exciting and thus decided to use about 200Hz (actually 199.9966Hz). Note that the function `OSTickISR()` found in `OS_CPU_A.ASM` contains code to call the DOS tick handler one time out of 11. This is done to ensure that some of the housekeeping needed in DOS is maintained. You do not need to do this if you set the tick rate to 20Hz. Before returning to DOS, `PC_SetTickRate()` is called by specifying `18` as the desired frequency. `PC_SetTickRate()` will know that you actually mean 18.2Hz and will correctly set the 82C54.

The last two functions in `PC.C` are used to get and set an interrupt vector. Again, I used Borland C/C++ library functions do accomplish this, but `PC_VectGet()` and `PC_VectSet()` can easily be changed to accommodate a different compiler.

1.06 μC/OS-II Examples

The examples provided in this chapter were compiled using the Borland C/C++ V3.1 compiler in a DOS box on a Windows 95 platform. The executable code is found in the `OBJ` subdirectory of each example's directory. The code was actually compiled under the Borland IDE (Integrated Development Environment) with the options listed in Table 1.1.

Table 1.1   Compilation options in the IDE.

Code generation	
Model	: Large
Options	: Treat `enums` as `ints`
Assume `SS` Equals `DS`	: Default for memory model
Advanced code generation	
Floating point	: Emulation
Instruction set	: 80186
Options	: Generate underbars
	Debug info in OBJs
	Fast floating point
Optimizations	
Optimizations	Global register allocation
	Invariant code motion
	Induction variables
	Loop optimization
	Suppress redundant loads
	Copy propagation
	Dead code elimination
	Jump optimization
	In-line intrinsic functions
Register variables	Automatic
Common subexpressions	Optimize globally
Optimize for	Speed

I assume that the Borland C/C++ compiler is installed in the C:\CPP directory. If your compiler is located in a different directory, you need to change the path in the Options/Directories menu of the IDE.

µC/OS-II is a scalable operating system, which means that the code size of µC/OS-II can be reduced if you are not using all of its services. Code reduction is done by setting the #defines OS_???_EN to 0 in OS_CFG.H. This disables code generation for the services that you will not be using. The examples in this chapter make use of this feature, so each example declares its OS_???_EN appropriately.

1.07 Example 1

The first example is found in \SOFTWARE\uCOS-II\EX1_x86L and basically consists of 13 tasks (including the µC/OS-II idle task). µC/OS-II creates two internal tasks: the idle task and a task that determines CPU usage. Example 1 creates 11 other tasks. The TaskStart() task is created by main(); its function is to create the other tasks and display the following statistics on the screen:

- the number of task switches in one second,
- the CPU usage in %,
- the number of context switches,
- the current date and time, and
- the µC/OS-II version.

TaskStart() also checks to see if you have pressed the Esc key to exit the example and return to DOS.

The other 10 tasks are based on the same code; that is, the function Task(). Each of the 10 tasks displays a number (each task has its own number from 0 to 9) at random locations on the screen.

1.07.01 *main()*

Example 1 does basically the same thing as the first example provided in the first edition of *µC/OS*; however, I cleaned up some of the code, and output to the screen is in color. Also, I decided to use the old data types (i.e., UBYTE, UWORD, etc.) to show that µC/OS-II is backward compatible.

main() starts by clearing the screen to ensure that no characters are left over from the previous DOS session [L1.5(1)]. Note that I have specified white letters on a black background. Since the screen will be cleared, I simply could have specified a black background and not specified a foreground. If I did this, and you decided to return to DOS, you would not see anything on the screen! It's always better to specify a visible foreground just for this reason.

A requirement of µC/OS-II is that you call OSInit() [L1.5(2)] before you invoke any of its other services. OSInit() creates two tasks: an idle task, which executes when no other task is ready to run, and a statistic task, which computes CPU usage.

Listing 1.5 main().

```
void main (void)
{
    PC_DispClrScr(DISP_FGND_WHITE + DISP_BGND_BLACK);            (1)
    OSInit();                                                    (2)
    PC_DOSSaveReturn();                                          (3)
    PC_VectSet(uCOS, OSCtxSw);                                   (4)
    RandomSem = OSSemCreate(1);                                  (5)
```

Listing 1.5   *main(). (Continued)*

```
    OSTaskCreate(TaskStart,                                            (6)
                 (void *)0,
                 (void *)&TaskStartStk[TASK_STK_SIZE-1],
                 0);
    OSStart();                                                         (7)
}
```

The current DOS environment is saved by calling PC_DOSSaveReturn() [L1.5(3)]. This allows you to return to DOS as if you had never started μC/OS-II. A lot happens in PC_DOSSaveReturn(), so you may need to look at the code in Listing 1.6 to follow along. PC_DOSSaveReturn() starts by setting the flag PC_ExitFlag to FALSE [L1.6(1)], indicating that you are not returning to DOS, then initializes OSTickDOSCtr to 1 [L1.6(2)] because this variable is decremented in OSTickISR(). A value of 0 would cause this value to wrap around to 255 when decremented by OSTickISR(). PC_DOSSaveReturn() then saves the DOS tick handler in a free vector table [L1.6(3)–(4)] entry so that it can be called by the μC/OS-II tick handler. Next, PC_DOSSaveReturn() calls setjmp() [L1.6(5)], which captures the state of the processor (i.e., the contents of all its registers) into a structure called PC_JumpBuf. Capturing the processor's context allows you to return to PC_DOSSaveReturn() and execute the code immediately following the call to setjmp(). Because PC_ExitFlag was initialized to FALSE [L1.6(1)], PC_DOSSaveReturn() skips the code in the if statement [L1.6(6)–(9)] and returns to the caller [main()]. When you want to return to DOS, all you have to do is call PC_DOSReturn() (Listing 1.7), which sets PC_ExitFlag to TRUE [L1.7(1)] and executes a longjmp() [L1.7(2)]. This brings the processor back in PC_DOSSaveReturn() [just after the call to setjmp()] [L1.6(5)]. This time, however, PC_ExitFlag is TRUE, and the code following the if statement is executed. PC_DOSSaveReturn() changes the tick rate back to 18.2Hz [L1.6(6)], restores the PC tick ISR handler [L1.6(7)], clears the screen [L1.6(8)], and returns to the DOS prompt through the exit(0) function [L1.6(9)].

Listing 1.6   *Saving the DOS environment.*

```
void PC_DOSSaveReturn (void)
{
    PC_ExitFlag  = FALSE;                                              (1)
    OSTickDOSCtr =     8;                                              (2)
    PC_TickISR   = PC_VectGet(VECT_TICK);                             (3)


    OS_ENTER_CRITICAL();
    PC_VectSet(VECT_DOS_CHAIN, PC_TickISR);                           (4)
    OS_EXIT_CRITICAL();


    setjmp(PC_JumpBuf);                                               (5)
```

Listing 1.6   Saving the DOS environment. (Continued)

```
    if (PC_ExitFlag == TRUE) {
        OS_ENTER_CRITICAL();
        PC_SetTickRate(18);                                     (6)
        PC_VectSet(VECT_TICK, PC_TickISR);                      (7)
        OS_EXIT_CRITICAL();
        PC_DispClrScr(DISP_FGND_WHITE + DISP_BGND_BLACK);       (8)
        exit(0);                                                (9)
    }
}
```

Listing 1.7   Setting up to return to DOS.

```
void PC_DOSReturn (void)
{
    PC_ExitFlag = TRUE;                                         (1)
    longjmp(PC_JumpBuf, 1);                                     (2)
}
```

Now go back to main() in Listing 1.5. main() calls PC_VectSet() [L1.5(4)] to install the µC/OS-II context switch handler. Task-level context switching is done by issuing an 80x86 INT instruction to this vector location. I decided to use vector 0x80 (i.e., 128) because it's not used by either DOS or the BIOS.

A binary semaphore is created [L1.5(5)] to guard access to the random number generator provided by the Borland C/C++ library. I decided to use a semaphore because I didn't know whether or not this function was reentrant. I assumed it was not. By initializing the semaphore to 1, I indicate that only one task can access the random number generator at a time.

Before starting multitasking, I create one task [L1.5(6)] called TaskStart(). It is very important that you create at least one task before multitasking begins with OSStart() [L1.5(7)]. Failure to do this will certainly make your application crash. In fact, you may always want to create only a single task if you are planning on using the CPU usage statistic task. The µC/OS-II statistic task assumes that no other task is running for a whole second. If, however, you need to create additional tasks before multitasking, you must ensure that your task code will monitor the global variable OSStatRdy and delay execution [i.e., call OSTimeDly()] until this variable becomes TRUE. This indicates that µC/OS-II has collected its data for CPU usage statistics.

1.07.02   *TaskStart()*

A major portion of the work in Example 1 is done by TaskStart(). The pseudocode for this function is shown in Listing 1.8. The task starts by displaying a banner on top of the screen identifying it as Example 1 [L1.8(1)]. Next, you disable interrupts to change the tick ISR (Interrupt Service Routine) vector so that it now points to the µC/OS-II tick handler [L1.8(2)] and, change the tick rate from the default DOS 18.2Hz to 200Hz [L1.8(3)]. You don't want to be interrupted while in the process of changing an interrupt vector! Note that main() (see Listing 1.5) purposely didn't set the interrupt vector to the µC/OS-II tick handler because you don't want a tick interrupt to occur before the operating system is fully initialized and running. If you run code in an embedded application, you should always enable the ticker (as I have done here) from within the first task.

Listing 1.8   Task that creates the other tasks.

```
void TaskStart (void *data)
{
    Prevent compiler warning by assigning 'data' to itself;
    Display banner identifying this as EXAMPLE #1;                    (1)


    OS_ENTER_CRITICAL();
    PC_VectSet(0x08, OSTickISR);                                      (2)
    PC_SetTickRate(200);                                             (3)
    OS_EXIT_CRITICAL();


    Initialize the statistic task by calling 'OSStatInit()';         (4)


    Create 10 identical tasks;                                       (5)


    for (;;) {
        Display the number of tasks created;
        Display the % of CPU used;
        Display the number of task switches in 1 second;
        Display uC/OS-II's version number
        if (key was pressed) {
            if (key pressed was the ESCAPE key) {
                PC_DOSReturn();
            }
        }
        Delay for 1 Second;
    }
}
```

Before you create any other tasks, you need to determine how fast your particular PC is by calling OSStatInit() [L1.8(4)]. OSStatInit() is shown in Listing 1.9 and starts by delaying itself for two clock ticks so that it can be synchronized to the tick interrupt [L1.9(1)]. Because of this, OSStat-Init() must occur after the ticker has been installed; otherwise, your application will crash! When µC/OS-II returns control to OSStatInit(), a 32-bit counter called OSIdleCtr is cleared [L1.9(2)] and another delay is initiated, which again suspends OSStatInit(). At this point, µC/OS-II doesn't have anything else to execute, so it runs the Idle Task (internal to µC/OS-II). The idle task is an infinite loop that increments OSIdleCtr and increments it for one full second [L1.9(3)]. After one second,

1

µC/OS-II resumes OSStatInit(), which saves OSIdleCtr in a variable called OSIdleCtrMax [L1.9(4)]. OSIdleCtrMax now contains the largest value that OSIdleCtr can ever reach. When you start adding application code, the idle task will get less of the processor's time, so OSIdleCtr will not be allowed to count as high (assuming you reset OSIdleCtr every second). CPU utilization is computed by a task provided by µC/OS-II called OSStatTask(), which executes every second. OSStatRdy is set to TRUE to indicate that µC/OS-II collected the information it needed to peform CPU usage statistics [L1.9(5)]

Listing 1.9   Determining the PC's speed.

```
void OSStatInit (void)
{
    OSTimeDly(2);                                                    (1)
    OS_ENTER_CRITICAL();
    OSIdleCtr    = 0L;                                               (2)
    OS_EXIT_CRITICAL();
    OSTimeDly(OS_TICKS_PER_SEC);                                     (3)
    OS_ENTER_CRITICAL();
    OSIdleCtrMax = OSIdleCtr;                                        (4)
    OSStatRdy    = TRUE;                                             (5)
    OS_EXIT_CRITICAL();
}
```

1.07.03   TaskN()

OSStatInit() returns to TaskStart(); you can now create 10 identical tasks (all running the same code) [L1.8(5)]. TaskStart() creates all the tasks, and no context switch occurs because TaskStart() has a priority of 0 (the highest priority). When all the tasks are created, TaskStart() enters the infinite loop portion of the task and continuously displays statistics on the screen, checks to see if the Esc key is pressed, then delays for one second before starting the loop again. If you press Esc, TaskStart() calls PC_DOSReturn() and you return to the DOS prompt gracefully.

The task code is shown in Listing 1.10. When it executes, it tries to acquire a semaphore [L1.10(1)] so that you can call the Borland C/C++ library function random() [L1.10(2)]. I assume that random() is non-reentrant, so each of the 10 tasks must have exclusive access to this code in order to proceed. Release the semaphore when *x* and *y* coordinates are obtained [L1.10(3)]. The task displays a number (between 0 and 9), which is passed to the task when it is created [L1.10(4)]. Finally, each task delays itself for one tick [L1.10(5)]; thus, each task executes 200 times per second! With 10 tasks, µC/OS-II will context switch between these tasks 2,000 times per second.

Listing 1.10   Task that displays a number at random locations on the screen.

```
void Task (void *data)
{
    UBYTE x;
    UBYTE y;
    UBYTE err;


    for (;;) {
        OSSemPend(RandomSem, 0, &err);                                  (1)
        x = random(80);                                                (2)
        y = random(16);
        OSSemPost(RandomSem);                                          (3)
        PC_DispChar(x, y + 5, *(char *)data, DISP_FGND_LIGHT_GRAY);    (4)
        OSTimeDly(1);                                                  (5)
    }
}
```

1.08 Example 2

Example 2 makes use of the extended task create function and the µC/OS-II stack-checking feature. Stack checking is useful when you don't actually know ahead of time how much stack space you need to allocate for each task. In this case, allocate much more stack space than you think you need and let µC/OS-II tell you exactly how much stack space is actually used. You obviously need to run the application long enough and under your worst case conditions to get the proper numbers. Your final stack size should accommodate system expansion, so make sure you allocate between 10 and 25 percent more. In safety-critical applications, however, you may want to consider 100 percent more. What you get from stack checking is a ballpark figure; you are not looking for an exact stack usage.

The µC/OS-II stack-checking function assumes that the stack is filled with zeros when the task is created. You accomplish this by telling OSTaskCreateExt() to clear the stack upon task creation (i.e., by setting OS_TASK_OPT_STK_CHK and OS_TASK_OPT_STK_CLR for the opt argument). If you intend to create and delete tasks, you should set these options so that a new stack is cleared every time the task is created. You should note that having OSTaskCreateExt() clear the stack increases execution overhead, which obviously depends on the stack size. µC/OS-II scans the stack starting at the bottom until it finds a nonzero entry (see Figure 1.1). As the stack is scanned, µC/OS-II increments a counter that indicates how many entries are free (Stack Free).

Example 2 is found in \SOFTWARE\uCOS-II\EX2_x86L and consists of nine tasks. Again, µC/OS-II creates two internal tasks: the idle task and the task that determines CPU usage. EX2L.C creates the other seven tasks. As with Example 1, TaskStart() is created by main(); its function is to create the other tasks and display the following statistics on the screen:

- the number of task switches in one second,
- the CPU usage in %,
- the number of context switches,
- the current date and time, and
- the µC/OS-II version.

Figure 1.1   µC/OS-II stack checking.

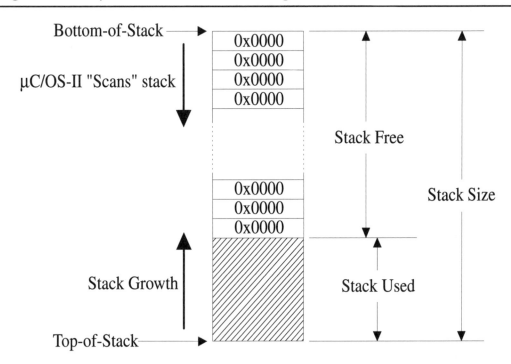

1.08.01 main()

main() looks just like the code for Example 1 (see Listing 1.11), except for two small differences. First, main() calls PC_ElapsedInit() [L1.11(1)] to initialize the elapsed time measurement function used to measure the execution time of OSTaskStkChk(). Second, all tasks are created using the extended task create function instead of OSTaskCreate() [L1.11(2)]. This allows you to perform, among other things, stack checking on each task.

Listing 1.11 `main()` for Example 2.

```
void main (void)
{
    PC_DispClrScr(DISP_FGND_WHITE + DISP_BGND_BLACK);
    OSInit();
    PC_DOSSaveReturn();
    PC_VectSet(uCOS, OSCtxSw);
    PC_ElapsedInit();                                              (1)
    OSTaskCreateExt(TaskStart,                                     (2)
                    (void *)0,
                    &TaskStartStk[TASK_STK_SIZE-1],
                    TASK_START_PRIO,
                    TASK_START_ID,
                    &TaskStartStk[0],
                    TASK_STK_SIZE,
                    (void *)0,
                    OS_TASK_OPT_STK_CHK | OS_TASK_OPT_STK_CLR);
    OSStart();
}
```

In addition to the same four arguments needed by OSTaskCreate(), OSTaskCreateExt() requires five additional arguments: a task ID, a pointer to the bottom of the stack, the stack size (in number of elements), a pointer to a user-supplied Task Control Block (TCB) extension, and a variable used to specify options to the task. One of the options is used to tell μC/OS-II that stack checking is allowed on the created task. Example 2 doesn't make use of the TCB (Task Control Block) extension pointer.

1.08.02 `TaskStart()`

Listing 1.12 shows the pseudocode for TaskStart(). The first five operations are similar to those found in Example 1. TaskStart() creates two mailboxes used by Task 4 and Task 5 [L1.12(1)]. A task that displays the current date and time is created [L1.12(2)] as well as five application tasks.

Listing 1.12 Pseudocode for `TaskStart()`.

```
void TaskStart (void *data)
{
    Prevent compiler warning by assigning 'data' to itself;
    Display a banner and non-changing text;
    Install uC/OS-II's tick handler;
    Change the tick rate to 200 Hz;
    Initialize the statistics task;
    Create 2 mailboxes which are used by Task #4 and #5;          (1)
    Create a task that will display the date and time on the screen;  (2)
    Create 5 application tasks;
```

1

Listing 1.12   Pseudocode for *TaskStart* (). (Continued)

```
for (;;) {
    Display #tasks running;
    Display CPU usage in %;
    Display #context switches per seconds;
    Clear the context switch counter;
    Display uC/OS-II's version;
    if (Key was pressed) {
        if (Key pressed was the ESCAPE key) {
            Return to DOS;
        }
    }
    Delay for 1 second;
}
}
```

1.08.03   *TaskN()*

The code for Task1() checks the size of the stack for each of the seven application tasks. The execution time of OSTaskStkChk() is measured [L1.13(1)–(2)] and displayed along with the stack size information. Note that all stack size data are displayed in number of bytes. This task executes 10 times per second [L1.13(3)] (i.e., every 100ms).

Listing 1.13   Example 2, Task 1.

```
void  Task1 (void *pdata)
{
    INT8U       err;
    OS_STK_DATA data;
    INT16U      time;
    INT8U       i;
    char        s[80];


    pdata = pdata;
    for (;;) {
        for (i = 0; i < 7; i++) {
            PC_ElapsedStart();                              (1)
            err  = OSTaskStkChk(TASK_START_PRIO+i, &data)
            time = PC_ElapsedStop();                        (2)
```

Listing 1.13   Example 2, Task 1. (Continued)

```
        if (err == OS_NO_ERR) {
            sprintf(s, "%31d      %31d      %31d      %5d",
                    data.OSFree + data.OSUsed,
                    data.OSFree,
                    data.OSUsed,
                    time);
            PC_DispStr(19, 12+i, s, DISP_FGND_YELLOW);
        }
    }
    OSTimeDlyHMSM(0, 0, 0, 100);                                    (3)
    }
}
```

Task2() in Listing 1.14 displays a clockwise-rotating wheel on the screen. Each rotation completes in 200ms (i.e., 4 x 10 ticks x 5ms/tick).

Listing 1.14   Clockwise-rotating wheel task.

```
void  Task2 (void *data)
{
    data = data;
    for (;;) {
        PC_DispChar(70, 15, '|',  DISP_FGND_WHITE + DISP_BGND_RED);
        OSTimeDly(10);
        PC_DispChar(70, 15, '/',  DISP_FGND_WHITE + DISP_BGND_RED);
        OSTimeDly(10);
        PC_DispChar(70, 15, '-',  DISP_FGND_WHITE + DISP_BGND_RED);
        OSTimeDly(10);
        PC_DispChar(70, 15, '\\', DISP_FGND_WHITE + DISP_BGND_RED);
        OSTimeDly(10);
    }
}
```

Task3() (Listing 1.15) also displays a rotating wheel, but the rotation is in the opposite direction. Also, Task3() allocates storage on the stack. I decided to fill the dummy array to show that OSTaskStkChk() takes less time to determine stack usage when the stack is close to being full [L1.15(1)].

1

Listing 1.15   Counterclockwise-roating wheel task.

```c
void  Task3 (void *data)
{
    char      dummy[500];
    INT16U  i;
    data = data;
    for (i = 0; i < 499; i++) {
        dummy[i] = '?';
    }
    for (;;) {
        PC_DispChar(70, 16, '|',  DISP_FGND_WHITE + DISP_BGND_BLUE);
        OSTimeDly(20);
        PC_DispChar(70, 16, '\\',  DISP_FGND_WHITE + DISP_BGND_BLUE);
        OSTimeDly(20);
        PC_DispChar(70, 16, '-',  DISP_FGND_WHITE + DISP_BGND_BLUE);
        OSTimeDly(20);
        PC_DispChar(70, 16, '/',  DISP_FGND_WHITE + DISP_BGND_BLUE);
        OSTimeDly(20);
    }
}
```

Task4() (Listing 1.16) sends a message to Task5() and waits for an acknowledgment [L1.16(1)]. The message sent is simply a pointer to a character. Every time Task4() receives an acknowledgment from Task5() [L1.16(2)], Task4() increments the ASCII character value before sending the next message [L1.16(3)].

Listing 1.16   Task 4 communicates with Task 5.

```c
void  Task4 (void *data)
{
    char    txmsg;
    INT8U   err;
```

Listing 1.16   Task 4 communicates with Task 5. (Continued)

```
    data  = data;
    txmsg = 'A';
    for (;;) {
        while (txmsg <= 'Z') {
            OSMboxPost(TxMbox, (void *)&txmsg);          (1)
            OSMboxPend(AckMbox, 0, &err);                (2)
            txmsg++;                                     (3)
        }
        txmsg = 'A';
    }
}
```

When Task5() (Listing 1.17) receives the message [L1.17(1)] (i.e., the character), it displays the character on the screen [L1.17(2)] then waits one second [L1.17(3)] before acknowledging it to Task 4 [L1.17(4)].

Listing 1.17   Task 5 receives and displays a message.

```
void  Task5 (void *data)
{
    char  *rxmsg;
    INT8U  err;


    data = data;
    for (;;) {
        rxmsg = (char *)OSMboxPend(TxMbox, 0, &err);                    (1)
        PC_DispChar(70, 18, *rxmsg, DISP_FGND_YELLOW+DISP_BGND_RED);    (2)
        OSTimeDlyHMSM(0, 0, 1, 0);                                      (3)
        OSMboxPost(AckMbox, (void *)1);                                 (4)
    }
}
```

TaskClk() (Listing 1.18) displays the current date and time every second.

1

Listing 1.18   Clock display task.

```
void  TaskClk (void *data)
{
    struct time now;
    struct date today;
    char        s[40];


    data = data;
    for (;;) {
        PC_GetDateTime(s);
        PC_DispStr(0, 24, s, DISP_FGND_BLUE + DISP_BGND_CYAN);
        OSTimeDly(OS_TICKS_PER_SEC);
    }
}
```

1.09   Example 3

Example 3 demonstrates some additional features of μC/OS-II. Specifically, Example 3 uses the TCB (Task Control Block) extension capability of OSTaskCreateExt(), the user-defined context switch hook [OSTaskSwHook()], the user-defined statistic task hook [OSTaskStatHook()], and message queues.

Example 3 is found in \SOFTWARE\uCOS-II\EX3_x86L and again consists of nine tasks. μC/OS-II creates two internal tasks: the idle task and the task that determines CPU usage. EX3L.C creates the other seven tasks. As with Examples 1 and 2, TaskStart() is created by main(); its function is to create the other tasks and display statistics on the screen.

1.09.01   main()

main() (Listing 1.19) looks just like the code for Example 2, except the task is given a name saved in a user-defined TCB extension [L1.19(1)]. (The declaration for the extension is found in INCLUDES.H and is shown in Listing 1.20.) I decided to allocate 30 characters for the task name (including the NUL character) to show that you can have fairly descriptive task names [L1.20(1)]. I disabled stack checking for TaskStart() because you do not use that feature in this example [L1.19(2)].

Listing 1.19   main() for Example 3.

```
void main (void)
{
    PC_DispClrScr(DISP_FGND_WHITE + DISP_BGND_BLACK);
    OSInit();
    PC_DOSSaveReturn();
    PC_VectSet(uCOS, OSCtxSw);
    PC_ElapsedInit();

    strcpy(TaskUserData[TASK_START_ID].TaskName, "StartTask");        (1)
    OSTaskCreateExt(TaskStart,
                    (void *)0,
                    &TaskStartStk[TASK_STK_SIZE-1],
                    TASK_START_PRIO,
                    TASK_START_ID,
                    &TaskStartStk[0],
                    TASK_STK_SIZE,
                    &TaskUserData[TASK_START_ID],
                    0);                                               (2)
    OSStart();
}
```

Listing 1.20   TCB extension data structure.

```
typedef struct {
    char    TaskName[30];                                            (1)
    INT16U  TaskCtr;
    INT16U  TaskExecTime;
    INT32U  TaskTotExecTime;
} TASK_USER_DATA;
```

1.09.02   Tasks

The pseudocode for TaskStart() is shown in Listing 1.21. The code is different from Example 2 in three ways:

• a message queue is created [L1.21(1)] for use by Task1(), Task2(), and Task3();

• each task has a name which is stored in the TCB extension [L1.21(2)]; and

• stack checking is not allowed.

Listing 1.21   Pseudocode for `TaskStart()`, Example 3.

```
void TaskStart (void *data)
{
    Prevent compiler warning by assigning 'data' to itself;
    Display a banner and non-changing text;
    Install uC/OS-II's tick handler;
    Change the tick rate to 200 Hz;
    Initialize the statistics task;
    Create a message queue;                                          (1)
    Create a task that will display the date and time on the screen;
    Create 5 application tasks with a name stored in the TCB ext.;   (2)
    for (;;) {
        Display #tasks running;
        Display CPU usage in %;
        Display #context switches per seconds;
        Clear the context switch counter;
        Display uC/OS-II's version;
        if (Key was pressed) {
            if (Key pressed was the ESCAPE key) {
                Return to DOS;
            }
        }
        Delay for 1 second;
    }
}
```

Task1() writes messages into the message queue [L1.22(1)] and delays itself whenever a message is sent [L1.22(2)]. This allows the receiver to display the message at a readable rate. Three different messages are sent.

Listing 1.22   Example 3, Task 1.

```
void  Task1 (void *data)
{
    char one   = '1';
    char two   = '2';
    char three = '3';
```

Listing 1.22   Example 3, Task 1. (Continued)

```
    data = data;
    for (;;) {
        OSQPost(MsgQueue, (void *)&one);                              (1)
        OSTimeDlyHMSM(0, 0, 1,   0);                                  (2)
        OSQPost(MsgQueue, (void *)&two);
        OSTimeDlyHMSM(0, 0, 0, 500);
        OSQPost(MsgQueue, (void *)&three);
        OSTimeDlyHMSM(0, 0, 1,   0);
    }
}
```

Task2() pends on the message queue with no timeout [L1.23(1)]. This means that the task will wait forever for a message to arrive. When the message is received, Task2() displays the message on the screen [L1.23(2)] and delays itself for 500ms [L1.23(3)]. This allows Task3() to receive a message because Task2() does not check the queue for 500ms.

Listing 1.23   Example 3, Task 2.

```
void  Task2 (void *data)
{
    INT8U *msg;
    INT8U  err;


    data = data;
    for (;;) {
        msg = (INT8U *)OSQPend(MsgQueue, 0, &err);                   (1)
        PC_DispChar(70, 14, *msg, DISP_FGND_YELLOW+DISP_BGND_BLUE);  (2)
        OSTimeDlyHMSM(0, 0, 0, 500);                                 (3)
    }
}
```

Task3() also pends on the message queue, but it is willing to wait only 250ms [L1.24(1)]. If a message is received, Task3() displays the message number [L1.24(3)]. If a timeout occurs, Task3() displays a "T" (for timeout) instead [L1.24(2)].

Listing 1.24   Example 3, Task 3.

```
void  Task3 (void *data)
{
    INT8U *msg;
    INT8U  err;



    data = data;
    for (;;) {
        msg = (INT8U *)OSQPend(MsgQueue, OS_TICKS_PER_SEC/4, &err);          (1)
        if (err == OS_TIMEOUT) {
            PC_DispChar(70,15,'T',DISP_FGND_YELLOW+DISP_BGND_RED);           (2)
        } else {
            PC_DispChar(70,15,*msg,DISP_FGND_YELLOW+DISP_BGND_BLUE);         (3)
        }
    }
}
```

Task4() doesn't do much except post [L1.25(1)] and pend [L1.25(2)] on a mailbox. This basically allows you to measure the time it takes these calls to execute on your particular PC. Task4() executes every 10ms [L1.25(3)].

Listing 1.25   Example 3, Task 4.

```
void  Task4 (void *data)
{
    OS_EVENT *mbox;
    INT8U      err;



    data = data;
    mbox = OSMboxCreate((void *)0);
    for (;;) {
        OSMboxPost(mbox, (void *)1);                                        (1)
        OSMboxPend(mbox, 0, &err);                                          (2)
        OSTimeDlyHMSM(0, 0, 0, 10);                                         (3)
    }
}
```

Task5() does nothing useful except delay itself for one clock tick [L1.26(1)]. Note that all µC/OS-II tasks must call a service provided by µC/OS-II to wait either for time to expire or for an event to occur. If this is not done, the task prevents all lower priority tasks from running.

Listing 1.26   Example 3, Task 5.

```
void  Task5 (void *data)
{
    data = data;
    for (;;) {
        OSTimeDly(1);                                          (1)
    }
}
```

Also, TaskClk() (Listing 1.18) displays the current date and time every second.

1.09.03   Notes

Events happen behind the scenes that are not apparent just by looking at EX3L.C. EX3L.C contains code for OSTaskSwHook() that measures the execution time of each task, keeps track of how often each task executes, and accumulates total execution time of each task. This information is stored in the TCB extension so that it can be displayed. OSTaskSwHook() is called every time a context switch occurs.

A timer on the PC obtains the execution time of the task being switched out through PC_Elapsed-Stop() [L1.27(1)]. It is assumed that the timer was started by calling PC_ElapsedStart() when the task was switched in [L1.27(2)]. The first context switch will probably read an incorrect value, but this is not critical. OSTaskSwHook() retrieves the pointer to the TCB extension [L1.27(3)], and if an extension exists [L1.27(4)] for the task, a counter is incremented [L1.27(5)], indicating how often the current task has been switched out. Such a counter is useful to determine if a particular task is running. Next, the execution time of the task being switched out is saved in the TCB extension [L1.27(6)]. A separate accumulator is used to maintain the total execution time [L1.27(7)]. This allows you to determine the percent of time each task takes with respect to other tasks in an application. Note that these statistics are displayed by OSTaskStatHook().

1

Listing 1.27 User-defined *OSTaskSwHook()*.

```
void OSTaskSwHook (void)
{
    INT16U            time;
    TASK_USER_DATA *puser;


    time  = PC_ElapsedStop();                          (1)
    PC_ElapsedStart();                                 (2)
    puser = OSTCBCur->OSTCBExtPtr;                     (3)
    if (puser != (void *)0) {                          (4)
        puser->TaskCtr++;                              (5)
        puser->TaskExecTime     = time;               (6)
        puser->TaskTotExecTime += time;               (7)
    }
}
```

μC/OS-II always calls OSTaskStatHook() when you enable the statistic task (i.e., the configuration constant OS_TASK_STAT_EN in OS_CFG.H is set to 1). When enabled, the statistic task OSTaskStat() always calls the user-definable function OSTaskStatHook(). This happens every second. I decided to have OSTaskStatHook() display the statistics collected by OSTaskSwHook(). In addition, OSTaskStatHook() also computes the percent of time each task takes with respect to the others.

The total execution time of all tasks is computed [L1.28(1)]. Then, individual statistics are displayed at the proper location on the screen [L1.28(2)] by DispTaskStat(), which takes care of converting the values into ASCII. Next, percent execution time is computed for each task [L1.28(3)] and displayed [L1.28(4)].

Listing 1.28 User-defined *OSTaskStatHook()*.

```
void OSTaskStatHook (void)
{
    char    s[80];
    INT8U   i;
    INT32U total;
    INT8U   pct;


    total = 0L;
    for (i = 0; i < 7; i++) {
        total += TaskUserData[i].TaskTotExecTime;      (1)
        DispTaskStat(i);                               (2)
    }
```

Listing 1.28   User-defined *OSTaskStatHook()*. *(Continued)*

```
    if (total > 0) {
        for (i = 0; i < 7; i++) {
            pct = 100 * TaskUserData[i].TaskTotExecTime / total;              (3)
            sprintf(s, "%3d %%", pct);
            PC_DispStr(62, i + 11, s, DISP_FGND_YELLOW);                      (4)
        }
    }
    if (total > 1000000000L) {
        for (i = 0; i < 7; i++) {
            TaskUserData[i].TaskTotExecTime = 0L;
        }
    }
}
```

Real-Time Systems Concepts

Real-time systems are characterized by the severe consequences that result if logical as well as timing correctness properties of the system are not met. There are two types of real-time systems: SOFT and HARD. In a SOFT real-time system, tasks are performed by the system as fast as possible, but the tasks don't have to finish by specific times. In HARD real-time systems, tasks have to be performed not only correctly but on time. Most real-time systems have a combination of SOFT and HARD requirements. Real-time applications cover a wide range, but most real-time systems are *embedded*. This means that the computer is built into a system and is not seen by the user as being a computer. The following list shows a few examples of embedded systems.

Process control
    Food processing
    Chemical plants
Automotive
    Engine controls
    Antilock braking systems
Office automation
    FAX machines
    Copiers
Computer peripherals
    Printers
    Terminals
    Scanners
    Modems

Communication
    Switches
    Routers
Robots
Aerospace
    Flight management systems
    Weapons systems
    Jet engine controls
Domestic
    Microwave ovens
    Dishwashers
    Washing machines
    Thermostats

Real-time software applications are typically more difficult to design than non-real-time applications. This chapter describes real-time concepts.

2.00 Foreground/Background Systems

Small systems of low complexity are generally designed as shown in Figure 2.1. These systems are called *foreground/background* or *super-loops*. An application consists of an infinite loop that calls modules (i.e., functions) to perform the desired operations (background). Interrupt Service Routines (ISRs) handle asynchronous events (foreground). Foreground is also called *interrupt level*; background is called *task level*. Critical operations must be performed by the ISRs to ensure that they are dealt with in a timely fashion. Because of this, ISRs have a tendency to take longer than they should. Also, information for a background module made available by an ISR is not processed until the background routine gets its turn to execute. This is called the *task level response*. The worst case task-level response time depends on how long the background loop takes to execute. Because the execution time of typical code is not constant, the time for successive passes through a portion of the loop is nondeterministic. Furthermore, if a code change is made, the timing of the loop is affected.

Figure 2.1   Foreground/background systems.

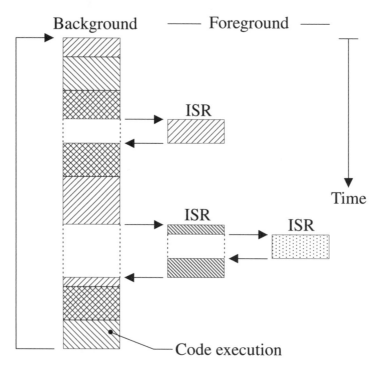

Most high-volume microcontroller-based applications (e.g., microwave ovens, telephones, toys, and so on) are designed as foreground/background systems. Also, in microcontroller-based applications, it may be better (from a power consumption point of view) to halt the processor and perform all of the processing in ISRs.

2.01 Critical Section of Code

A critical section of code, also called a *critical region*, is code that needs to be treated indivisibly. Once the section of code starts executing, it must not be interrupted. To ensure this, interrupts are typically disabled before the critical code is executed and enabled when the critical code is finished (see also section 2.03, Shared Resource).

2.02 Resource

A resource is any entity used by a task. A resource can thus be an I/O device, such as a printer, a keyboard, or a display, or a variable, a structure, or an array.

2.03 Shared Resource

A shared resource is a resource that can be used by more than one task. Each task should gain exclusive access to the shared resource to prevent data corruption. This is called *mutual exclusion*, and techniques to ensure mutual exclusion are discussed in section 2.18, Mutual Exclusion.

2.04 Multitasking

Multitasking is the process of scheduling and switching the CPU (Central Processing Unit) between several tasks; a single CPU switches its attention between several sequential tasks. Multitasking is like foreground/background with multiple backgrounds. Multitasking maximizes the utilization of the CPU and also provides for modular construction of applications. One of the most important aspects of multitasking is that it allows the application programmer to manage complexity inherent in real-time applications. Application programs are typically easier to design and maintain if multitasking is used.

2.05 Task

A task, also called a *thread*, is a simple program that thinks it has the CPU all to itself. The design process for a real-time application involves splitting the work to be done into tasks responsible for a portion of the problem. Each task is assigned a priority, its own set of CPU registers, and its own stack area (as shown in Figure 2.2).

Each task typically is an infinite loop that can be in any one of five states: *DORMANT, READY, RUNNING, WAITING* (for an event), or *ISR* (interrupted) (Figure 2.3). The DORMANT state corresponds to a task that resides in memory but has not been made available to the multitasking kernel. A task is READY when it can execute but its priority is less than the currently running task. A task is RUNNING when it has control of the CPU. A task is WAITING when it requires the occurrence of an event (waiting for an I/O operation to complete, a shared resource to be available, a timing pulse to occur, time to expire, etc.). Finally, a task is in the ISR state when an interrupt has occurred and the CPU is in the process of servicing the interrupt. Figure 2.3 also shows the functions provided by µC/OS-II to make a task move from one state to another.

Figure 2.2   Multiple tasks.

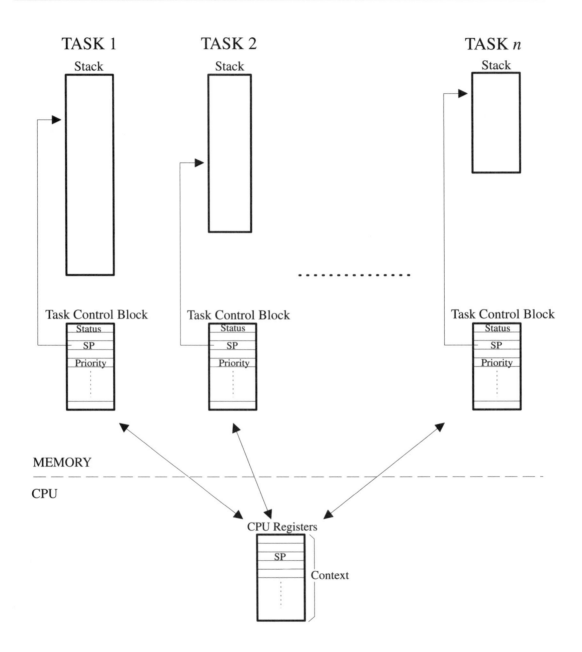

Figure 2.3   Task states.

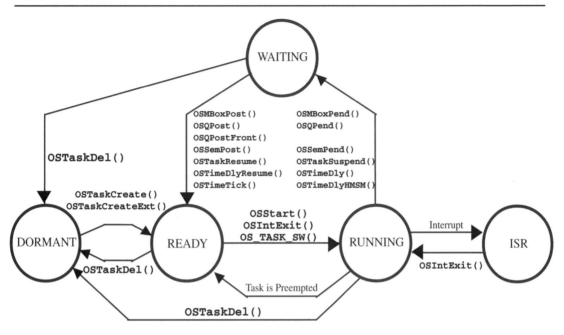

2.06 *Context Switch (or Task Switch)*

When a multitasking kernel decides to run a different task, it simply saves the current task's *context* (CPU registers) in the current task's context storage area — its stack (Figure 2.2). Once this operation is performed, the new task's context is restored from its storage area then resumes execution of the new task's code. This process is called a *context switch* or a *task switch.* Context switching adds overhead to the application. The more registers a CPU has, the higher the overhead. The time required to perform a context switch is determined by how many registers have to be saved and restored by the CPU. Performance of a real-time kernel should not be judged by how many context switches the kernel is capable of doing per second.

2.07 *Kernel*

The kernel is the part of a multitasking system responsible for the management of tasks (i.e., for managing the CPU's time) and communication between tasks. The fundamental service provided by the kernel is context switching. The use of a real-time kernel generally simplifies the design of systems by allowing the application to be divided into multiple tasks managed by the kernel. A kernel adds overhead to your system because it requires extra ROM (code space) and additional RAM for the kernel data structures. But most importantly, each task requires its own stack space, which has a tendency to eat up RAM quite quickly. A kernel will also consume CPU time (typically between 2 and 5 percent).

Single-chip microcontrollers are generally not able to run a real-time kernel because they have very little RAM. A kernel allows you to make better use of your CPU by providing you with indispensable services such as semaphore management, mailboxes, queues, time delays, etc. Once you design a system using a real-time kernel, you will not want to go back to a foreground/background system.

2.08 Scheduler

The scheduler, also called the *dispatcher*, is the part of the kernel responsible for determining which task will run next. Most real-time kernels are priority based. Each task is assigned a priority based on its importance. The priority for each task is application specific. In a priority-based kernel, control of the CPU is always given to the highest priority task ready to run. *When* the highest priority task gets the CPU, however, is determined by the type of kernel used. There are two types of priority-based kernels: *non-preemptive* and *preemptive*.

2.09 Non-Preemptive Kernel

Non-preemptive kernels require that each task does something to explicitly give up control of the CPU. To maintain the illusion of concurrency, this process must be done frequently. Non-preemptive scheduling is also called *cooperative multitasking*; tasks cooperate with each other to share the CPU. Asynchronous events are still handled by ISRs. An ISR can make a higher priority task ready to run, but the ISR always returns to the interrupted task. The new higher priority task will gain control of the CPU only when the current task gives up the CPU.

One of the advantages of a non-preemptive kernel is that interrupt latency is typically low (see the later discussion on interrupts). At the task level, non-preemptive kernels can also use non-reentrant functions (discussed later). Non-reentrant functions can be used by each task without fear of corruption by another task. This is because each task can run to completion before it relinquishes the CPU. However, non-reentrant functions should not be allowed to give up control of the CPU.

Task-level response using a non-preemptive kernel can be much lower than with foreground/background systems because task-level response is now given by the time of the longest task.

Another advantage of non-preemptive kernels is the lesser need to guard shared data through the use of semaphores. Each task owns the CPU, and you don't have to fear that a task will be preempted. This is not an absolute rule, and in some instances, semaphores should still be used. Shared I/O devices may still require the use of mutual exclusion semaphores; for example, a task might still need exclusive access to a printer.

The execution profile of a non-preemptive kernel is shown in Figure 2.4. A task is executing [F2.4(1)] but gets interrupted. If interrupts are enabled, the CPU vectors (jumps) to the ISR [L2.4(2)]. The ISR handles the event [F2.4(3)] and makes a higher priority task ready to run. Upon completion of the ISR, a *Return From Interrupt* instruction is executed, and the CPU returns to the interrupted task [F2.4(4)]. The task code resumes at the instruction following the interrupted instruction [F2.4(5)]. When the task code completes, it calls a service provided by the kernel to relinquish the CPU to another task [F2.4(6)]. The new higher priority task then executes to handle the event signaled by the ISR [F2.4(7)].

Figure 2.4   Non-preemptive kernel.

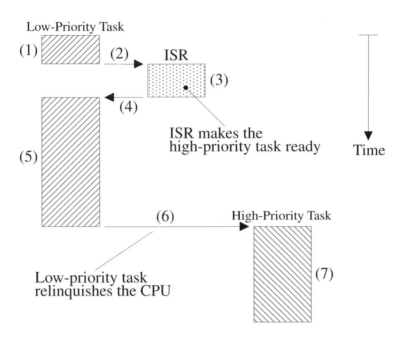

The most important drawback of a non-preemptive kernel is responsiveness. A higher priority task that has been made ready to run may have to wait a long time to run because the current task must give up the CPU when it is ready to do so. As with background execution in foreground/background systems, task-level response time in a non-preemptive kernel is nondeterministic; you never really know when the highest priority task will get control of the CPU. It is up to your application to relinquish control of the CPU.

To summarize, a non-preemptive kernel allows each task to run until it voluntarily gives up control of the CPU. An interrupt preempts a task. Upon completion of the ISR, the ISR returns to the interrupted task. Task-level response is much better than with a foreground/background system but is still nondeterministic. Very few commercial kernels are non-preemptive.

2.10 Preemptive Kernel

A preemptive kernel is used when system responsiveness is important. Because of this, μC/OS-II and most commercial real-time kernels are preemptive. The highest priority task ready to run is always given control of the CPU. When a task makes a higher priority task ready to run, the current task is preempted (suspended) and the higher priority task is *immediately* given control of the CPU. If an ISR makes a higher priority task ready, when the ISR completes, the interrupted task is suspended and the new higher priority task is resumed. This is illustrated in Figure 2.5.

Figure 2.5   Preemptive kernel.

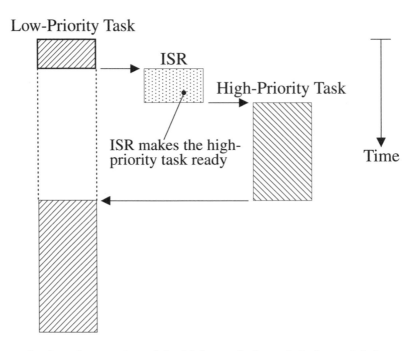

With a preemptive kernel, execution of the highest priority task is deterministic; you can determine when it will get control of the CPU. Task-level response time is thus minimized by using a preemptive kernel.

Application code using a preemptive kernel should not use non-reentrant functions, unless exclusive access to these functions is ensured through the use of mutual exclusion semaphores, because both a low- and a high-priority task can use a common function. Corruption of data may occur if the higher priority task preempts a lower priority task that is using the function.

To summarize, a preemptive kernel always executes the highest priority task that is ready to run. An interrupt preempts a task. Upon completion of an ISR, the kernel resumes execution to the highest priority task ready to run (not the interrupted task). Task-level response is optimum and deterministic. μC/OS-II is a preemptive kernel.

2.11 Reentrancy

A *reentrant function* can be used by more than one task without fear of data corruption. A reentrant function can be interrupted at any time and resumed at a later time without loss of data. Reentrant functions either use local variables (i.e., CPU registers or variables on the stack) or protect data when global variables are used. An example of a reentrant function is shown in Listing 2.1.

Listing 2.1   Reentrant function.

```
void strcpy(char *dest, char *src)
{
    while (*dest++ = *src++) {
        ;
    }
    *dest = NUL;
}
```

Because copies of the arguments to `strcpy()` are placed on the task's stack, `strcpy()` can be invoked by multiple tasks without fear that the tasks will corrupt each other's pointers.

An example of a non-reentrant function is shown in Listing 2.2. `swap()` is a simple function that swaps the contents of its two arguments. For the sake of discussion, I assume that you are using a pre-emptive kernel, that interrupts are enabled, and that `Temp` is declared as a global integer:

Listing 2.2   Non-reentrant function.

```
int Temp;

void swap(int *x, int *y)
{
    Temp = *x;
    *x   = *y;
    *y   = Temp;
}
```

The programmer intended to make `swap()` usable by any task. Figure 2.6 shows what could happen if a low-priority task is interrupted while `swap()` [F2.6(1)] is executing. Note that at this point `Temp` contains 1. The ISR makes the higher priority task ready to run, so at the completion of the ISR [F2.6(2)], the kernel (assuming µC/OS-II) is invoked to switch to this task [F2.6(3)]. The high-priority task sets `Temp` to 3 and swaps the contents of its variables correctly (i.e., z is 4 and t is 3). The high-priority task eventually relinquishes control to the low-priority task [F2.6(4)] by calling a kernel service to delay itself for one clock tick (described later). The lower priority task is thus resumed [F2.6(5)]. Note that at this point, `Temp` is still set to 3! When the low-priority task resumes execution, it sets y to 3 instead of 1.

Note that this a simple example, so it is obvious how to make the code reentrant. However, other situations are not as easy to solve. An error caused by a non-reentrant function may not show up in your application during the testing phase; it will most likely occur once the product has been delivered! If you are new to multitasking, you will need to be careful when using non-reentrant functions.

You can make `swap()` reentrant with one of the following techniques:

- Declare `Temp` local to `swap()`.
- Disable interrupts before the operation and enable them afterwards.
- Use a semaphore (described later).

Figure 2.6   Non-reentrant function.

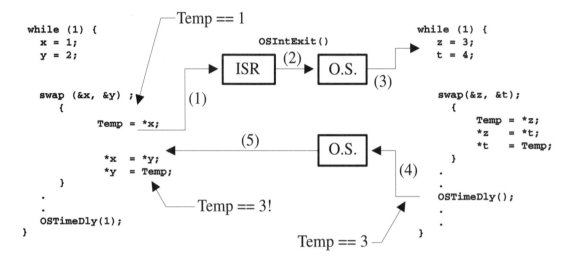

If the interrupt occurs either before or after swap(), the x and y values for both tasks will be correct.

2.12 Round-Robin Scheduling

When two or more tasks have the same priority, the kernel allows one task to run for a predetermined amount of time, called a *quantum*, then selects another task. This is also called *time slicing*. The kernel gives control to the next task in line if

- the current task has no work to do during its time slice or
- the current task completes before the end of its time slice.

µC/OS-II does not currently support round-robin scheduling. Each task must have a unique priority in your application.

2.13 Task Priority

A priority is assigned to each task. The more important the task, the higher the priority given to it.

2.14 Static Priorities

Task priorities are said to be *static* when the priority of each task does not change during the application's execution. Each task is thus given a fixed priority at compile time. All the tasks and their timing constraints are known at compile time in a system where priorities are static.

2.15 Dynamic Priorities

Task priorities are said to be dynamic if the priority of tasks can be changed during the application's execution; each task can change its priority at run time. This is a desirable feature to have in a real-time kernel to avoid priority inversions.

2.16 Priority Inversions   *see Sec 4.06 Pg 124*

Priority inversion is a problem in real-time systems and occurs mostly when you use a real-time kernel. Figure 2.7 illustrates a priority inversion scenario. Task 1 has a higher priority than Task 2, which in turn has a higher priority than Task 3. Task 1 and Task 2 are both waiting for an event to occur and Task 3 is executing [F2.7(1)]. At some point, Task 3 acquires a semaphore (see section 2.18.04, Semaphores), which it needs before it can access a shared resource [F2.7(2)]. Task 3 performs some operations on the acquired resource [F2.7(4)] until it is preempted by the high-priority task, Task 1 [F2.7(3)]. Task 1 executes for a while until it also wants to access the resource [F2.7(5)]. Because Task 3 owns the resource, Task 1 has to wait until Task 3 releases the semaphore. As Task 1 tries to get the semaphore, the kernel notices that the semaphore is already owned; thus, Task 1 is suspended and Task 3 is resumed [F2.7(6)]. Task 3 continues execution until it is preempted by Task 2 because the event that Task2 was waiting for occurred [F2.7(7)]. Task 2 handles the event [F2.7(8)] and when it's done, Task 2 relinquishes the CPU back to Task 3 [F2.7(9)]. Task 3 finishes working with the resource [F2.7(10)] and releases the semaphore [F2.7(11)]. At this point, the kernel knows that a higher priority task is waiting for the semaphore, and a context switch is done to resume Task 1. At this point, Task 1 has the semaphore and can access the shared resource [F2.7(12)].

The priority of Task 1 has been virtually reduced to that of Task 3 because it was waiting for the resource that Task 3 owned. The situation was aggravated when Task 2 preempted Task 3, which further delayed the execution of Task 1.

You can correct this situation by raising the priority of Task 3, just for the time it takes to access the resource, then restoring the original priority level when the task is finished. The priority of Task 3 must be raised up to or above the highest priority of the other tasks competing for the resource. A multitasking kernel should allow task priorities to change dynamically to help prevent priority inversions. However, it takes some time to change a task's priority. What if Task 3 had completed access of the resource before it was preempted by Task 1 and then by Task 2? Had you raised the priority of Task 3 before accessing the resource and then lowered it back when done, you would have wasted valuable CPU time. What is really needed to avoid priority inversion is a kernel that changes the priority of a task automatically. This is called *priority inheritance*, which μC/OS-II unfortunately does not support. There are, however, some commercial kernels that do.

Figure 2.7   Priority inversion problem.

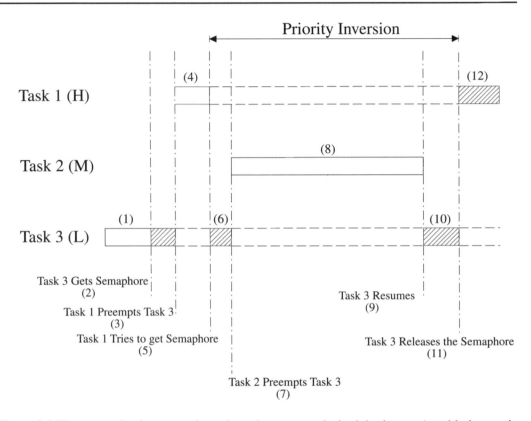

Figure 2.8 illustrates what happens when a kernel supports priority inheritance. As with the previous example, Task 3 is running [F2.8(1)] and acquires a semaphore to access a shared resource [F2.8(2)]. Task 3 accesses the resource [F2.8(3)] and then is preempted by Task 1 [F2.8(4)]. Task 1 executes [F2.8(5)] and tries to obtain the semaphore [F2.8(6)]. The kernel sees that Task 3 has the semaphore but has a lower priority than Task 1. In this case, the kernel raises the priority of Task 3 to the same level as Task 1. The kernel then switches back to Task 3 so that this task can continue with the resource [F2.8(7)]. When Task 3 is done with the resource, it releases the semaphore [F2.8(8)]. At this point, the kernel reduces the priority of Task 3 to its original value and gives the semaphore to Task 1 which is now free to continue [F2.8(9)]. When Task 1 is done executing [F2.8(10)], the medium-priority task (i.e., Task 2) gets the CPU [F2.8(11)]. Note that Task 2 could have been ready to run any time between F2.8(3) and (10) without affecting the outcome. There is still some level of priority inversion that cannot be avoided.

Figure 2.8   *Kernel that supports priority inheritance.*

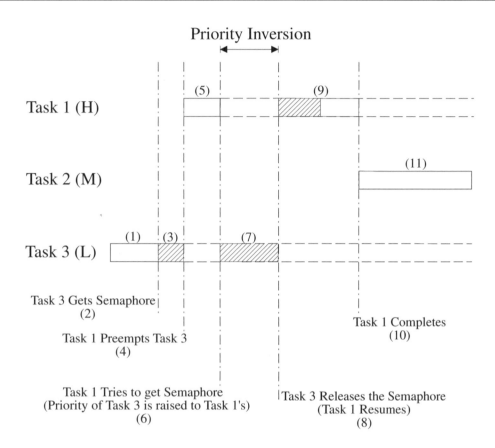

2.17 *Assigning Task Priorities*

Assigning task priorities is not a trivial undertaking because of the complex nature of real-time systems. In most systems, not all tasks are considered critical. Noncritical tasks should obviously be given low priorities. Most real-time systems have a combination of SOFT and HARD requirements. In a SOFT real-time system, tasks are performed as quickly as possible, but they don't have to finish by specific times. In HARD real-time systems, tasks have to be performed not only correctly, but on time.

An interesting technique called *Rate Monotonic Scheduling* (RMS) has been established to assign task priorities based on how often tasks execute. Simply put, tasks with the highest rate of execution are given the highest priority (Figure 2.9).

Figure 2.9   Assigning task priorities based on task execution rate.

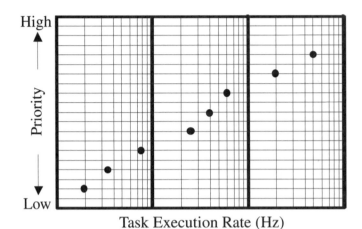

RMS makes a number of assumptions:

- All tasks are periodic (they occur at regular intervals).
- Tasks do not synchronize with one another, share resources, or exchange data.
- The CPU must always execute the highest priority task that is ready to run. In other words, preemptive scheduling must be used.

Given a set of *n* tasks that are assigned RMS priorities, the basic RMS theorem states that all task HARD real-time deadlines will always be met if the inequality in Equation [2.1] is verified.

[2.1] $$\sum_i \frac{E_i}{T_i} \le n(2^{1/n} - 1)$$

where, E_i corresponds to the maximum execution time of task *i* and T_i corresponds to the execution period of task *i*. In other words, E_i/T_i corresponds to the fraction of CPU time required to execute task *i*. Table 2.1 shows the value for size $n(2^{1/n} - 1)$ based on the number of tasks. The upper bound for an infinite number of tasks is given by ln(2), or 0.693. This means that to meet all HARD real-time deadlines based on RMS, CPU utilization of all time-critical tasks should be less than 70 percent! Note that you can still have non-time-critical tasks in a system and thus use 100 percent of the CPU's time. Using 100 percent of your CPU's time is not a desirable goal because it does not allow for code changes and added features. As a rule of thumb, you should always design a system to use less than 60 to 70 percent of your CPU.

RMS says that the highest rate task has the highest priority. In some cases, the highest rate task may not be the most important task. Your application will thus dictate how you need to assign priorities. However, RMS is an interesting starting point.

Table 2.1   Allowable CPU utilization based on number of tasks.

Number of Tasks	$n(2^{1/n} - 1)$
1	1.000
2	0.828
3	0.779
4	0.756
5	0.743
.	.
.	.
.	.
∞	0.693

2.18 Mutual Exclusion

The easiest way for tasks to communicate with each other is through shared data structures. This is especially easy when all tasks exist in a single address space and can reference global variables, pointers, buffers, linked lists, ring buffers, etc. Although sharing data simplifies the exchange of information, you must ensure that each task has exclusive access to the data to avoid contention and data corruption. The most common methods of obtaining exclusive access to shared resources are

- disabling interrupts,
- performing test-and-set operations,
- disabling scheduling, and
- using semaphores.

2.18.01   Disabling and Enabling Interrupts

The easiest and fastest way to gain exclusive access to a shared resource is by disabling and enabling interrupts, as shown in the pseudocode in Listing 2.3.

Listing 2.3   Disabling and enabling interrupts.

```
Disable interrupts;
Access the resource (read/write from/to variables);
Reenable interrupts;
```

μC/OS-II uses this technique (as do most, if not all, kernels) to access internal variables and data structures. In fact, μC/OS-II provides two macros that allow you to disable and then enable interrupts from your C code: OS_ENTER_CRITICAL() and OS_EXIT_CRITICAL(), respectively [see section 8.03.02, OS_ENTER_CRITICAL(), and OS_EXIT_CRITICAL()]. You need to use these macros in tandem, as shown in Listing 2.4.

Listing 2.4   Using µC/OS-II macros to disable and enable interrupts.

```
void Function (void)
{
    OS_ENTER_CRITICAL();
    .
    .      /* You can access shared data in here */
    .
    OS_EXIT_CRITICAL();
}
```

You must be careful, however, not to disable interrupts for too long because this affects the response of your system to interrupts. This is known as *interrupt latency*. You should consider this method when you are changing or copying a few variables. Also, this is the only way that a task can share variables or data structures with an ISR. In all cases, you should keep interrupts disabled for as little time as possible.

If you use a kernel, you are basically allowed to disable interrupts for as much time as the kernel does without affecting interrupt latency. Obviously, you need to know how long the kernel will disable interrupts. Any good kernel vendor will provide you with this information. After all, if they sell a real-time kernel, time is important!

2.18.02   Test-And-Set

If you are not using a kernel, two functions could 'agree' that to access a resource, they must check a global variable and if the variable is 0, the function has access to the resource. To prevent the other function from accessing the resource, however, the first function that gets the resource simply sets the variable to 1. This is commonly called a *Test-And-Set* (or TAS) operation. Either the TAS operation must be performed indivisibly (by the processor) or you must disable interrupts when doing the TAS on the variable, as shown in Listing 2.5.

Listing 2.5   Using Test-And-Set to access a resource.

```
Disable interrupts;
if ('Access Variable' is 0) {
    Set variable to 1;
    Reenable interrupts;
    Access the resource;
    Disable interrupts;
    Set the 'Access Variable' back to 0;
    Reenable interrupts;
} else {
    Reenable interrupts;
    /* You don't have access to the resource, try back later; */
}
```

Some processors actually implement a TAS operation in hardware (e.g., the 68000 family of processors have the TAS instruction).

2.18.03 Disabling and Enabling the Scheduler

If your task is not sharing variables or data structures with an ISR, you can disable and enable scheduling (see section 3.06, Locking and Unlocking the Scheduler), as shown in Listing 2.6 (using µC/OS-II as an example). In this case, two or more tasks can share data without the possibility of contention. You should note that while the scheduler is locked, interrupts are enabled, and if an interrupt occurs while in the critical section, the ISR is executed immediately. At the end of the ISR, the kernel always returns to the interrupted task, even if a higher priority task has been made ready to run by the ISR. The scheduler is invoked when OSSchedUnlock() is called to see if a higher priority task has been made ready to run by the task or an ISR. A context switch results if a higher priority task is ready to run. Although this method works well, you should avoid disabling the scheduler because it defeats the purpose of having a kernel in the first place. The next method should be chosen instead.

Listing 2.6   Accessing shared data by disabling and enabling scheduling.

```
void Function (void)
{
    OSSchedLock();
    .
    .    /* You can access shared data in here (interrupts are recognized) */
    .
    OSSchedUnlock();
}
```

2.18.04 Semaphores

The semaphore was invented by Edgser Dijkstra in the mid-1960s. It is a protocol mechanism offered by most multitasking kernels. Semaphores are used to

- control access to a shared resource (mutual exclusion),
- signal the occurrence of an event, and
- allow two tasks to synchronize their activities.

A semaphore is a key that your code acquires in order to continue execution. If the semaphore is already in use, the requesting task is suspended until the semaphore is released by its current owner. In other words, the requesting task says: "Give me the key. If someone else is using it, I am willing to wait for it!" There are two types of semaphores: *binary* semaphores and *counting* semaphores. As its name implies, a binary semaphore can only take two values: 0 or 1. A counting semaphore allows values between 0 and 255, 65535, or 4294967295, depending on whether the semaphore mechanism is implemented using 8, 16, or 32 bits, respectively. The actual size depends on the kernel used. Along with the semaphore's value, the kernel also needs to keep track of tasks waiting for the semaphore's availability.

Generally, only three operations can be performed on a semaphore: INITIALIZE (also called *CREATE*), WAIT (also called *PEND*), and SIGNAL (also called *POST*). The initial value of the semaphore must be provided when the semaphore is initialized. The waiting list of tasks is always initially empty.

A task desiring the semaphore will perform a WAIT operation. If the semaphore is available (the semaphore value is greater than 0), the semaphore value is decremented and the task continues execution. If the semaphore's value is 0, the task performing a WAIT on the semaphore is placed in a waiting list. Most kernels allow you to specify a timeout; if the semaphore is not available within a certain amount of time, the requesting task is made ready to run and an error code (indicating that a timeout has occurred) is returned to the caller.

A task releases a semaphore by performing a SIGNAL operation. If no task is waiting for the semaphore, the semaphore value is simply incremented. If any task is waiting for the semaphore, however, one of the tasks is made ready to run and the semaphore value is not incremented; the key is given to one of the tasks waiting for it. Depending on the kernel, the task that receives the semaphore is either

- the highest priority task waiting for the semaphore or
- the first task that requested the semaphore (First In First Out, or FIFO).

NOT AN OPTION

Some kernels have an option that allows you to choose either method when the semaphore is initialized. µC/OS-II only supports the first method. If the readied task has a higher priority than the current task (the task releasing the semaphore), a context switch occurs (with a preemptive kernel) and the higher priority task resumes execution; the current task is suspended until it again becomes the highest priority task ready to run.

Listing 2.7 shows how you can share data using a semaphore (in µC/OS-II). Any task needing access to the same shared data calls OSSemPend(), and when the task is done with the data, the task calls OSSemPost(). Both of these functions are described later. You should note that a semaphore is an object that needs to be initialized before it's used; for mutual exclusion, a semaphore is initialized to a value of 1. Using a semaphore to access shared data doesn't affect interrupt latency. If an ISR or the current task makes a higher priority task ready to run while accessing shared data, the higher priority task executes immediately.

Listing 2.7   *Accessing shared data by obtaining a semaphore.*

```
OS_EVENT *SharedDataSem;
void Function (void)
{
    INT8U err;
    OSSemPend(SharedDataSem, 0, &err);
        WAIT
        .
        .    /* You can access shared data in here (interrupts are recognized) */
        .
    OSSemPost(SharedDataSem);
}       Signal
```

Semaphores are especially useful when tasks share I/O devices. Imagine what would happen if two tasks were allowed to send characters to a printer at the same time. The printer would contain interleaved data from each task. For instance, the printout from Task 1 printing "I am Task 1!" and Task 2 printing "I am Task 2!" could result in:

I Ia amm T Tasask k1 !2!

In this case, use a semaphore and initialize it to 1 (i.e., a binary semaphore). The rule is simple: to access the printer each task first must obtain the resource's semaphore. Figure 2.10 shows tasks competing for a semaphore to gain exclusive access to the printer. Note that the semaphore is represented symbolically by a key, indicating that each task must obtain this key to use the printer.

Figure 2.10   Using a semaphore to get permission to access a printer.

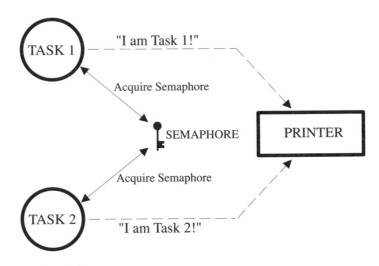

The above example implies that each task must know about the existence of the semaphore in order to access the resource. There are situations when it is better to encapsulate the semaphore. Each task would thus not know that it is actually acquiring a semaphore when accessing the resource. For example, an RS-232C port is used by multiple tasks to send commands and receive responses from a device connected at the other end (Figure 2.11).

The function CommSendCmd() is called with three arguments: the ASCII string containing the command, a pointer to the response string from the device, and finally, a timeout in case the device doesn't respond within a certain amount of time. The pseudocode for this function is shown in Listing 2.8.

Listing 2.8   Encapsulating a semaphore.

```
INT8U CommSendCmd(char *cmd, char *response, INT16U timeout)
{
    Acquire port's semaphore;
    Send command to device;
    Wait for response (with timeout);
    if (timed out) {
        Release semaphore;
        return (error code);
    } else {
        Release semaphore;
        return (no error);
    }
}
```

Each task that needs to send a command to the device has to call this function. The semaphore is assumed to be initialized to 1 (i.e., available) by the communication driver initialization routine. The first task that calls CommSendCmd() acquires the semaphore, proceeds to send the command, and waits for a response. If another task attempts to send a command while the port is busy, this second task is suspended until the semaphore is released. The second task appears simply to have made a call to a normal function that will not return until the function has performed its duty. When the semaphore is released by the first task, the second task acquires the semaphore and is allowed to use the RS-232C port.

Figure 2.11   Hiding a semaphore from tasks.

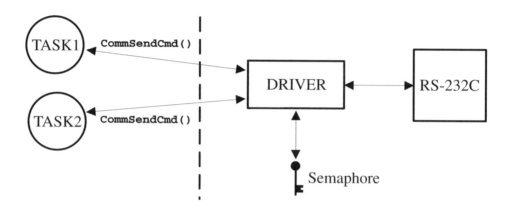

A counting semaphore is used when a resource can be used by more than one task at the same time. For example, a counting semaphore is used in the management of a buffer pool as shown in Figure 2.12. Assume that the buffer pool initially contains 10 buffers. A task would obtain a buffer from the buffer manager by calling BufReq(). When the buffer is no longer needed, the task would return the buffer to the buffer manager by calling BufRel(). The pseudocode for these functions is shown in Listing 2.9.

∴ COUNTING SEMAPHORE IS INITIALIZED WITH

Listing 2.9   Buffer management using a semaphore.   *VALUE OF 10.*

```
BUF *BufReq(void)
{
    BUF *ptr;

    Acquire a semaphore;          — This is the global resource.
    Disable interrupts;             ∴ disable/enable interrupts
    ptr          = BufFreeList;
    BufFreeList = ptr->BufNext;
    Enable interrupts;
    return (ptr);
}
```

Listing 2.9   *Buffer management using a semaphore. (Continued)*

```
void BufRel(BUF *ptr)
{
    Disable interrupts;
    ptr->BufNext = BufFreeList;
    BufFreeList = ptr;
    Enable interrupts;
    Release semaphore;
}
```

2

Figure 2.12   *Using a counting semaphore.*

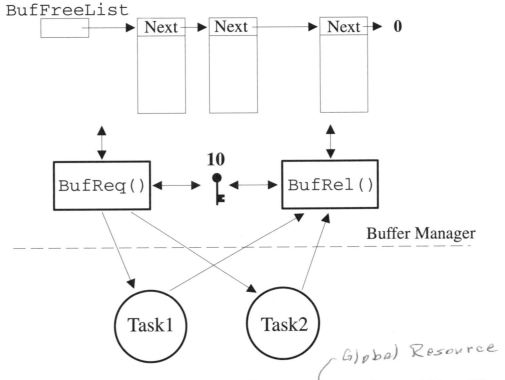

The buffer manager will satisfy the first 10 buffer requests because there are 10 keys. When all semaphores are used, a task requesting a buffer is suspended until a semaphore becomes available. Interrupts are disabled to gain exclusive access to the linked list (this operation is very quick). When a task is finished with the buffer it acquired, it calls BufRel() to return the buffer to the buffer manager; the buffer is inserted into the linked list before the semaphore is released. By encapsulating the interface to the buffer manager in BufReq() and BufRel(), the caller doesn't need to be concerned with the actual implementation details.

Semaphores are often overused. The use of a semaphore to access a simple shared variable is over-kill in most situations. The overhead involved in acquiring and releasing the semaphore can consume valuable time. You can do the job just as efficiently by disabling and enabling interrupts (see section 2.18.01, Disabling and Enabling Interrupts). Suppose that two tasks are sharing a 32-bit integer vari-able. The first task increments the variable while the other task clears it. If you consider how long a pro-cessor takes to perform either operation, you will realize that you do not need a semaphore to gain exclusive access to the variable. Each task simply needs to disable interrupts before performing its oper-ation on the variable and enable interrupts when the operation is complete. A semaphore should be used, however, if the variable is a floating-point variable and the microprocessor doesn't support floating point in hardware. In this case, the processing time involved in processing the floating-point variable could have affected interrupt latency if you had disabled interrupts.

2.19 Deadlock (or Deadly Embrace)

A deadlock, also called a *deadly embrace*, is a situation in which two tasks are each unknowingly wait-ing for resources held by the other. Assume task T1 has exclusive access to resource R1 and task T2 has exclusive access to resource R2. If T1 needs exclusive access to R2 and T2 needs exclusive access to R1, neither task can continue. They are deadlocked. The simplest way to avoid a deadlock is for tasks to

- acquire all resources before proceeding,
- acquire the resources in the same order, and
- release the resources in the reverse order.

Most kernels allow you to specify a timeout when acquiring a semaphore. This feature allows a deadlock to be broken. If the semaphore is not available within a certain amount of time, the task requesting the resource resumes execution. Some form of error code must be returned to the task to notify it that a timeout occurred. A return error code prevents the task from thinking it has obtained the resource. Deadlocks generally occur in large multitasking systems, not in embedded systems.

2.20 Synchronization

A task can be synchronized with an ISR (or another task when no data is being exchanged) by using a semaphore as shown in Figure 2.13. Note that, in this case, the semaphore is drawn as a flag to indicate that it is used to signal the occurrence of an event (rather than to ensure mutual exclusion, in which case it would be drawn as a key). When used as a synchronization mechanism, the semaphore is initialized to 0. Using a semaphore for this type of synchronization is called a *unilateral rendezvous*. A task initiates an I/O operation and waits for the semaphore. When the I/O operation is complete, an ISR (or another task) signals the semaphore and the task is resumed.

Figure 2.13   Synchronizing tasks and ISRs.

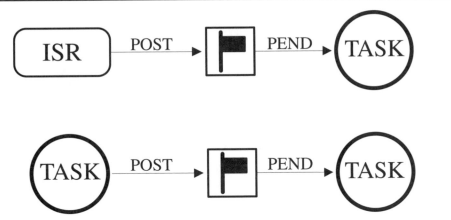

If the kernel supports counting semaphores, the semaphore would accumulate events that have not yet been processed. Note that more than one task can be waiting for an event to occur. In this case, the kernel could signal the occurrence of the event either to

- the highest priority task waiting for the event to occur or
- the first task waiting for the event.

Depending on the application, more than one ISR or task could signal the occurrence of the event.

Two tasks can synchronize their activities by using two semaphores, as shown in Figure 2.14. This is called a *bilateral rendezvous*. A bilateral rendezvous is similar to a unilateral rendezvous, except both tasks must synchronize with one another before proceeding.

For example, two tasks are executing as shown in Listing 2.10. When the first task reaches a certain point, it signals the second task [L2.10(1)] then waits for a return signal [L2.10(2)]. Similarly, when the second task reaches a certain point, it signals the first task [L2.10(3)] and waits for a return signal [L2.10(4)]. At this point, both tasks are synchronized with each other. A bilateral rendezvous cannot be performed between a task and an ISR because an ISR cannot wait on a semaphore.

Figure 2.14   Tasks synchronizing their activities.

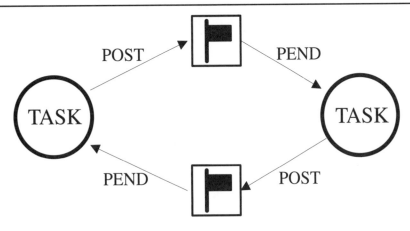

Listing 2.10   Bilateral rendezvous.

```
Task1()
{
    for (;;) {
        Perform operation;
        Signal task #2;                                              (1)
        Wait for signal from task #2;                                (2)
        Continue operation;
    }
}


Task2()
{
    for (;;) {
        Perform operation;
        Signal task #1;                                              (3)
        Wait for signal from task #1;                                (4)
        Continue operation;
    }
}
```

2.21 Event Flags — NOT CURRENTLY AVAILABLE (V2.04)
5/10/03   WAS ADDED IN V2.51 ?

Event flags are used when a task needs to synchronize with the occurrence of multiple events. The task can be synchronized when any of the events have occurred. This is called disjunctive synchronization (logical OR). A task can also be synchronized when all events have occurred. This is called conjunctive synchronization (logical AND). Disjunctive and conjunctive synchronization are shown in Figure 2.15.

Common events can be used to signal multiple tasks, as shown in Figure 2.16. Events are typically grouped. Depending on the kernel, a group consists of 8, 16, or 32 events, each represented by a bit. (mostly 32 bits, though). Tasks and ISRs can set or clear any event in a group. A task is resumed when all the events it requires are satisfied. The evaluation of which task will be resumed is performed when a new set of events occurs (i.e., during a SET operation).

Kernels supporting event flags offer services to SET event flags, CLEAR event flags, and WAIT for event flags (conjunctively or disjunctively). µC/OS-II does not currently support event flags.

2

Figure 2.15   Disjunctive and conjunctive synchronization.

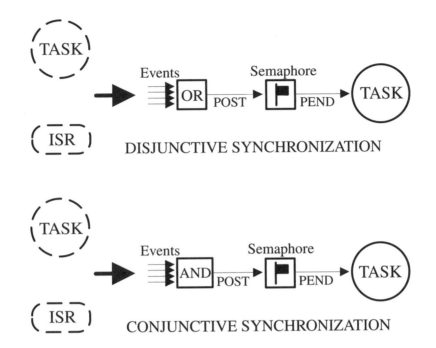

DISJUNCTIVE SYNCHRONIZATION

CONJUNCTIVE SYNCHRONIZATION

2.22 Intertask Communication

It is sometimes necessary for a task or an ISR to communicate information to another task. This information transfer is called *intertask communication.* Information may be communicated between tasks in two ways: through global data or by sending messages.

When using global variables, each task or ISR must ensure that it has exclusive access to the variables. If an ISR is involved, the only way to ensure exclusive access to the common variables is to disable interrupts. If two tasks are sharing data, each can gain exclusive access to the variables either by disabling and enabling interrupts or with the use of a semaphore (as we have seen). Note that a task can only communicate information to an ISR by using global variables. A task is not aware when a global variable is changed by an ISR, unless the ISR signals the task by using a semaphore or unless the task polls the contents of the variable periodically. To correct this situation, you should consider using either a *message mailbox* or a *message queue.*

An ISR cannot wait on a semaphore.

P. 59, too

Figure 2.16   Event flags.

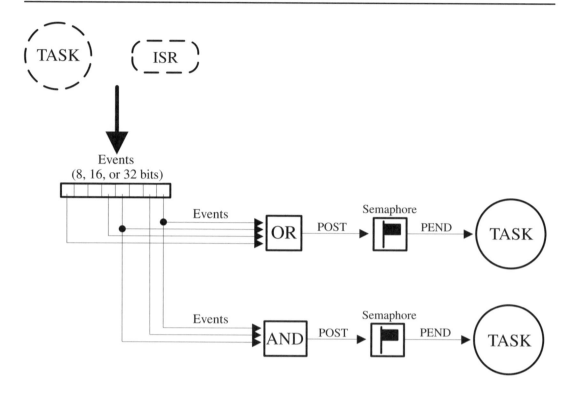

2.23 Message Mailboxes

Messages can be sent to a task through kernel services. A Message Mailbox, also called a message exchange, is typically a pointer-size variable. Through a service provided by the kernel, a task or an ISR can deposit a message (the pointer) into this mailbox. Similarly, one or more tasks can receive messages through a service provided by the kernel. Both the sending task and receiving task agree on what the pointer is actually pointing to.

A waiting list is associated with each mailbox in case more than one task wants to receive messages through the mailbox. A task desiring a message from an empty mailbox is suspended and placed on the waiting list until a message is received. Typically, the kernel allows the task waiting for a message to specify a timeout. If a message is not received before the timeout expires, the requesting task is made ready to run and an error code (indicating that a timeout has occurred) is returned to it. When a message is deposited into the mailbox, either the highest priority task waiting for the message is given the message (*priority based*) or the first task to request a message is given the message (*First-In-First-Out*, or FIFO). Figure 2.17 shows a task depositing a message into a mailbox. Note that the mailbox is represented by an I-beam and the timeout is represented by an hourglass. The number next to the hourglass represents the number of clock ticks (described later) the task will wait for a message to arrive.

Kernels typically provide the following mailbox services.

- Initialize the contents of a mailbox. The mailbox initially may or may not contain a message.
- Deposit a message into the mailbox (POST).
- Wait for a message to be deposited into the mailbox (PEND).
- Get a message from a mailbox if one is present, but do not suspend the caller if the mailbox is empty (ACCEPT). If the mailbox contains a message, the message is extracted from the mailbox. A return code is used to notify the caller about the outcome of the call.

Message mailboxes can also simulate binary semaphores. A message in the mailbox indicates that the resource is available, and an empty mailbox indicates that the resource is already in use by another task.

Figure 2.17   Message mailbox.

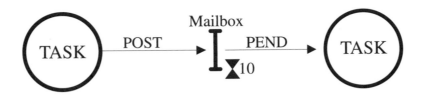

2.24 Message Queues

A message queue is used to send one or more messages to a task. A message queue is basically an array of mailboxes. Through a service provided by the kernel, a task or an ISR can deposit a message (the pointer) into a message queue. Similarly, one or more tasks can receive messages through a service provided by the kernel. Both the sending task and receiving task agree as to what the pointer is actually pointing to. Generally, the first message inserted in the queue will be the first message extracted from the queue (FIFO). In addition, to extract messages in a FIFO fashion, µC/OS-II allows a task to get messages Last-In-First-Out (LIFO).

As with the mailbox, a waiting list is associated with each message queue, in case more than one task is to receive messages through the queue. A task desiring a message from an empty queue is suspended and placed on the waiting list until a message is received. Typically, the kernel allows the task waiting for a message to specify a timeout. If a message is not received before the timeout expires, the requesting task is made ready to run and an error code (indicating a timeout has occurred) is returned to it. When a message is deposited into the queue, either the highest priority task or the first task to wait for the message is given the message. Figure 2.18 shows an ISR (Interrupt Service Routine) depositing a message into a queue. Note that the queue is represented graphically by a double I-beam. The "10" indicates the number of messages that can accumulate in the queue. A "0" next to the hourglass indicates that the task will wait forever for a message to arrive.

Kernels typically provide the message queue services listed below.

*   Initialize the queue. The queue is always assumed to be empty after initialization.
*   Deposit a message into the queue (POST).
*   Wait for a message to be deposited into the queue (PEND).
*   Get a message from a queue if one is present, but do not suspend the caller if the queue is empty (ACCEPT). If the queue contains a message, the message is extracted from the queue. A return code is used to notify the caller about the outcome of the call.

Figure 2.18   Message queue.

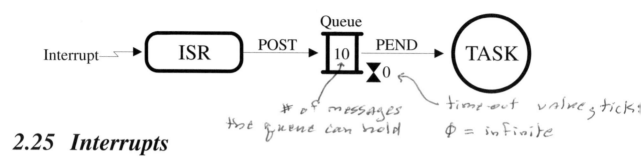

2.25 Interrupts

An interrupt is a hardware mechanism used to inform the CPU that an asynchronous event has occurred. When an interrupt is recognized, the CPU saves part (or all) of its context (i.e., registers) and jumps to a special subroutine called an *Interrupt Service Routine*, or ISR. The ISR processes the event, and upon completion of the ISR, the program returns to

*   the background for a foreground/background system,
*   the interrupted task for a non-preemptive kernel, or
*   the highest priority task ready to run for a preemptive kernel.

Interrupts allow a microprocessor to process events when they occur. This prevents the microprocessor from continuously *polling* an event to see if it has occurred. Microprocessors allow interrupts to be ignored and recognized through the use of two special instructions: *disable interrupts* and *enable interrupts*, respectively. In a real-time environment, interrupts should be disabled as little as possible. Disabling interrupts affects interrupt latency (see section 2.26, Interrupt Latency) and may cause interrupts to be missed. Processors generally allow interrupts to be *nested*. This means that while servicing an interrupt, the processor will recognize and service other (more important) interrupts, as shown in Figure 2.19.

2.26 Interrupt Latency

Probably the most important specification of a real-time kernel is the amount of time interrupts are disabled. All real-time systems disable interrupts to manipulate critical sections of code and reenable interrupts when the critical section has executed. The longer interrupts are disabled, the higher the *interrupt latency.* Interrupt latency is given by Equation [2.2].

[2.2]   Maximum amount of time interrupts are disabled *in the normal course of Processing.*
         + Time to start executing the first instruction in the ISR
              ↳ *strictly the hardware response time*

Figure 2.19 Interrupt nesting.

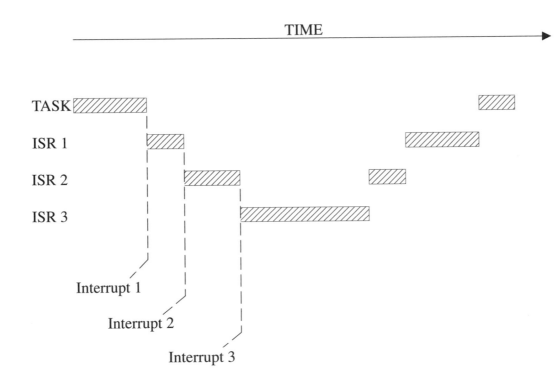

2.27 Interrupt Response

Interrupt response is defined as the time between the reception of the interrupt and the start of the user code that handles the interrupt. The interrupt response time accounts for all the overhead involved in handling an interrupt. Typically, the processor's context (CPU registers) is saved on the stack before the user code is executed.

For a foreground/background system, the user ISR code is executed immediately after saving the processor's context. The response time is given by Equation [2.3].

[2.3]   Interrupt latency + Time to save the CPU's context

For a non-preemptive kernel, the user ISR code is executed immediately after the processor's context is saved. The response time to an interrupt for a non-preemptive kernel is given by Equation [2.4].

[2.4]   Interrupt latency + Time to save the CPU's context

For a preemptive kernel, a special function provided by the kernel needs to be called. This function notifies the kernel that an ISR is in progress and allows the kernel to keep track of interrupt nesting. For μC/OS-II, this function is called `OSIntEnter()`. The response time to an interrupt for a preemptive kernel is given by Equation [2.5].

[2.5] Interrupt latency
+ Time to save the CPU's context
+ Execution time of the kernel ISR entry function

A system's worst case interrupt response time is its only response. Your system may respond to interrupts in 50μs 99 percent of the time, but if it responds to interrupts in 250μs the other 1 percent, you must assume a 250μs interrupt response time.

2.28 Interrupt Recovery

Interrupt recovery is defined as the time required for the processor to return to the interrupted code. Interrupt recovery in a foreground/background system simply involves restoring the processor's context and returning to the interrupted task. Interrupt recovery is given by Equation [2.6].

[2.6] Time to restore the CPU's context
+ Time to execute the return from interrupt instruction

As with a foreground/background system, interrupt recovery with a non-preemptive kernel (Equation [2.7]) simply involves restoring the processor's context and returning to the interrupted task.

[2.7] Time to restore the CPU's context
+ Time to execute the return from interrupt instruction

For a preemptive kernel, interrupt recovery is more complex. Typically, a function provided by the kernel is called at the end of the ISR. For μC/OS-II, this function is called `OSIntExit()` and allows the kernel to determine if all interrupts have nested. If they have nested (i.e., a return from interrupt would return to task-level code), the kernel determines if a higher priority task has been made ready to run as a result of the ISR. If a higher priority task is ready to run as a result of the ISR, this task is resumed. Note that, in this case, the interrupted task will resume only when it again becomes the highest priority task ready to run. For a preemptive kernel, interrupt recovery is given by Equation [2.8].

[2.8] Time to determine if a higher priority task is ready
+ Time to restore the CPU's context of the highest priority task
+ Time to execute the return from interrupt instruction

2.29 Interrupt Latency, Response, and Recovery

Figures 2.20 through 2.22 show the interrupt latency, response, and recovery for a foreground/background system, a non-preemptive kernel, and a preemptive kernel, respectively.

You should note that for a preemptive kernel, the exit function either decides to return to the interrupted task [F2.22(A)] or to a higher priority task that the ISR has made ready to run [F2.22(B)]. In the later case, the execution time is slightly longer because the kernel has to perform a context switch. I made the difference in execution time somewhat to scale assuming μC/OS-II on an Intel 80186 processor (see Table 9.3, Execution times of μC/OS-II services on 33MHz 80186). This allows you to see the cost (in execution time) of switching context.

2.30 ISR Processing Time

Although ISRs should be as short as possible, there are no absolute limits on the amount of time for an ISR. One cannot say that an ISR must always be less than 100µs, 500µs, or 1ms. If the ISR code is the most important code that needs to run at any given time, it could be as long as it needs to be. In most cases, however, the ISR should recognize the interrupt, obtain data or a status from the interrupting device, and signal a task to perform the actual processing. You should also consider whether the overhead involved in signaling a task is more than the processing of the interrupt. Signaling a task from an ISR (i.e., through a semaphore, a mailbox, or a queue) requires some processing time. If processing your interrupt requires less than the time required to signal a task, you should consider processing the interrupt in the ISR itself and possibly enabling interrupts to allow higher priority interrupts to be recognized and serviced.

option 1

option 2a

option 2 b.

Figure 2.20   Interrupt latency, response, and recovery (foreground/background).

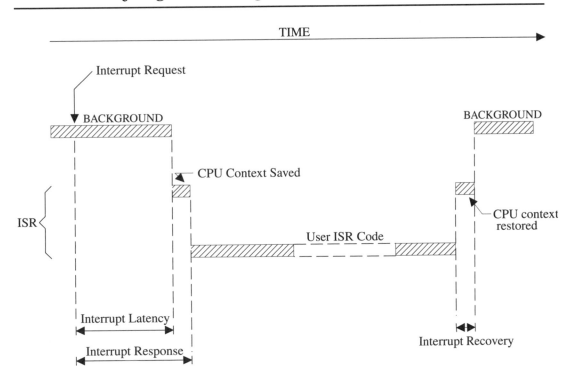

2.31 Nonmaskable Interrupts (NMIs)

Sometimes, an interrupt must be serviced as quickly as possible and cannot afford to have the latency imposed by a kernel. In these situations, you may be able to use the *Nonmaskable Interrupt* (NMI) provided on most microprocessors. Because the NMI cannot be disabled, interrupt latency, response, and recovery are minimal. The NMI is generally reserved for drastic measures such as saving important information during a power down. If, however, your application doesn't have this requirement, you could use the NMI to service your most time-critical ISR. The following equations show how to determine the interrupt latency [2.9], response [2.10], and recovery [2.11], respectively, of an NMI.

[2.9]   Time to execute longest instruction + Time to start executing the NMI ISR

[2.10]   Interrupt latency + Time to save the CPU's context

[2.11]   Time to restore the CPU's context
              + Time to execute the return from interrupt instruction

I have used the NMI in an application to respond to an interrupt that could occur every 150µs. The processing time of the ISR took from 80 to 125µs, and the kernel I used disabled interrupts for about 45µs. As you can see, if I had used maskable interrupts, the ISR could have been late by 20µs.

When you are servicing an NMI, you cannot use kernel services to signal a task because NMIs cannot be disabled to access critical sections of code. However, you can still pass parameters to and from the NMI. Parameters passed must be global variables and the size of these variables must be read or written indivisibly; that is, not as separate byte read or write instructions.

Figure 2.21   *Interrupt latency, response, and recovery (non-preemptive kernel).*

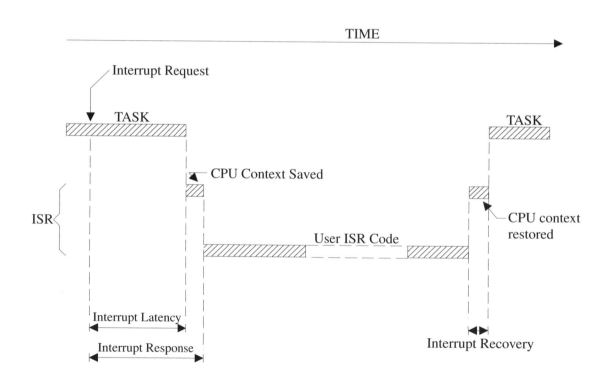

Figure 2.22 *Interrupt latency, response, and recovery (preemptive kernel).*

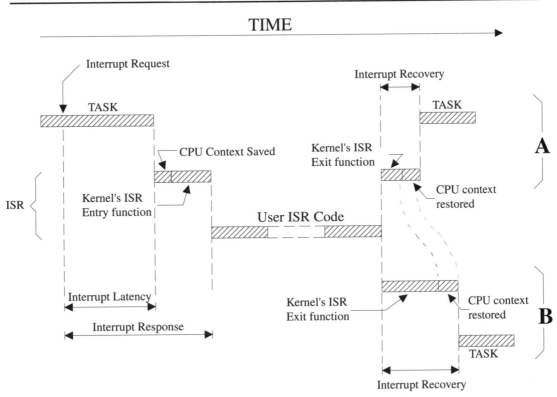

NMIs can be disabled by adding external circuitry, as shown in Figure 2.23. Assuming that both the interrupt and the NMI are positive-going signals, a simple AND gate is inserted between the interrupt source and the processor's NMI input. Interrupts are disabled by writing a 0 to an output port. You wouldn't want to disable interrupts to use kernel services, but you could use this feature to pass parameters (i.e., larger variables) to and from the ISR and a task.

Figure 2.23 *Disabling nonmaskable interrupts.*

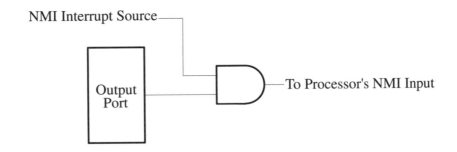

Now, suppose that the NMI service routine needs to signal a task every 40 times it executes. If the NMI occurs every 150µs, a signal would be required every 6ms (40 x 150µs). From a NMI ISR, you cannot use the kernel to signal the task, but you could use the scheme shown in Figure 2.24. In this case, the NMI service routine would generate a hardware interrupt through an output port (i.e., bring an output high). Since the NMI service routine typically has the highest priority and interrupt nesting is typically not allowed while servicing the NMI ISR, the interrupt would not be recognized until the end of the NMI service routine. At the completion of the NMI service routine, the processor would be interrupted to service this hardware interrupt. This ISR would clear the interrupt source (i.e., bring the port output low) and post to a semaphore that would wake up the task. As long as the task services the semaphore well within 6ms, your deadline would be met.

Figure 2.24   Signaling a task from a nonmaskable interrupt.

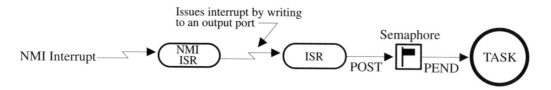

2.32 Clock Tick

A *clock tick* is a special interrupt that occurs periodically. This interrupt can be viewed as the system's heartbeat. The time between interrupts is application specific and is generally between 10 and 200ms. The clock tick interrupt allows a kernel to delay tasks for an integral number of clock ticks and to provide timeouts when tasks are waiting for events to occur. The faster the tick rate, the higher the overhead imposed on the system.

All kernels allow tasks to be delayed for a certain number of clock ticks. The resolution of delayed tasks is one clock tick; however, this does not mean that its accuracy is one clock tick.

Figures 2.25 through 2.27 are timing diagrams showing a task delaying itself for one clock tick. The shaded areas indicate the execution time for each operation being performed. Note that the time for each operation varies to reflect typical processing, which would include loops and conditional statements (i.e., if/else, switch, and ?:). The processing time of the Tick ISR has been exaggerated to show that it too is subject to varying execution times.

Case 1 (Figure 2.25) shows a situation where higher priority tasks and ISRs execute prior to the task, which needs to delay for one tick. As you can see, the task attempts to delay for 20ms but because of its priority, actually executes at varying intervals. This causes the execution of the task to *jitter*.

Figure 2.25 Delaying a task for one tick (Case 1).

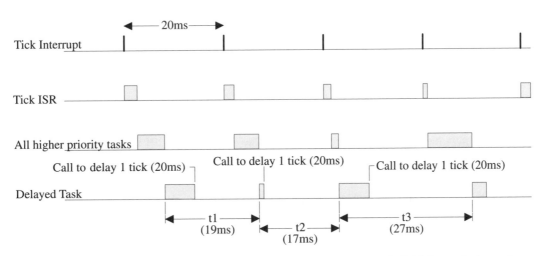

Case 2 (Figure 2.26) shows a situation where the execution times of all higher priority tasks and ISRs are slightly less than one tick. If the task delays itself just before a clock tick, the task will execute again almost immediately! Because of this, if you need to delay a task at least one clock tick, you must specify one extra tick. In other words, if you need to delay a task for at least five ticks, you must specify six ticks!

Figure 2.26 Delaying a task for one tick (Case 2).

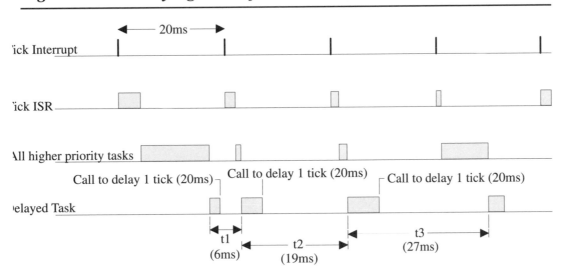

Case 3 (Figure 2.27) shows a situation in which the execution times of all higher priority tasks and ISRs extend beyond one clock tick. In this case, the task that tries to delay for one tick actually executes two ticks later and misses its deadline. This might be acceptable in some applications, but in most cases it isn't.

These situations exist with all real-time kernels. They are related to CPU processing load and possibly incorrect system design. Here are some possible solutions to these problems:

• Increase the clock rate of your microprocessor.

• Increase the time between tick interrupts.

• Rearrange task priorities.

• Avoid using floating-point math (if you must, use single precision).

• Get a compiler that performs better code optimization.

• Write time-critical code in assembly language.

• If possible, upgrade to a faster microprocessor in the same family; that is, 8086 to 80186, 68000 to 68020, etc.

Regardless of what you do, jitter will always occur.

Figure 2.27   Delaying a task for one tick (Case 3).

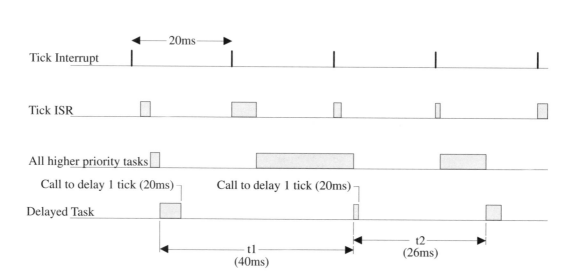

2.33 Memory Requirements

If you are designing a foreground/background system, the amount of memory required depends solely on your application code. With a multitasking kernel, things are quite different. To begin with, a kernel requires extra code space (ROM). The size of the kernel depends on many factors. Depending on the features provided by the kernel, you can expect anywhere from 1 to 100Kb. A minimal kernel for an 8-bit CPU that provides only scheduling, context switching, semaphore management, delays, and time-outs should require about 1 to 3Kb of code space. The total code space is given by Equation [2.12].

[2.12]   Application code size + Kernel code size

Because each task runs independently of the others, it must be provided with its own stack area (RAM). As a designer, you must determine the stack requirement of each task as closely as possible (this is sometimes a difficult undertaking). The stack size must not only account for the task requirements (local variables, function calls, etc.), it must also account for maximum interrupt nesting (saved registers, local storage in ISRs, etc.). Depending on the target processor and the kernel used, a separate stack can be used to handle all interrupt-level code. This is a desirable feature because the stack requirement for each task can be substantially reduced. Another desirable feature is the ability to specify the stack size of each task on an individual basis (μC/OS-II permits this). Conversely, some kernels require that all task stacks be the same size. All kernels require extra RAM to maintain internal variables, data structures, queues, etc. The total RAM required if the kernel does not support a separate interrupt stack is given by Equation [2.13].

[2.13] Application code requirements
+ Data space (i.e., RAM) needed by the kernel
+ SUM(task stacks + MAX(ISR nesting))

If the kernel supports a separate stack for interrupts, the total RAM required is given by Equation [2.14].

[2.14] Application code requirements
+ Data space (i.e., RAM) needed by the kernel
+ SUM(task stacks)
+ MAX(ISR nesting)

Unless you have large amounts of RAM to work with, you need to be careful how you use the stack space. To reduce the amount of RAM needed in an application, you must be careful how you use each task's stack for

- large arrays and structures declared locally to functions and ISRs,
- function (i.e., subroutine) nesting,
- interrupt nesting,
- library functions stack usage, and
- function calls with many arguments.

To summarize, a multitasking system requires more code space (ROM) and data space (RAM) than a foreground/background system. The amount of extra ROM depends only on the size of the kernel, and the amount of RAM depends on the number of tasks in your system.

2.34 Advantages and Disadvantages of Real-Time Kernels

A real-time kernel, also called a *Real-Time Operating System*, or *RTOS*, allows real-time applications to be designed and expanded easily; functions can be added without requiring major changes to the software. The use of an RTOS simplifies the design process by splitting the application code into separate tasks. With a preemptive RTOS, all time-critical events are handled as quickly and as efficiently as possible. An RTOS allows you to make better use of your resources by providing you with valuable services, such as semaphores, mailboxes, queues, time delays, timeouts, etc.

You should consider using a real-time kernel if your application can afford the extra requirements: extra cost of the kernel, more ROM/RAM, and 2 to 4 percent additional CPU overhead.

The one factor I haven't mentioned so far is the cost associated with the use of a real-time kernel. In some applications, cost is everything and would preclude you from even considering an RTOS.

There are currently about 80+ RTOS vendors. Products are available for 8-, 16-, 32-, and even 64-bit microprocessors. Some of these packages are complete operating systems and include not only the real-time kernel but also an input/output manager, windowing systems (display), a file system, networking, language interface libraries, debuggers, and cross-platform compilers. The cost of an RTOS varies from $70 to well over $30,000. The RTOS vendor may also require royalties on a per-target-system basis. This is like buying a chip from the RTOS vendor that you include with each unit sold. The RTOS vendors call this *silicon software*. The royalty fee varies between $5 to about $250 per unit. Like any other software package these days, you also need to consider the maintenance cost, which can set you back another $100 to $5,000 per year!

2.35 Real-Time Systems Summary

Table 2.2 summarizes the three types of real-time systems: foreground/background, non-preemptive kernel, and preemptive kernel.

Table 2.2   *Real-time systems summary.*

	Foreground/ Background	Non-Preemptive Kernel	Preemptive Kernel
Interrupt latency (Time)	MAX(Longest instruction, User int. disable) + Vector to ISR	MAX(Longest instruction, User int. disable, Kernel int. disable) + Vector to ISR	MAX(Longest instruction, User int. disable, Kernel int. disable) + Vector to ISR
Interrupt response (Time)	Int. latency + Save CPU's context	Int. latency + Save CPU's context	Interrupt latency + Save CPU's context + Kernel ISR entry function
Interrupt recovery (Time)	Restore background's context + Return from int.	Restore task's context + Return from int.	Find highest priority task + Restore highest priority task's context + Return from interrupt
Task response (Time)	Background	Longest task + Find highest priority task + Context switch	Find highest priority task + Context switch
ROM size	Application code	Application code + Kernel code	Application code + Kernel code
RAM size	Application code	Application code + Kernel RAM + SUM(Task stacks + MAX(ISR stack))	Application code + Kernel RAM + SUM(Task stacks + MAX(ISR stack))
Services available?	Application code must provide	Yes	Yes

Chapter 3

Kernel Structure

This chapter describes some of the structural aspects of µC/OS-II. You will learn

- how µC/OS-II handles access to critical sections of code,
- what a task is, and how µC/OS-II knows about your tasks,
- how tasks are scheduled,
- how µC/OS-II determines the percent CPU your application is using,
- how to write Interrupt Service Routines (ISRs),
- what a clock tick is and how µC/OS-II handles it,
- how to initialize µC/OS-II, and
- how to start multitasking.

    This chapter also describes the following application services:
- `OS_ENTER_CRITICAL()` and `OS_EXIT_CRITICAL()`,   76
- `OSInit()`,
- `OSStart()`,
- `OSIntEnter()` and `OSIntExit()`,   94
- `OSSchedLock()` and `OSSchedUnlock()`, and
- `OSVersion()`.

3.00 Critical Sections

µC/OS-II, like all real-time kernels, needs to disable interrupts in order to access critical sections of code and to reenable interrupts when done. This allows µC/OS-II to protect critical code from being entered simultaneously from either multiple tasks or ISRs. The interrupt disable time is one of the most important specifications that a real-time kernel vendor can provide because it affects the responsiveness of your system to real-time events. µC/OS-II tries to keep the interrupt disable time to a minimum, but with µC/OS-II, interrupt disable time is largely dependent on the processor architecture and the quality of the code generated by the compiler. Processors generally provide instructions to disable/enable interrupts, and your C compiler must have a mechanism to perform these operations directly from C. Some compilers allow you to insert in-line assembly language statements into your C source code. This makes it quite easy to insert processor instructions to enable and disable interrupts. Other compilers contain language extensions to enable and disable interrupts directly from C. To hide the implementation method chosen by the compiler manufacturer, µC/OS-II defines two macros to disable and enable interrupts: OS_ENTER_CRITICAL() and OS_EXIT_CRITICAL(), respectively. Because these macros are processor specific, they are found in a file called OS_CPU.H. Each processor port thus has its own OS_CPU.H file.

Chapter 8, Porting µC/OS-II, and Chapter 9, 80x86, Large Model Port, provide additional details with regard to these two macros.

3.01 Tasks

A task is typically an infinite loop function [L3.1(2)] as shown in Listing 3.1. A task looks just like any other C function containing a return type and an argument, but it never returns. The return type must always be declared void [L3.1(1)].

Listing 3.1   A task is an infinite loop.

```
   void YourTask (void *pdata)                                        (1)
   {
       for (;;) {                                                     (2)
           /* USER CODE */
           Call one of uC/OS-II's services:
           OSMboxPend();
           OSQPend();
           OSSemPend();
           OSTaskDel(OS_PRIO_SELF);
           OSTaskSuspend(OS_PRIO_SELF);
           OSTimeDly();
           OSTimeDlyHMSM();
           /* USER CODE */
       }
   }
```

Alternatively, the task can delete itself upon completion as shown in Listing 3.2. Note that the task code is not actually deleted; µC/OS-II simply doesn't know about the task anymore, so the task code will not run. Also, if the task calls OSTaskDel(), the task never returns.

Listing 3.2   A task that deletes itself when done.

```
void YourTask (void *pdata)
{
    /* USER CODE */
    OSTaskDel(OS_PRIO_SELF);
}
```

The argument [L3.1(1)] is passed to your task code when the task first starts executing. Notice that the argument is a pointer to a void. This allows your application to pass just about any kind of data to your task. The pointer is a "universal" vehicle used to pass your task the address of a variable, a structure, or even the address of a function if necessary! It is possible (see Example 1 in Chapter 1) to create many identical tasks, all using the same function (or task body). For example, you could have four serial ports that each are managed by their own task. However, the task code is actually identical. Instead of copying the code four times, you can create a task that receives a pointer to a data structure that defines the serial port's parameters (baud rate, I/O port addresses, interrupt vector number, etc.) as an argument.

μC/OS-II can manage up to 64 tasks; however, the current version of μC/OS-II uses two tasks for system use. Also, I decided to reserve priorities 0, 1, 2, 3, OS_LOWEST_PRIO-3, OS_LOWEST_PRIO-2, OS_LOWEST_PRIO-1, and OS_LOWEST_PRIO for future use. OS_LOWEST_PRIO is a #define constant defined in the file OS_CFG.H. Therefore, you can have up to 56 application tasks. Each task of your application must be assigned a unique priority level from 0 to OS_LOWEST_PRIO-2. The lower the priority number, the higher the priority of the task. μC/OS-II always executes the highest priority task ready to run. In the current version of μC/OS-II, the task priority number also serves as the task identifier. The priority number (i.e., task identifier) is used by some kernel services such as OSTaskChangePrio() and OSTaskDel().

In order for μC/OS-II to manage your task, you must "create" a task by passing its address along with other arguments to one of two functions: OSTaskCreate() or OSTaskCreateExt(). OSTaskCreateExt() is an extended version of OSTaskCreate() and provides additional features. These two functions are explained in Chapter 4, Task Management.

3.02   Task States

Figure 3.1 shows the state transition diagram for tasks under μC/OS-II. At any given time, a task can be in any one of five states.

The *DORMANT* state corresponds to a task (see Listing 3.1 or 3.2) that resides in program space (ROM or RAM) but has not been made available to μC/OS-II. A task is made available to μC/OS-II by calling either OSTaskCreate() or OSTaskCreateExt(). When a task is created, it is made *READY* to run. Tasks may be created before multitasking starts or dynamically by a running task. If a task created by another task has a higher priority than its creator, the created task is given control of the CPU immediately. A task can return itself or another task to the dormant state by calling OSTaskDel().

Multitasking is started by calling OSStart(). OSStart() runs the highest priority task that is READY to run. This task is thus placed in the *RUNNING* state. Only one task can be running at any given time. A ready task will not run until all higher priority tasks are either placed in the wait state or are deleted.

Figure 3.1   Task states.

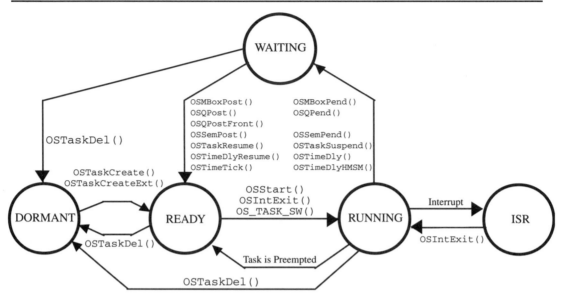

The running task may delay itself for a certain amount of time by calling either OSTimeDly() or OSTimeDlyHMSM(). This task is *WAITING* for some time to expire and the next highest priority task that is ready to run is given control of the CPU immediately. The delayed task is made ready to run by OSTimeTick() when the desired time delay expires (see section 3.10, Clock Tick).

The running task may also need to wait until an event occurs by calling either OSSemPend(), OSMboxPend(), or OSQPend(). The task is WAITING for the occurrence of the event. When a task pends on an event, the next highest priority task is given control of the CPU immediately. The task is made ready when the event occurs. The occurrence of an event may be signaled by either another task or an ISR.

A running task can always be interrupted, unless the task or µC/OS-II disables interrupts. The task thus enters the *ISR* state. When an interrupt occurs, execution of the task is suspended and the ISR takes control of the CPU. The ISR may make one or more tasks ready to run by signaling one or more events. In this case, before returning from the ISR, µC/OS-II determines if the interrupted task is still the highest priority task ready to run. If a higher priority task is made ready to run by the ISR, the new highest priority task is resumed; otherwise, the interrupted task is resumed.

When all tasks are waiting either for events or for time to expire, µC/OS-II executes the idle task, OSTaskIdle().

3.03 *Task Control Blocks (OS_TCBs)*

When a task is created, it is assigned a Task Control Block, OS_TCB (Listing 3.3). A task control block is a data structure that is used by µC/OS-II to maintain the state of a task when it is preempted. When the task regains control of the CPU, the task control block allows the task to resume execution exactly where it left off. All OS_TCBs reside in RAM. You will notice that I organized its fields to allow for data structure packing while maintaining a logical grouping of members. An OS_TCB is initialized when a task is created (see Chapter 4, Task Management).

Listing 3.3   The µC/OS-II task control block.

```
typedef struct os_tcb {
    OS_STK         *OSTCBStkPtr;        Pg )07

#if OS_TASK_CREATE_EXT_EN
    void           *OSTCBExtPtr;
    OS_STK         *OSTCBStkBottom;
    INT32U          OSTCBStkSize;
    INT16U          OSTCBOpt;
    INT16U          OSTCBId;
#endif

    struct os_tcb *OSTCBNext;
    struct os_tcb *OSTCBPrev;

#if (OS_Q_EN && (OS_MAX_QS >= 2)) || OS_MBOX_EN || OS_SEM_EN
    OS_EVENT       *OSTCBEventPtr;
#endif

#if (OS_Q_EN && (OS_MAX_QS >= 2)) || OS_MBOX_EN
    void           *OSTCBMsg;
#endif

    INT16U          OSTCBDly;
    INT8U           OSTCBStat;
    INT8U           OSTCBPrio;

    INT8U           OSTCBX;
    INT8U           OSTCBY;
    INT8U           OSTCBBitX;
    INT8U           OSTCBBitY;

#if OS_TASK_DEL_EN
    BOOLEAN         OSTCBDelReq;
#endif
} OS_TCB;
```

.OSTCBStkPtr contains a pointer to the current top-of-stack for the task. µC/OS-II allows each task to have its own stack, but just as important, each stack can be any size. Some commercial kernels assume that all stacks are the same size unless you write complex hooks. This limitation wastes RAM when all tasks have different stack requirements because the largest anticipated stack size has to be allocated for all tasks. .OSTCBStkPtr should be the only field in the OS_TCB data structure that is accessed from assembly language code (from the context-switching code). Placing .OSTCBStkPtr at the first entry in the structure makes accessing this field easier from assembly language code.

.OSTCBExtPtr is a pointer to a user-definable task control block extension. This allows you or the user of µC/OS-II to extend the task control block without having to change the source code for µC/OS-II. .OSTCBExtPtr is only used by OSTaskCreateExt(), so you need to set OS_TASK_CREATE_EXT_EN to 1 to enable this field. You could create a data structure that contains the name of each task or keep track of the execution time of the task or the number of times a task has been switched-in (see Example 3). Notice that I decided to place this pointer immediately after the stack pointer in case you need to access this field from assembly language. This makes calculating the offset from the beginning of the data structure easier.

.OSTCBStkBottom is a pointer to the bottom of the task's stack. If the processor's stack grows from high to low memory locations, then .OSTCBStkBottom will point at the lowest valid memory location for the stack. Similarly, if the processor's stack grows from low to high memory locations, then .OSTCBStkBottom will point at the highest valid stack address. .OSTCBStkBottom is used by OSTaskStkChk() to check the size of a task's stack at run time. This allows you determine the amount of free stack space available for each stack. Stack checking can only occur if you create a task with OSTaskCreateExt(), so you need to set OS_TASK_CREATE_EXT_EN to 1 to enable this field.

.OSTCBStkSize holds the size of the stack in number of elements instead of bytes. This means that if a stack contains 1,000 entries and each entry is 32 bits wide, then the actual size of the stack is 4,000 bytes. Similarly, a stack where entries are 16 bits wide would contain 2,000 bytes for the same 1,000 entries. .OSTCBStkSize is used by OSTaskStkChk(). Again, this field is valid only if you set OS_TASK_CREATE_EXT_EN to 1.

.OSTCBOpt holds "options" that can be passed to OSTaskCreateExt(), so this field is valid only if you set OS_TASK_CREATE_EXT_EN to 1. µC/OS-II currently defines only three options (see uCOS_II.H): OS_TASK_OPT_STK_CHK, OS_TASK_OPT_STK_CLR, and OS_TASK_OPT_SAVE_FP. OS_TASK_OPT_STK_CHK is used to specify to OSTaskCreateExt() that stack checking is enabled for the task being created. OS_TASK_OPT_STK_CLR indicates that the stack needs to be cleared when the task is created. The stack only needs to be cleared if you intend to do stack checking. If you do not specify OS_TASK_OPT_STK_CLR and you then create and delete tasks, stack checking will report incorrect stack usage. If you never delete a task once it's created and your startup code then clears all RAM, you can save valuable execution time by NOT specifying this option. Passing OS_TASK_OPT_STK_CLR increases the execution time of OSTaskCreateExt() because it clears the content of the stack. The larger your stack, the longer it takes. Finally, OS_TASK_OPT_SAVE_FP tells OSTaskCreateExt() that the task will be doing floating-point computations. If the processor provides hardware-assisted floating-point capability, the floating-point registers need to be saved for the task being created and during a context switch.

.OSTCBId is used to hold an identifier for the task. This field is currently not used and has only been included for future expansion.

.OSTCBNext and **.OSTCBPrev** are used to doubly link OS_TCBs. This chain of OS_TCBs is used by OSTimeTick() to update the .OSTCBDly field for each task. The OS_TCB for each task is linked when the task is created, and the OS_TCB is removed from the list when the task is deleted. A doubly linked list permits an element in the chain to be quickly inserted or removed.

.OSTCBEventPtr is a pointer to an event control block and is described later (see Chapter 6, Intertask Communication & Synchronization).

.OSTCBMsg is a pointer to a message that is sent to a task. The use of this field is described later (see Chapter 6, Intertask Communication & Synchronization).

.OSTCBDly is used when a task needs to be delayed for a certain number of clock ticks or a task needs to pend for an event to occur with a timeout. In this case, this field contains the number of clock ticks the task is allowed to wait for the event to occur. When this variable is 0, the task is not delayed or has no timeout when waiting for an event.

.OSTCBStat contains the state of the task. When .OSTCBStat is 0, the task is ready to run. Other values can be assigned to .OSTCBStat, and these values are described in uCOS_II.H.

.OSTCBPrio contains the task priority. A high-priority task has a low .OSTCBPrio value (i.e., the lower the number, the higher the actual priority).

.OSTCBX, **.OSTCBY**, **.OSTCBBitX**, and **.OSTCBBitY** are used to accelerate the process of making a task ready to run or to make a task wait for an event (to avoid computing these values at run time). The values for these fields are computed when the task is created or when the task's priority is changed. The values are obtained as shown in Listing 3.4.

Listing 3.4   Calculating OS_TCB members.

```
OSTCBY            = priority >> 3;
OSTCBBitY         = OSMapTbl[priority >> 3];
OSTCBX            = priority & 0x07;
OSTCBBitX         = OSMapTbl[priority & 0x07];
```

.OSTCBDelReq is a boolean used to indicate whether or not a task requested that the current task be deleted. The use of this field is described later (see Chapter 4, Task Management).

The maximum number of tasks (OS_MAX_TASKS) that an application can have is specified in OS_CFG.H and determines the number of OS_TCBs allocated by μC/OS-II for your application. You can reduce the amount of RAM needed by setting OS_MAX_TASKS to the actual number of tasks needed in your application. All OS_TCBs are placed in OSTCBTbl[]. Note that μC/OS-II allocates OS_N_SYS_TASKS (see uCOS_II.H) extra OS_TCBs for internal use. Currently, one is used for the idle task, and another is used for the statistic task (if OS_TASK_STAT_EN is set to 1). When μC/OS-II is initialized, all OS_TCBs in the table are linked in a singly linked list of free OS_TCBs, as shown in Figure 3.2. When a task is created, the OS_TCB pointed to by OSTCBFreeList is assigned to the task, and OSTCBFreeList is adjusted to point to the next OS_TCB in the chain. When a task is deleted, its OS_TCB is returned to the list of free OS_TCBs.

Figure 3.2   List of free OS_TCBs.

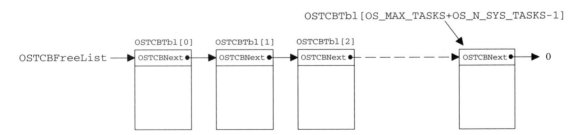

3.04 Ready List

→ by programmer (handwritten)

Each task is assigned a unique priority level between 0 and OS_LOWEST_PRIO, inclusive (see OS_CFG.H). Task priority OS_LOWEST_PRIO is always assigned to the idle task when µC/OS-II is initialized. Note that OS_MAX_TASKS and OS_LOWEST_PRIO are unrelated. You can have only 10 tasks in an application while still having 32 priority levels (if you set OS_LOWEST_PRIO to 31).

Each task that is ready to run is placed in a ready list consisting of two variables, OSRdyGrp and OSRdyTbl[]. Task priorities are grouped (eight tasks per group) in OSRdyGrp. Each bit in OSRdyGrp indicates when a task in a group is ready to run. When a task is ready to run, it also sets its corresponding bit in the ready table, OSRdyTbl[]. The size of OSRdyTbl[] depends on OS_LOWEST_PRIO (see uCOS_II.H). This allows you to reduce the amount of RAM (data space) needed by µC/OS-II when your application requires few task priorities.

To determine which priority (and thus which task) will run next, the scheduler determines the lowest priority number that has its bit set in OSRdyTbl[]. The relationship between OSRdyGrp and OSRdyTbl[] is shown in Figure 3.3 and is given by the following rules.

Bit 0 in OSRdyGrp is 1 when any bit in OSRdyTbl[0] is 1.
Bit 1 in OSRdyGrp is 1 when any bit in OSRdyTbl[1] is 1.
Bit 2 in OSRdyGrp is 1 when any bit in OSRdyTbl[2] is 1.
Bit 3 in OSRdyGrp is 1 when any bit in OSRdyTbl[3] is 1.
Bit 4 in OSRdyGrp is 1 when any bit in OSRdyTbl[4] is 1.
Bit 5 in OSRdyGrp is 1 when any bit in OSRdyTbl[5] is 1.
Bit 6 in OSRdyGrp is 1 when any bit in OSRdyTbl[6] is 1.
Bit 7 in OSRdyGrp is 1 when any bit in OSRdyTbl[7] is 1.

The code in Listing 3.5 is used to place a task in the ready list. prio is the task's priority.

Listing 3.5   Making a task ready to run.

(handwritten annotations: = YYY, = XXX, "Turn on 1 bit in OSRdyGrp, on if it's not on already")

```
OSRdyGrp            |= OSMapTbl[prio >> 3];
OSRdyTbl[prio >> 3] |= OSMapTbl[prio & 0x07];
```

(handwritten annotations: "Turn on 1 bit in the row associated with the OSRdyGrp bit turned on above")

(left margin handwritten: bit function, "OR-EQUAL", A |= 4 means A = A | 4, OR)

Table 3.1   Contents of OSMapTbl[].

Index (value of YYY or XXX)	Bit Mask (Binary)
0	00000001
1	00000010
2	00000100
3	00001000
4	00010000
5	00100000
6	01000000
7	10000000

As you can see from Figure 3.3, the lower three bits of the task's priority are used to determine the bit position in OSRdyTbl[], and the next three most significant bits are used to determine the index into OSRdyTbl[]. Note that OSMapTbl[] (see OS_CORE.C) is in ROM and is used to equate an index from 0 to 7 to a bit mask, as shown in Table 3.1.

Figure 3.3   The µC/OS-II ready list.

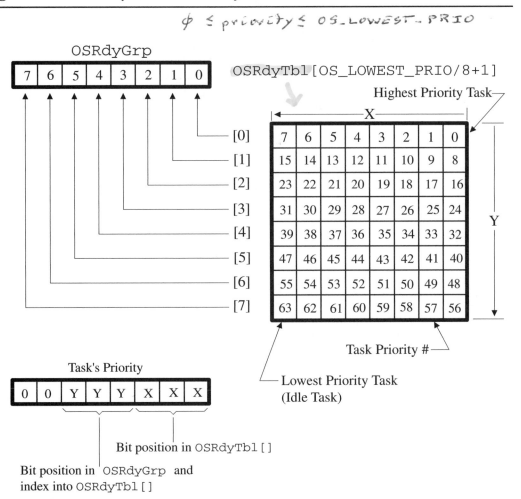

$\phi \leq priority \leq OS\_LOWEST\_PRIO$

Values for OS Rdy Grp & OSRdy Tbl[ ] are derived from Task Priority, which is assigned by programmer.

This turns a single bit off in ∧one row it OSRdyTbl. If, as as result, no bits remain on sb that row, then set the corresponding bit in OSRdyGrp to φ.

turn this bit off.

A task is removed from the ready list by reversing the process using the code in Listing 3.6.

ex. ~(0001 0000) = (1 1 1 0 φ 1 1 1)

Listing 3.6 *Removing a task from the ready list.*

```
if ((OSRdyTbl[prio >> 3] &= ~OSMapTbl[prio & 0x07]) == 0)
    OSRdyGrp &= ~OSMapTbl[prio >> 3];
```

This code clears the ready bit of the task in OSRdyTbl[] and clears the bit in OSRdyGrp only if all tasks in a group are not ready to run; that is, all bits in OSRdyTbl[prio >> 3] are 0. Another table lookup is performed, rather than scanning through the table starting with OSRdyTbl[0], to find the highest priority task ready to run. OSUnMapTbl[256] is a priority resolution table (see OS_CORE.C). Eight bits represent when tasks are ready in a group. The least significant bit has the highest priority. Using this byte to index the table returns the bit position of the highest priority bit set — a number between 0 and 7. Determining the priority of the highest priority task ready to run is accomplished with the code in Listing 3.7.

Listing 3.7 *Finding the highest priority task ready to run.*

```
y    = OSUnMapTbl[OSRdyGrp];
x    = OSUnMapTbl[OSRdyTbl[y]];
prio = (y << 3) + x;
```

For example, if OSRdyGrp contains 01101000 (binary), then the table lookup OSUn-MapTbl[OSRdyGrp] yields a value of 3, which corresponds to bit 3 in OSRdyGrp. Note that bit positions are assumed to start on the right with bit 0 being the rightmost bit. Similarly, if OSRdyTbl[3] contains 11100100 (binary), then OSUnMapTbl[OSRdyTbl[3]] results in a value of 2 (bit 2). The task priority (prio) is then 26(3 x 8 + 2). Getting a pointer to the OS_TCB for the corresponding task is done by indexing into OSTCBPrioTbl[] using the task's priority.

where is this initialized? Pg. 109 OSTCBInit

3.05 Task Scheduling

μC/OS-II always executes the highest priority task ready to run. The determination of which task has the highest priority, and thus which task will be next to run, is determined by the scheduler. Task-level scheduling is performed by OSSched(). ISR-level scheduling is handled by another function [OSIntExit()] described later. The code for OSSched() is shown in Listing 3.8.

μC/OS-II task-scheduling time is constant irrespective of the number of tasks created in an application. OSSched() exits if called from an ISR (i.e., OSIntNesting > 0) or if scheduling has been disabled because your application called OSSchedLock() at least once (i.e., OSLockNesting > 0) [L3.8(1)]. If OSSched() is not called from an ISR and the scheduler is enabled, then OSSched() determines the priority of the highest priority task that is ready to run [L3.8(2)]. A task that is ready to run has its corresponding bit set in OSRdyTbl[]. Once the highest priority task has been found, OSSched() verifies that the highest priority task is not the current task. This is done to avoid an unnecessary context switch [L3.8(3)]. Note that μC/OS used to obtain OSTCBHighRdy and compared it with OSTCBCur. On 8- and some 16-bit processors, this operation was relatively slow because a comparison was made of pointers instead of 8-bit integers as it is now done in μC/OS-II. Also, there is no point in looking up OSTCBHighRdy in OSTCBPrioTbl[] unless you actually need to do a context switch. The combination of comparing 8-bit values instead of pointers and looking up OSTCBHighRdy only when needed should make µC/OS-II faster than µC/OS on 8- and some 16-bit processors.

Listing 3.8   Task scheduler.

[handwritten: disabled.]

[handwritten: if >0 ⇒ Scheduler was ... ; if >0 ⇒ called from ISR.]

```
void OSSched (void)
{
    INT8U y;


    OS_ENTER_CRITICAL();
    if ((OSLockNesting | OSIntNesting) == 0) {                        (1)
        y          = OSUnMapTbl[OSRdyGrp];                            (2)
        OSPrioHighRdy = (INT8U)((y << 3) + OSUnMapTbl[OSRdyTbl[y]]);  (2)
        if (OSPrioHighRdy != OSPrioCur) {                             (3)
            OSTCBHighRdy = OSTCBPrioTbl[OSPrioHighRdy];               (4)
            OSCtxSwCtr++;                                             (5)
            OS_TASK_SW();                                             (6)
        }
    }
    OS_EXIT_CRITICAL();
}
```

[handwritten annotations: "Priority of Task is index into Table"; "Table of Pointers to TCB's. It is initialized in OSTCB Init - Pg 109"; "MACRO Pg 197"; "where is this established? in OSStart Pg 102"; "done by OSCtxSw() ... see below"]

To perform a context switch, OSTCBHighRdy must point to the OS_TCB of the highest priority task, which is done by indexing into OSTCBPrioTbl[] using OSPrioHighRdy [L3.8(4)]. Next, the statistic counter OSCtxSwCtr is incremented to keep track of the number of context switches [L3.8(5)]. Finally, the macro OS_TASK_SW() is invoked to do the actual context switch [L3.8(6)].

A context switch simply consists of saving the processor registers on the stack of the task being suspended and restoring the registers of the higher priority task from its stack. In µC/OS-II, the stack frame for a ready task always looks as if an interrupt has just occurred and all processor registers were saved onto it. In other words, all that µC/OS-II has to do to run a ready task is restore all processor registers from the task's stack and execute a return from interrupt. To switch context, implement OS_TASK_SW() so that you simulate an interrupt. Most processors provide either software interrupt or TRAP instructions to accomplish this. The interrupt service routine (ISR) or trap handler (also called the exception handler) must vector to the assembly language function OSCtxSw(). OSCtxSw() expects to have OSTCB-HighRdy point to the OS_TCB of the task to be switched-in and OSTCBCur point to the OS_TCB of the task being suspended. Refer to Chapter 8, Porting µC/OS-II, for additional details on OSCtxSw().

*[handwritten: * , Pg 197 - 199]*

All of the code in OSSched() is considered a critical section. Interrupts are disabled to prevent ISRs from setting the ready bit of one or more tasks during the process of finding the highest priority task ready to run. Note that OSSched() could be written entirely in assembly language to reduce scheduling time. OSSched() was written in C for readability and portability and to minimize assembly language.

3.06 Locking and Unlocking the Scheduler

The OSSchedLock() function (Listing 3.9) is used to prevent task rescheduling until its counterpart, OSSchedUnlock() (Listing 3.10), is called. The task that calls OSSchedLock() keeps control of the CPU even though other higher priority tasks are ready to run. Interrupts, however, are still recognized and serviced (assuming interrupts are enabled). OSSchedLock() and OSSchedUnlock() must be used in pairs. The variable OSLockNesting keeps track of the number of times OSSchedLock() has been called. This allows nested functions to contain critical code that other tasks cannot access. µC/OS-II allows nesting up to 255 levels deep. Scheduling is re-enabled when OSLockNesting is 0. OSSchedLock() and OSSchedUnlock() must be used with caution because they affect the normal management of tasks by µC/OS-II.

OSSchedUnlock() calls the scheduler [L3.10(2)] when OSLockNesting has decremented to 0 [L3.10(1)]. OSSchedUnlock() is called from a task because events could have made higher priority tasks ready to run while scheduling was locked.

After calling OSSchedLock(), your application must not make any system calls that suspend execution of the current task; that is, your application cannot call OSMboxPend(), OSQPend(), OSSemPend(), OSTaskSuspend(OS_PRIO_SELF), OSTimeDly(), or OSTimeDlyHMSM() until OSLockNesting returns to 0. No other task is allowed to run, because the scheduler is locked out and your system will lock up.

You may want to disable the scheduler when a low-priority task needs to post messages to multiple mailboxes, queues, or semaphores (see Chapter 6, Intertask Communication & Synchronization) and you don't want a higher priority task to take control until all mailboxes, queues, and semaphores have been posted to.

Listing 3.9 Locking the scheduler.

```
void OSSchedLock (void)
{
    if (OSRunning == TRUE) {
        OS_ENTER_CRITICAL();
        OSLockNesting++;
        OS_EXIT_CRITICAL();
    }
}
```

Listing 3.10   Unlocking the scheduler.

```
void OSSchedUnlock (void)
{
    if (OSRunning == TRUE) {
        OS_ENTER_CRITICAL();
        if (OSLockNesting > 0) {
            OSLockNesting--;
            if ((OSLockNesting | OSIntNesting) == 0) {                    (1)
                OS_EXIT_CRITICAL();
                OSSched();                                                (2)
            } else {
                OS_EXIT_CRITICAL();
            }
        } else {
            OS_EXIT_CRITICAL();
        }
    }
}
```

3.07 Idle Task

μC/OS-II always creates a task (a.k.a. the *idle task*) that is executed when none of the other tasks is ready to run. The idle task [OSTaskIdle()] is always set to the lowest priority, OS_LOWEST_PRIO. OSTaskIdle() does nothing but increment a 32-bit counter called OSIdleCtr, which is used by the statistics task (see section 3.08, Statistics Task) to determine the percent CPU time actually being consumed by the application software. The code for the idle task is shown in Listing 3.11. Interrupts are disabled then enabled around the increment because on 8- and most 16-bit processors, a 32-bit increment requires multiple instructions that must be protected from being accessed by higher priority tasks or an ISR. The idle task can never be deleted by application software.

Listing 3.11   The μC/OS-II idle task.

```
void OSTaskIdle (void *pdata)
{
    pdata = pdata;
    for (;;) {
        OS_ENTER_CRITICAL();
        OSIdleCtr++;
        OS_EXIT_CRITICAL();
    }
}
```

3.08 Statistics Task

µC/OS-II contains a task that provides run-time statistics. This task is called OSTaskStat() and is created if you set the configuration constant OS_TASK_STAT_EN (see OS_CFG.H) to 1. When enabled, OSTaskStat() (see OS_CORE.C) executes every second and computes the percent CPU usage. In other words, OSTaskStat() tells you how much of the CPU time is used by your application, as a percentage. This value is placed in the signed 8-bit integer variable OSCPUUsage. The resolution of OSCPUUsage is 1 percent.

If your application is to use the statistic task, you must call OSStatInit() (see OS_CORE.C) from the first and only task created in your application during initialization. In other words, your startup code must create only one task before calling OSStart(). From this one task, you must call OSStatInit() before you create your other application tasks. The pseudocode in Listing 3.12 shows what needs to be done.

Listing 3.12 Initializing the statistic task.

```
void main (void)
{
    OSInit();                       /* Initialize uC/OS-II                       (1)*/
    /* Install uC/OS-II's context switch vector                                   */
    /* Create your startup task (for sake of discussion, TaskStart())           (2)*/
    OSStart();                      /* Start multitasking                        (3)*/
}




void TaskStart (void *pdata)
{
    /* Install and initialize µC/OS-II's ticker                                  (4)*/
    OSStatInit();                   /* Initialize statistics task                (5)*/
    /* Create your application task(s)                                            */
    for (;;) {
        /* Code for TaskStart() goes here!                                        */
    }
}
```

Because your application must create only one task [TaskStart()], µC/OS-II has only three tasks to manage when main() calls OSStart(): TaskStart(), OSTaskIdle(), and OSTaskStat(). Please note that you don't have to call the startup task TaskStart() — you can call it anything you like. Your startup task will have the highest priority because µC/OS-II sets the priority of the idle task to OS_LOWEST_PRIO and the priority of the statistic task to OS_LOWEST_PRIO - 1 internally.

Figure 3.4 illustrates the flow of execution when initializing the statistic task. The first function that you must call in µC/OS-II is OSInit(), which initializes µC/OS-II [F3.4(1)]. Next, you need to install the interrupt vector that will be used to perform context switches [F3.4(2)]. Note that on some processors (specifically the Motorola 68HC11), there is no need to "install" a vector because the vector is already resident in ROM. You must create `TaskStart()` by calling either `OSTaskCreate()` or `OSTaskCreateExt()` [F3.4(3)]. Once you are ready to multitask, call `OSStart()`, which schedules `TaskStart()` for execution because it has the highest priority [F3.4(4)].

Figure 3.4   Statistic task initialization.

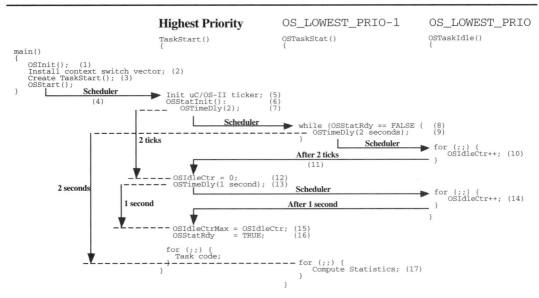

`TaskStart()` is responsible for initializing and starting the ticker [F3.4(5)]. This is necessary because you don't want to receive a tick interrupt until you are actually multitasking. Next, `TaskStart()` calls `OSStatInit()` [F3.4(6)]. `OSStatInit()` determines how high the idle counter (`OSIdleCtr`) can count if no other task in the application is executing. A Pentium II running at 333MHz increments this counter to a value of about 15,000,000. `OSIdleCtr` is still far from wrapping around the 4,294,967,296 limit of a 32-bit value. As processors get faster, you may want to keep an eye on this potential problem.

`OSStatInit()` starts off by calling `OSTimeDly()` [F3.4(7)], which puts `TaskStart()` to sleep for two ticks. This is done to synchronize `OSStatInit()` to the ticker. μC/OS-II then picks the next highest priority task that is ready to run, which happens to be `OSTaskStat()`. You will see the code for `OSTaskStat()` later, but as a preview, the very first thing `OSTaskStat()` does is check to see if the flag `OSStatRdy` is set to `FALSE` [F3.4(8)] and delays for two seconds if it is. It so happens that `OSStatRdy` is initialized to `FALSE` by `OSInit()`, so `OSTaskStat()` in fact puts itself to sleep for two seconds [F3.4(9)]. This causes a context switch to the only task that is ready to run, `OSTaskIdle()`. The CPU stays in `OSTaskIdle()` [F3.4(10)] until the two ticks of `TaskStart()` expire. After two ticks, `TaskStart()` resumes [F3.4(11)] execution in `OSStatInit()` and `OSIdleCtr` is cleared [F3.4(12)]. Then, `OSStatInit()` delays itself for one full second [F3.4(13)]. Because no other task is ready to run, `OSTaskIdle()` again gets control of the CPU. During that time, `OSIdleCtr` is continuously incremented [F3.4(14)]. After one second, `TaskStart()` is resumed, still in `OSStatInit()`, and the value that `OSIdleCtr` reached during that one second is saved in `OSIdleCtrMax` [F3.4(15)]. `OSStatInit()` sets `OSStatRdy` to `TRUE` [F3.4(16)], which allows `OSTaskStat()` to perform a CPU usage computation [F3.4(17)] after its delay of two seconds expires.

The code for OSStatInit() is shown in Listing 3.13.

Listing 3.13 Initializing the statistic task.

```
void OSStatInit (void)
{
    OSTimeDly(2);
    OS_ENTER_CRITICAL();
    OSIdleCtr    = 0L;
    OS_EXIT_CRITICAL();
    OSTimeDly(OS_TICKS_PER_SEC);
    OS_ENTER_CRITICAL();
    OSIdleCtrMax = OSIdleCtr;
    OSStatRdy    = TRUE;
    OS_EXIT_CRITICAL();
}
```

The code for OSTaskStat() is shown in Listing 3.14. I've already discussed why OSTaskStat() has to wait for OSStatRdy [L3.14(1)] in the previous paragraphs. The task code executes every second and basically determines how much CPU time is actually consumed by all the application tasks. When you start adding application code, the idle task will get less of the processor's time, and OSIdleCtr will not be allowed to count as high as it did when nothing else was running. Remember that OSStatInit() saved this maximum value in OSIdleCtrMax. CPU utilization (Equation [3.1]) is stored in the variable OSCPUUsage [L3.14(2)]:

[3.1]
$$\text{OSCPUUsage}_{(\%)} = 100\left(1 - \frac{\text{OSIdleCtr}}{\text{OSIdleCtrMax}}\right)$$

Once the above computation is performed, OSTaskStat() calls OSTaskStatHook() [L3.14(3)], a user-definable function that allows the statistic task to be expanded. Indeed, your application could compute and display the total execution time of all tasks, the percent time actually consumed by each task, and more (see section 1.09, Example 3).

Listing 3.14 Statistics task.

```
void OSTaskStat (void *pdata)
{
    INT32U run;
    INT8S usage;


    pdata = pdata;
    while (OSStatRdy == FALSE) {                              (1)
        OSTimeDly(2 * OS_TICKS_PER_SEC);
    }
```

Listing 3.14   Statistics task. (Continued)

```
for (;;) {
    OS_ENTER_CRITICAL();
    OSIdleCtrRun = OSIdleCtr;
    run          = OSIdleCtr;
    OSIdleCtr    = 0L;
    OS_EXIT_CRITICAL();
    if (OSIdleCtrMax > 0L) {
        usage = (INT8S)(100L - 100L * run / OSIdleCtrMax);      (2)
        if (usage > 100) {
            OSCPUUsage = 100;
        } else if (usage < 0) {
            OSCPUUsage = 0;
        } else {
            OSCPUUsage = usage;
        }
    } else {
        OSCPUUsage = 0;
    }
    OSTaskStatHook();                                           (3)
    OSTimeDly(OS_TICKS_PER_SEC);
}
}
```

3.09 Interrupts under µC/OS-II

because you can't access CPU registers from C   *Pg 96*

µC/OS-II requires that an Interrupt Service Routine (ISR) be written in assembly language. However, if your C compiler supports in-line assembly language, you can put the ISR code directly in a C source file. The pseudocode for an ISR is shown in Listing 3.15.

Listing 3.15   ISRs under µC/OS-II.

```
YourISR:
    Save all CPU registers;                                    (1)
    Call OSIntEnter() or, increment OSIntNesting directly;     (2)
    Execute user code to service ISR;                          (3)
    Call OSIntExit();                                          (4)
    Restore all CPU registers;                                 (5)
    Execute a return from interrupt instruction;               (6)
```

Your code should save all CPU registers onto the current task stack [L3.15(1)]. Note that on some processors, like the Motorola 68020 (and higher), a different stack is used when servicing an interrupt. µC/OS-II can work with such processors as long as the registers are saved on the interrupted task's stack when a context switch occurs.

µC/OS-II needs to know that you are servicing an ISR, so you need to either call OSIntEnter() or increment the global variable OSIntNesting [L3.15(2)]. OSIntNesting can be incremented directly if your processor performs an increment operation to memory using a single instruction. If your processor forces you to read OSIntNesting in a register, increment the register, store the result back in OSIntNesting, then call OSIntEnter(). OSIntEnter() wraps these three instructions with code to disable and then enable interrupts, thus ensuring exclusive access to OSIntNesting, which is considered a shared resource. Incrementing OSIntNesting directly is much faster than calling OSIntEnter() and is thus the preferred way. One word of caution: some implementations of OSIntEnter() cause interrupts to be enabled when OSIntEnter() returns. In these cases, you need to clear the interrupt source before calling OSIntEnter(); otherwise, your interrupt will be re-entered continuously and your application will crash!

Once the previous two steps have been accomplished, you can start servicing the interrupting device [L3.15(3)]. This section is obviously application specific. µC/OS-II allows you to nest interrupts because it keeps track of nesting in OSIntNesting. To allow for interrupt nesting in most cases, however, you will need to clear the interrupt source before you enable interrupts.

The conclusion of the ISR is marked by calling OSIntExit() [L3.15(4)], which decrements the interrupt nesting counter. When the nesting counter reaches 0, all nested interrupts have completed and µC/OS-II needs to determine whether a higher priority task has been awakened by the ISR (or any other nested ISR). If a higher priority task is ready to run, µC/OS-II returns to the higher priority task rather than to the interrupted task. If the interrupted task is still the most important task to run, OSIntExit() returns to its caller [L3.15(5)]. At that point the saved registers are restored and a return from interrupt instruction is executed [L3.15(6)]. Note that µC/OS-II will return to the interrupted task if scheduling has been disabled (OSLockNesting > 0).

The above description is further illustrated in Figure 3.5. The interrupt is received [F3.5(1)] but is not recognized by the CPU, either because interrupts have been disabled by µC/OS-II or your application or because the CPU has not completed executing the current instruction. Once the CPU recognizes the interrupt [F3.5(2)], the CPU vectors (at least on most microprocessors) to the ISR [F3.5(3)]. As described above, the ISR saves the CPU registers [F3.5(4)] (i.e., the CPU's context). Once this is done, your ISR notifies µC/OS-II by calling OSIntEnter() or by incrementing OSIntNesting [F3.5(5)]. Your ISR code then gets to execute [F3.5(6)]. Your ISR should do as little work as possible and defer most of the work to the task. A task is notified of the ISR by calling either OSMboxPost(), OSQPost(), OSQPostFront(), or OSSemPost(). The receiving task may or may not be pending at the mailbox, queue, or semaphore when the ISR occurs and the post is made. Once the user ISR code has completed, your need to call OSIntExit() [F3.5(7)]. As can be seen from the timing diagram, OSIntExit() takes less time to return to the interrupted task when there is no higher priority task (HPT) readied by the ISR. Furthermore, in this case, the CPU registers are then simply restored [F3.5(8)] and a return from interrupt instruction is executed [F3.5(9)]. If the ISR makes a higher priority task ready to run, then OSIntExit() takes longer to execute because a context switch is now needed [F3.5(10)]. The registers of the new task are restored [F3.5(11)], and a return from interrupt instruction is executed [F3.5(12)].

Figure 3.5   Servicing an interrupt.

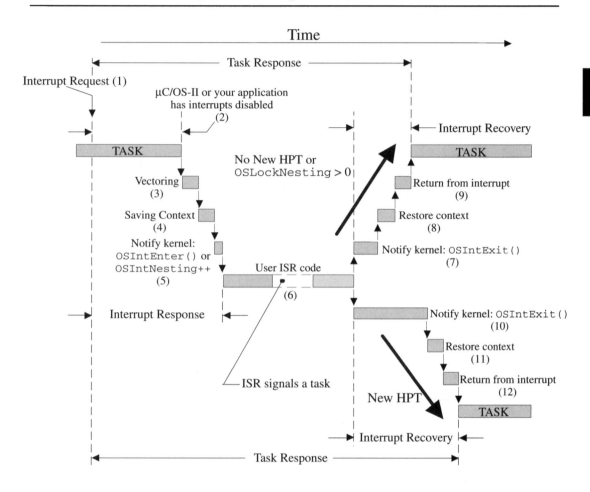

The code for OSIntEnter() is shown in Listing 3.16 and the code for OSIntExit() is shown in Listing 3.17. Very little needs to be said about OSIntEnter().

Listing 3.16   Notify µC/OS-II about beginning an ISR.

```
void OSIntEnter (void)
{
    OS_ENTER_CRITICAL();
    OSIntNesting++;
    OS_EXIT_CRITICAL();
}
```

Listing 3.17   Notify µC/OS-II about leaving an ISR.

```
void OSIntExit (void)
{
    OS_ENTER_CRITICAL();                                              (1)
    if ((--OSIntNesting | OSLockNesting) == 0) {                      (2)
        OSIntExitY   = OSUnMapTbl[OSRdyGrp];                          (3)
        OSPrioHighRdy = (INT8U)((OSIntExitY << 3) +
                        OSUnMapTbl[OSRdyTbl[OSIntExitY]]);
        if (OSPrioHighRdy != OSPrioCur) {
            OSTCBHighRdy  = OSTCBPrioTbl[OSPrioHighRdy];
            OSCtxSwCtr++;
            OSIntCtxSw();                                             (4)
        }
    }
    OS_EXIT_CRITICAL();
}
```

OSIntExit() looks strangely like OSSched() except for three differences. First, the interrupt nesting counter is decremented in OSIntExit() [L3.17(2)] and rescheduling occurs when both the interrupt nesting counter and the lock nesting counter (OSLockNesting) are 0. The second difference is that the Y index needed for OSRdyTbl[] is stored in the global variable OSIntExitY [L3.17(3)] This is done to avoid allocating a local variable on the stack, which would need to be accounted for in OSIntCtxSw() [see section 9.04.03 "OSIntCtxSw()" on page 224]. Finally, If a context switch is needed, OSIntExit() calls OSIntCtxSw() [L3.17(4)] instead of OS_TASK_SW() as it did in OSSched().

There are two reasons for calling OSIntCtxSw() instead of OS_TASK_SW(). First, half the work is already done because the ISR has already saved the CPU registers onto the task stack, as shown in Listing 3.15(1) and Figure 3.6(1). Second, calling OSIntExit() from the ISR pushes the return address of the ISR onto the stack [L3.15(4) and F3.6(2)]. Depending on how interrupts are disabled (see Chapter 8, Porting µC/OS-II), the processor's status word may be pushed onto the stack [L3.17(1) and F3.6(3)] by OS_ENTER_CRITICAL() in OSIntExit(). Finally, the return address of the call to OSIntCtxSw() is also pushed onto the stack [L3.17(4) and F3.6(4)]. The stack frame is as µC/OS-II expects when a task is suspended, except for the extra elements on the stack [F3.6(2)–(4)]. OSIntCtxSw() simply needs to adjust the processor's stack pointer (SP), as shown in [F3.6(5)]. In other words, adjusting the stack frame ensures that all the stack frames of the suspended tasks look the same.

Implementation details about `OSIntCtxSw()` are provided in Chapter 8, Porting μC/OS-II.

Figure 3.6 Cleanup by OSIntCtxSw().

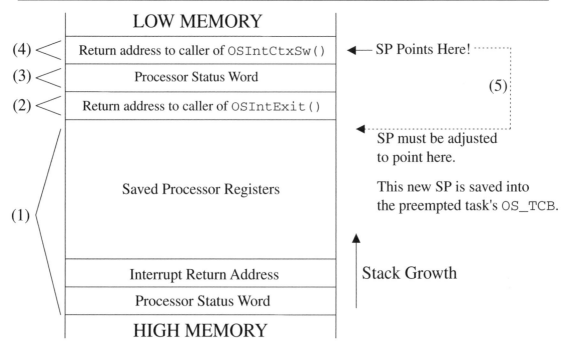

Some processors, like the Motorola 68HC11, require that you implicitly re-enable interrupts in order to allow nesting. This can be used to your advantage. Indeed, if your ISR needs to be serviced quickly and it doesn't need to notify a task about itself, you don't need to call `OSIntEnter()` (or increment `OSIntNesting`) or `OSIntExit()` as long as you don't enable interrupts within the ISR. The pseudocode in Listing 3.18 shows this situation. The only way a task and this ISR can communicate is through global variables.

In lieu of listing 3.15, by 91

Listing 3.18 ISRs on a Motorola 68HC11.

```
M68HC11_ISR:                    /* Fast ISR, MUST NOT enable interrupts */
    All register saved automatically by the CPU;
    Execute user code to service the interrupt;
    Execute a return from interrupt instruction;
```

3.10 Clock Tick

µC/OS-II requires that you provide a periodic time source to keep track of time delays and timeouts. A tick should occur between 10 and 100 times per second, or Hertz. The faster the tick rate, the higher the overhead imposed on the system. The actual frequency of the clock tick depends on the desired tick resolution of your application. You can obtain a tick source either by dedicating a hardware timer or generating an interrupt from an AC power line (50/60Hz) signal.

You MUST enable ticker interrupts AFTER multitasking has started; that is, after calling OSStart(). In other words, you should initialize ticker interrupts in the first task that executes following a call to OSStart(). A common mistake is to enable ticker interrupts after OSInit() and before OSStart() as shown in Listing 3.19.

Listing 3.19   Incorrect way to start the ticker.

```
void main(void)
{
    .
    .
    OSInit();                  /* Initialize µC/OS-II                      */
    .
    .
    /* Application initialization code ...                                 */
    /* ... Create at least one task by calling OSTaskCreate()             */
    .
    .
    Enable TICKER interrupts; /* DO NOT DO THIS HERE!!!                    */
    .
    .
    OSStart();                 /* Start multitasking                      */
}
```

Potentially, the tick interrupt could be serviced before µC/OS-II starts the first task. At this point, µC/OS-II is in an unknown state and your application will crash.

The µC/OS-II clock tick is serviced by calling OSTimeTick() from a *tick ISR*. The tick ISR follows all the rules described in the previous section. The pseudocode for the tick ISR is shown in Listing 3.20. This code must be written in assembly language because you cannot access CPU registers directly from C.

Listing 3.20   Pseudocode for tick ISR.

```
void OSTickISR(void)
{
    Save processor registers;
    Call OSIntEnter() or increment OSIntNesting;
```

[handwritten: Similar to OSSched() Pg 94]

Listing 3.20 Pseudocode for tick ISR. (Continued)

```
    Call OSTimeTick();
    Call OSIntExit();
    Restore processor registers;
    Execute a return from interrupt instruction;
}
```

[handwritten annotations: → Can An ISR call a C. function? ; Pg 94 → If higher priority task has been made ready, OSIntExit() perform context switch.]

The code for OSTimeTick() is shown in Listing 3.21. OSTimeTick() starts by calling the user-definable function OSTimeTickHook(), which can be used to extend the functionality of OSTimeTick() [L3.21(1)]. I decided to call OSTimeTickHook() first to give your application a chance to do something as soon as the tick is serviced because you may have some time-critical work to do. Most of the work done by OSTimeTick() basically consists of decrementing the OSTCBDly field for each OS_TCB (if it's nonzero). OSTimeTick() follows the chain of OS_TCB, starting at OSTCB-List [L3.21(2)], until it reaches the idle task [L3.21(3)]. When the OSTCBDly field of a task's OS_TCB is decremented to 0, the task is made ready to run [L3.21(5)]. The task is not readied, however, if it was explicitly suspended by OSTaskSuspend() [L3.21(4)]. The execution time of OSTimeTick() is directly proportional to the number of tasks created in an application.

[handwritten: — Task is added to Ready List]

Listing 3.21 Service a tick, **OSTimeTick()**.

```
void OSTimeTick (void)
{
    OS_TCB *ptcb;

    OSTimeTickHook();                                              (1)
    ptcb = OSTCBList;                                              (2)
    while (ptcb->OSTCBPrio != OS_IDLE_PRIO) {                      (3)
        OS_ENTER_CRITICAL();
        if (ptcb->OSTCBDly != 0) {
            if (--ptcb->OSTCBDly == 0) {
                if (!(ptcb->OSTCBStat & OS_STAT_SUSPEND)) {        (4)
                    OSRdyGrp                |= ptcb->OSTCBBitY;    (5)
                    OSRdyTbl[ptcb->OSTCBY]  |= ptcb->OSTCBBitX;
                } else {
                    ptcb->OSTCBDly = 1;
                }
            }
        }
        ptcb = ptcb->OSTCBNext;
        OS_EXIT_CRITICAL();
    }
```

[handwritten annotations: 'state' of TCB; a bit flag in OSTCBStat; Pg 81; Pg 127]

Listing 3.21 Service a tick, `OSTimeTick()`. (Continued)

```
    OS_ENTER_CRITICAL();                                        (6)
    OSTime++;                                                   (7)
    OS_EXIT_CRITICAL();
}
```

OSTimeTick() also accumulates the number of clock ticks since power-up in an unsigned 32-bit variable called OSTime [L3.21(7)]. Note that I disable interrupts [L3.21(6)] before incrementing OSTime because on some processors, a 32-bit increment will most likely be done using multiple instructions.

If you don't like to make ISRs any longer than they must be, OSTimeTick() can be called at the task level as shown in Listing 3.22. To do this, create a task that has a higher priority than all your other application tasks. The tick ISR needs to signal this high-priority task by using either a semaphore or a message mailbox.

Listing 3.22 Service a tick, `TickTask()`.

```
void TickTask (void *pdata)
{
    pdata = pdata;
    for (;;) {
        OSMboxPend(...);        /* Wait for signal from Tick ISR */
        OSTimeTick();
    }
}
```

You obviously need to create a mailbox (initialized to NULL) that will be used to signal the task that a tick interrupt has occurred (Listing 3.23).

Listing 3.23 Service a tick, `OSTickISR()`. ← This replaces listing 3.20

```
void OSTickISR(void)
{
    Save processor registers;
    Call OSIntEnter() or increment OSIntNesting;

    Post a 'dummy' message (e.g. (void *)1) to the tick mailbox;

    Call OSIntExit();
    Restore processor registers;
    Execute a return from interrupt instruction;
}
```

3.11 µC/OS-II Initialization

A requirement of µC/OS-II is that you call OSInit() before you call any of its other services. OSInit() initializes all µC/OS-II variables and data structures (see OS_CORE.C).

OSInit() creates the idle task OSTaskIdle(), which is always ready to run. The priority of OSTaskIdle() is always set to OS_LOWEST_PRIO. If OS_TASK_STAT_EN and OS_TASK_CREATE_EXT_EN (see OS_CFG.H) are both set to 1, OSInit() also creates the statistic task OSTaskStat() and makes it ready to run. The priority of OSTaskStat() is always set to OS_LOWEST_PRIO-1.

Figure 3.7 shows the relationship between some µC/OS-II variables and data structures after calling OSInit(). The illustration assumes that

- OS_TASK_STAT_EN is set to 1 in OS_CFG.H,
- OS_LOWEST_PRIO is set to 63 in OS_CFG.H, and
- OS_MAX_TASKS is set greater than 2 in OS_CFG.H.

The task control blocks (OS_TCBs) of these two tasks are chained together in a doubly linked list. OSTCBList points to the beginning of this chain. When a task is created, it is always placed at the beginning of the list. In other words, OSTCBList always points to the OS_TCB of last task created. The ends of the chain points to NULL (i.e., 0).

Because both tasks are ready to run, their corresponding bits in OSRdyTbl[] are set to 1. Also, because the bits of both tasks are on the same row in OSRdyTbl[], only one bit in OSRdyGrp is set to 1.

µC/OS-II also initializes four pools of free data structures as shown in Figure 3.8. Each of these pools is a singly linked list and allows µC/OS-II to obtain and return an element from and to a pool quickly. Note that the number of free OS_TCBs in the free pool is determined by OS_MAX_TASKS, specified in OS_CFG.H. µC/OS-II automatically allocates OS_N_SYS_TASKS (see uCOS_II.H) OS_TCB entries automatically. This, of course, allows sufficient task control blocks for the statistic task and the idle task. The lists pointed to by OSEventFreeList and OSQFreeList are discussed in Chapter 6, Intertask Communication & Synchronization. The list pointed to by OSMemFreeList is discussed in Chapter 7, Memory Management.

3.12 Starting µC/OS-II

You start multitasking by calling OSStart(). However, before you start µC/OS-II, you must create at least one of your application tasks as shown in Listing 3.24.

Listing 3.24 Initializing and starting µC/OS-II.

```
void main (void)
{
    OSInit();            /* Initialize uC/OS-II                 */
    .
    .
    Create at least 1 task using either OSTaskCreate() or OSTaskCreateExt();
    .
    .
    OSStart();           /* Start multitasking!  OSStart() will not return */
}
```

Figure 3.7   *Data structures after calling* `OSInit()`.

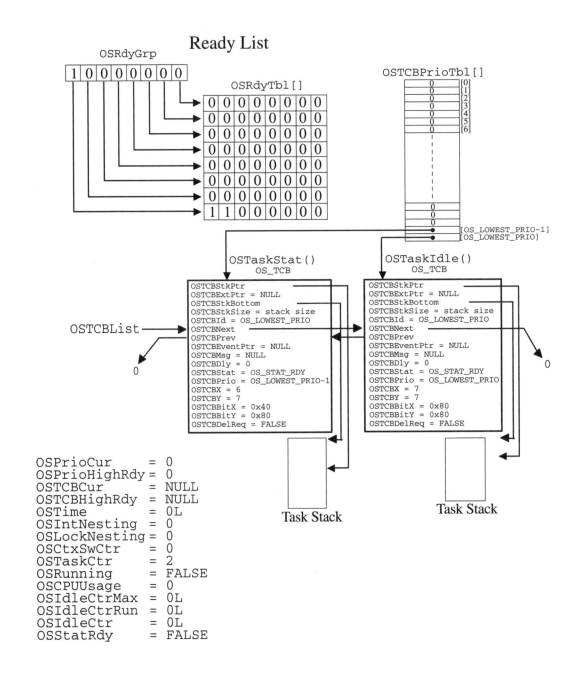

Figure 3.8   Free pools.

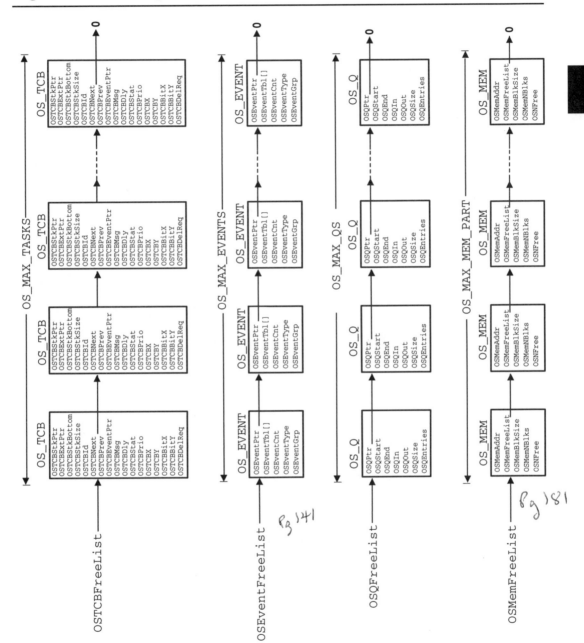

The code for `OSStart()` is shown in Listing 3.25. When called, `OSStart()` finds the `OS_TCB` (from the ready list) of the highest priority task that you have created [L3.25(1)]. Then, `OSStart()` calls `OSStartHighRdy()` [L3.25(2)] (see OS_CPU_A.ASM) for the processor being used. Basically, `OSStartHighRdy()` restores the CPU registers by popping them off the task's stack then executes a return from interrupt instruction, which forces the CPU to execute your task's code. (See section 9.04.01 "`OSStartHighRdy()`" on page 221) for details on how this is done for the 80x86.) Note that `OSStartHighRdy()` will never return to `OSStart()`.

Listing 3.25   Starting multitasking.

```
void OSStart (void)
{
    INT8U y;
    INT8U x;


    if (OSRunning == FALSE) {
        y             = OSUnMapTbl[OSRdyGrp];
        x             = OSUnMapTbl[OSRdyTbl[y]];
        OSPrioHighRdy = (INT8U)((y << 3) + x);
        OSPrioCur     = OSPrioHighRdy;
        OSTCBHighRdy  = OSTCBPrioTbl[OSPrioHighRdy];                        (1)
        OSTCBCur      = OSTCBHighRdy;
        OSStartHighRdy();                                                   (2)
    }
}
```

Figure 3.9 shows the contents of the variables and data structures after multitasking has started. Here, I assume that the task you created has a priority of 6. Notice that `OSTaskCtr` indicates that three tasks have been created: `OSRunning` is set to `TRUE`, indicating that multitasking has started, `OSPrioCur` and `OSPrioHighRdy` contain the priority of your application task, and `OSTCBCur` and `OSTCBHighRdy` both point to the `OS_TCB` of your task.

3.13   Obtaining the Current µC/OS-II Version

You can obtain the current version of µC/OS-II from your application by calling `OSVersion()` (Listing 3.26). `OSVersion()` returns the version number multiplied by 100. In other words, version 2.00 is returned as 200.

Listing 3.26   Getting the current µC/OS-II version.

```
INT16U OSVersion (void)
{
    return (OS_VERSION);
}
```

To find out about the latest version of µC/OS-II and how to obtain an upgrade, you should either contact the publisher or check the official µC/OS-II Web site at www.uCOS-II.com.

Figure 3.9   Variables and data structures after calling OSStart().

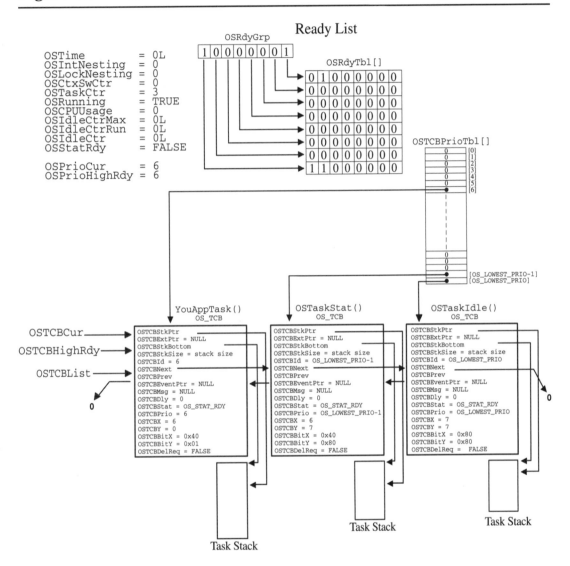

3.14 OSEvent???() Functions

You probably noticed that OS_CORE.C has four functions that were not mentioned in this chapter. These functions are OSEventWaitListInit(), OSEventTaskRdy(), OSEventTaskWait(), and OSEventTO(). I placed these functions in OS_CORE.C, but I explain their use in Chapter 6, Intertask Communication & Synchronization.

Chapter 4

Task Management

In the previous chapter I specified that a task is either an infinite loop function or a function that deletes itself when it is done executing. Note that the task code is not actually deleted — µC/OS-II simply doesn't know about the task anymore, so that code will not run. A task looks just like any other C function, containing a return type and an argument, but it must never return. The return type of a task must always be declared void. The functions described in this chapter are found in the file OS_TASK.C. To review, a task must have one of the two structures:

```
void YourTask (void *pdata)
{
    for (;;) {
        /* USER CODE */
        Call one of uC/OS-II's services:
            OSMboxPend();
            OSQPend();
            OSSemPend();
            OSTaskDel(OS_PRIO_SELF);
            OSTaskSuspend(OS_PRIO_SELF);
            OSTimeDly();
            OSTimeDlyHMSM();
        /* USER CODE */
    }
}
```

or

```
void YourTask (void *pdata)
{
    /* USER CODE */
    OSTaskDel(OS_PRIO_SELF);
}
```

This chapter describes the services that allow your application to create a task, delete a task, change a task's priority, suspend and resume a task, and allow your application to obtain information about a task.

µC/OS-II can manage up to 64 tasks, although µC/OS-II reserves the four highest priority tasks and the four lowest priority tasks for its own use. This leaves you with up to 56 application tasks. The lower the value of the priority, the higher the priority of the task. In the current version of µC/OS-II, the task priority number also serves as the task identifier.

4.00 Creating a Task, *OSTaskCreate()*

In order for µC/OS-II to manage your task, you must create it. You create a task by passing its address and other arguments to one of two functions: OSTaskCreate() or OSTaskCreateExt(). OSTaskCreate() is backward compatible with µC/OS, and OSTaskCreateExt() is an extended version of OSTaskCreate(), providing additional features. A task can be created using either function. A task can be created prior to the start of multitasking or by another task. You must create at least one task before you start multitasking [i.e., before you call OSStart()]. A task cannot be created by an ISR.

The code for OSTaskCreate() is shown in Listing 4.1. As can be seen, OSTaskCreate() requires four arguments. task is a pointer to the task code, pdata is a pointer to an argument that is passed to your task when it starts executing, ptos is a pointer to the top of the stack that is assigned to the task (see section 4.02, Task Stacks), and prio is the desired task priority.

Listing 4.1   *OSTaskCreate()*.

```
INT8U OSTaskCreate (void (*task)(void *pd), void *pdata, OS_STK *ptos, INT8U prio)
{
    void    *psp;
    INT8U    err;



    if (prio > OS_LOWEST_PRIO) {                                             (1)
        return (OS_PRIO_INVALID);
    }
```

Listing 4.1   *OSTaskCreate(). (Continued)*

```
    OS_ENTER_CRITICAL();
    if (OSTCBPrioTbl[prio] == (OS_TCB *)0) {                          (2)
        OSTCBPrioTbl[prio] = (OS_TCB *)1;                            (3)
        OS_EXIT_CRITICAL();                                          (4)
        psp = (void *)OSTaskStkInit(task, pdata, ptos, 0);          (5)
        err = OSTCBInit(prio, psp, (void *)0, 0, 0, (void *)0, 0);  (6)
        if (err == OS_NO_ERR) {                                      (7)
            OS_ENTER_CRITICAL();
            OSTaskCtr++;                                             (8)
            OSTaskCreateHook(OSTCBPrioTbl[prio]);                   (9)
            OS_EXIT_CRITICAL();
            if (OSRunning) {                                         (10)
                OSSched();                                          (11)
            }
        } else {
            OS_ENTER_CRITICAL();
            OSTCBPrioTbl[prio] = (OS_TCB *)0;                       (12)
            OS_EXIT_CRITICAL();
        }
        return (err);
    } else {
        OS_EXIT_CRITICAL();
        return (OS_PRIO_EXIST);
    }
}
```

OSTaskCreate() starts by checking that the task priority is valid [L4.1(1)]. The priority of a task must be a number between 0 and OS_LOWEST_PRIO, inclusive. Next, OSTaskCreate() makes sure that a task has not already been created at the desired priority [L4.1(2)]. With µC/OS-II, all tasks must have a unique priority. If the desired priority is free, µC/OS-II reserves the priority by placing a non-NULL pointer in OSTCBPrioTbl[] [L4.1(3)]. This allows OSTaskCreate() to re-enable interrupts [L4.1(4)] while it sets up the rest of the data structures for the task.

OSTaskCreate() then calls OSTaskStkInit() [L4.1(5)], which is responsible for setting up the task stack. This function is processor specific and is found in OS_CPU_C.C. Refer to Chapter 8, Porting µC/OS-II, for details on how to implement OSTaskStkInit(). If you already have a port of µC/OS-II for the processor you are intending to use, you don't need to be concerned about implementation details. OSTaskStkInit() returns the new top-of-stack (psp), which is saved in the task's OS_TCB. You should note that the fourth argument (opt) to OSTaskStkInit() is set to 0. This is because, unlike OSTaskCreateExt(), OSTaskCreate() does not support options, so there are no options to pass to OSTaskStkInit().

µC/OS-II supports processors that have stacks that grow either from high to low memory or from low to high memory. When you call OSTaskCreate(), you must know how the stack grows (see

OS_STACK_GROWTH in OS_CPU.H of the processor you are using) because you must pass the task's top-of-stack to OSTaskCreate(), which can be either the lowest or the highest memory location of the stack.

Once OSTaskStkInit() has completed setting up the stack, OSTaskCreate() calls OSTCB-Init()[L4.1(6)] to obtain and initialize an OS_TCB from the pool of free OS_TCBs. The code for OSTCBInit() is shown in Listing 4.2 but is found in OS_CORE.C instead of OS_TASK.C. OSTCB-Init() first tries to obtain an OS_TCB from the OS_TCB pool [L4.2(1)]. If the pool contains a free OS_TCB [L4.2(2)], it is initialized [L4.2(3)]. Note that once an OS_TCB is allocated, OSTCBInit() can re-enable interrupts because at this point the creator of the task owns the OS_TCB and it cannot be corrupted by another concurrent task creation. OSTCBInit() can thus proceed to initialize some of the OS_TCB fields with interrupts enabled.

Listing 4.2   *OSTCBInit().*

```
INT8U OSTCBInit (INT8U   prio,      OS_STK *ptos,     OS_STK *pbos, INT16U id,
                 INT16U stk_size, void    *pext,     INT16U  opt)
{
    OS_TCB *ptcb;


    OS_ENTER_CRITICAL();
    ptcb = OSTCBFreeList;                                                   (1)
    if (ptcb != (OS_TCB *)0) {                                              (2)
        OSTCBFreeList        = ptcb->OSTCBNext;
        OS_EXIT_CRITICAL();
        ptcb->OSTCBStkPtr    = ptos;                                        (3)
        ptcb->OSTCBPrio      = (INT8U)prio;
        ptcb->OSTCBStat      = OS_STAT_RDY;
        ptcb->OSTCBDly       = 0;
#if OS_TASK_CREATE_EXT_EN
        ptcb->OSTCBExtPtr    = pext;
        ptcb->OSTCBStkSize   = stk_size;
        ptcb->OSTCBStkBottom = pbos;
        ptcb->OSTCBOpt       = opt;
        ptcb->OSTCBId        = id;
#else
        pext                 = pext;
        stk_size             = stk_size;
        pbos                 = pbos;
        opt                  = opt;
        id                   = id;
#endif
```

Listing 4.2   *OSTCBInit().* *(Continued)*

```
#if OS_TASK_DEL_EN
        ptcb->OSTCBDelReq     = OS_NO_ERR;
#endif


        ptcb->OSTCBY          = prio >> 3;
        ptcb->OSTCBBitY       = OSMapTbl[ptcb->OSTCBY];
        ptcb->OSTCBX          = prio & 0x07;
        ptcb->OSTCBBitX       = OSMapTbl[ptcb->OSTCBX];


#if     OS_MBOX_EN || (OS_Q_EN && (OS_MAX_QS >= 2)) || OS_SEM_EN
        ptcb->OSTCBEventPtr   = (OS_EVENT *)0;
#endif


#if     OS_MBOX_EN || (OS_Q_EN && (OS_MAX_QS >= 2))
        ptcb->OSTCBMsg        = (void *)0;
#endif


        OS_ENTER_CRITICAL();                                          (4)
        OSTCBPrioTbl[prio]    = ptcb;                                 (5)
        ptcb->OSTCBNext       = OSTCBList;
        ptcb->OSTCBPrev       = (OS_TCB *)0;
        if (OSTCBList != (OS_TCB *)0) {
            OSTCBList->OSTCBPrev = ptcb;
        }
        OSTCBList             = ptcb;
        OSRdyGrp             |= ptcb->OSTCBBitY;                      (6)
        OSRdyTbl[ptcb->OSTCBY] |= ptcb->OSTCBBitX;
        OS_EXIT_CRITICAL();
        return (OS_NO_ERR);                                          (7)
    } else {
        OS_EXIT_CRITICAL();
        return (OS_NO_MORE_TCB);
    }
}
```

Handwritten annotations: "re: Pg 84" and "when would OSTCBList ever be ∅?" ; "initialize new TCB" ; "update previous 'new' TCB"

OSTCBInit() disables interrupts [L4.2(4)] when it needs to insert the OS_TCB into the doubly linked list of tasks that have been created [L4.2(5)]. The list starts at OSTCBList, and the OS_TCB of a new task is always inserted at the beginning of the list. Finally, the task is made ready to run [L4.2(6)], and OSTCBInit() returns to its caller [OSTaskCreate()] with a code indicating that an OS_TCB has been allocated and initialized [L4.2(7)].

I can now continue the discussion of OSTaskCreate() (Listing 4.1). Upon return from OSTC-BInit(), OSTaskCreate() checks the return code [L4.1(7)] and, upon success, increments OSTaskCtr which keeps track of the number of tasks created [L4.1(8)]. If OSTCBInit() failed, the priority level is relinquished by setting the entry in OSTCBPrioTbl[prio] to 0 [L4.1(12)]. OSTaskCreate() then calls OSTaskCreateHook() [L4.1(9)], which is a user-specified function that allows you to extend the functionality of OSTaskCreate(). For example, you could initialize and store the contents of floating-point registers, MMU registers, or anything else that can be associated with a task. However, you would typically store this additional information in memory that would be allocated by your application. OSTaskCreateHook() can be declared either in OS_CPU_C.C (if OS_CPU_HOOKS_EN is set to 1) or elsewhere. Note that interrupts are disabled when OSTaskCreate() calls OSTaskCreateHook(). Because of this, you should keep the code in this function to a minimum because it can directly affect interrupt latency. When called, OSTaskCreateHook() receives a pointer to the OS_TCB of the task being created. This means that the hook function can access all members of the OS_TCB data structure.

Finally, if OSTaskCreate() is called from a task (i.e., OSRunning is set to TRUE [L4.1(10)]), the scheduler is called [L4.1(11)] to determine whether the created task has a higher priority than its creator. Creating a higher priority task results in a context switch to the new task. If the task was created before multitasking has started [i.e., you did not call OSStart() yet], the scheduler is not called.

4.01 Creating a Task, *OSTaskCreateExt()*

Creating a task using OSTaskCreateExt() offers more flexibility, but at the expense of additional overhead. The code for OSTaskCreateExt() is shown in Listing 4.3.

As can be seen, OSTaskCreateExt() requires nine arguments! The first four arguments (task, pdata, ptos, and prio) are exactly the same as in OSTaskCreate(), and they are located in the same order. I did this to make it easier to migrate your code to use OSTaskCreateExt().

The id establishes a unique identifier for the task being created. This argument has been added for future expansion and is otherwise unused by µC/OS-II. This identifier will allow me to extend µC/OS-II beyond its limit of 64 tasks. For now, simply set the task's ID to the same value as the task's priority.

pbos is a pointer to the task's bottom-of-stack and this argument is used to perform stack checking.

stk_size specifies the size of the stack in number of elements. This means that if a stack entry is four bytes wide, then a stk_size of 1000 means that the stack will have 4,000 bytes. Again, this argument is used for stack checking.

pext is a pointer to a user-supplied data area that can be used to extend the OS_TCB of the task. For example, you can add a name to a task (see Example 3), storage for the contents of floating-point registers during a context switch, a port address to trigger an oscilloscope during a context switch, and more.

Finally, opt specifies options to OSTaskCreateExt(), specifying whether stack checking is allowed, whether the stack will be cleared, whether floating-point operations are performed by the task, etc. uCOS_II.H contains a list of available options (OS_TASK_OPT_STK_CHK, OS_TASK_OPT_STK_CLR, and OS_TASK_OPT_SAVE_FP). Each option consists of a bit. The option is selected when the bit is set (simply OR the above OS_TASK_OPT_??? constants).

Listing 4.3   *OSTaskCreateExt().*

```
INT8U OSTaskCreateExt (void    (*task)(void *pd),
                       void    *pdata,
                       OS_STK  *ptos,
                       INT8U   prio,
                       INT16U  id,
                       OS_STK  *pbos,
                       INT32U  stk_size,
                       void    *pext,
                       INT16U  opt)
{
    void    *psp;
    INT8U   err;
    INT16U  i;
    OS_STK  *pfill;



    if (prio > OS_LOWEST_PRIO) {                            (1)
        return (OS_PRIO_INVALID);
    }
    OS_ENTER_CRITICAL();
    if (OSTCBPrioTbl[prio] == (OS_TCB *)0) {                (2)
        OSTCBPrioTbl[prio] = (OS_TCB *)1;                  (3)
        OS_EXIT_CRITICAL();                                (4)
```

↓ Additional (handwritten annotation)

new (handwritten annotation)

4

OSTaskCreateExt() starts by checking that the task priority is valid [L4.3(1)]. The priority of a task must be a number between 0 and OS_LOWEST_PRIO, inclusive. Next, OSTaskCreateExt() makes sure that a task has not already been created at the desired priority [L4.3(2)]. With µC/OS-II, all tasks must have a unique priority. If the desired priority is free, then µC/OS-II reserves the priority by placing a non-NULL pointer in OSTCBPrioTbl[] [L4.3(3)]. This allows OSTaskCreateExt() to re-enable interrupts [L4.3(4)] while it sets up the rest of the data structures for the task.

In order to perform stack checking on a task [see section 4.03, Stack Checking, OSTaskStkChk()], you must set the OS_TASK_OPT_STK_CHK flag in the opt argument. Also, stack checking requires that the stack contain zeros (i.e., it is cleared) when the task is created. To specify that a task gets cleared when it is created, set OS_TASK_OPT_STK_CLR in the opt argument. When both of these flags are set, OSTaskCreateExt() clears the stack [L4.3(5)].

Listing 4.3 **OSTaskCreateExt(). (Continued)**

```
        if (opt & OS_TASK_OPT_STK_CHK) {                               (5)
            if (opt & OS_TASK_OPT_STK_CLR) {
                pfill = pbos;
                for (i = 0; i < stk_size; i++) {
                    #if OS_STK_GROWTH == 1
                    *pfill++ = (OS_STK)0;
                    #else
                    *pfill-- = (OS_STK)0;
                    #endif
                }
            }
        }
        psp = (void *)OSTaskStkInit(task, pdata, ptos, opt);           (6)
        err = OSTCBInit(prio, psp, pbos, id, stk_size, pext, opt);     (7)
        if (err == OS_NO_ERR) {                                        (8)
            OS_ENTER_CRITICAL;
            OSTaskCtr++;                                               (9)
            OSTaskCreateHook(OSTCBPrioTbl[prio]);                      (10)
            OS_EXIT_CRITICAL();
            if (OSRunning) {                                           (11)
                OSSched();                                             (12)
            }
        } else {
            OS_ENTER_CRITICAL();
            OSTCBPrioTbl[prio] = (OS_TCB *)0;                          (13)
            OS_EXIT_CRITICAL();
        }
        return (err);
    } else {
        OS_EXIT_CRITICAL();
        return (OS_PRIO_EXIST);
    }
}
```

NEW

OSTaskCreateExt() then calls OSTaskStkInit() [L4.3(6)], which is responsible for setting up the task stack. This function is processor specific and is found in OS_CPU_C.C. Refer to Chapter 8, Porting µC/OS-II, for details on how to implement OSTaskStkInit(). If you already have a port of µC/OS-II for the processor you are intending to use, then you don't need to be concerned about implementation details. OSTaskStkInit() returns the new top-of-stack (psp) which will be saved in the task's OS_TCB.

µC/OS-II supports processors that have stacks that grow either from high to low memory or from low to high memory (see section 4.02, Task Stacks). When you call OSTaskCreateExt(), you must know how the stack grows (see OS_CPU.H of the processor you are using) because you must pass the task's top-of-stack, which can either be the lowest memory location of the stack (when OS_STK_GROWTH is 0) or the highest memory location of the stack (when OS_STK_GROWTH is 1), to OSTaskCreateExt().

Once OSTaskStkInit() has completed setting up the stack, OSTaskCreateExt() calls OSTCB-Init() [L4.3(7)] to obtain and initialize an OS_TCB from the pool of free OS_TCBs. The code for OSTCBInit() is shown and described with OSTaskCreate() (see section 4.00). Upon return from OSTCBInit(), OSTaskCreateExt() checks the return code [L4.3(8)] and, upon success, increments OSTaskCtr which keeps track of the number of tasks created, [L4.3(9)]. If OSTCBInit() failed, the priority level is relinquished by setting the entry in OSTCBPrioTbl[prio] to 0 [L4.3(13)]. OSTaskCreateExt() then calls OSTaskCreateHook() [L4.3(10)], which is a user-specified function that allows you to extend the functionality of OSTaskCreateExt(). OSTaskCreateHook() can be declared either in OS_CPU_C.C (if OS_CPU_HOOKS_EN is set to 1) or elsewhere (if OS_CPU_HOOKS_EN is set to 0). Note that interrupts are disabled when OSTaskCreateExt() calls OSTaskCreateHook(). Because of this, you should keep the code in this function to a minimum because it can directly affect interrupt latency. When called, OSTaskCreateHook() receives a pointer to the OS_TCB of the task being created. This means that the hook function can access all members of the OS_TCB data structure.

Finally, if OSTaskCreateExt() is called from a task (i.e., OSRunning is set to TRUE [L4.3(11)]), the scheduler is called [L4.3(12)] to determine whether the created task has a higher priority than its creator. Creating a higher priority task results in a context switch to the new task. If the task was created before multitasking started [i.e., you did not call OSStart() yet], the scheduler is not called.

4.02 Task Stacks

Each task must have its own stack space. A stack must be declared as being of type OS_STK and must consist of contiguous memory locations. You can allocate stack space either statically (at compile time) or dynamically (at run time). A static stack declaration is shown in Listings 4.4 and 4.5. Either declaration is made outside a function.

Listing 4.4   Static stack.

```
static OS_STK  MyTaskStack[stack_size];
```

or

Listing 4.5   Static stack.

```
OS_STK  MyTaskStack[stack_size];
```

You can allocate stack space dynamically by using the C compiler's `malloc()` function as shown in Listing 4.6. However, you must be careful with fragmentation. Specifically, if you create and delete tasks, your memory allocator may not be able to return a stack for your task(s) because the heap eventually becomes fragmented.

Listing 4.6   Using `malloc()` to allocate stack space for a task.

```
OS_STK   *pstk;



pstk = (OS_STK *)malloc(stack_size);
if (pstk != (OS_STK *)0) {              /* Make sure malloc() has enough space */
    Create the task;
}
```

Figure 4.1 illustrates a heap containing 3Kb of available memory that can be allocated with `malloc()` [F4.1(1)]. For the sake of discussion, you create three tasks (tasks A, B, and C), each requiring 1Kb. Assume that the first 1Kb is given to task A, the second to task B, and the third to task C [F4.1(2)]. Your application then deletes task A and task C and relinquishes the memory to the heap using `free()` [F4.1(3)]. Your heap now has 2Kb of memory free, but it's not contiguous. This means that you cannot create another task (i.e., task D) that requires 2 Kb because your heap is fragmented. If, however, you never delete a task, the use of `malloc()` is perfectly acceptable.

Figure 4.1   Fragmentation.

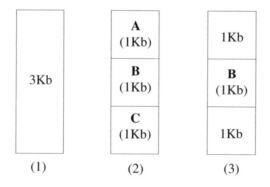

(1)   (2)   (3)

Because μC/OS-II supports processors with stacks that grow either from high to low memory or from low to high memory, you must know how the stack grows when you call either `OSTaskCreate()` or `OSTaskCreateExt()` because you need to pass the task's top-of-stack to these functions. When OS_STK_GROWTH is set to 0 in OS_CPU.H, you need to pass the lowest memory location of the stack to the task create function as shown in Listing 4.7.

beginning

Stack grows from Low to High

Listing 4.7   Stack grows from low to high memory.

```
OS_STK   TaskStack[TASK_STACK_SIZE];


OSTaskCreate(task, pdata, &TaskStack[0], prio);
```
← STACK Grows from High to Low (handwritten)

When OS_STK_GROWTH is set to 1 in OS_CPU.H, you need to pass the highest memory location of the stack to the task create function as shown in Listing 4.8.

beginning of stack (handwritten)

Listing 4.8   Stack grows from high to low memory.

```
OS_STK   TaskStack[TASK_STACK_SIZE];


OSTaskCreate(task, pdata, &TaskStack[TASK_STACK_SIZE-1], prio);
```

This requirement affects code portability. If you need to port your code from a processor architecture that supports a downward-growing stack to one that supports an upward-growing stack, you may need to make your code handle both cases. Specifically, Listings 4.7 and 4.8 are rewritten as shown in Listing 4.9.

Listing 4.9   Supporting stacks that grow in either direction.

```
OS_STK   TaskStack[TASK_STACK_SIZE];



#if OS_STK_GROWTH == 0
    OSTaskCreate(task, pdata, &TaskStack[0], prio);
#else
    OSTaskCreate(task, pdata, &TaskStack[TASK_STACK_SIZE-1], prio);
#endif
```

The size of the stack needed by your task is application specific. When sizing the stack, however, you must account for nesting of all the functions called by your task, the number of local variables that will be allocated by all functions called by your task, and the stack requirements for all nested interrupt service routines. In addition, your stack must be able to store all CPU registers.

4.03 Stack Checking, OSTaskStkChk()

Sometimes it is necessary to determine how much stack space a task actually uses. This allows you to reduce the amount of RAM needed by your application code by not overallocating stack space. µC/OS-II provides OSTaskStkChk(), which provides you with this valuable information.

In Figure 4.2, I assume that the stack grows from high memory to low memory (i.e., OS_STK_GROWTH is set to 1) but the following discussion applies equally well to a stack growing in the opposite direction [F4.2(1)]. µC/OS-II determines stack growth by looking at the contents of the stack itself. Stack checking is performed on demand as opposed to continuously. To perform stack checking, µC/OS-II requires that the stack be filled with zeros when the task is created [F4.2(2)]. Also, µC/OS-II needs to know the location of the bottom-of-stack (BOS) [F4.2(3)] and the size of the stack you assigned to the task [F4.2(4)]. These two values are stored in the task's OS_TCB when the task is created.

In order to use the µC/OS-II stack-checking facilities, you must do the following.

- Set OS_TASK_CREATE_EXT to 1 in OS_CFG.H.

- Create a task using OSTaskCreateExt() and give the task much more space than you think it really needs.

- Set the opt argument in OSTaskCreateExt() to OS_TASK_OPT_STK_CHK + OS_TASK_OPT_STK_CLR. Note that if your startup code clears all RAM and you never delete tasks once they are created, you don't need to set the OS_TASK_OPT_STK_CLR option. This reduces the execution time of OSTaskCreateExt().

- Call OSTaskStkChk() by specifying the priority of the task you want to check.

Figure 4.2   Stack checking.

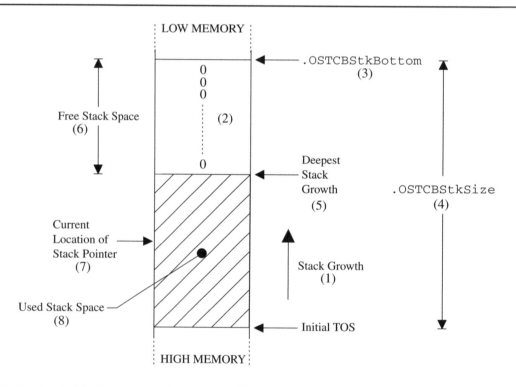

OSTaskStkChk() computes the amount of free stack space by "walking" from the bottom of the stack and counting the number of zero-value entries on the stack until a nonzero value is found [F4.2(5)]. Note that stack entries are checked using the data type of the stack (see OS_STK in OS_CPU.H). In other words, if a stack entry is 32 bits wide, the comparison for a zero value is done using 32 bits. The amount of stack space used [F4.2(8)] is obtained by subtracting the number of zero-value entries [F4.2(6)] from the stack size you specified in OSTaskCreateExt(). OSTaskStkChk() actually places the number of bytes free and the number of bytes used in a data structure of type OS_STK_DATA (see uCOS_II.H) . Note that at any given time, the stack pointer for the task being checked may

4

be pointing somewhere between the initial top-of-stack (TOS) and the deepest stack growth [F4.2(7)]. Also, every time you call OSTaskStkChk(), you may get a different value for the amount of free space on the stack until your task has reached its deepest growth [F4.2(5)].

You need to run the application long enough and under your worst case conditions to get proper numbers. Once OSTaskStkChk() provides you with the worst case stack requirement, you can go back and set the final size of your stack. You should accommodate system expansion, so make sure you allocate between 10 and 100 percent more stack. What you should get from stack checking is a ballpark figure; you are not looking for an exact stack usage.

The code for OSTaskStkChk() is shown in Listing 4.10. The data structure OS_STK_DATA (see uCOS_II.H) is used to hold information about the task stack. I decided to use a data structure for two reasons. First, I consider OSTaskStkChk() to be a query-type function, and I wanted to have all query functions work the same way — return data about the query in a data structure. Second, passing data in a data structure is efficient and allows me to add additional fields in the future without changing the API (Application Programming Interface) of OSTaskStkChk(). For now, OS_STK_DATA only contains two fields: OSFree and OSUsed. As you can see, you invoke OSTaskStkChk() by specifying the priority of the task you want to perform stack checking on. If you specify OS_PRIO_SELF [L4.10(1)], it is assumed that you want to know the stack information about the current task. Obviously, the task must exist [L4.10(2)]. To perform stack checking, you must have created the task using OSTaskCreate-Ext() and you must have passed the option OS_TASK_OPT_STK_CHK [L4.10(3)]. If all the proper conditions are met, OSTaskStkChk() computes the free stack space as described above by walking from the bottom of stack until a nonzero stack entry is encountered [L4.10(4)]. Finally, the information that is stored in OS_STK_DATA is computed [L4.10(5)]. Note that the function computes the actual number of bytes free and the number of bytes used on the stack as opposed to the number of elements. Obviously, the actual stack size (in bytes) can be obtained by adding these two values.

Listing 4.10   Stack-checking function.

```
INT8U OSTaskStkChk (INT8U prio, OS_STK_DATA *pdata)
{
    OS_TCB   *ptcb;
    OS_STK   *pchk;
    INT32U   free;
    INT32U   size;


    pdata->OSFree = 0;
    pdata->OSUsed = 0;
    if (prio > OS_LOWEST_PRIO && prio != OS_PRIO_SELF) {
        return (OS_PRIO_INVALID);
    }
    OS_ENTER_CRITICAL();
    if (prio == OS_PRIO_SELF) {                                       (1)
        prio = OSTCBCur->OSTCBPrio;
    }
    ptcb = OSTCBPrioTbl[prio];
```

Listing 4.10   Stack-checking function. (Continued)

```
    if (ptcb == (OS_TCB *)0) {                              (2)
        OS_EXIT_CRITICAL();
        return (OS_TASK_NOT_EXIST);
    }
    if ((ptcb->OSTCBOpt & OS_TASK_OPT_STK_CHK) == 0) {      (3)
        OS_EXIT_CRITICAL();
        return (OS_TASK_OPT_ERR);
    }
    free = 0;                                               (4)
    size = ptcb->OSTCBStkSize;
    pchk = ptcb->OSTCBStkBottom;
    OS_EXIT_CRITICAL();
#if OS_STK_GROWTH == 1
    while (*pchk++ == 0) {
        free++;
    }
#else
    while (*pchk-- == 0) {
        free++;
    }
#endif
    pdata->OSFree = free * sizeof(OS_STK);                  (5)
    pdata->OSUsed = (size - free) * sizeof(OS_STK);
    return (OS_NO_ERR);
}
```

4.04 Deleting a Task, `OSTaskDel()`

Sometimes it is necessary to delete a task. Deleting a task means that the task will be returned to the DORMANT state (see section 3.02, Task States) and does not mean that the code for the task will be deleted. The task code is simply no longer scheduled by µC/OS-II. Delete a task by calling OSTaskDel() (Listing 4.11). OSTaskDel() starts by making sure that you are not attempting to delete an idle task because this is not allowed [L4.11(1)]. However, you are allowed to delete the statistic task [L4.11(2)]. OSTaskDel() then checks to make sure you are not attempting to delete a task from within an ISR, which is again not allowed [L4.11(3)]. The caller can delete itself by specifying OS_PRIO_SELF as the argument [L4.11(4)]. OSTaskDel() verifies that the task to delete does in fact exist [L4.11(5)]. This test obviously will pass if you specified OS_PRIO_SELF. I didn't want to create a separate case for this situation because it would have increased code size and thus execution time.

Listing 4.11   Task delete.

```
INT8U OSTaskDel (INT8U prio)
{
    OS_TCB   *ptcb;
    OS_EVENT *pevent;

    if (prio == OS_IDLE_PRIO) {                                          (1)
        return (OS_TASK_DEL_IDLE);
    }
    if (prio >= OS_LOWEST_PRIO && prio != OS_PRIO_SELF) {               (2)
        return (OS_PRIO_INVALID);
    }
    OS_ENTER_CRITICAL();
    if (OSIntNesting > 0) {                                             (3)
        OS_EXIT_CRITICAL();
        return (OS_TASK_DEL_ISR);
    }
    if (prio == OS_PRIO_SELF) {                                         (4)
        prio = OSTCBCur->OSTCBPrio;
    }
    if ((ptcb = OSTCBPrioTbl[prio]) != (OS_TCB *)0) {                   (5)
        if ((OSRdyTbl[ptcb->OSTCBY] &= ~ptcb->OSTCBBitX) == 0) {       (6)
            OSRdyGrp &= ~ptcb->OSTCBBitY;
        }
        if ((pevent = ptcb->OSTCBEventPtr) != (OS_EVENT *)0) {          (7)
            if ((pevent->OSEventTbl[ptcb->OSTCBY] &= ~ptcb->OSTCBBitX) == 0) {
                pevent->OSEventGrp &= ~ptcb->OSTCBBitY;
            }
        }
        ptcb->OSTCBDly  = 0;                                            (8)
        ptcb->OSTCBStat = OS_STAT_RDY;                                  (9)
        OSLockNesting++;                                               (10)
        OS_EXIT_CRITICAL();                                           (11)
        OSDummy();                                                    (12)
        OS_ENTER_CRITICAL();
        OSLockNesting--;                                              (13)
        OSTaskDelHook(ptcb);                                          (14)
        OSTaskCtr--;
        OSTCBPrioTbl[prio] = (OS_TCB *)0;                             (15)
```

4

Listing 4.11   Task delete. (Continued)

```
        if (ptcb->OSTCBPrev == (OS_TCB *)0) {                        (16)
            ptcb->OSTCBNext->OSTCBPrev = (OS_TCB *)0;
            OSTCBList                  = ptcb->OSTCBNext;
        } else {
            ptcb->OSTCBPrev->OSTCBNext = ptcb->OSTCBNext;
            ptcb->OSTCBNext->OSTCBPrev = ptcb->OSTCBPrev;
        }
        ptcb->OSTCBNext = OSTCBFreeList;                             (17)
        OSTCBFreeList   = ptcb;
        OS_EXIT_CRITICAL();
        OSSched();                                                  (18)
        return (OS_NO_ERR);
    } else {
        OS_EXIT_CRITICAL();
        return (OS_TASK_DEL_ERR);
    }
}
```

Once all conditions are satisfied, the OS_TCB is removed from all possible µC/OS-II data structures. OSTaskDel() does this in two parts to reduce interrupt latency. First, if the task is in the ready list, it is removed [L4.11(6)]. If the task is in a list waiting for a mailbox, queue, or semaphore, it is removed from that list [L4.11(7)]. Next, OSTaskDel() forces the delay count to zero to make sure that the tick ISR will not ready this task once you re-enable interrupts [L4.11(8)]. Finally, OSTaskDel() sets the task's .OSTCBStat flag to OS_STAT_RDY. Note that OSTaskDel() is not trying to make the task ready, it is simply preventing another task or an ISR from resuming this task [i.e., in case the other task or ISR calls OSTaskResume() [L4.11(9)]]. This situation could occur because OSTaskDel() will be re-enabling interrupts [L4.11(11)], so an ISR can make a higher priority task ready, which could resume the task you are trying to delete. Instead of setting the task's .OSTCBStat flag to OS_STAT_RDY, I simply could have cleared the OS_STAT_SUSPEND bit (which would have been clearer), but this takes slightly more processing time.

At this point, the task to delete cannot be made ready to run by another task or an ISR because it's been removed from the ready list, it's not waiting for an event to occur, it's not waiting for time to expire, and it cannot be resumed. For all intents and purposes, the task is DORMANT. Because of this, OSTaskDel() must prevent the scheduler [L4.11(10)] from switching to another task because if the current task is almost deleted, it could not be rescheduled! At this point, OSTaskDel() re-enables interrupts in order to reduce interrupt latency [L4.11(11)]. OSTaskDel() could thus service an interrupt, but because it incremented OSLockNesting, the ISR would return to the interrupted task. Note that OSTaskDel() is still not done with the deletion process because it needs to unlink the OS_TCB from the TCB chain and return the OS_TCB to the free OS_TCB list.

Note also that I call the dummy function OSDummy() immediately after calling OS_EXIT_CRITI-CAL() [L4.11(12)]. I do this because I want to make sure that the processor executes at least one instruction with interrupts enabled. On many processors, executing an interrupt enable instruction forces the CPU to have interrupts *disabled* until the end of the next instruction! The Intel 80x86 and

Zilog Z-80 processors actually work like this. Enabling and immediately disabling interrupts would behave just as if I didn't enable interrupts. This would of course increase interrupt latency. Calling OSDummy() thus ensures that I execute a call and a return instruction before re-disabling interrupts. You could certainly replace OSDummy() with a macro that executes a "no-operation" instruction and thus slightly reduce the execution time of OSTaskDel(). I didn't think it was worth the effort of creating yet another macro that would require porting.

OSTaskDel() can now continue with the deletion process of the task. After OSTaskDel() re-disables interrupts, OSTaskDel() re-enables scheduling by decrementing the lock nesting counter [L4.11(13)], OSTaskDel() then calls the user-definable task delete hook OSTaskDelHook() [L4.11(14)]. This allows user-defined TCB extensions to be relinquished. Next, OSTaskDel() decrements the task counter to indicate that there is one less task being managed by µC/OS-II. OSTaskDel() removes the OS_TCB from the priority table by simply replacing the link to the OS_TCB of the task being deleted with a NULL pointer [L4.11(15)], OSTaskDel() then removes the OS_TCB of the task being deleted from the doubly linked list of OS_TCBs that starts at OSTCBList [L4.11(16)]. Note that there is no need to check for the case where ptcb->OSTCBNext == 0 because OSTaskDel() cannot delete the idle task, which always happens to be at the end of the chain. The OS_TCB is returned to the free list of OS_TCBs to allow another task to be created [L4.11(17)]. Last, but not least, the scheduler [L4.11(18)] is called to see if a higher priority task has been made ready to run by an ISR that would have occurred when OSTaskDel() re-enabled interrupts at step [L4.11(11)].

4.05 Requesting to Delete a Task, *OSTaskDelReq()*

Sometimes, a task owns resources such as memory buffers or a semaphore. If another task attempts to delete this task, the resources are not freed and thus are lost. In this type of situation, you somehow need to tell the task that owns these resources to delete itself when it's done with the resources. You can accomplish this with the OSTaskDelReq() function.

Both the requestor and the task to be deleted need to call OSTaskDelReq(). The requestor code is shown in Listing 4.12. The task that makes the request needs to determine what conditions would cause a request for the task to be deleted [L4.12(1)]. In other words, your application determines what conditions lead to this decision. If the task needs to be deleted, call OSTaskDelReq() by passing the priority of the task to be deleted [L4.12(2)]. If the task to delete does not exist, OSTaskDelReq() returns OS_TASK_NOT_EXIST. You would get this if the task to delete has already been deleted or has not been created yet. If the return value is OS_NO_ERR, the request has been accepted but the task has not been deleted yet. You may want to wait until the task to be deleted does in fact delete itself. You can do this by delaying the requestor for a certain amount of time, as I did in [L4.12(3)]. I decided to delay for one tick, but you can certainly wait longer if needed. When the requested task eventually deletes itself, the return value in [L4.12(2)] is OS_TASK_NOT_EXIST and the loop exits [L4.12(4)].

Listing 4.12   Requester code requesting a task to delete itself.

```
void RequestorTask (void *pdata)
{
    INT8U err;


    pdata = pdata;
    for (;;) {
        /* Application code */
        if ('TaskToBeDeleted()' needs to be deleted) {                    (1)
            while (OSTaskDelReq(TASK_TO_DEL_PRIO) != OS_TASK_NOT_EXIST) {  (2)
                OSTimeDly(1);                                              (3)
            }
        }
        /* Application code */                                            (4)
    }
}
```

Listing 4.13   Task requesting to delete itself.

```
void TaskToBeDeleted (void *pdata)
{
    INT8U err;


    pdata = pdata;
    for (;;) {
        /* Application code */
        if (OSTaskDelReq(OS_PRIO_SELF) == OS_TASK_DEL_REQ) {   (1)
            Release any owned resources;                       (2)
            De-allocate any dynamic memory;
            OSTaskDel(OS_PRIO_SELF);                           (3)
        } else {
            /* Application code */
        }
    }
}
```

The pseudocode for the task that needs to delete itself is shown in Listing 4.13. This task basically polls a flag that resides inside the task's OS_TCB. The value of this flag is obtained by calling OSTaskDelReq(OS_PRIO_SELF). When OSTaskDelReq() returns OS_TASK_DEL_REQ [L4.13(1)] to its caller, it indicates that another task has requested that this task needs to be deleted. In this case, the task to be deleted releases any resources owned [L4.13(2)] and calls OSTaskDel(OS_PRIO_SELF) to delete itself [L4.13(3)]. As previously mentioned, the code for the task is not actually deleted. Instead, µC/OS-II simply does not schedule the task for execution. In other words, the task code will no longer run. You can, however, recreate the task by calling either OSTaskCreate() or OSTaskCreateExt().

The code for OSTaskDelReq() is shown in Listing 4.14. As usual, OSTaskDelReq() needs to check for boundary conditions. First, OSTaskDelReq() notifies the caller in case he requests to delete the idle task [L4.14(1)]. Next, it must ensure that the caller is not trying to request to delete an invalid priority [L4.14(2)]. If the caller is the task to be deleted, the flag stored in the OS_TCB is returned [L4.14(3)]. If you specified a task with a priority other than OS_PRIO_SELF and the task exists [L4.14(4)], OSTaskDelReq() sets the internal flag for that task [L4.14(5)]. If the task does not exist, OSTaskDelReq() returns OS_TASK_NOT_EXIST to indicate that the task must have deleted itself [L4.14(6)].

4

Listing 4.14 OSTaskDelReq().

```
INT8U OSTaskDelReq (INT8U prio)
{
    BOOLEAN  stat;
    INT8U    err;
    OS_TCB   *ptcb;


    if (prio == OS_IDLE_PRIO) {                                       (1)
        return (OS_TASK_DEL_IDLE);
    }
    if (prio >= OS_LOWEST_PRIO && prio != OS_PRIO_SELF) {             (2)
        return (OS_PRIO_INVALID);
    }
    if (prio == OS_PRIO_SELF) {                                       (3)
        OS_ENTER_CRITICAL();
        stat = OSTCBCur->OSTCBDelReq;
        OS_EXIT_CRITICAL();
        return (stat);
    } else {
        OS_ENTER_CRITICAL();
        if ((ptcb = OSTCBPrioTbl[prio]) != (OS_TCB *)0) {             (4)
            ptcb->OSTCBDelReq = OS_TASK_DEL_REQ;                      (5)
            err              = OS_NO_ERR;
        } else {
            err              = OS_TASK_NOT_EXIST;                     (6)
```

Listing 4.14 `OSTaskDelReq()`. *(Continued)*

```
        }
        OS_EXIT_CRITICAL();
        return (err);
    }
}
```

4.06 *Changing a Task's Priority,* `OSTaskChangePrio()`

When you create a task, you assign the task a priority. At run time, you can change the priority of any task by calling OSTaskChangePrio(). In other words, µC/OS-II allows you to change priorities dynamically.

The code for OSTaskChangePrio() is shown in Listing 4.15. You cannot change the priority of the idle task [L4.15(1)]. You can change either the priority of the calling task or another task. To change the priority of the calling task, either specify the old priority of that task or specify OS_PRIO_SELF, and OSTaskChangePrio() will determine what the priority of the calling task is for you. You must also specify the new (i.e., desired) priority. Because µC/OS-II cannot have multiple tasks running at the same priority, OSTaskChangePrio() needs to check that the desired priority is available [L4.15(2)]. If the desired priority is available, µC/OS-II reserves the priority by loading something into OSTCBPrioTbl[newprio], thus reserving that entry [L4.15(3)]. This allows OSTaskChangePrio() to re-enable interrupts and know that no other task either can create a task at the desired priority or have another task call OSTaskChangePrio() by specifying the same new priority. This is done so that OSTaskChangePrio() can precompute some values that are stored in the task's OS_TCB [L4.15(4)]. These values are used to put or remove the task in or from the ready list (see section 3.04, Ready List).

OSTaskChangePrio() then checks to see if the current task is attempting to change its priority [L4.15(5)]. Next, we see if the task for which OSTaskChangePrio() is trying to change the priority exists [L4.15(6)]. Obviously, if it's the current task, this test will succeed. However, if OSTaskChangePrio() is trying to change the priority of a task that doesn't exist, it must relinquish the "reserved" priority back to the priority table, OSTCBPrioTbl[] [L4.15(17)], and return an error code to the caller.

OSTaskChangePrio() now removes the pointer to the OS_TCB of the task from the priority table by inserting a NULL pointer [L4.15(7)]. This makes the old priority available for reuse. Then, we check to see if the task for which OSTaskChangePrio() is changing the priority is ready to run [L4.15(8)]. If it is, it must be removed from the ready list at the current priority [L4.15(9)] and inserted back into the ready list at the new priority [L4.15(10)]. Note here that OSTaskChangePrio() uses the precomputed values [L4.15(4)] to insert the task in the ready list

If the task is ready, it could be waiting on a semaphore, mailbox, or queue. OSTaskChangePrio() knows that the task is waiting for one of these events if the OSTCBEventPtr is non-NULL [L4.15(11)]. If the task is waiting for an event, OSTaskChangePrio() must remove the task from the wait list (at the old priority) of the event control block (see section 6.00, Event Control Blocks) and insert the task back into the wait list, but this time at the new priority [L4.15(12)]. The task could be waiting for time to expire (see Chapter 5, Task Management) or the task could be suspended [see section 4.07, Suspending a Task, OSTaskSuspend()]. In these cases, items L4.15(8) through L4.15(12) would be skipped.

Next, OSTaskChangePrio() stores a pointer to the task's OS_TCB in OSTCBPrioTbl[] [L4.15(13)]. The new priority is saved in the OS_TCB [L4.15(14)], and the precomputed values are also saved in the OS_TCB [L4.15(15)]. After OSTaskChangePrio() exits the critical section, the scheduler is called in case the new priority is higher than the old priority or the priority of the calling task [L4.15(16)].

Listing 4.15 *OSTaskChangePrio()*.

```
INT8U OSTaskChangePrio (INT8U oldprio, INT8U newprio)
{
    OS_TCB   *ptcb;
    OS_EVENT *pevent;
    INT8U    x;
    INT8U    y;
    INT8U    bitx;
    INT8U    bity;


    if ((oldprio >= OS_LOWEST_PRIO && oldprio != OS_PRIO_SELF) ||      (1)
         newprio >= OS_LOWEST_PRIO) {
        return (OS_PRIO_INVALID);
    }
    OS_ENTER_CRITICAL();
    if (OSTCBPrioTbl[newprio] != (OS_TCB *)0) {                        (2)
        OS_EXIT_CRITICAL();
        return (OS_PRIO_EXIST);
    } else {
        OSTCBPrioTbl[newprio] = (OS_TCB *)1;                          (3)
        OS_EXIT_CRITICAL();
        y    = newprio >> 3;                                          (4)
        bity = OSMapTbl[y];
        x    = newprio & 0x07;
        bitx = OSMapTbl[x];
        OS_ENTER_CRITICAL();
        if (oldprio == OS_PRIO_SELF) {                                (5)
            oldprio = OSTCBCur->OSTCBPrio;
        }
        if ((ptcb = OSTCBPrioTbl[oldprio]) != (OS_TCB *)0) {          (6)
            OSTCBPrioTbl[oldprio] = (OS_TCB *)0;                      (7)
            if (OSRdyTbl[ptcb->OSTCBY] & ptcb->OSTCBBitX) {          (8)
                if ((OSRdyTbl[ptcb->OSTCBY] &= ~ptcb->OSTCBBitX) == 0) {  (9)
                    OSRdyGrp &= ~ptcb->OSTCBBitY;
                }
                OSRdyGrp    |= bity;                                  (10)
```

4

Listing 4.15 *OSTaskChangePrio().* *(Continued)*

```
                OSRdyTbl[y]  |= bitx;
        } else {
            if ((pevent = ptcb->OSTCBEventPtr) != (OS_EVENT *)0) {          (11)
                if ((pevent->OSEventTbl[ptcb->OSTCBY] &=
                        ~ptcb->OSTCBBitX) == 0) {
                    pevent->OSEventGrp &= ~ptcb->OSTCBBitY;
                }
                pevent->OSEventGrp   |= bity;                               (12)
                pevent->OSEventTbl[y] |= bitx;
            }
        }
        OSTCBPrioTbl[newprio] = ptcb;                                       (13)
        ptcb->OSTCBPrio       = newprio;                                    (14)
        ptcb->OSTCBY          = y;                                          (15)
        ptcb->OSTCBX          = x;
        ptcb->OSTCBBitY       = bity;
        ptcb->OSTCBBitX       = bitx;
        OS_EXIT_CRITICAL();
        OSSched();                                                         (16)
        return (OS_NO_ERR);
    } else {
        OSTCBPrioTbl[newprio] = (OS_TCB *)0;                               (17)
        OS_EXIT_CRITICAL();
        return (OS_PRIO_ERR);
    }
  }
}
}
```

4.07 Suspending a Task, *OSTaskSuspend()*

Sometimes it is useful to explicitly suspend the execution of a task. This is accomplished with the OSTaskSuspend() function call. A suspended task can only be resumed by calling the OSTaskResume() function call. Task suspension is additive. This means that if the task being suspended is also waiting for time to expire, the suspension needs to be removed and the time needs to expire in order for the task to be ready to run. A task can suspend either itself or another task.

The code for OSTaskSuspend() is shown in Listing 4.16. As usual, OSTaskSuspend() checks for boundary conditions. First, OSTaskSuspend() ensures that your application is not attempting to suspend the idle task [L4.16(1)]. Next, you must specify a valid priority [L4.16(2)]. Remember that the highest valid priority number (i.e., lowest priority) is OS_LOWEST_PRIO. Note that you can suspend the statistic task. You may have noticed that the first test [L4.16(1)] is replicated in [L4.16(2)]. I did this to be backward compatible with μC/OS. The first test could be removed to save a little bit of processing time, but this is really insignificant so I decided to leave it.

Next, OSTaskSuspend() checks to see if you specified to suspend the calling task [L4.16(3)] by specifying OS_PRIO_SELF. You could also decided to suspend the calling task by specifying its priority [L4.16(4)]. In both of these cases, the scheduler needs to be called. This is why I created the local variable self, which will be examined at the appropriate time. If you are not suspending the calling task, then OSTaskSuspend() does not need to run the scheduler because the calling task is suspending a lower priority task.

OSTaskSuspend() then checks to see that the task to suspend exists [L4.16(5)]. If so, it is removed from the ready list [L4.16(6)]. Note that the task to suspend may not be in the ready list because it could be waiting for an event or for time to expire. In this case, the corresponding bit for the task to suspend in OSRdyTbl[] would already be cleared (i.e., 0). Clearing it again is faster than checking to see if it's clear and then clearing it if it's not. Now OSTaskSuspend() sets the OS_STAT_SUSPEND flag in the task's OS_TCB to indicate that the task is now suspended [L4.16(7)]. Finally, OSTaskSuspend() calls the scheduler only if the task being suspended is the calling task [L4.16(8)].

Listing 4.16 *OSTaskSuspend()*.

```
INT8U OSTaskSuspend (INT8U prio)
{
    BOOLEAN   self;
    OS_TCB    *ptcb;


    if (prio == OS_IDLE_PRIO) {                                          (1)
        return (OS_TASK_SUSPEND_IDLE);
    }
    if (prio >= OS_LOWEST_PRIO && prio != OS_PRIO_SELF) {                (2)
        return (OS_PRIO_INVALID);
    }
    OS_ENTER_CRITICAL();
    if (prio == OS_PRIO_SELF) {                                         (3)
        prio = OSTCBCur->OSTCBPrio;
```

Listing 4.16 *OSTaskSuspend().* (Continued)

```
            self = TRUE;
        } else if (prio == OSTCBCur->OSTCBPrio) {                     (4)
            self = TRUE;
        } else {
            self = FALSE;
        }
        if ((ptcb = OSTCBPrioTbl[prio]) == (OS_TCB *)0) {             (5)
            OS_EXIT_CRITICAL();
            return (OS_TASK_SUSPEND_PRIO);
        } else {
            if ((OSRdyTbl[ptcb->OSTCBY] &= ~ptcb->OSTCBBitX) == 0) {  (6)
                OSRdyGrp &= ~ptcb->OSTCBBitY;
            }
            ptcb->OSTCBStat |= OS_STAT_SUSPEND;                       (7)
            OS_EXIT_CRITICAL();
            if (self == TRUE) {                                      (8)
                OSSched();
            }
            return (OS_NO_ERR);
        }
    }
}
```

4.08 *Resuming a Task,* **OSTaskResume()**

As mentioned in the previous section, a suspended task can only be resumed by calling OSTaskResume(). The code for OSTaskResume() is shown in Listing 4.17. Because OSTaskSuspend() cannot suspend the idle task, it must verify that your application is not attempting to resume this task [L4.17(1)].   Note that this test also ensures that you are not trying to resume OS_PRIO_SELF (OS_PRIO_SELF is #defined to 0xFF, which is always greater than OS_LOWEST_PRIO), which wouldn't make sense.

    The task to resume must exist because you will be manipulating its OS_TCB [L4.17(2)], and it must also have been suspended [L4.17(3)]. OSTaskResume() removes the suspension by clearing the OS_STAT_SUSPEND bit in the OSTCBStat field [L4.17(4)]. For the task to be ready to run, the OSTCBDly field must be 0 [L4.17(5)] because there are no flags in OSTCBStat to indicate that a task is waiting for time to expire. The task is made ready to run only when both conditions are satisfied [L4.17(6)]. Finally, the scheduler is called to see if the resumed task has a higher priority than the calling task [L4.17(7)].

Listing 4.17   `OSTaskResume()`.

```
INT8U OSTaskResume (INT8U prio)
{
    OS_TCB    *ptcb;


    if (prio >= OS_LOWEST_PRIO) {                                              (1)
        return (OS_PRIO_INVALID);
    }
    OS_ENTER_CRITICAL();
    if ((ptcb = OSTCBPrioTbl[prio]) == (OS_TCB *)0) {                          (2)
        OS_EXIT_CRITICAL();
        return (OS_TASK_RESUME_PRIO);
    } else {
        if (ptcb->OSTCBStat & OS_STAT_SUSPEND) {                              (3)
            if (((ptcb->OSTCBStat &= ~OS_STAT_SUSPEND) == OS_STAT_RDY) &&     (4)
                (ptcb->OSTCBDly  == 0)) {                                     (5)
                OSRdyGrp                 |= ptcb->OSTCBBitY;                   (6)
                OSRdyTbl[ptcb->OSTCBY] |= ptcb->OSTCBBitX;
                OS_EXIT_CRITICAL();
                OSSched();                                                    (7)
            } else {
                OS_EXIT_CRITICAL();
            }
            return (OS_NO_ERR);
        } else {
            OS_EXIT_CRITICAL();
            return (OS_TASK_NOT_SUSPENDED);
        }
    }
}
```

4.09   Getting Information about a Task, OSTaskQuery()

Your application can obtain information about itself or other application tasks by calling OSTaskQuery(). In fact, OSTaskQuery() obtains a copy of the contents of the desired task's OS_TCB. The fields available to you in the OS_TCB depend on the configuration of your application (see OS_CFG.H). Indeed, because µC/OS-II is scalable, it only includes the features that your application requires.

To call OSTaskQuery(), your application must allocate storage for an OS_TCB, as shown in Listing 4.18. This OS_TCB is in a totally different data space from the OS_TCBs allocated by µC/OS-II. After calling OSTaskQuery(), this OS_TCB contains a snapshot of the OS_TCB for the desired task. You need to be careful with the links to other OS_TCBs (i.e., OSTCBNext and OSTCBPrev); you don't want to change what these links are pointing to! In general, only use this function to see what a task is doing — a great tool for debugging.

Listing 4.18   Obtaining information about a task.

```
OS_TCB MyTaskData;


void MyTask (void *pdata)
{
    pdata = pdata;
    for (;;) {
        /* User code                    */
        err = OSTaskQuery(10, &MyTaskData);
        /* Examine error code ..        */
        /* User code                    */
    }
}
```

The code for OSTaskQuery() is shown in Listing 4.19. Note that I allow you to examine ALL the tasks, including the idle task [L4.19(1)]. You need to be especially careful not to change what OSTCB-Next and OSTCBPrev are pointing to. As usual, OSTaskQuery() checks to see if you want information about the current task [L4.19(2)] and that the task has been created [L4.19(3)]. All fields are copied using the assignment shown instead of field by field [L4.19(4)]. This is much faster because the compiler will most likely generate memory copy instructions.

Listing 4.19   OSTaskQuery().

```
INT8U OSTaskQuery (INT8U prio, OS_TCB *pdata)
{
    OS_TCB *ptcb;
                                                         0+ff

    if (prio > OS_LOWEST_PRIO && prio != OS_PRIO_SELF) {                    (1)
        return (OS_PRIO_INVALID);
    }
```

Listing 4.19 `OSTaskQuery()`. *(Continued)*

```
    OS_ENTER_CRITICAL();
    if (prio == OS_PRIO_SELF) {                              (2)
        prio = OSTCBCur->OSTCBPrio;
    }
    if ((ptcb = OSTCBPrioTbl[prio]) == (OS_TCB *)0) {        (3)
        OS_EXIT_CRITICAL();
        return (OS_PRIO_ERR);
    }
    *pdata = *ptcb;                                          (4)
    OS_EXIT_CRITICAL();
    return (OS_NO_ERR);
}
```

4

5

Time Management

Section 3.10, Clock Tick, established that µC/OS-II requires (as do other kernels) that you provide a periodic interrupt to keep track of time delays and timeouts. This periodic time source is called a *clock tick* and should occur between 10 and 100 times per second, or Hertz. The actual frequency of the clock tick depends on the desired tick resolution of your application. However, the higher the frequency of the ticker, the higher the overhead.

Section 3.10 discussed the tick ISR (Interrupt Service Routine) as well as the function that it needs to call to notify µC/OS-II about the tick interrupt — OSTimeTick(). This chapter describes five services that deal with time issues:

- OSTimeDly(),
- OSTimeDlyHMSM(),
- OSTimeDlyResume(),
- OSTimeGet(), and
- OSTimeSet().

The functions described in this chapter are found in the file OS_TIME.C.

5.00 Delaying a Task, OSTimeDly()

µC/OS-II provides a service that allows the calling task to delay itself for a user-specified number of clock ticks. This function is called OSTimeDly(). Calling this function causes a context switch and forces µC/OS-II to execute the next highest priority task that is ready to run. The task calling OSTimeDly() is made ready to run as soon as the time specified expires or if another task cancels the delay by calling OSTimeDlyResume(). Note that this task will run only when it's the highest priority task.

Listing 5.1 shows the code for OSTimeDly(). Your application calls this function by supplying the number of ticks to delay — a value between 1 and 65535. If you specify a value of 0 [L5.1(1)], you are indicating that you don't want to delay the task, and the function immediately returns to the caller. A nonzero value causes OSTimeDly() to remove the current task from the ready list [L5.1(2)]. Next, the number of ticks are stored in the OS_TCB of the current task [L5.1(3)], where it is decremented on every clock tick by `OSTimeTick()`. Finally, since the task is no longer ready, the scheduler is called [L5.1(4)] so that the next highest priority task that is ready to run gets executed.

Listing 5.1   *OSTimeDly().*

```
void OSTimeDly (INT16U ticks)
{
    if (ticks > 0) {                                                    (1)
        OS_ENTER_CRITICAL();
        if ((OSRdyTbl[OSTCBCur->OSTCBY] &= ~OSTCBCur->OSTCBBitX) == 0) {  (2)
            OSRdyGrp &= ~OSTCBCur->OSTCBBitY;
        }
        OSTCBCur->OSTCBDly = ticks;                                     (3)
        OS_EXIT_CRITICAL();
        OSSched();                                                      (4)
    }
}
```

It is important to realize that the resolution of a delay is between zero and one tick. In other words, if you try to delay for only one tick, you could end up with an intermediate delay between 0 and 1 tick. This is assuming, however, that your processor is not heavily loaded. Figure 5.1 illustrates what happens. A tick interrupt occurs every 10ms [F5.1(1)]. Assuming that you are not servicing any other interrupts and that you have interrupts enabled, the tick ISR will be invoked [F5.1(2)]. You may have a few high-priority tasks (HPTs) waiting for time to expire, so they will execute next [F5.1(3)]. The low-priority task (LPT) shown in Figure 5.1 then gets a chance to execute and, upon completion, calls `OSTimeDly(1)` at the moment shown [F5.1(4)]. µC/OS-II puts the task to sleep until the next tick. When the next tick arrives, the tick ISR executes [F5.1(5)], but this time there are no HPTs to execute, and µC/OS-II executes the task that delayed itself for one tick [F5.1(6)]. As you can see, the task actually delayed for less than one tick! On heavily loaded systems, the task may call `OSTimeDly(1)` a few tens of microseconds before the tick occurs and thus the delay results in almost no delay because the task is immediately rescheduled. If your application must delay for at least one tick, you must call `OSTimeDly(2)`, specifying a delay of two ticks!

5.01 *Delaying a Task,* `OSTimeDlyHMSM()`

`OSTimeDly()` is a very useful function, but your application needs to know time in terms of ticks. You can use the global #define constant `OS_TICKS_PER_SEC` (see `OS_CFG.H`) to convert time to ticks, but this is somewhat awkward. I added the function `OSTimeDlyHMSM()` so that you can specify time in hours (H), minutes (M), seconds (S), and milliseconds (m), which is more natural. Like `OSTimeDly()`, calling this function causes a context switch and forces µC/OS-II to execute the next highest priority task that is ready to run. The task calling `OSTimeDlyHMSM()` is made ready to run as soon as the time specified expires or if another task cancels the delay by calling `OSTimeDlyResume()` [see section 5.02, Resuming a Delayed Task, `OSTimeDlyResume()`]. Again, this task runs only when it again becomes the highest priority task.

Figure 5.1   *Delay resolution.*

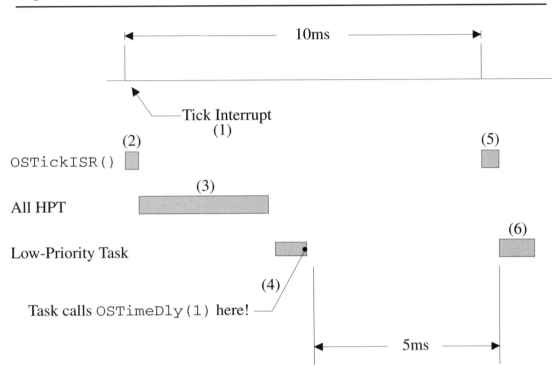

Listing 5.2 shows the code for OSTimeDlyHMSM(). As you can see, your application calls this function by supplying the delay in hours, minutes, seconds, and milliseconds. In practice, you should avoid delaying a task for long periods of time because it's always a good idea to get some feedback activity from a task (increment a counter, blink an LED, etc.). However, if you do need long delays, μC/OS-II can delay a task for 256 hours (close to 11 days).

OSTimeDlyHMSM() starts by checking that you have specified valid values for its arguments [L5.2(1)]. As with OSTimeDly(), OSTimeDlyHMSM() exits if you specify no delay [L5.2(9)]. Because μC/OS-II only knows about ticks, the total number of ticks is computed from the specified time [L5.2(3)]. The code shown in Listing 5.2 is obviously not very efficient. I just showed the equation this way so you can see how the total ticks are computed. The actual code efficiently factors in OS_TICKS_PER_SEC. [L5.2(3)] determines the number of ticks given the specified milliseconds with rounding to the nearest tick. The value 500/OS_TICKS_PER_SECOND basically corresponds to 0.5 ticks converted to milliseconds. For example, if the tick rate (OS_TICKS_PER_SEC) is set to 100Hz (10ms), a delay of 4ms would result in no delay! A delay of 5ms would result in a delay of 10ms, and so on.

μC/OS-II only supports delays of up to 65,535 ticks. To support longer delays, obtained by L5.2(2), OSTimeDlyHMSM() determines how many times you need to delay for more than 65,535 ticks [L5.2(4)], as well as the remaining number of ticks [L5.2(5)]. For example, if OS_TICKS_PER_SEC is 100 and you want a delay of 15 minutes, then OSTimeDlyHMSM() would have to delay for 15 x 60 x 100 = 90,000 ticks. This delay is broken down into two delays of 32,768 ticks (because you can't delay 65,536 ticks, only 65,535) and one delay of 24,464 ticks. In this case, OSTimeDlyHMSM() takes care of the remainder [L5.2(6)] first, then the number of times 65,535 is exceeded [L5.2(7) and (8)] (i.e., two 32,768-tick delays).

Listing 5.2 *OSTimeDlyHMSM()*.

```
INT8U OSTimeDlyHMSM (INT8U hours, INT8U minutes, INT8U seconds, INT16U milli)
{
    INT32U ticks;
    INT16U loops;


    if (hours > 0 || minutes > 0 || seconds > 0 || milli > 0) {        (1)
        if (minutes > 59) {
            return (OS_TIME_INVALID_MINUTES);
        }
        if (seconds > 59) {
            return (OS_TIME_INVALID_SECONDS);
        }
        if (milli > 999) {
            return (OS_TIME_INVALID_MILLI);
        }
        ticks = (INT32U)hours    * 3600L * OS_TICKS_PER_SEC           (2)
              + (INT32U)minutes  *   60L * OS_TICKS_PER_SEC
              + (INT32U)seconds  *          OS_TICKS_PER_SEC
              + OS_TICKS_PER_SEC * ((INT32U)milli
              + 500L/OS_TICKS_PER_SEC) / 1000L;                       (3)
        loops = ticks / 65536L;                                      (4)
        ticks = ticks % 65536L;                                      (5)
        OSTimeDly(ticks);                                            (6)
        while (loops > 0) {                                          (7)
            OSTimeDly(32768);                                        (8)
            OSTimeDly(32768);
            loops--;
        }
        return (OS_NO_ERR);
    } else {
        return (OS_TIME_ZERO_DLY);                                   (9)
    }
}
```

Because of the way OSTimeDlyHMSM() is implemented, you cannot resume (see next section) a task that calls OSTimeDlyHMSM() with a combined time that exceeds 65,535 clock ticks. In other words, if the clock tick runs at 100Hz, you cannot resume a delayed task that calls OSTimeDly-HMSM(0, 10, 55, 350) or higher.

5.02 *Resuming a Delayed Task,* `OSTimeDlyResume()`

µC/OS-II allows you to resume a task that delays itself. Instead of waiting for time to expire, a delayed task can be made ready to run by another task that cancels the delay. This is done by calling `OSTime-DlyResume()` and specifying the priority of the task to resume. In fact, `OSTimeDlyResume()` also can resume a task that is waiting for an event (see Chapter 6, Intertask Communication & Synchronization), although this is not recommended. In this case, the task pending on the event thinks it timed out waiting for the event.

The code for `OSTimeDlyResume()` is shown in Listing 5.3 and begins by making sure the task has a valid priority [L5.3(1)]. Next, `OSTimeDlyResume()` verifies that the task to resume does in fact exist [L5.3(2)]. If the task exists, `OSTimeDlyResume()` checks to see if the task is waiting for time to expire [L5.3(3)]. Whenever the `OS_TCB` field `OSTCBDly` contains a nonzero value, the task is waiting for time to expire because the task called either `OSTimeDly()`, `OSTimeDlyHMSM()`, or any of the PEND functions described in Chapter 6. The delay is then canceled by forcing `OSTCBDly` to 0 [L5.3(4)]. A delayed task may also have been suspended; thus, the task is only made ready to run if the task was not suspended [L5.3(5)]. The task is placed in the ready list when the above conditions are satisfied [L5.3(6)]. At this point, `OSTimeDlyResume()` calls the scheduler to see if the resumed task has a higher priority than the current task [L5.3(7)]. This would result in a context switch.

Listing 5.3   Resuming a delayed task.

```
INT8U OSTimeDlyResume (INT8U prio)
{
    OS_TCB *ptcb;

    if (prio >= OS_LOWEST_PRIO) {                                        (1)
        return (OS_PRIO_INVALID);
    }
    OS_ENTER_CRITICAL();
    ptcb = (OS_TCB *)OSTCBPrioTbl[prio];
    if (ptcb != (OS_TCB *)0) {                                          (2)
        if (ptcb->OSTCBDly != 0) {                                      (3)
            ptcb->OSTCBDly = 0;                                         (4)
            if (!(ptcb->OSTCBStat & OS_STAT_SUSPEND)) {                 (5)
                OSRdyGrp                 |= ptcb->OSTCBBitY;            (6)
                OSRdyTbl[ptcb->OSTCBY] |= ptcb->OSTCBBitX;
                OS_EXIT_CRITICAL();
                OSSched();                                              (7)
            } else {
                OS_EXIT_CRITICAL();
            }
            return (OS_NO_ERR);
        } else {
```

5

Listing 5.3   Resuming a delayed task. (Continued)

```
            OS_EXIT_CRITICAL();
            return (OS_TIME_NOT_DLY);
        }
    } else {
        OS_EXIT_CRITICAL();
        return (OS_TASK_NOT_EXIST);
    }
}
```

Note that you could also have a task delay itself by waiting on a semaphore, mailbox, or queue with a timeout (see Chapter 6). You would resume such a task by simply posting to the semaphore, mailbox, or queue, respectively. The only problem with this scenario is that it requires you to allocate an event control block (see section 6.00), so your application would consume a little bit more RAM.

5.03   System Time, *OSTimeGet()* and *OSTimeSet()*

Whenever a clock tick occurs, µC/OS-II increments a 32-bit counter. This counter starts at zero when you initiate multitasking by calling OSStart() and rolls over after 4,294,967,295 ticks. At a tick rate of 100Hz, this 32-bit counter rolls over every 497 days. You can obtain the current value of this counter by calling OSTimeGet(). You can also change the value of the counter by calling OSTimeSet(). The code for both functions is shown in Listing 5.4. Note that interrupts are disabled when accessing OSTime. This is because incrementing and copying a 32-bit value on most 8-bit processors requires multiple instructions that must be treated indivisibly.

Listing 5.4   Obtaining and setting the system time.

```
INT32U OSTimeGet (void)
{
    INT32U ticks;

    OS_ENTER_CRITICAL();
    ticks = OSTime;
    OS_EXIT_CRITICAL();
    return (ticks);
}


void OSTimeSet (INT32U ticks)
{
    OS_ENTER_CRITICAL();
    OSTime = ticks;
    OS_EXIT_CRITICAL();
}
```

Chapter 6

Intertask Communication & Synchronization

μC/OS-II provides many mechanisms to protect shared data and provide intertask communication. You already have seen two such mechanisms:

- Disabling and enabling interrupts through the macros OS_ENTER_CRITICAL() and OS_EXIT_ CRITICAL(), respectively. You use these macros when two tasks or a task and an ISR need to share data. See section 3.00, Critical Sections, section 8.03.02, OS_ENTER_CRITICAL(), and OS_EXIT_ CRITICAL(), and section 9.03.02 Critical Sections, OS_CPU.H..

- Locking and unlocking μC/OS-II's scheduler with OSSchedLock() and OSSchedUnlock(), respectively. Again, you can use these services to access shared data. See section 3.06, Locking and Unlocking the Scheduler.

In this chapter I discuss the other three types of services provided by μC/OS-II: semaphores, message mailboxes, and message queues.

Figure 6.1 shows how tasks and Interrupt Service Routines (ISRs) can interact with each other. A task or an ISR *signals* a task [F6.1A(1)] through a kernel object called an *Event Control Block* (ECB). The signal is considered to be an event, which explains my choice of this name. A task can *wait* for another task or an ISR to signal the object [F6.1A(2)]. You should note that only tasks are allowed to wait for events to occur – an ISR is not allowed to wait on an ECB. An optional *timeout* [F6.1A(3)] can be specified by the waiting task in case the object is not signaled within a specified time period. Multiple tasks can wait for a task or an ISR to signal an ECB [F6.1B]. When the ECB is signaled, only the highest priority task waiting on the ECB will be "signaled" and made ready to run. An ECB can be either a semaphore, a message mailbox, or a message queue, as discussed later. When an ECB is used as a semaphore, tasks can both wait on and signal the ECB [F6.1C(4)].

Figure 6.1   Use of event control blocks.

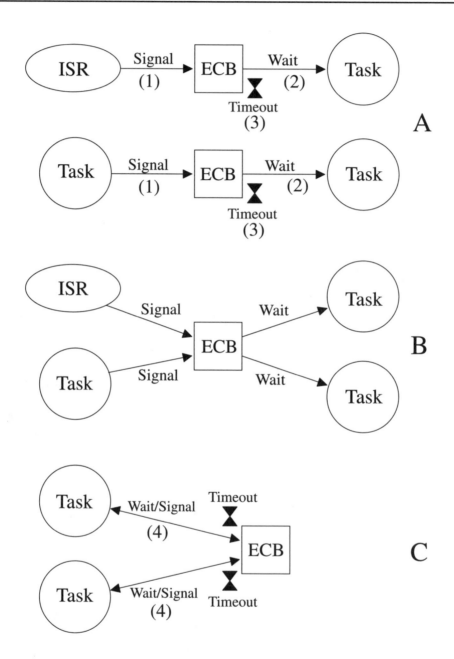

6.00 Event Control Blocks

also see pg 101

μC/OS-II maintains the state of an ECB in a data structure called OS_EVENT (see uCOS_II.H). The state of an event consists of the event itself (a counter for a semaphore, a pointer for a message mailbox, or an array of pointers for a queue) and a list of tasks waiting for the event to occur. Each semaphore, mailbox, and queue is assigned an ECB. The data structure for an ECB is shown in Listing 6.1.

Listing 6.1   Event control block data structure.

```
typedef struct {
    void    *OSEventPtr;                     /* Ptr to message or queue structure */
    INT8U   OSEventTbl[OS_EVENT_TBL_SIZE];   /* Wait list for event to occur      */
    INT16U  OSEventCnt;                      /* Count (when event is a semaphore)  */
    INT8U   OSEventType;                     /* Event type                         */
    INT8U   OSEventGrp;                      /* Group for wait list                */
} OS_EVENT;
```

.OSEventPtr is only used when the ECB is assigned to a mailbox or a queue. It points to the message when used for a mailbox or to a data structure when used for a queue (see section 6.06, Message Mailboxes, and 6.07, Message Queues).

.OSEventTbl[] and **.OSEventGrp** are similar to OSRdyTbl[] and OSRdyGrp, respectively, except that they contain a list of tasks waiting on the event instead of a list of tasks ready to run (see section 3.04, Ready List).

.OSEventCnt is used to hold the semaphore count when the ECB is used for a semaphore (see section 6.05, Semaphores).

.OSEventType contains the type associated with the ECB and can have the following values: OS_EVENT_SEM, OS_EVENT_TYPE_MBOX, or OS_EVENT_TYPE_Q. This field is used to make sure you are accessing the proper object when you perform operations on these objects through μC/OS-II's service calls.

Each task that needs to wait for the event to occur is placed in the wait list consisting of the two variables, .OSEventGrp and .OSEventTbl[]. Note that I used a dot (.) in front of the variable name to indicate that the variable is part of a data structure. Task priorities are grouped (eight tasks per group) in .OSEventGrp. Each bit in .OSEventGrp is used to indicate when any task in a group is waiting for the event to occur. When a task is waiting, its corresponding bit is set in the wait table, .OSEventTbl[]. The size (in bytes) of .OSEventTbl[] depends on OS_LOWEST_PRIO (see uCOS_II.H). This allows μC/OS-II to reduce the amount of RAM (i.e., data space) when your application requires just a few task priorities.

6

The task that is resumed when the event occurs is the highest priority task waiting for the event and corresponds to the lowest priority number that has a bit set in .OSEventTbl[]. The relationship between .OSEventGrp and .OSEventTbl[] is shown in Figure 6.2 and is given by the following rules.

Bit 0 in .OSEventGrp is 1 when any bit in .OSEventTbl[0] is 1.
Bit 1 in .OSEventGrp is 1 when any bit in .OSEventTbl[1] is 1.
Bit 2 in .OSEventGrp is 1 when any bit in .OSEventTbl[2] is 1.
Bit 3 in .OSEventGrp is 1 when any bit in .OSEventTbl[3] is 1.
Bit 4 in .OSEventGrp is 1 when any bit in .OSEventTbl[4] is 1.
Bit 5 in .OSEventGrp is 1 when any bit in .OSEventTbl[5] is 1.
Bit 6 in .OSEventGrp is 1 when any bit in .OSEventTbl[6] is 1.
Bit 7 in .OSEventGrp is 1 when any bit in .OSEventTbl[7] is 1.

Figure 6.2   Wait list for task waiting for an event to occur.

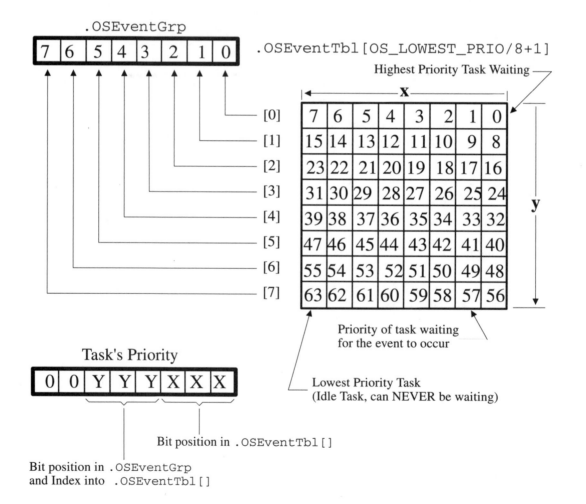

The following code places a task in the wait list:

Listing 6.2   *Making a task wait for an event.*

```
pevent->OSEventGrp            |= OSMapTbl[prio >> 3];
pevent->OSEventTbl[prio >> 3] |= OSMapTbl[prio & 0x07];
```

prio is the task's priority, and pevent is a pointer to the event control block.

You should realize from Listing 6.2 that inserting a task in the wait list always takes the same amount of time and does not depend on how many tasks are in your system. Also, from Figure 6.2, the lower 3 bits of the task's priority are used to determine the bit position in .OSEventTbl[], and the next three most significant bits are used to determine the index into .OSEventTbl[]. Note that OSMapTbl[] (see OS_CORE.C) is a table in ROM, used to equate an index from 0 to 7 to a bit mask as shown in the Table 6.1.

Table 6.1   *Content of OSMapTbl[].*

Index	Bit Mask (Binary)
0	00000001
1	00000010
2	00000100
3	00001000
4	00010000
5	00100000
6	01000000
7	10000000

A task is removed from the wait list by reversing the process (Listing 6.3).

Listing 6.3   *Removing a task from a wait list.*

```
if ((pevent->OSEventTbl[prio >> 3] &= ~OSMapTbl[prio & 0x07]) == 0) {
    pevent->OSEventGrp &= ~OSMapTbl[prio >> 3];
}
```

This code clears the bit corresponding to the task in .OSEventTbl[] and clears the bit in .OSEventGrp only if all tasks in a group are not waiting; that is, all bits in .OSEventTbl[prio >> 3] are 0. Another table lookup is performed, rather than scanning through the table starting with .OSEventTbl[0], to find the highest priority task waiting for the event. OSUnMapTbl[256] is a priority resolution table (see OS_CORE.C). Eight bits are used to represent when tasks are waiting in a group. The least significant bit has the highest priority. Using this byte to index, the table returns the bit position of the highest priority bit set — a number between 0 and 7. The code in Listing 6.4 determines the priority of the highest priority task waiting for the event.

Listing 6.4   Finding the highest priority task waiting for the event.

```
y    = OSUnMapTbl[pevent->OSEventGrp];
x    = OSUnMapTbl[pevent->OSEventTbl[y]];
prio = (y << 3) + x;
```

For example, if .OSEventGrp contains 01101000 (binary), OSUnMapTbl[.OSEventGrp] yields a value of 3, which corresponds to bit 3 in .OSEventGrp. Note that bit positions are assumed to start on the right with bit 0 being the rightmost bit. Similarly, if .OSEventTbl[3] contains 11100100 (binary), OSUnMapTbl[.OSEventTbl[3]] result s in a value of 2 (bit 2). The priority of the task waiting (prio) is now 26 (3*8 + 2)!

The number of ECBs to allocate depends on the number of semaphores, mailboxes, and queues needed for your application. The number of ECBs is established by the #define OS_MAX_EVENTS, which you define in OS_CFG.H. When OSInit() is called (see section 3.11, µC/OS-II Initialization), all ECBs are linked in a singly linked list — the list of free ECBs (Figure 6.3). When a semaphore, mailbox, or queue is created, an ECB is removed from this list and initialized. ECBs cannot be returned to the list of free ECBs because semaphores, mailboxes, and queues cannot be deleted.

Figure 6.3   List of free ECBs.

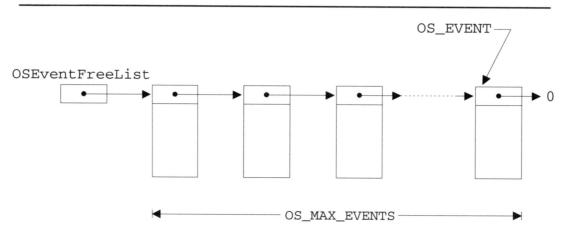

Four common operations can be performed on ECBs:

- initialize an ECB,
- make a task ready,
- make a task wait for an event, and
- make a task ready because a timeout occurred while waiting for an event.

To avoid duplicating code and thus to reduce code size, four functions have been created to performs these operations: OSEventWaitListInit(), OSEventTaskRdy(), OSEventWait(), and OSEventTO(), respectively.

6.01 *Initializing an ECB,* `OSEventWaitListInit()`

Listing 6.5 shows the code for OSEventWaitListInit(), which is a function called when a sema-phore, message mailbox, or message queue is created [see OSSemCreate(), OSMboxCreate(), or OSQCreate()]. All that is accomplished by OSEventWaitListInit() is to indicate that no task is waiting on the ECB. OSEventWaitListInit() is passed a pointer to an event control block, which is assigned when the semaphore, message mailbox, or message queue is created.

149
156
160

Listing 6.5 *Initializing the wait list.*

```
void OSEventWaitListInit (OS_EVENT *pevent)
{
    INT8U i;


    pevent->OSEventGrp = 0x00;
    for (i = 0; i < OS_EVENT_TBL_SIZE; i++) {
        pevent->OSEventTbl[i] = 0x00;
    }
}
```

6

6.02 *Making a Task Ready,* `OSEventTaskRdy()`

Listing 6.6 shows the code for OSEventTaskRdy(). This function is called by OSSemPost(), OSMboxPost(), OSQPost(), and OSQPostFront() when an ECB is signaled and the highest priority task waiting on the ECB needs to be made ready to run. In other words, OSEventTaskRdy() removes the highest priority task (HPT) from the wait list of the ECB and makes this task ready to run. Figure 6.4 illustrates the first four operations performed in OSEventTaskRdy().

but does not call OSSched. Pg 85
— ? misprint

OSEventTaskRdy() starts by determining the index into .OSEventTbl[] of the HPT [L6.6/F6.4(1)], a number between 0 and OS_LOWEST_PRIO/8 + 1. Then the bit mask of the HPT in .OSEventGrp is obtained [L6.6/F6.4(2)] (see Table 6.1, page 143, for possible values). OSEventTaskRdy() determines the bit position of the task in .OSEventTbl[] [L6.6/F6.4(3)], a value between 0 and OS_LOWEST_PRIO/8 + 1, and the bit mask of the HPT in .OSEventTbl[] [L6.6/F6.4(4)] (see Table 6.1 for possible values). The priority of the task being made ready to run is determined by combining the x and y indices [L6.6(5)]. At this point, you can extract the task from the wait list [L6.6(6)].

The task control block (TCB) of the task being readied contains information that needs to be changed. Knowing the task's priority, you can obtain a pointer to that TCB [L6.6(7)]. Because the HPT is not waiting anymore, you need to make sure that OSTimeTick() will not attempt to decrement the .OSTCBDly value of that task. OSEventTaskRdy() prevents this by forcing this field to 0 [L6.6(8)]. It then forces the pointer to the ECB to NULL because the HPT is no longer waiting on this ECB [L6.6(9)]. A message is sent to the HPT if OSEventTaskRdy() is called by either OSMboxPost() or OSQPost(). This message is passed as an argument and needs to be placed in the task's TCB [L6.6(10)]. When OSEventTaskRdy() is called, the msk argument contains the appropriate bit mask to clear the bit in .OSTCBStat, which corresponds to the type of event signaled (OS_STAT_SEM, OS_STAT_MBOX,

MASK

or OS_STAT_Q; see uCOS_II.H) [L6.6(11)]. Finally, if .OSTCBStat indicates that the task is ready to run [L6.6(12)], OSEventTaskRdy() inserts this task in µC/OS-II's ready list [L6.6(13)]. Note that the task may not be ready to run because it could have been explicitly suspended [see sections 4.07, Suspending a Task, OSTaskSuspend(), and 4.08, Resuming a Task, OSTaskResume()].

Note that OSEventTaskRdy() is called with interrupts disabled.

Listing 6.6   *Making a task ready to run.*

```c
void OSEventTaskRdy (OS_EVENT *pevent, void *msg, INT8U msk)
{
    OS_TCB *ptcb;
    INT8U   x;
    INT8U   y;
    INT8U   bitx;
    INT8U   bity;
    INT8U   prio;


    y     = OSUnMapTbl[pevent->OSEventGrp];                      (1)
    bity = OSMapTbl[y];                                          (2)
    x     = OSUnMapTbl[pevent->OSEventTbl[y]];                   (3)
    bitx = OSMapTbl[x];                                          (4)
    prio = (INT8U)((y << 3) + x);                                (5)
    if ((pevent->OSEventTbl[y] &= ~bitx) == 0) {                 (6)
        pevent->OSEventGrp &= ~bity;
    }
    ptcb                = OSTCBPrioTbl[prio];                    (7)
    ptcb->OSTCBDly      = 0;                                     (8)
    ptcb->OSTCBEventPtr = (OS_EVENT *)0;                         (9)
#if (OS_Q_EN && (OS_MAX_QS >= 2)) || OS_MBOX_EN
    ptcb->OSTCBMsg      = msg;                                   (10)
#else
    msg                 = msg;
#endif
    ptcb->OSTCBStat     &= ~msk;                                 (11)
    if (ptcb->OSTCBStat == OS_STAT_RDY) {                        (12)
        OSRdyGrp     |= bity;                                    (13)
        OSRdyTbl[y]  |= bitx;
    }
}
```

Figure 6.4 Making a task ready to run.

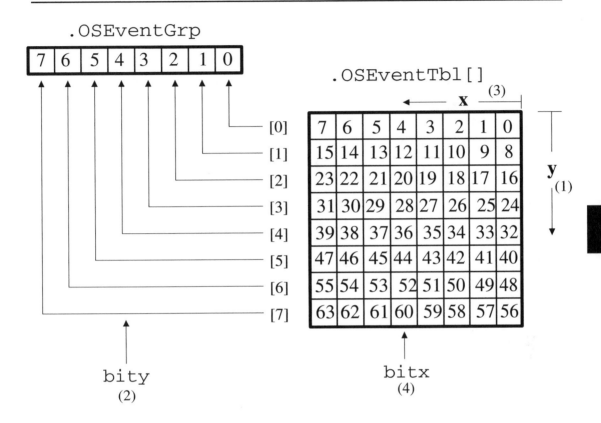

6.03 Making a Task Wait for an Event,
OSEventTaskWait()

Listing 6.7 shows the code for OSEventTaskWait(). This function is called by OSSemPend(), OSMboxPend(), and OSQPend() when a task must wait on an ECB. In other words, OSEventTaskWait() removes the current task from the ready list and places it in the wait list of the ECB.

Pg 83

A TASK THAT IS running is, by defn, the highest priority tASk.

Listing 6.7   Making a task wait on an ECB.

```
void OSEventTaskWait (OS_EVENT *pevent)
{
    OSTCBCur->OSTCBEventPtr = pevent;                                        (1)
    if ((OSRdyTbl[OSTCBCur->OSTCBY] &= ~OSTCBCur->OSTCBBitX) == 0) {        (2)
        OSRdyGrp &= ~OSTCBCur->OSTCBBitY;
    }
    pevent->OSEventTbl[OSTCBCur->OSTCBY]  |= OSTCBCur->OSTCBBitX;           (3)
    pevent->OSEventGrp                    |= OSTCBCur->OSTCBBitY;
}
```

The pointer to the ECB is placed in the task's TCB, linking the task to the event control block [L6.7(1)]. Next, the task is removed from the ready list [L6.7(2)] and placed in the wait list for the ECB [L6.7(3)].

6.04 Making a Task Ready because of a Timeout, *OSEventTO()*

Listing 6.8 shows the code for OSEventTO(). This function is called by OSSemPend(), OSMbox-Pend(), and OSQPend() when a task has been made ready to run by OSTimeTick(), which means that the ECB was not signaled within the specified timeout period. In this case, OSEventTO() must remove the task from the wait list of the ECB [L6.8(1)] and mark the task as being ready [L6.8(2)]. Finally, the link to the ECB is removed from the task's TCB [L6.8(3)]. You should note that OSEventTO() is also called with interrupts disabled.

Listing 6.8   Making a task ready because of a timeout.

```
void  OSEventTO (OS_EVENT *pevent)
{
    if ((pevent->OSEventTbl[OSTCBCur->OSTCBY] &= ~OSTCBCur->OSTCBBitX) == 0) {   (1)
        pevent->OSEventGrp &= ~OSTCBCur->OSTCBBitY;
    }
    OSTCBCur->OSTCBStat       = OS_STAT_RDY;  ←                                  (2)
    OSTCBCur->OSTCBEventPtr = (OS_EVENT *)0;                                     (3)
}
```

If task were suspended when this line is executed, it reset "suspended bit". ∴ NO LONGER SUSPENDED.

6.05 Semaphores

OSEventCnt

µC/OS-II semaphores consist of two elements: a 16-bit unsigned integer used to hold the semaphore count (0 to 65535) and a list of tasks waiting for the semaphore count to be greater than 0. To enable µC/OS-II semaphore services, you must set the configuration constant OS_SEM_EN to 1 (see file OS_CFG.H).

OS Event Grp
OS EventTbl[]

A semaphore needs to be created before it can be used. Create a semaphore by calling OSSemCreate() (see next section) and specifying the initial count of the semaphore. The initial value of a semaphore can be between 0 and 65535. If you use the semaphore to signal the occurrence of one or more events, initialize the semaphore to 0. If you use the semaphore to access a shared resource, initialize the semaphore to 1 (i.e., use it as a binary semaphore). Finally, if the semaphore allows your application to obtain any one of *n* identical resources, initialize the semaphore to *n* and use it as a counting semaphore.

μC/OS-II provides five services to access semaphores: OSSemCreate(), OSSemPend(), OSSemPost(), OSSemAccept(), and OSSemQuery(). Figure 6.5 shows a flow diagram to illustrate the relationship between tasks, ISRs, and a semaphore. Note that the symbology used to represent a semaphore is either a key or a flag. Use a key symbol if the semaphore is used to access shared resources. The N next to the key represents how many resources are available. N is 1 for a binary semaphore. Use a flag symbol when a semaphore is used to signal the occurrence of an event. N in this case represents the number of times the event can be signaled. As you can see from Figure 6.5 a task or an ISR can call OSSemPost(). However, only tasks are allowed to call OSSemPend() and OSSemQuery().

Figure 6.5   *Relationships between tasks, ISRs, and a semaphore.*

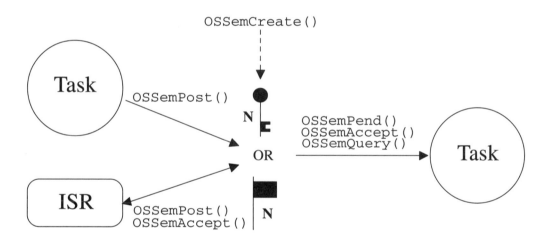

6.05.01   *Creating a Semaphore, OSSemCreate()*

The code to create a semaphore is shown in Listing 6.9. OSSemCreate() starts by obtaining an ECB from the free list of ECBs (see Figure 6.3) [L6.9(1)]. The linked list of free ECBs is adjusted to point to the next free ECB [L6.9(2)]. If there is an ECB available [L6.9(3)], the ECB type is set to OS_EVENT_TYPE_SEM [L6.9(4)]. Other OSSem???() function calls check this field to make sure that the ECB is of the proper type. This prevents you from calling OSSemPost() on an ECB that was created for use as a message mailbox (see 6.06, Message Mailboxes). Next, the desired initial count for the semaphore is stored in the ECB [L6.9(5)]. The wait list is then initialized by calling OSEventWaitListInit() [see 6.01, Initializing an ECB, OSEventWaitListInit()] [L6.9(6)]. Because the semaphore is being initialized, there are no tasks waiting for it. Finally, OSSemCreate() returns a pointer to the ECB [L6.9(7)]. This pointer must be used in subsequent calls to manipulate semaphores [OSSemPend(), OSSemPost(), OSSemAccept(), and OSSemQuery()]. The pointer is basically used as the semaphore's handle. If there are no more ECBs, OSSemCreate() returns a NULL pointer.

You should note that once a semaphore has been created, it cannot be deleted. In other words, there is no way in µC/OS-II to return an ECB back to the free list of ECBs. It would be dangerous to delete a semaphore object if tasks were waiting on the semaphore and/or relying on the presence of the semaphore. What would those tasks do?

Listing 6.9   Creating a semaphore.

```
OS_EVENT *OSSemCreate (INT16U cnt)         // 0 if to signal occurrence of
{                                          //      1 or more events
    OS_EVENT *pevent;                      // 1 if to control access to
                                           //      shared resource
                                           // n
    OS_ENTER_CRITICAL();
    pevent = OSEventFreeList;                                              (1)
    if (OSEventFreeList != (OS_EVENT *)0) {                                (2)
        OSEventFreeList = (OS_EVENT *)OSEventFreeList->OSEventPtr;
    }
    OS_EXIT_CRITICAL();
    if (pevent != (OS_EVENT *)0) {                                        (3)
        pevent->OSEventType = OS_EVENT_TYPE_SEM;                          (4)
        pevent->OSEventCnt  = cnt;                                        (5)
        OSEventWaitListInit(pevent);   // sets all entries                (6)
    }                                  //   in Event Table to ∅.
    return (pevent);                   // ie, no events are waiting.      (7)
}
```

6.05.02   Waiting on a Semaphore, OSSemPend()

The code to wait on a semaphore is shown in Listing 6.10. OSSemPend() starts by checking that the ECB being pointed to by pevent has been created by OSSemCreate() [L6.10(1)]. If the semaphore is available (its count is nonzero) [L6.10(2)], the count is decremented [L6.10(3)] and the function returns to its caller with an error code indicating success. Obviously, if you want the semaphore, this is the outcome you are looking for. This also happens to be the fastest path through OSSemPend().

If the semaphore is not available (the count is zero), OSSemPend() checks to see if the function was called by an ISR [L6.10(4)]. Under normal circumstances, you should not call OSSemPend() from an ISR because an ISR cannot be made to wait. I decided to add this check just in case. However, if the semaphore is in fact available, the call to OSSemPend() would be successful even if called by an ISR!

If the semaphore count is zero and OSSemPend() was not called by an ISR, the calling task needs to be put to sleep until another task (or an ISR) signals the semaphore (see the next section). OSSemPend() allows you to specify a timeout value as one of its arguments (i.e., timeout). This feature is useful to avoid waiting indefinitely for the semaphore. If the value passed is nonzero, OSSemPend() suspends the task until the semaphore is signaled or the specified timeout period expires. Note that a timeout value of 0 indicates that the task is willing to wait forever for the semaphore to be signaled. To put the calling task to sleep, OSSemPend() sets the status flag in the task's TCB (Task Control Block) to indicate that the task is suspended waiting for a semaphore [L6.10(5)]. The timeout is also stored in the TCB [L6.10(6)] ~NOT SO~ so that it can be decremented by OSTimeTick(). You should recall (see section 3.10, Clock Tick) that OSTimeTick() decrements each of the created task's .OSTCBDly field if it's nonzero. The actual work of putting the task to sleep is done by OSEventTaskWait() [see section 6.03, Making a Task Wait for an Event, OSEventTaskWait()] [L6.10(7)]. *— MUST BE*

Because the calling task is no longer ready to run, the scheduler is called to run the next highest priority task that is ready to run [L6.10(8)]. When the semaphore is signaled (or the timeout period expires) and the task that called OSSemPend() is again the highest priority task, OSSched() returns. OSSemPend() then checks to see if the TCB status flag is still set to indicate that the task is waiting for the semaphore [L6.10(9)]. If the task is still waiting for the semaphore, it must not have been signaled by an OSSemPost() call. Indeed, the task must have be readied by OSTimeTick(), indicating that the timeout period has expired. In this case, the task is removed from the wait list for the semaphore by calling OSEventTO() [L6.10(10)], and an error code is returned to the task that called OSSemPend() to indicate that a timeout occurred. If the status flag in the task's TCB doesn't have the OS_STAT_SEM bit set, then the semaphore must have been signaled and the task that called OSSemPend() can now conclude that it has the semaphore. Also, the link to the ECB is removed [L6.10(11)].

Listing 6.10   Waiting for a semaphore.

6

```
void OSSemPend (OS_EVENT *pevent, INT16U timeout, INT8U *err)
{
    OS_ENTER_CRITICAL();
    if (pevent->OSEventType != OS_EVENT_TYPE_SEM) {              (1)
        OS_EXIT_CRITICAL();
        *err = OS_ERR_EVENT_TYPE;
    }
    if (pevent->OSEventCnt > 0) {                                (2)
        pevent->OSEventCnt--;                                    (3)
        OS_EXIT_CRITICAL();
        *err = OS_NO_ERR;
    } else if (OSIntNesting > 0) {                               (4)
        OS_EXIT_CRITICAL();
        *err = OS_ERR_PEND_ISR;
    } else {
        OSTCBCur->OSTCBStat  |= OS_STAT_SEM;                     (5)
        OSTCBCur->OSTCBDly    = timeout;                         (6)
        OSEventTaskWait(pevent);                                 (7)
        OS_EXIT_CRITICAL();
        OSSched();                                               (8)
        OS_ENTER_CRITICAL();
        if (OSTCBCur->OSTCBStat & OS_STAT_SEM) {                 (9)
            OSEventTO(pevent);                                   (10)
            OS_EXIT_CRITICAL();
            *err = OS_TIMEOUT;
        } else {
```

— why doesn't this return immediately? OSMBoxPend() does — pg 157.

Reverse the order of these tests. ALSO pg 157 ✱

Set bit in OSRdyTbl to ∅.

pg 148 — Removes Task from Ready List.

The actual WAIT occurs here. *Pg 85*

{ Task is running because of Timeout. Need to clean up TCB & event Table

Listing 6.10   Waiting for a semaphore. (Continued)

```
                    OSTCBCur->OSTCBEventPtr = (OS_EVENT *)0;          (11)
                    OS_EXIT_CRITICAL();
                    *err = OS_NO_ERR;
            }
        }
    }
```

6.05.03   Signaling a Semaphore, OSSemPost()

The code to signal a semaphore is shown in Listing 6.11. OSSemPost() starts by checking that the ECB being pointed to by pevent has been created by OSSemCreate() [L6.11(1)]. Next, it checks to see if any tasks are waiting on the semaphore [L6.11(2)]. There are tasks waiting when the .OSEvent-Grp field in the ECB contains a nonzero value. The highest priority task waiting for the semaphore is removed from the wait list by OSEventTaskRdy() [see section 6.02, Making a Task Ready, OSEv-entTaskRdy()] [L6.11(3)] and made ready to run. OSSched() is then called [L6.11(4)] to see if the task made ready is now the highest priority task ready to run. If it is, a context switch results [only if OSSemPost() is called from a task] and the readied task is executed. If the readied task is not the high-est priority task, OSSched() returns and the task that called OSSemPost()continues execution. If there are no tasks waiting on the semaphore, the semaphore count simply gets incremented [L6.11(5)].

Note that a context switch does not occur if OSSemPost() is called by an ISR because context switching from an ISR can only occur when OSIntExit() is called at the completion of the ISR from the last nested ISR (see section 3.09, Interrupts under µC/OS-II).

Listing 6.11   Signaling a semaphore.

```
INT8U OSSemPost (OS_EVENT *pevent)
{
    OS_ENTER_CRITICAL();
    if (pevent->OSEventType != OS_EVENT_TYPE_SEM) {          (1)
        OS_EXIT_CRITICAL();
        return (OS_ERR_EVENT_TYPE);
    }
    if (pevent->OSEventGrp) {                                 (2)
        OSEventTaskRdy(pevent, (void *)0, OS_STAT_SEM);       (3)
        OS_EXIT_CRITICAL();
        OSSched();
        return (OS_NO_ERR);                                  (4)
    } else {
        if (pevent->OSEventCnt < 65535) {
            pevent->OSEventCnt++;
            OS_EXIT_CRITICAL();                              (5)
            return (OS_NO_ERR);
```

Listing 6.11   Signaling a semaphore. (Continued)

```
        } else {
            OS_EXIT_CRITICAL();
            return (OS_SEM_OVF);
        }
    }
}
```

6.05.04   *Getting a Semaphore without Waiting,* OSSemAccept()

It is possible to obtain a semaphore(without putting a task to sleep if the semaphore is not available.) This is accomplished by calling OSSemAccept(), shown in Listing 6.12. OSSemAccept() starts by checking that the ECB being pointed to by pevent has been created by OSSemCreate() [L6.12(1)]. OSSemAccept() then gets the current semaphore count [L6.12(2)] to determine whether the semaphore is available (i.e., a nonzero value) [L6.12(3)]. The count is decremented only if the semaphore was available [L6.12(4)]. Finally, the original count of the semaphore is returned to the caller [L6.12(5)]. The code that called OSSemAccept() needs to examine the returned value. A returned value of zero indicates that the semaphore is not available; a nonzero value indicates that the semaphore is available. Furthermore, a nonzero value indicates to the caller the number of resources that are available. Keep in mind that, in this case, one of the resources has been allocated to the calling task because the count has been decremented. An ISR must use OSSemAccept() instead of OSSemPend().

6

Listing 6.12   Getting a semaphore without waiting.

```
INT16U OSSemAccept (OS_EVENT *pevent)
{
    INT16U cnt;


    OS_ENTER_CRITICAL();
    if (pevent->OSEventType != OS_EVENT_TYPE_SEM) {          (1)
        OS_EXIT_CRITICAL();
        return (0);      ←——— why return 0?
    }
    cnt = pevent->OSEventCnt;                                (2)
    if (cnt > 0) {                                           (3)
        pevent->OSEventCnt--;                                (4)
    }
    OS_EXIT_CRITICAL();
    return (cnt);                                            (5)
}
```

6.05.05 *Obtaining the Status of a Semaphore,* *OSSemQuery()*

OSSemQuery() allows your application to take a "snapshot" of an ECB that is used as a semaphore (Listing 6.13). OSSemQuery() receives two arguments: pevent contains a pointer to the semaphore, which is returned by OSSemCreate() when the semaphore is created, and pdata is a pointer to a data structure (OS_SEM_DATA, see uCOS_II.H) that holds information about the semaphore. Your application will thus need to allocate a variable of type OS_SEM_DATA that will be used to receive the information about the desired semaphore. I decided to use a new data structure because the caller should only be concerned with semaphore-specific data as opposed to the more generic OS_EVENT data structure, which contain two additional fields (.OSEventType and .OSEventPtr). OS_SEM_DATA contains the current semaphore count (.OSCnt) and the list of tasks waiting on the semaphore (.OSEventTbl[] and .OSEventGrp).

As always, OSSemQuery() checks that pevent points to an ECB containing a semaphore [L6.13(1)]. OSSemQuery() then copies the wait list [L6.13(2)] followed by the current semaphore count [L6.13(3)] from the OS_EVENT structure to the OS_SEM_DATA structure.

Listing 6.13   Obtaining the status of a semaphore.

```
INT8U OSSemQuery (OS_EVENT *pevent, OS_SEM_DATA *pdata)
{
    INT8U  i;
    INT8U *psrc;
    INT8U *pdest;


    OS_ENTER_CRITICAL();
    if (pevent->OSEventType != OS_EVENT_TYPE_SEM) {              (1)
        OS_EXIT_CRITICAL();
        return (OS_ERR_EVENT_TYPE);
    }
    pdata->OSEventGrp = pevent->OSEventGrp;                      (2)
    psrc              = &pevent->OSEventTbl[0];
    pdest             = &pdata->OSEventTbl[0];
    for (i = 0; i < OS_EVENT_TBL_SIZE; i++) {
        *pdest++ = *psrc++;
    }
    pdata->OSCnt      = pevent->OSEventCnt;                      (3)
    OS_EXIT_CRITICAL();
    return (OS_NO_ERR);
}
```

6.06 Message Mailboxes

A message mailbox (or simply a mailbox) is a µC/OS-II object that allows a task or an ISR to send a pointer-sized variable to another task. The pointer is typically initialized to point to some application specific data structure containing a "message." To enable µC/OS-II's message mailbox services, you must set the configuration constant OS_MBOX_EN to 1 (see file OS_CFG.H).

A mailbox needs to be created before it can be used. Creating a mailbox is accomplished by calling OSMboxCreate() (see next section) and specifying the initial value of the pointer. Typically, the initial value is a NULL pointer, but a mailbox can initially contain a message. If you use the mailbox to signal the occurrence of an event (i.e., send a message), you typically initialize it to a NULL pointer because the event (most likely) has not occurred. If you use the mailbox to access a shared resource, you initialize the mailbox with a non-NULL pointer. In this case, you basically use the mailbox as a binary semaphore.

µC/OS-II provides five services to access mailboxes: OSMboxCreate(), OSMboxPend(), OSMboxPost(), OSMboxAccept(), and OSMboxQuery(). Figure 6.6 shows a flow diagram to illustrate the relationship between tasks, ISRs, and a message mailbox. Note that the symbology used to represent a mailbox is an I-beam. The content of the mailbox is a pointer to a message. What the pointer points to is application specific. A mailbox can only contain one pointer (mailbox is full) or a pointer to NULL (mailbox is empty). As you can see from Figure 6.6, a task or an ISR can call OSMboxPost(). However, only tasks are allowed to call OSMboxPend() and OSMboxQuery().

6

Figure 6.6   ***Relationships between tasks, ISRs, and a message mailbox.***

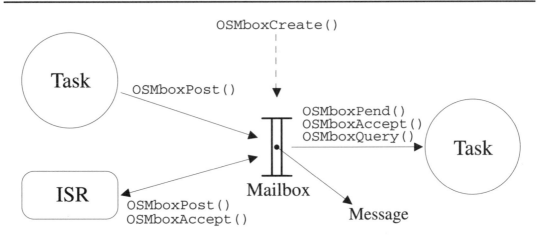

6.06.01 Creating a Mailbox, OSMboxCreate()

The code to create a mailbox is shown in Listing 6.14 and is basically identical to OSSemCreate() except that the ECB type is set to OS_EVENT_TYPE_MBOX [L6.14(1)] and, instead of using the .OSEventCnt field, I use the .OSEventPtr field to hold the message pointer [L6.14(2)].

OSMboxCreate() returns a pointer to the ECB [L6.14(3)]. This pointer must be used in subsequent calls to access the mailbox [OSMboxPend(), OSMboxPost(), OSMboxAccept(), and OSMboxQuery()]. The pointer is basically used as the mailbox handle. Note that if there are no more ECBs, OSMboxCreate() returns a NULL pointer.

Once a mailbox has been created, it cannot be deleted. It would be dangerous to delete a message mailbox object if tasks were waiting on the mailbox.

Listing 6.14 Creating a mailbox.

```
OS_EVENT *OSMboxCreate (void *msg)
{
    OS_EVENT *pevent;


    OS_ENTER_CRITICAL();
    pevent = OSEventFreeList;
    if (OSEventFreeList != (OS_EVENT *)0) {
        OSEventFreeList = (OS_EVENT *)OSEventFreeList->OSEventPtr;
    }
    OS_EXIT_CRITICAL();
    if (pevent != (OS_EVENT *)0) {
        pevent->OSEventType = OS_EVENT_TYPE_MBOX;                        (1)
        pevent->OSEventPtr = msg;                                       (2)
        OSEventWaitListInit(pevent);
    }
    return (pevent);                                                    (3)
}
```

(Handwritten annotations: "You can "initialize" mailbox msg, must at LEAST initialize it to NULL." / "initialize the msg." / "→ Pointer to ECB")

6.06.02 Waiting for a Message at a Mailbox, OSMboxPend()

The code to wait for a message to arrive at a mailbox is shown in Listing 6.15. Again, the code is very similar to OSSemPend() so I only discuss the differences. OSMboxPend() verifies that the ECB being pointed to by pevent has been created by OSMboxCreate() [L6.15(1)]. A message is available when .OSEventPtr contains a non-NULL pointer [L6.15(2)]. In this case, OSMboxPend() stores the pointer to the message in msg and places a NULL pointer in .OSEventPtr to empty the mailbox [L6.15(3)]. Again, this is the outcome you are looking for. This also happens to be the fastest path through OSMboxPend().

If a message is not available (.OSEventPtr contains a NULL pointer), OSMboxPend() checks to see if the function was called by an ISR [L6.15(4)]. As with OSSemPend(), you should not call OSMboxPend() from an ISR because an ISR cannot be made to wait. Again, I decided to add this check just in case. However, if the message is in fact available, the call to OSMboxPend() would be successful even if called from an ISR!

If a message is not available, the calling task must be suspended until either a message is posted or the specified timeout period expires [L6.15(5)]. When a message is posted to the mailbox (or the timeout period expires) and the task that called OSMboxPend() is again the highest priority task, OSSched() returns. OSMboxPend() checks to see if a message was placed in the task's TCB by OSMboxPost() [L6.15(6)]. If so, the call is successful and the message is returned to the caller.

Pg 79-80

Listing 6.15   *Waiting for a message to arrive at a mailbox.*

```
void *OSMboxPend (OS_EVENT *pevent, INT16U timeout, INT8U *err)
{
    void  *msg;

    OS_ENTER_CRITICAL();
    if (pevent->OSEventType != OS_EVENT_TYPE_MBOX) {                    (1)
        OS_EXIT_CRITICAL();
        *err = OS_ERR_EVENT_TYPE;
        return ((void *)0);
    }
    msg = pevent->OSEventPtr;
    if (msg != (void *)0) {                                            (2)
        pevent->OSEventPtr = (void *)0;                                (3)
        OS_EXIT_CRITICAL();
        *err = OS_NO_ERR;
    } else if (OSIntNesting > 0) {                                     (4)
        OS_EXIT_CRITICAL();
        *err = OS_ERR_PEND_ISR;
    } else {
        OSTCBCur->OSTCBStat  |= OS_STAT_MBOX;
        OSTCBCur->OSTCBDly    = timeout;
        OSEventTaskWait(pevent);                                       (5)
        OS_EXIT_CRITICAL();
        OSSched();
        OS_ENTER_CRITICAL();
        if ((msg = OSTCBCur->OSTCBMsg) != (void *)0) {                 (6)
            OSTCBCur->OSTCBMsg      = (void *)0;
            OSTCBCur->OSTCBStat     = OS_STAT_RDY;
            OSTCBCur->OSTCBEventPtr = (OS_EVENT *)0;
            OS_EXIT_CRITICAL();
            *err                    = OS_NO_ERR;
```

[handwritten annotations:]

immediately is available.

if msg is non-NULL, a msg is available

Empty the mailbox.

reverse these two tests?

Pg 248 → Removes Tasbe from Ready List

This statement moves the message into msg.

Clears the message area in TCB.

← TCB no longer linked to ECB

Listing 6.15 Waiting for a message to arrive at a mailbox. (Continued)

```
        } else if (OSTCBCur->OSTCBStat & OS_STAT_MBOX) {         (7)
            OSEventTO(pevent);                                   (8)
            OS_EXIT_CRITICAL();
            msg                  = (void *)0;                    (9)
            *err                 = OS_TIMEOUT;
        } else {
            msg                  = pevent->OSEventPtr;           (10)
            pevent->OSEventPtr   = (void *)0;                    (11)
            OSTCBCur->OSTCBEventPtr = (OS_EVENT *)0;             (12)
            OS_EXIT_CRITICAL();
            *err                 = OS_NO_ERR;
        }
    }
    return (msg);
}
```

A timeout is detected by looking at the .OSTCBStat field in the task's TCB to see if the OS_STAT_ MBOX bit is still set. A timeout occurs when the bit is set [L6.15(7)]. The task is removed from the mailbox's wait list by calling OSEventTO() [L6.15(8)]. Note that the returned pointer is set to NULL [L6.15(9)] because there is no message. If the status flag in the task's TCB doesn't have the OS_STAT_ MBOX bit set, then a message must have been sent. The task that called OSMboxPend() thus receives the pointer to the message [L6.15(10)]. Note that OSMboxPend() needs to clear the mailbox's content by placing a NULL pointer in .OSEventPtr. Also, the link to the ECB is removed [L6.15(12)].

6.06.03 Sending a Message to a Mailbox, OSMboxPost()

The code to deposit a message in a mailbox is shown in Listing 6.16. After making sure that the ECB is used as a mailbox [L6.16(1)], OSMboxPost() checks to see if any task is waiting for a message to arrive at the mailbox [L6.16(2)]. There are tasks waiting when the OSEventGrp field in the ECB contains a nonzero value. The highest priority task waiting for the message is removed from the wait list by OSEventTaskRdy() [see section 6.02, Making a Task Ready, OSEventTaskRdy()] [L6.16(3)], and this task is made ready to run. OSSched() is then called [L6.16(4)] to see if the task made ready is now the highest priority task ready to run. If it is, a context switch results [only if OSMboxPost() is called from a task] and the readied task is executed. If the readied task is not the highest priority task, OSSched() returns and the task that called OSMboxPost() continues execution. If there are no tasks waiting for a message to arrive at the mailbox, then the pointer to the message is saved in the mailbox [L6.16(6)], assuming there isn't already a non-NULL pointer [L6.16(5)]. Storing the pointer in the mailbox allows the next task to call OSMboxPend() to get the message immediately.

Note that a context switch does not occur if OSMboxPost() is called by an ISR because context switching from an ISR only occurs when OSIntExit() is called at the completion of the ISR and from the last nested ISR (see section 3.09, Interrupts under μC/OS-II).

Listing 6.16   Depositing a message in a mailbox.

```
INT8U OSMboxPost (OS_EVENT *pevent, void *msg)
{
    OS_ENTER_CRITICAL();
    if (pevent->OSEventType != OS_EVENT_TYPE_MBOX) {          (1)
        OS_EXIT_CRITICAL();
        return (OS_ERR_EVENT_TYPE);
    }
    if (pevent->OSEventGrp) {                                 (2)
        OSEventTaskRdy(pevent, msg, OS_STAT_MBOX);            (3)
        OS_EXIT_CRITICAL();
        OSSched();                                           (4)
        return (OS_NO_ERR);
    } else {
        if (pevent->OSEventPtr != (void *)0) {               (5)
            OS_EXIT_CRITICAL();
            return (OS_MBOX_FULL);
        } else {
            pevent->OSEventPtr = msg;
            OS_EXIT_CRITICAL();                              (6)
            return (OS_NO_ERR);
        }
    }
}
```

[Handwritten annotations: "puts this msg into OS_TCBMsg of TCB associated w/event" pointing to line (1); "Pg) 46"; "← if no task is waiting for msg, save it anyway. It will be immediately available to next task to call OSMboxPend()."]

6.06.04   *Getting a Message without Waiting,* `OSMboxAccept()`

You can obtain a message from a mailbox without putting a task to sleep if the mailbox is empty. This is accomplished by calling `OSMboxAccept()`, shown in Listing 6.17. `OSMboxAccept()` starts by checking that the ECB being pointed to by `pevent` has been created by `OSMboxCreate()` [L6.17(1)]. `OSMboxAccept()` then gets the current contents of the mailbox [L6.17(2)] in order to determine whether a message is available (i.e., a non-`NULL` pointer) [L6.17(3)]. If a message is available, the mailbox is emptied [L6.17(4)]. Finally, the original contents of the mailbox is returned to the caller [L6.17(5)]. The code that called `OSMboxAccept()` must examine the returned value. If `OSMboxAccept()` returns a `NULL` pointer, then a message was not available. A non-`NULL` pointer indicates that a message was deposited in the mailbox. An ISR should use `OSMboxAccept()` instead of `OSMboxPend()`.

You can use `OSMboxAccept()` to flush the contents of a mailbox.

Listing 6.17   Getting a message without waiting.

```
void *OSMboxAccept (OS_EVENT *pevent)
{
    void  *msg;



    OS_ENTER_CRITICAL();
    if (pevent->OSEventType != OS_EVENT_TYPE_MBOX) {                    (1)
        OS_EXIT_CRITICAL();
        return ((void *)0);
    }
    msg = pevent->OSEventPtr;                                          (2)
    if (msg != (void *)0) {                                           (3)
        pevent->OSEventPtr = (void *)0;                               (4)
    }
    OS_EXIT_CRITICAL();
    return (msg);                                                     (5)
}
```

6.06.05   Obtaining the Status of a Mailbox, OSMboxQuery()

OSMboxQuery() allows your application to take a snapshot of an ECB used for a message mailbox. The code for this function is shown in Listing 6.18. OSMboxQuery() is passed two arguments: pevent contains a pointer to the message mailbox, which is returned by OSMboxCreate() when the mailbox is created, and pdata is a pointer to a data structure (OS_MBOX_DATA, see uCOS_II.H) that holds information about the message mailbox. Your application thus needs to allocate a variable of type OS_MBOX_DATA that will be used to receive the information about the desired mailbox. I decided to use a new data structure because the caller should only be concerned with mailbox-specific data, as opposed to the more generic OS_EVENT data structure, which contains two additional fields (.OSEventCnt and .OSEventType). OS_MBOX_DATA contains the current contents of the message (.OSMsg) and the list of tasks waiting for a message to arrive (.OSEventTbl[] and .OSEventGrp).

As always, the function checks that pevent points to an ECB containing a mailbox [L6.18(1)]. OSMboxQuery() then copies the wait list [L6.18(2)], followed by the current message [L6.18(3)], from the OS_EVENT structure to the OS_MBOX_DATA structure.

Listing 6.18   Obtaining the status of a mailbox.

```
INT8U OSMboxQuery (OS_EVENT *pevent, OS_MBOX_DATA *pdata)
{
    INT8U  i;
    INT8U *psrc;
    INT8U *pdest;
```

Listing 6.18 Obtaining the status of a mailbox. (Continued)

```
    OS_ENTER_CRITICAL();
    if (pevent->OSEventType != OS_EVENT_TYPE_MBOX) {                      (1)
        OS_EXIT_CRITICAL();
        return (OS_ERR_EVENT_TYPE);
    }
    pdata->OSEventGrp = pevent->OSEventGrp;                               (2)
    psrc              = &pevent->OSEventTbl[0];
    pdest             = &pdata->OSEventTbl[0];
    for (i = 0; i < OS_EVENT_TBL_SIZE; i++) {
        *pdest++ = *psrc++;
    }
    pdata->OSMsg      = pevent->OSEventPtr;                               (3)
    OS_EXIT_CRITICAL();
    return (OS_NO_ERR);
}
```

6

6.06.06   Using a Mailbox as a Binary Semaphore

A message mailbox can be used as a binary semaphore by initializing the mailbox with a non-NULL pointer [(void *1) works well]. A task requesting the "semaphore" calls OSMboxPend() and releases the "semaphore" by calling OSMboxPost(). Listing 6.19 shows how this works. Use this technique to conserve code space if your application only needs binary semaphores and mailboxes. In this case, set OS_SEM_EN to 0 and use only mailboxes instead of both mailboxes and semaphores.

Listing 6.19 Using a mailbox as a binary semaphore.

```
OS_EVENT *MboxSem;


void Task1 (void *pdata)
{
    INT8U err;


    for (;;) {
        OSMboxPend(MboxSem, 0, &err);   /* Obtain access to resource(s)   */
        .
        .       /* Task has semaphore, access resource(s)                 */
        .
        OSMboxPost(MboxSem, (void*)1);  /* Release access to resource(s) */
    }
}
```

6.06.07   Using a Mailbox instead of OSTimeDly()

The timeout feature of a mailbox can be used to simulate a call to OSTimeDly(). As shown in Listing 6.20, Task1() resumes execution after the time period expires if no message is received within the specified TIMEOUT period. This is basically identical to OSTimeDly(TIMEOUT). However, the task can be resumed by Task2() when Task(2) post a "dummy" message to the mailbox before the time-out expires. This is the same as calling OSTimeDlyResume() had Task1() called OSTimeDly(). Note that the returned message is ignored because you are not actually looking to get a message from another task or an ISR.

Listing 6.20   Using a mailbox as a time delay.

```
OS_EVENT *MboxTimeDly;


void Task1 (void *pdata)
{
    INT8U err;


    for (;;) {
        OSMboxPend(MboxTimeDly, TIMEOUT, &err);    /* Delay task                */
        .
        .    /* Code executed after time delay                                  */
        .
    }
}



void Task2 (void *pdata)
{
    INT8U err;


    for (;;) {
        OSMboxPost(MboxTimeDly, (void *)1);          /* Cancel delay for Task1  */
        .
        .
    }
}
```

6.07 Message Queues

A message queue (or simply a queue) is a µC/OS-II object that allows a task or an ISR to send pointer-sized variables to another task. Each pointer typically is initialized to point to some application-specific data structure containing a message. To enable µC/OS-II's message queue services, you must set the configuration constant OS_Q_EN to 1 (see file OS_CFG.H) and determine how many message queues µC/OS-II needs to support by setting the configuration constant OS_MAX_QS, also found in OS_CFG.H.

A queue needs to be created before it can be used. Creating a queue is accomplished by calling OSQCreate() (see section 6.07.01) and specifying the number of entries (i.e., pointers) a queue can hold.

µC/OS-II provides seven services to access message queues: OSQCreate(), OSQPend(), OSQ-Post(), OSQPostFront(), OSQAccept(), OSQFlush(), and OSQQuery(). Figure 6.7 shows a flow diagram to illustrate the relationship between tasks, ISRs, and a message queue. Note that the symbology used to represent a queue looks like a mailbox with multiple entries. In fact, you can think of a queue as an array of mailboxes, except that there is only one wait list associated with the queue. Again, what the pointers point to is application specific. N represents the number of entries the queue holds. The queue is full when your application calls OSQPost() [or OSQPostFront()] N times before your application has called OSQPend() or OSQAccept(). As you can see from Figure 6.7, a task or an ISR can call OSQPost(), OSQPostFront(), OSQFlush(), or OSQAccept(). However, only tasks are allowed to call OSQPend() and OSQQuery().

Figure 6.7   Relationships between tasks, ISRs, and a message queue.

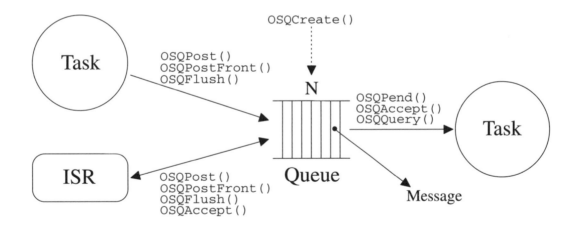

Figure 6.8 shows the different data structures needed to implement a message queue. An ECB is required because you need a wait list [F6.8(1)], and using an ECB allows queue services to use some of the same code used by semaphores and mailboxes. When a message queue is created, a queue control block (i.e., an OS_Q, see OS_Q.C) is allocated and linked to the ECB using the .OSEventPtr field in OS_EVENT, [F6.8(2)]. Before you create a queue, however, you need to allocate an array of pointers [F6.8(3)] that contains the desired number of queue entries. In other words, the number of elements in the array corresponds to the number of entries in the queue. The starting address of the array is passed to OSQCreate() as an argument as well as the size (in number of elements) of the array. In fact, you don't actually need to use an array as long as the memory occupies contiguous locations.

The configuration constant OS_MAX_QS in OS_CFG.H specifies how many queues you are allowed to have in your application and must be set at least to 2. When µC/OS-II is initialized, a list of free queue control blocks is created as shown in Figure 6.9.

Figure 6.8   Data structures used in a message queue.

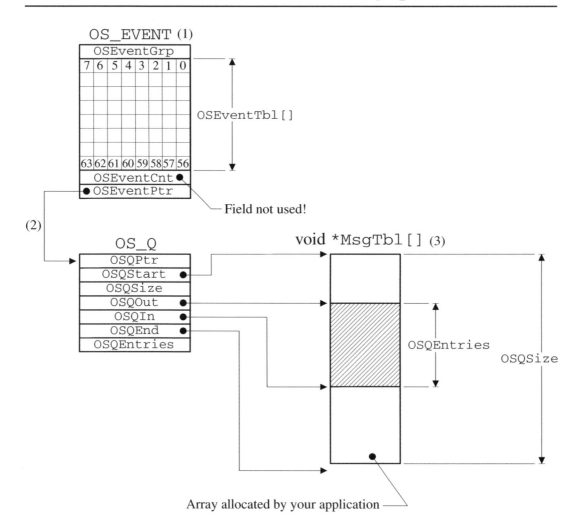

Figure 6.9   List of free queue control blocks.

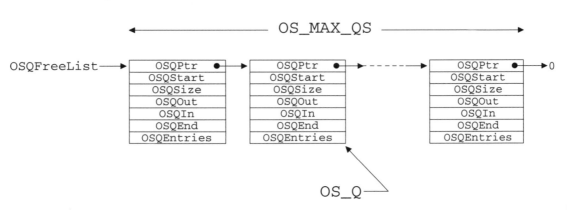

A queue control block is a data structure used to maintain information about the queue. It contains the fields described below. Note that the fields are preceded with a dot to show that they are members of a structure as opposed to simple variables.

.OSQPtr links queue control blocks in the list of free queue control blocks. Once the queue is created, this field is not used.

.OSQStart contains a pointer to the start of the message queue storage area. Your application must declare this storage area before creating the queue.

.OSQEnd is a pointer to one location past the end of the queue. This pointer is used to make the queue a circular buffer.

.OSQIn is a pointer to the location in the queue where the next message will be inserted. .OSQIn is adjusted back to the beginning of the message storage area when .OSQIn equals .OSQEnd.

.OSQOut is a pointer to the next message to be extracted from the queue. .OSQOut is adjusted back to the beginning of the message storage area when .OSQOut equals .OSQEnd. .OSQOut is also used to insert a message [see OSQPostFront()].

.OSQSize contains the size of the message storage area. The size of the queue is determined by your application when the queue is created. Note that μC/OS-II allows the queue to contain up to 65,535 entries.

.OSQEntries contains the current number of entries in the message queue. The queue is empty when .OSQEntries is 0 and full when it equals .OSQSize. The message queue is empty when the queue is created.

6

A message queue is basically a circular buffer as shown in Figure 6.10. Each entry contains a pointer. The pointer to the next message is deposited at the entry pointed to by .OSQIn [F6.10(1)] unless the queue is full (i.e., .OSQEntries == .OSQSize) [F6.10(3)]. Depositing the pointer at .OSQIn implements a FIFO (First-In-First-Out) queue. You can implement a LIFO (Last-In-First-Out) queue by pointing to the entry preceeding .OSQOut [F6.10(2)] and depositing the pointer at that location. The pointer is also considered full when .OSQEntries == .OSQSize. Message pointers are always extracted from the entry pointed to by .OSQOut [F6.10(4)]. The pointers .OSQStart and .OSQEnd [F6.10(5)] are simply markers used to establish the beginning and end of the array so that .OSQIn and .OSQOut can wrap around to implement this circular motion.

Figure 6.10   A message queue is a circular buffer of pointers.

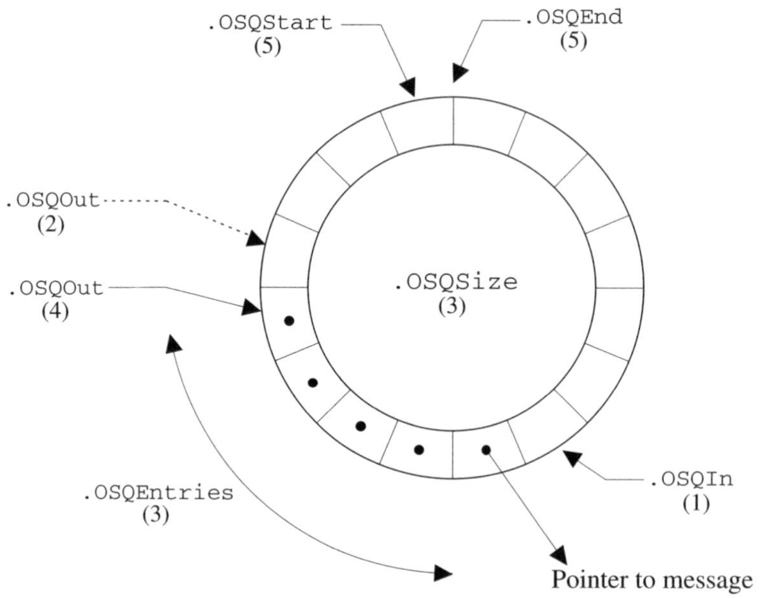

6.07.01   Creating a Queue, OSQCreate()

The code to create a message queue is shown in Listing 6.21. OSQCreate() requires you to allocate an array of pointers that will hold the message. The array must be declared as an array of pointers to void.

OSQCreate() starts by obtaining an ECB from the free list of ECBs (see Figure 6.3) [L6.21(1)]. The linked list of free ECBs is adjusted to point to the next free ECB [L6.21(2)]. Next, OSQCreate() obtains a queue control block from the free list [L6.21(3)]. OSQCreate() initializes the queue control block [L6.21(4)] (if one is available), sets the ECB type to OS_EVENT_TYPE_Q [L6.21(5)] and makes .OSEventPtr point to the queue control block [L6.21(6)]. The wait list is initialized by calling OSEventWaitListInit() [see section 6.01, Initializing an ECB, OSEventWaitListInit()] [L6.21(7)]. Because the queue is being initialized, no tasks are waiting. Finally, OSQCreate() returns a pointer to the allocated ECB [L6.21(9)]. This pointer must be used in subsequent calls that operate on message queues [OSQPend(), OSQPost(), OSQPostFront(), OSQFlush(), OSQAccept(), and OSQQuery()]. The pointer is basically used as the queue's handle. Note that if there were no more

ECBs, OSQCreate() would return a NULL pointer. If a queue control block is not available, OSQCreate() returns the ECB back to the list of free ECBs [L6.21(8)] (there is no point in wasting the ECB).

Note that once a message queue has been created, it cannot be deleted. It would be dangerous to delete a message queue object if tasks were waiting for messages from it.

Listing 6.21 *Creating a queue.*

```
OS_EVENT *OSQCreate (void **start, INT16U size)
{
    OS_EVENT  *pevent;
    OS_Q      *pq;


    OS_ENTER_CRITICAL();
    pevent = OSEventFreeList;                                            (1)
    if (OSEventFreeList != (OS_EVENT *)0) {
        OSEventFreeList = (OS_EVENT *)OSEventFreeList->OSEventPtr;       (2)
    }
    OS_EXIT_CRITICAL();
    if (pevent != (OS_EVENT *)0) {
        OS_ENTER_CRITICAL();
        pq = OSQFreeList;                                                (3)
        if (OSQFreeList != (OS_Q *)0) {
            OSQFreeList = OSQFreeList->OSQPtr;
        }
        OS_EXIT_CRITICAL();
        if (pq != (OS_Q *)0) {
            pq->OSQStart        = start;                                 (4)
            pq->OSQEnd          = &start[size];
            pq->OSQIn           = start;
            pq->OSQOut          = start;
            pq->OSQSize         = size;
            pq->OSQEntries      = 0;
            pevent->OSEventType = OS_EVENT_TYPE_Q;                       (5)
            pevent->OSEventPtr  = pq;                                    (6)
            OSEventWaitListInit(pevent);                                 (7)
        } else {
            OS_ENTER_CRITICAL();
            pevent->OSEventPtr = (void *)OSEventFreeList;                (8)
```

6

Listing 6.21   Creating a queue. (Continued)

```
            OSEventFreeList    = pevent;
            OS_EXIT_CRITICAL();
            pevent = (OS_EVENT *)0;
        }
    }
    return (pevent);                                                        (9)
}
```

6.07.02   Waiting for a Message at a Queue, OSQPend()

The code to wait for a message to arrive at a queue is shown in Listing 6.22. OSQPend() verifies that the ECB being pointed to by pevent has been created by OSQCreate() [L6.22(1)]. A message is available when .OSQEntries is greater than 0 [L6.22(2)]. In this case, OSQPend() stores the pointer to the message in msg, moves the .OSQOut pointer so that it points to the next entry in the queue [L6.22(3)], and decrements the number of entries left in the queue [L6.22(4)]. Because it is a circular buffer, OSQPend() needs to check that .OSQOut has not moved past the last valid entry in the array [L6.22(5)]. When this happens, however, .OSQOut is adjusted to point back to the beginning of the array [L6.22(6)]. This is the path you are looking for when calling OSQPend(), and it also happens to be the fastest path.

Listing 6.22   Waiting for a message to arrive at a queue.

```
void *OSQPend (OS_EVENT *pevent, INT16U timeout, INT8U *err)
{
    void   *msg;
    OS_Q   *pq;


    OS_ENTER_CRITICAL();
    if (pevent->OSEventType != OS_EVENT_TYPE_Q) {                           (1)
        OS_EXIT_CRITICAL();
        *err = OS_ERR_EVENT_TYPE;
        return ((void *)0);
    }
    pq = pevent->OSEventPtr;
    if (pq->OSQEntries != 0) {                                              (2)
        msg = *pq->OSQOut++;                                                (3)
        pq->OSQEntries--;                                                   (4)
        if (pq->OSQOut == pq->OSQEnd) {                                     (5)
            pq->OSQOut = pq->OSQStart;                                      (6)
        }
        OS_EXIT_CRITICAL();
```

Listing 6.22   Waiting for a message to arrive at a queue. (Continued)

```
        *err = OS_NO_ERR;
    } else if (OSIntNesting > 0) {                                      (7)
        OS_EXIT_CRITICAL();
        *err = OS_ERR_PEND_ISR;
    } else {
        OSTCBCur->OSTCBStat     |= OS_STAT_Q;                           (8)
        OSTCBCur->OSTCBDly       = timeout;
        OSEventTaskWait(pevent);
        OS_EXIT_CRITICAL();
        OSSched();                                                      (9)
        OS_ENTER_CRITICAL();
        if ((msg = OSTCBCur->OSTCBMsg) != (void *)0) {                  (10)
            OSTCBCur->OSTCBMsg      = (void *)0;
            OSTCBCur->OSTCBStat     = OS_STAT_RDY;
            OSTCBCur->OSTCBEventPtr = (OS_EVENT *)0;                    (11)
            OS_EXIT_CRITICAL();
            *err                    = OS_NO_ERR;
        } else if (OSTCBCur->OSTCBStat & OS_STAT_Q) {                   (12)
            OSEventTO(pevent);                                          (13)
            OS_EXIT_CRITICAL();
            msg                     = (void *)0;                        (14)
            *err                    = OS_TIMEOUT;
        } else {
```

6

If a message is not available (.OSEventEntries is 0), OSQPend() checks to see if the function was called by an ISR [L6.22(7)]. As with OSSemPend() and OSMboxPend(), you should not call OSQPend() from an ISR because an ISR cannot be made to wait. However, if the message is in fact available, the call to OSQPend() would be successful even if called from an ISR!

If a message is not available, the calling task must be suspended until either a message is posted or the specified timeout period expires [L6.22(8)]. When a message is posted to the queue (or the timeout period expires) and the task that called OSQPend() is again the highest priority task, then OSSched() returns [L6.22(9)]. OSQPend() then checks to see if a message was placed in the task's TCB by OSQ-Post()[L6.22(10)]. If this is the case, the call is successful, some cleanup work is done to unlink the message queue from the TCB [L6.22(11)] and the message is returned to the caller [L6.22(17)].

A timeout is detected by looking at the .OSTCBStat field in the task's TCB to see if the OS_STAT_Q bit is still set. A timeout occurs when the bit is set [L6.22(12)]. The task is removed from the queue's wait list by calling OSEventTO()[L6.22(13)]. Note that the returned pointer is set to NULL [L6.22(14)] (no message was available).

Listing 6.22   Waiting for a message to arrive at a queue. (Continued)

```
            msg = *pq->OSQOut++;                                              (15)

            pq->OSQEntries--;

            if (pq->OSQOut == pq->OSQEnd) {

                pq->OSQOut = pq->OSQStart;

            }

            OSTCBCur->OSTCBEventPtr = (OS_EVENT *)0;                          (16)

            OS_EXIT_CRITICAL();

            *err = OS_NO_ERR;

        }

    }

    return (msg);                                                            (17)

}
```

If the status flag in the task's TCB doesn't have the OS_STAT_Q bit set, a message must have been sent, so the message is extracted from the queue [L6.22(15)]. Also, the link to the ECB is removed because the task will no longer wait on that message queue [L6.22(16)].

6.07.03   Sending a Message to a Queue (FIFO), OSQPost()

The code to deposit a message in a queue is shown in Listing 6.23. After making sure that the ECB is used as a queue [L6.23(1)], OSQPost() checks to see if any task is waiting for a message to arrive at the queue [L6.23(2)]. There are tasks waiting when the .OSEventGrp field in the ECB contains a non-zero value. The highest priority task waiting for the message is removed from the wait list by OSEventTaskRdy() [see section 6.02, Making a Task Ready, OSEventTaskRdy()] [L6.23(3)], and this task is made ready to run. OSSched() is then called [L6.23(4)] to see if the task made ready is now the highest priority task ready to run. If it is, a context switch results [only if OSQPost() is called from a task] and the readied task is executed. If the readied task is not the highest priority task, OSSched() returns and the task that called OSQPost() continues execution.

Listing 6.23   Depositing a message in a queue (FIFO).

```
INT8U OSQPost (OS_EVENT *pevent, void *msg)
{
    OS_Q    *pq;



    OS_ENTER_CRITICAL();
    if (pevent->OSEventType != OS_EVENT_TYPE_Q) {                            (1)
        OS_EXIT_CRITICAL();
        return (OS_ERR_EVENT_TYPE);
    }
    if (pevent->OSEventGrp) {                                                (2)
```

Listing 6.23 Depositing a message in a queue (FIFO). (Continued)

```
            OSEventTaskRdy(pevent, msg, OS_STAT_Q);                    (3)
            OS_EXIT_CRITICAL();
            OSSched();                                                 (4)
            return (OS_NO_ERR);
        } else {
            pq = pevent->OSEventPtr;
            if (pq->OSQEntries >= pq->OSQSize) {                       (5)
                OS_EXIT_CRITICAL();
                return (OS_Q_FULL);
            } else {
                *pq->OSQIn++ = msg;                                    (6)
                pq->OSQEntries++;
                if (pq->OSQIn == pq->OSQEnd) {
                    pq->OSQIn = pq->OSQStart;
                }
                OS_EXIT_CRITICAL();
            }
            return (OS_NO_ERR);
        }
    }
```

If no tasks are waiting for a message to arrive at the queue, then the pointer to the message is saved in the queue [L6.23(6)] unless the queue is already full [L6.23(5)]. You should note that if the queue is full, the message is not inserted in the queue, and thus the message is basically lost. Storing the pointer to the message in the queue allows the next task that calls OSQPend() (on this queue) to immediately get the pointer.

Note that a context switch does not occur if OSQPost() is called by an ISR because context switching from an ISR only occurs when OSIntExit() is called at the completion of the ISR, from the last nested ISR (see section 3.09, Interrupts under μC/OS-II).

6.07.04 Sending a Message to a Queue (LIFO), *OSQPostFront ()*

OSQPostFront() is basically identical to OSQPost(), except that OSQPostFront() uses .OSQOut instead of .OSQIn as the pointer to the next entry to insert. The code is shown in Listing 6.24. You should note, however, that .OSQOut points to an already inserted entry, so .OSQOut must be made to point to the previous entry. If .OSQOut points at the beginning of the array [L6.24(1)], then a decrement really means positioning .OSQOut at the end of the array [L6.24(2)]. However, .OSQEnd points to one entry past the array and thus .OSQOut needs to be adjusted to be within range [L6.24(3)].

`OSQPostFront()` implements a LIFO queue because the next message extracted by `OSQPend()` is the last message inserted by `OSQPostFront()`.

Listing 6.24 *Depositing a message in a queue (LIFO).*

```c
INT8U OSQPostFront (OS_EVENT *pevent, void *msg)
{
    OS_Q    *pq;


    OS_ENTER_CRITICAL();
    if (pevent->OSEventType != OS_EVENT_TYPE_Q) {
        OS_EXIT_CRITICAL();
        return (OS_ERR_EVENT_TYPE);
    }
    if (pevent->OSEventGrp) {
        OSEventTaskRdy(pevent, msg, OS_STAT_Q);
        OS_EXIT_CRITICAL();
        OSSched();
        return (OS_NO_ERR);
    } else {
        pq = pevent->OSEventPtr;
        if (pq->OSQEntries >= pq->OSQSize) {
            OS_EXIT_CRITICAL();
            return (OS_Q_FULL);
        } else {
            if (pq->OSQOut == pq->OSQStart) {                    (1)
                pq->OSQOut = pq->OSQEnd;                         (2)
            }
            pq->OSQOut--;                                        (3)
            *pq->OSQOut = msg;
            pq->OSQEntries++;
            OS_EXIT_CRITICAL();
        }
        return (OS_NO_ERR);
    }
}
```

6.07.05 *Getting a Message without Waiting,* `OSQAccept()`

You can obtain a message from a queue without putting a task to sleep by calling OSQAccept() if the queue is empty. The code for this function is shown in Listing 6.25. OSQAccept() starts by checking that the ECB being pointed to by pevent has been created by OSQCreate() [L6.25(1)]. OSQAccept() then checks to see if there are any entries in the queue [L6.25(2)]. If the queue contains at least one message, the next pointer (i.e., message) is extracted from the queue [L6.25(3)]. The code that calls OSQAccept() needs to examine the returned value. If OSQAccept() returns a NULL pointer, then a message is not available [L6.25(4)]. A non-NULL pointer indicates that a message pointer is available. An ISR should use OSQAccept() instead of OSQPend(). If an entry is available, OSQAccept() extracts the entry from the queue.

Listing 6.25 *Getting a message without waiting.*

```
void *OSQAccept (OS_EVENT *pevent)
{
    void  *msg;
    OS_Q  *pq;


    OS_ENTER_CRITICAL();
    if (pevent->OSEventType != OS_EVENT_TYPE_Q) {        (1)
        OS_EXIT_CRITICAL();
        return ((void *)0);
    }
    pq = pevent->OSEventPtr;
    if (pq->OSQEntries != 0) {                           (2)
        msg = *pq->OSQOut++;                             (3)
        pq->OSQEntries--;
        if (pq->OSQOut == pq->OSQEnd) {
            pq->OSQOut = pq->OSQStart;
        }
    } else {
        msg = (void *)0;                                (4)
    }
    OS_EXIT_CRITICAL();
    return (msg);
}
```

6.07.06   *Flushing a Queue,* `OSQFlush()`

`OSQFlush()` allows you to remove all the messages posted to a queue and basically start with a fresh queue. The code for this function is shown in Listing 6.26. As usual, µC/OS-II checks to ensure that `pevent` is pointing to a message queue [L6.26(1)]. The In and Out pointers are reset to the beginning of the array and the number of entries is cleared [L6.26(2)]. I decided not to check to see if any tasks were pending on the queue because it would be irrelevant anyway. In other words, if tasks are waiting on the queue, then `.OSQEntries` would already be set to 0. The only difference is that `.OSQIn` and `.OSQOut` may be pointing elsewhere in the array.

Listing 6.26   *Flushing the contents of a queue.*

```
INT8U OSQFlush (OS_EVENT *pevent)
{
    OS_Q  *pq;


    OS_ENTER_CRITICAL();
    if (pevent->OSEventType != OS_EVENT_TYPE_Q) {            (1)
        OS_EXIT_CRITICAL();
        return (OS_ERR_EVENT_TYPE);
    }
    pq              = pevent->OSEventPtr;
    pq->OSQIn       = pq->OSQStart;                          (2)
    pq->OSQOut      = pq->OSQStart;
    pq->OSQEntries = 0;
    OS_EXIT_CRITICAL();
    return (OS_NO_ERR);
}
```

6.07.07   *Obtaining the Status of a Queue,* `OSQQuery()`

`OSQQuery()` allows your application to take a snapshot of the contents of a message queue. The code for this function is shown in Listing 6.27. `OSQQuery()` is passed two arguments: `pevent` contains a pointer to the message queue, which is returned by `OSQCreate()` when the queue is created, and `pdata` is a pointer to a data structure (`OS_Q_DATA`, see `uCOS_II.H`) that holds information about the message queue. Your application thus needs to allocate a variable of type `OS_Q_DATA` that will receive the information about the desired queue. `OS_Q_DATA` contains the following fields.

.OSMsg contains the contents pointed to by `.OSQOut` if there are entries in the queue. If the queue is empty, `.OSMsg` contains a `NULL` pointer.

.OSNMsgs contains the number of messages in the queue (i.e., a copy of `.OSQEntries`).

.OSQSize contains the size of the queue (in number of entries).

.OSEventTbl[] and **.OSEventGrp** contain a snapshot of the message queue wait list. The caller to `OSQQuery()` can thus determine how many tasks are waiting for the queue.

As always, the function checks that `pevent` points to an ECB containing a queue [L6.27(1)]. `OSQQuery()` then copies the wait list [L6.27(2)]. If the queue contains any entries [L6.27(3)], the next message pointer to be extracted from the queue is copied into the `OS_Q_DATA` structure [L6.27(4)]. If the queue is empty, a `NULL` pointer is placed in `OS_Q_DATA` [L6.27(5)]. Finally, the number of entries and the size of the message queue are copied [L6.27(6)].

Listing 6.27 *Obtaining the status of a queue.*

```
INT8U OSQQuery (OS_EVENT *pevent, OS_Q_DATA *pdata)
{
    OS_Q    *pq;
    INT8U   i;
    INT8U   *psrc;
    INT8U   *pdest;


    OS_ENTER_CRITICAL();
    if (pevent->OSEventType != OS_EVENT_TYPE_Q) {              (1)
        OS_EXIT_CRITICAL();
        return (OS_ERR_EVENT_TYPE);
    }
    pdata->OSEventGrp = pevent->OSEventGrp;                    (2)
    psrc              = &pevent->OSEventTbl[0];
    pdest             = &pdata->OSEventTbl[0];
    for (i = 0; i < OS_EVENT_TBL_SIZE; i++) {
        *pdest++ = *psrc++;
    }
    pq = (OS_Q *)pevent->OSEventPtr;
    if (pq->OSQEntries > 0) {                                  (3)
        pdata->OSMsg = pq->OSQOut;                             (4)
    } else {
        pdata->OSMsg = (void *)0;                              (5)
    }
    pdata->OSNMsgs = pq->OSQEntries;                           (6)
    pdata->OSQSize = pq->OSQSize;
    OS_EXIT_CRITICAL();
    return (OS_NO_ERR);
}
```

6

6.07.08 Using a Message Queue when Reading Analog Inputs

It is often useful in control applications to read analog inputs at a regular interval. To accomplish this, create a task, call OSTimeDly() [see section 5.00, Delaying a Task, OSTimeDly()], and specify the desired sampling period. As shown in Figure 6.11, you could use a message queue instead and have your task pend on the queue with a timeout. The timeout corresponds to the desired sampling period. If no other task sends a message to the queue, the task is resumed after the specified timeout, which basically emulates the OSTimeDly() function.

You are probably wondering why I decided to use a queue when OSTimeDly() does the trick just fine. By adding a queue, you can have other tasks abort the wait by sending a message, thus forcing an immediate conversion. If you add some intelligence to your messages, you can tell the ADC task to convert a specific channel, tell the task to increase the sampling rate, and more. In other words, you can say to the task: "Can you convert analog input 3 for me now?" After servicing the message, the task would initiate the pend on the queue, which would restart the scanning process.

Figure 6.11   Reading analog inputs.

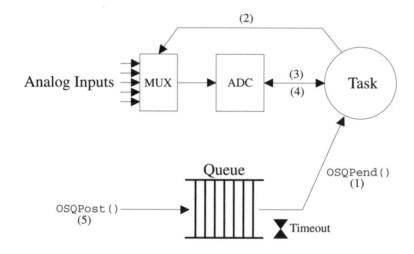

6.07.09 Using a Queue as a Counting Semaphore

A message queue can be used as a counting semaphore by initializing and loading a queue with as many non-NULL pointers [(void *1) works well] as there are resources available. A task requesting the "semaphore" calls OSQPend() and releases the "semaphore" by calling OSQPost(). Listing 6.28 shows how this works. Use this technique to conserve code space if your application only needs counting semaphores and message queues (you would then have no need for the semaphore services). In this case, set OS_SEM_EN to 0 and only use queues instead of both queues and semaphores. Note that this technique consumes a pointer-sized variable for each resource that the semaphore is guarding and requires a queue control block. In other words, you are sacrificing RAM space in order to save code space. Also, message queue services are slower than semaphore services. This technique would be very inefficient if your counting semaphore (in this case a queue) is guarding a large amount of resources (you would require a large array of pointers).

Listing 6.28   Using a queue as a counting semaphore.

```
OS_EVENT *QSem;
void     *QMsgTbl[N_RESOURCES]


void main (void)
{
    OSInit();
    .

    .
    QSem = OSQCreate(&QMsgTbl[0], N_RESOURCES);
    for (i = 0; i < N_RESOURCES; i++) {
        OSQPost(Qsem, (void *)1);
    }
    .

    .
    OSTaskCreate(Task1, .., .., ..);
    .

    .
    OSStart();
}


void Task1 (void *pdata)
{
    INT8U err;


    for (;;) {
        OSQPend(&QSem, 0, &err);        /* Obtain access to resource(s)    */
        .

        .    /* Task has semaphore, access resource(s)                    */
        .
        OSMQPost(QSem, (void*)1);       /* Release access to resource(s)   */
    }
}
```

6

Chapter 7

Memory Management

Your application can allocate and free dynamic memory using any ANSI C compiler's `malloc()` and `free()` functions, respectively. However, using `malloc()` and `free()` in an embedded real-time system is dangerous because, eventually, you may not be able to obtain a single contiguous memory area due to *fragmentation*. Fragmentation is the development of a large number of separate free areas (i.e., the total free memory is fragmented into small, non-contiguous pieces). I discussed the problem of fragmentation in section 4.02, Task Stacks, when I indicated that task stacks could be allocated using `malloc()`. Execution time of `malloc()` and `free()` are also generally nondeterministic because of the algorithms used to locate a contiguous block of free memory.

µC/OS-II provides an alternative to `malloc()` and `free()` by allowing your application to obtain fixed-sized *memory blocks* from a *partition* made of a contiguous memory area, as illustrated in Figure 7.1. All memory blocks are the same size and the partition contains an integral number of blocks. Allocation and deallocation of these memory blocks is done in constant time and is deterministic.

As shown in Figure 7.2, more than one memory partition can exist, so your application can obtain memory blocks of different sizes. However, a specific memory block must be returned to the partition from which it came. This type of memory management is not subject to fragmentation.

Figure 7.1 Memory partition.

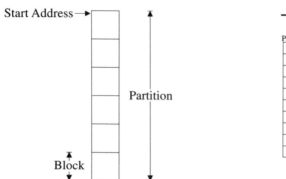

Figure 7.2 Multiple memory partitions.

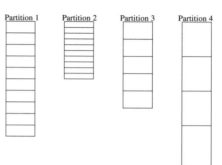

7.00 Memory Control Blocks

µC/OS-II keeps track of memory partitions through the use of a data structure called a *memory control block* (Listing 7.1). Each memory partition requires its own memory control block.

Listing 7.1 Memory control block data structure.

```
typedef struct {
    void    *OSMemAddr;
    void    *OSMemFreeList;
    INT32U  OSMemBlkSize;
    INT32U  OSMemNBlks;
    INT32U  OSMemNFree;
} OS_MEM;
```

One of these per partition.

must create at least 2 partitions.

.OSMemAddr is a pointer to the beginning (base) of the memory partition from which memory blocks will be allocated. This field is initialized when you create a partition [see section 7.01, Creating a Partition, OSMemCreate()] and is not used thereafter.

.OSMemFreeList is a pointer used by µC/OS-II to point to either the next free memory control block or to the next free memory block. The use depends on whether the memory partition has been created or not (see section 7.01).

.OSMemBlkSize determines the size of each memory block in the partition and is a parameter you specify when the memory partition is created (see section 7.01).

.OSMemNBlks establishes the total number of memory blocks available from the partition. This parameter is specified when the partition is created (see section 7.01).

.OSMemNFree is used to determine how many memory blocks are available from the partition.

Pg 99,101

µC/OS-II initializes the memory manager if you configure OS_MEM_EN to 1 in OS_CFG.H. Initialization is done by **OSMemInit()** [called by OSInit()] and consists of creating a linked list of memory control blocks, as shown in Figure 7.3. You specify the maximum number of memory partitions with the configuration constant OS_MAX_MEM_PART (see OS_CFG.H), which must be set at least to 2.

As you can see, the OSMemFreeList field of the control block is used to chain the free control blocks.

Figure 7.3 List of free memory control blocks.

Pg 101

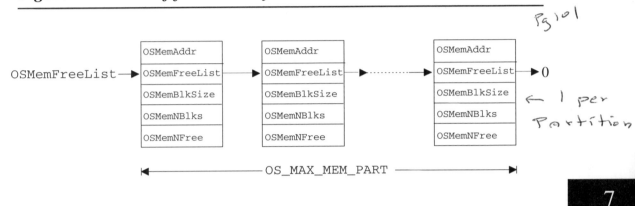

← 1 per Partition

7.01 Creating a Partition, *OSMemCreate()*

Your application must create each partition before it can be used. Create a memory partition by calling OSMemCreate(). Listing 7.2 shows how you could create a memory partition containing 100 blocks of 32 bytes each.

Listing 7.2 Creating a memory partition.

```
OS_MEM  *CommTxBuf;
INT8U    CommTxPart[100][32];



void main (void)
{
    INT8U err;



    OSInit();
    .

    .
    CommTxBuf = OSMemCreate(CommTxPart, 100, 32, &err);
    .

    .
    OSStart();
}
```

The code to create a memory partition is shown in Listing 7.3. OSMemCreate() requires four arguments: the beginning address of the memory partition, the number of blocks to be allocated from this partition, the size (in bytes) of each block, and a pointer to a variable that contains an error code. OSMemCreate() returns a NULL pointer if OSMemCreate() fails. On success, OSMemCreate() returns a pointer to the allocated memory control block. This pointer must be used in subsequent calls to memory management services [see OSMemGet(), OSMemPut(), and OSMemQuery() in sections 7.02 through 7.04].

Each memory partition must contain at least two memory blocks [L7.3(1)]. Also, each memory block must be able to hold the size of a pointer because a pointer is used to chain all the memory blocks together [L7.3(2)]. Next, OSMemCreate() obtains a memory control block from the list of free memory control blocks [L7.3(3)]. The memory control block contains run-time information about the memory partition. OSMemCreate() cannot create a memory partition unless a memory control block is available [L7.3(4)]. If a memory control block is available and all the previous conditions are satisfied, the memory blocks within the partition are linked together in a singly linked list [L7.3(5)]. When all the blocks are linked, the memory control block is filled with information about the partition [L7.3(6)]. OSMemCreate() returns the pointer to the memory control block so it can be used in subsequent calls to access the memory blocks from this partition [L7.3(7)].

Listing 7.3   OSMemCreate().

```
OS_MEM *OSMemCreate (void *addr, INT32U nblks, INT32U blksize, INT8U *err)
{
    OS_MEM   *pmem;
    INT8U    *pblk;
    void     **plink;
    INT32U   i;


    if (nblks < 2) {                                                        (1)
        *err = OS_MEM_INVALID_BLKS;
        return ((OS_MEM *)0);
    }
    if (blksize < sizeof(void *)) {                                         (2)
        *err = OS_MEM_INVALID_SIZE;
        return ((OS_MEM *)0);
    }
    OS_ENTER_CRITICAL();
    pmem = OSMemFreeList;                                                   (3)
    if (OSMemFreeList != (OS_MEM *)0) {
        OSMemFreeList = (OS_MEM *)OSMemFreeList->OSMemFreeList;
    }
    OS_EXIT_CRITICAL();
```

Should this be pmem?

Listing 7.3   *OSMemCreate(). (Continued)*

```
    if (pmem == (OS_MEM *)0) {                              (4)
        *err = OS_MEM_INVALID_PART;
        return ((OS_MEM *)0);
    }
    plink = (void **)addr;                                  (5)
    pblk  = (INT8U *)addr + blksize;
    for (i = 0; i < (nblks - 1); i++) {
        *plink = (void *)pblk;
        plink  = (void **)pblk;
        pblk   = pblk + blksize;
    }
    *plink = (void *)0;
    OS_ENTER_CRITICAL();
    pmem->OSMemAddr     = addr;                             (6)
    pmem->OSMemFreeList = addr;
    pmem->OSMemNFree    = nblks;
    pmem->OSMemNBlks    = nblks;
    pmem->OSMemBlkSize  = blksize;
    OS_EXIT_CRITICAL();
    *err   = OS_NO_ERR;
    return (pmem);                                          (7)
}
```

Figure 7.4 shows how the data structures look when OSMemCreate() completes successfully. Note that the memory blocks are shown linked one after the other. At run time, as you allocate and deallocate memory blocks, the blocks will most likely not be in this order.

7.02 Obtaining a Memory Block, OSMemGet()

Your application can get a memory block from one of the created memory partitions by calling OSMemGet(). Simply use the pointer returned by OSMemCreate() in the call to OSMemGet() to specify which partition the memory block will come from. Obviously, your application needs to know how big the memory block obtained is so that it doesn't exceed its storage capacity. In other words, you must not use more memory than is available from the memory block. For example, if a partition contains 32-byte blocks, then your application can use up to 32 bytes. When you are done using the block, you must return it to the proper memory partition [see section 7.03, Returning a Memory Block, OSMemPut()].

Figure 7.4   OSMemCreate().

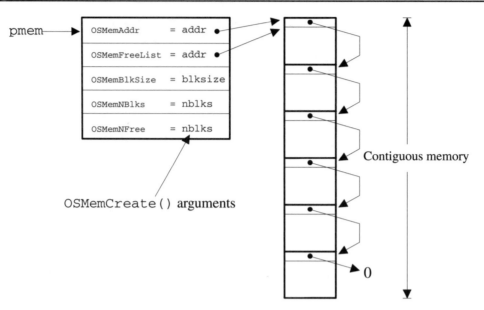

OSMemCreate() arguments

Listing 7.4 shows the code for OSMemGet(). The pointer specifies the partition from which you want to get a memory block [L7.4(1)]. OSMemGet() first checks to see if there are free blocks available [L7.4(2)]. If a block is available, it is removed from the free list [L7.4(3)]. The free list is then updated [L7.4(4)] so that it points to the next free memory block, and the number of blocks is decremented, indicating that it has been allocated [L7.4(5)]. The pointer to the allocated block is finally returned to your application [L7.4(6)].

Listing 7.4   OSMemGet().

```
void *OSMemGet (OS_MEM *pmem, INT8U *err)                          (1)
{
    void    *pblk;



    OS_ENTER_CRITICAL();
    if (pmem->OSMemNFree > 0) {                                    (2)
        pblk               = pmem->OSMemFreeList;                  (3)
        pmem->OSMemFreeList = *(void **)pblk;                      (4)
        pmem->OSMemNFree--;                                        (5)
        OS_EXIT_CRITICAL();
        *err = OS_NO_ERR;
        return (pblk);                                            (6)
    } else {
```

Listing 7.4   OSMemGet (). (Continued)

```
        OS_EXIT_CRITICAL();
        *err = OS_MEM_NO_FREE_BLKS;
        return ((void *)0);
    }
}
```

Note that you can call this function from an ISR because, if a memory block is not available, there is no waiting and the ISR simply receives a NULL pointer.

7.03 Returning a Memory Block, OSMemPut ()

When your application is done with a memory block, it must be returned to the appropriate partition. This is accomplished by calling OSMemPut(). You should note that OSMemPut() has no way of knowing whether the memory block returned to the partition belongs to that partition. In other words, if you allocate a memory block from a partition containing blocks of 32 bytes, then you should not return this block to a memory partition containing blocks of 120 bytes. The next time an application requests a block from the 120-byte partition, it will only get 32 valid bytes; the remaining 88 bytes may belong to some other task(s). This could certainly make your system crash.

Listing 7.5 shows the code for OSMemPut(). Simply pass OSMemPut() the address of the memory control block to which the memory block belongs [L7.5(1)]. OSMemPut() then checks to see that the memory partition is not already full [L7.5(2)]. This situation would certainly indicate that something went wrong during the allocation/deallocation process. If the memory partition can accept another memory block, it is inserted into the linked list of free blocks [L7.5(3)]. Finally, the number of memory blocks in the memory partition is incremented [L7.5(4)].

Listing 7.5   OSMemPut ().

```
INT8U OSMemPut (OS_MEM  *pmem, void *pblk)                          (1)
{
    OS_ENTER_CRITICAL();
    if (pmem->OSMemNFree >= pmem->OSMemNBlks) {                     (2)
        OS_EXIT_CRITICAL();
        return (OS_MEM_FULL);
    }
    *(void **)pblk       = pmem->OSMemFreeList;                     (3)
    pmem->OSMemFreeList = pblk;
    pmem->OSMemNFree++;                                             (4)
    OS_EXIT_CRITICAL();
    return (OS_NO_ERR);
}
```

7

7.04 Obtaining Status of a Memory Partition, `OSMemQuery()`

`OSMemQuery()` is used to obtain information about a memory partition. Specifically, your application can determine how many memory blocks are free, how many memory blocks have been used (i.e., allocated), the size of each memory block (in bytes), etc. This information is placed in a data structure called `OS_MEM_DATA`, as shown in Listing 7.6.

Listing 7.6   Data structure used to obtain status from a partition.

```
typedef struct {
    void   *OSAddr;       /* Points to beginning address of memory partition  */
    void   *OSFreeList;   /* Points to beginning of free list of memory blocks */
    INT32U OSBlkSize;     /* Size (in bytes) of each memory block             */
    INT32U OSNBlks;       /* Total number of blocks in the partition          */
    INT32U OSNFree;       /* Number of memory blocks free                     */
    INT32U OSNUsed;       /* Number of memory blocks used                     */
} OS_MEM_DATA;
```

The code for `OSMemQuery()` is shown in Listing 7.7. As you can see, all the fields found in `OS_MEM` are copied to the `OS_MEM_DATA` data structure with interrupts disabled [L7.7(1)]. This ensures that the fields will not be altered until they are all copied. You should also notice that computation of the number of blocks used is performed outside of the critical section because it's done using the local copy of the data [L7.7(2)].

Listing 7.7   `OSMemQuery()`.

```
INT8U OSMemQuery (OS_MEM *pmem, OS_MEM_DATA *pdata)
{
    OS_ENTER_CRITICAL();
    pdata->OSAddr     = pmem->OSMemAddr;                         (1)
    pdata->OSFreeList = pmem->OSMemFreeList;
    pdata->OSBlkSize  = pmem->OSMemBlkSize;
    pdata->OSNBlks    = pmem->OSMemNBlks;
    pdata->OSNFree    = pmem->OSMemNFree;
    OS_EXIT_CRITICAL();
    pdata->OSNUsed    = pdata->OSNBlks - pdata->OSNFree;         (2)
    return (OS_NO_ERR);
}
```

7.05 *Using Memory Partitions*

Figure 7.5 shows an example of how you can use the dynamic memory allocation feature of μC/OS-II, as well as its message-passing capability (see Chapter 6). Also, refer to Listing 7.8 for the pseudocode of the two tasks shown. The numbers in parenthesis in Figure 7.5 correspond to the appropriate action in Listing 7.8.

The first task reads and checks the value of analog inputs (pressures, temperatures, voltages) and sends a message to the second task if any of the analog inputs exceed a threshold. The message sent contains a time stamp, information about which channel had the error, an error code, an indication of the severity of the error, and any other information you can think of.

Error handling in this example is centralized. This means that other tasks, or even ISRs, can post error messages to the error-handling task. The error-handling task could be responsible for displaying error messages on a monitor (a display), logging errors to a disk, or dispatching other tasks that could take corrective actions based on the error.

Figure 7.5 *Using dynamic memory allocation.*

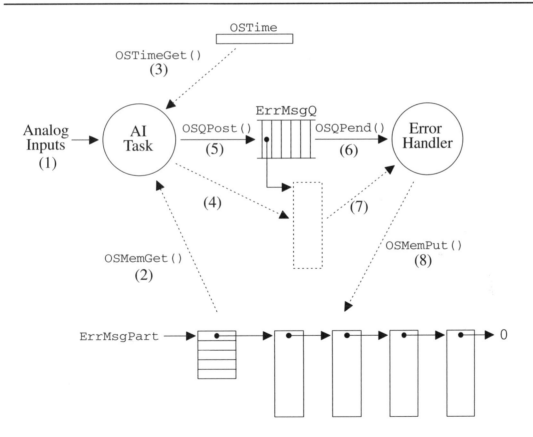

Listing 7.8   Scanning analog inputs and reporting errors.

```
AnalogInputTask()
{
    for (;;) {
        for (all analog inputs to read) {
            Read analog input;                                          (1)
            if (analog input exceed threshold) {
                Get memory block;                                       (2)
                Get current system time (in clock ticks);               (3)
                Store the following items in the memory block:          (4)
                    System time (i.e. a time stamp);
                    The channel that exceeded the threshold;
                    An error code;
                    The severity of the error;
                    Etc.
                Post the error message to error queue;                  (5)
                    (A pointer to the memory block containing the data)
            }
        }
        Delay task until it's time to sample analog inputs again;
    }
}




ErrorHandlerTask()
{
    for (;;) {
        Wait for message from error queue;                              (6)
            (Gets a pointer to a memory block containing information
             about the error reported)
        Read the message and take action based on error reported;       (7)
        Return the memory block to the memory partition;                (8)
    }
}
```

7.06 *Waiting for Memory Blocks from a Partition*

Sometimes it's useful to have a task wait for a memory block in case a partition runs out of blocks. µC/OS-II doesn't support "pending" on partitions, but you can support this requirement by adding a counting semaphore (see section 6.05, Semaphores) to guard the memory partition. To obtain a memory block, simply obtain a semaphore then call OSMemGet(). The whole process is shown in Listing 7.9.

First, declare your system objects [L7.9(1)]. Note that I used hard-coded constants for clarity. You would certainly create #define constants in a real application. Initialize µC/OS-II by calling OSInit() [L7.9(2)] then create a semaphore with an initial count corresponding to the number of blocks in the partition [L7.9(3)]. Next, create the partition [L7.9(4)] and one of the tasks [L7.9(5)] that will be accessing the partition. By now, you should be able to figure out what you need to do to add the other tasks. It would obviously not make much sense to use a semaphore if only one task is using memory blocks — there would be no need to ensure mutual exclusion! In fact, it wouldn't even make sense to use partitions unless you intend to share memory blocks with other tasks. Multitasking is then started by calling OSStart() [L7.9(6)]. When the task executes, it obtains a memory block [L7.9(8)] only if a semaphore is available [L7.9(7)]. Once the semaphore is available, the memory block is obtained. There is no need to check for an error code from OSSemPend() because the only way µC/OS-II will return to this task is if a memory block is released. Also, you don't need the error code from OSMemGet() for the same reason — you must have at least one block in the partition in order for the task to resume. When the task is finished with a memory block, it simply returns it to the partition [L7.9(9)] and signals the semaphore [L7.9(10)].

Listing 7.9 *Waiting for memory blocks from a partition.*

```
OS_EVENT   *SemaphorePtr;                                        (1)
OS_MEM     *PartitionPtr;
INT8U       Partition[100][32];
OS_STK      TaskStk[1000];


void main (void)
{
    INT8U err;

    OSInit();                                                    (2)
    .

    .

    SemaphorePtr = OSSemCreate(100);                             (3)
    PartitionPtr = OSMemCreate(Partition, 100, 32, &err);        (4)
    .

    OSTaskCreate(Task, (void *)0, &TaskStk[999], &err);          (5)
    .

    OSStart();                                                   (6)
}
```

Listing 7.9   Waiting for memory blocks from a partition. (Continued)

```
void Task (void *pdata)
{
    INT8U  err;
    INT8U *pblock;


    for (;;) {
        OSSemPend(SemaphorePtr, 0, &err);                    (7)
        pblock = OSMemGet(PartitionPtr, &err);               (8)
        .

        .   /* Use the memory block */

        .
        OSMemPut(PartitionPtr, pblock);                      (9)
        OSSemPost(SemaphorePtr);                             (10)
    }
}
```

8

Porting µC/OS-II

This chapter describes in general terms what needs to be done in order to adapt µC/OS-II to different processors. Adapting a real-time kernel to a microprocessor or a microcontroller is called a port. Most of µC/OS-II is written in C for portability; however, it is still necessary to write some processor-specific code in C and assembly language. Specifically, µC/OS-II manipulates processor registers, which can only be done through assembly language. Porting µC/OS-II to different processors is relatively easy because µC/OS-II was designed to be portable. If you already have a port for the processor you are intending to use, you don't need to read this chapter, unless of course you want to know how µC/OS-II processor-specific code works.

A processor can run µC/OS-II if it satisfies the following general requirements:

1. The processor has a C compiler that generates reentrant code.

2. Interrupts can be disabled and enabled from C.

3. The processor supports interrupts and can provide an interrupt that occurs at regular intervals (typically between 10 and 100Hz).

4. The processor supports a hardware stack that can accommodate a fair amount of data (possibly many kilobytes).

5. The processor has instructions to load and store the stack pointer and other CPU registers, either on the stack or in memory.

Processors like the Motorola 6805 series do not satisfy requirements number 4 and 5, so µC/OS-II cannot run on such processors.

Figure 8.1 shows the µC/OS-II architecture and its relationship with the hardware. When you use µC/OS-II in an application, you are responsible for providing the Application Software and the µC/OS-II Configuration sections. This book and diskette contain all the source code for the Processor-Independent Code section as well as the Processor-Specific Code section for the Intel 80x86, real mode, large model. If you intend to use µC/OS-II on a different processor, you need to either obtain a copy of a port for the processor you intend to use or write one yourself if the desired processor port is not available. Check the official µC/OS-II Web site at www.uCOS-II.com for a list of available ports.

Figure 8.1   µC/OS-II hardware/software architecture.

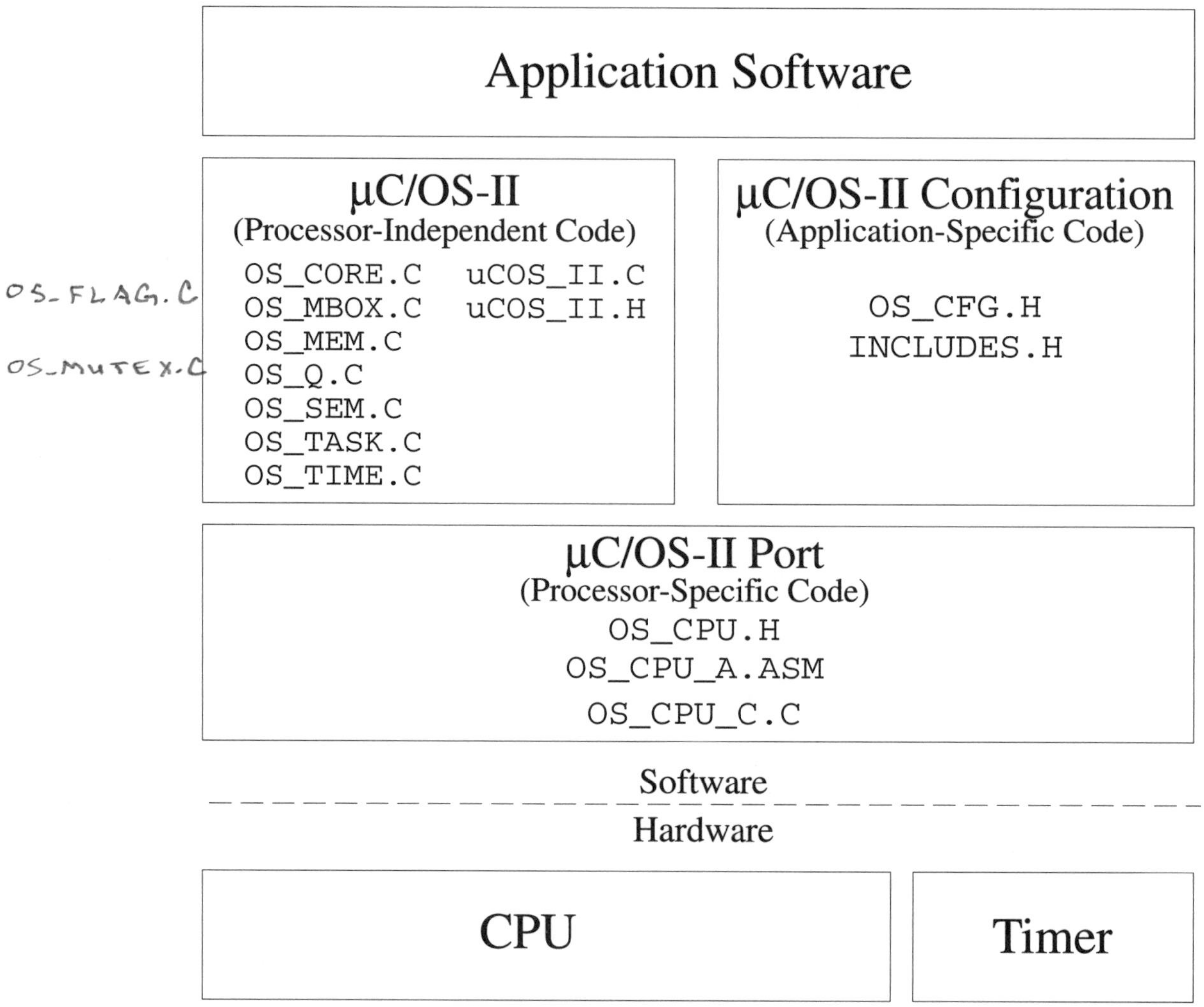

```
┌──────────────────────────────────────────────────────────────┐
│                    Application Software                        │
└──────────────────────────────────────────────────────────────┘

┌──────────────────────────┐  ┌──────────────────────────────────┐
│        µC/OS-II           │  │     µC/OS-II Configuration        │
│ (Processor-Independent    │  │    (Application-Specific Code)     │
│        Code)              │  │                                   │
│  OS_CORE.C    uCOS_II.C   │  │          OS_CFG.H                  │
│  OS_MBOX.C    uCOS_II.H   │  │          INCLUDES.H               │
│  OS_MEM.C                 │  │                                   │
│  OS_Q.C                   │  │                                   │
│  OS_SEM.C                 │  │                                   │
│  OS_TASK.C                │  │                                   │
│  OS_TIME.C                │  │                                   │
└──────────────────────────┘  └──────────────────────────────────┘

┌──────────────────────────────────────────────────────────────┐
│                      µC/OS-II Port                             │
│                 (Processor-Specific Code)                      │
│                       OS_CPU.H                                 │
│                      OS_CPU_A.ASM                              │
│                      OS_CPU_C.C                                │
└──────────────────────────────────────────────────────────────┘
                         Software
- - - - - - - - - - - - - - - - - - - - - - - - - - - - - - - -
                         Hardware
┌──────────────────────────────────┐  ┌────────────────────────┐
│              CPU                  │  │         Timer          │
└──────────────────────────────────┘  └────────────────────────┘
```

[handwritten annotations in left margin: OS_FLAG.C, OS_MUTEX.C]

Porting µC/OS-II is actually quite straightforward once you understand the subtleties of the target processor and the C compiler you are using. If your processor and compiler satisfy the µC/OS-II requirements and you have all the necessary tools at your disposal, porting consists of:

- setting the value of one #define constant (OS_CPU.H),
- declaring 10 data types (OS_CPU.H),
- declaring three #define macros (OS_CPU.H),
- writing six simple functions in C (OS_CPU_C.C), and
- writing four assembly language functions (OS_CPU_A.ASM).

Depending on the processor, a port can consist of writing or changing between 50 and 300 lines of code and could take anywhere from a few hours to about a week to accomplish.

Once you have a port of µC/OS-II for your processor, you need to verify its operation. Testing a multitasking real-time kernel such as µC/OS-II is not as complicated as you may think. You should test your port without application code. In other words, test the operations of the kernel by itself. There are two reasons to do this. First, you don't want to complicate things anymore than they need to be. Second, if something doesn't work, you know that the problem lies in the port as opposed to your application. Start with a couple of simple tasks and only the ticker interrupt service routine. Once you get multitasking going, it's quite simple to add your application tasks.

8.00 Development Tools

As previously stated, you need a C compiler for the processor you intend to use in order to port µC/OS-II. Because µC/OS-II is a preemptive kernel, you should only use a C compiler that generates reentrant code. It must also support assembly language programming. Most C compilers designed for embedded systems also include an assembler, a linker, and a locator. The linker is used to combine object files (compiled and assembled files) from different modules, and the locator allows you to place the code and data anywhere in the memory map of the target processor. Your C compiler must also provide a mechanism to disable and enable interrupts from C. Some compilers allow you to insert in-line assembly language statements into your C source code. This makes it quite easy to insert the proper processor instructions to enable and disable interrupts. Other compilers actually contain language extensions to enable and disable interrupts directly from C.

8.01 Directories and Files

The installation program provided on the distribution diskette installs µC/OS-II and the port for the Intel 80x86 (real mode, large model) on your hard disk. I devised a consistent directory structure that allows you to find the files for the desired target processor easily. If you add a port for another processor, you should consider following the same conventions.

All ports should be placed under \SOFTWARE\uCOS-II on your hard drive. The source code for each microprocessor or microcontroller port *must* be found in either two or three files: OS_CPU.H, OS_CPU_C.C, and, optionally, OS_CPU_A.ASM. The assembly language file is optional because some compilers allow you to have in-line assembly language, so you can place the needed assembly language code directly in OS_CPU_C.C. The directory in which the port is located determines which processor you are using. Examples of directories where different ports would be stored are shown in the table on page 194. Note that each directory contains the same filenames, even though they have totally different targets.

Intel/AMD 80186	\SOFTWARE\uCOS-II\Ix86S
	\OS_CPU.H
	\OS_CPU_A.ASM
	\OS_CPU_C.C
	\SOFTWARE\uCOS-II\Ix86L
	\OS_CPU.H
	\OS_CPU_A.ASM
	\OS_CPU_C.C
Motorola 68HC11	\SOFTWARE\uCOS-II\68HC11
	\OS_CPU.H
	\OS_CPU_A.ASM
	\OS_CPU_C.C

8.02 INCLUDES.H

As mentioned in Chapter 1, INCLUDES.H is a *master* include file found at the top of all .C files:

```
#include "includes.h".
```

INCLUDES.H allows every .C file in your project to be written without concern about which header file will actually be needed. The only drawback to having a master include file is that INCLUDES.H may include header files that are not pertinent to the actual .C file being compiled. This means that each file will require extra time to compile. This inconvenience is offset by code portability. You can edit INCLUDES.H to add your own header files, but your header files should be added at the end of the list.

8.03 OS_CPU.H   *Processor Specific Code*

OS_CPU.H contains processor- and implementation-specific #defines constants, macros, and type-defs. The general layout of OS_CPU.H is shown in Listing 8.1.

Listing 8.1   OS_CPU.H.

```
#ifdef   OS_CPU_GLOBALS
#define OS_CPU_EXT
#else
#define OS_CPU_EXT   extern
#endif
```

Listing 8.1 `OS_CPU.H.` *(Continued)*

```
/*
*********************************************************************************
*                              DATA TYPES
*                            (Compiler Specific)
*********************************************************************************
*/

typedef unsigned char   BOOLEAN;
typedef unsigned char   INT8U;     /* Unsigned  8 bit quantity          */   (1)
typedef signed   char   INT8S;     /* Signed    8 bit quantity          */
typedef unsigned int    INT16U;    /* Unsigned 16 bit quantity          */
typedef signed   int    INT16S;    /* Signed   16 bit quantity          */
typedef unsigned long   INT32U;    /* Unsigned 32 bit quantity          */
typedef signed   long   INT32S;    /* Signed   32 bit quantity          */
typedef float           FP32;      /* Single precision floating point */   (2)
typedef double          FP64;      /* Double precision floating point */


typedef unsigned int    OS_STK;    /* Each stack entry is 16-bit wide */


/*
*********************************************************************************
*                            Processor Specifics
*********************************************************************************
*/

#define  OS_ENTER_CRITICAL()   ???  /* Disable interrupts        */   (3)
#define  OS_EXIT_CRITICAL()    ???  /* Enable  interrupts        */

#define  OS_STK_GROWTH          1    /* Define stack growth: 1=Down, 0=Up */   (4)

#define  OS_TASK_SW()          ???                                    (5)
```

8.03.01 *Compiler-Specific Data Types*

Because different microprocessors have different word lengths, the port of µC/OS-II includes a series of type definitions that ensures portability. Specifically, µC/OS-II code never makes use of C's short, int, and long data types because they are inherently nonportable. Instead, I defined integer data types that are both portable and intuitive [L8.1(1)]. Also, for convenience, I have included floating-point data types [L8.1(2)] even though µC/OS-II doesn't make use of floating-point numbers.

The INT16U data type, for example, always represents a 16-bit unsigned integer. µC/OS-II and your application code can now assume that the range of values for variables declared with this type is from 0 to 65,535. A µC/OS-II port to a 32-bit processor could mean that an INT16U is actually declared as an unsigned short instead of an unsigned int. Where µC/OS-II is concerned, however, it still deals with an INT16U.

You must tell µC/OS-II the data type of a task's stack. This is done by declaring the proper C data type for OS_STK. If stack elements on your processor are 32 bits and your compiler documentation specifies that an int is 32 bits, declare OS_STK as being type unsigned int. All task stacks must be declared using OS_STK as its data type.

All you have to do is consult the compiler's manual and find the standard C data types that correspond to the types expected by µC/OS-II.

8.03.02 *OS_ENTER_CRITICAL(), and OS_EXIT_CRITICAL()*

µC/OS-II, like all real-time kernels, needs to disable interrupts in order to access critical sections of code and re-enable interrupts when done. This allows µC/OS-II to protect critical code from being entered simultaneously from either multiple tasks or Interrupt Service Routines (ISRs). The interrupt disable time is one of the most important specifications that a real-time kernel vendor can provide because it affects the responsiveness of your system to real-time events. µC/OS-II tries to keep the interrupt disable time to a minimum, but with µC/OS-II, interrupt disable time is largely dependent on the processor architecture and the quality of the code generated by the compiler. Every processor generally provides instructions to disable/enable interrupts, and your C compiler must have a mechanism to perform these operations directly from C. Some compilers allow you to insert in-line assembly language statements into your C source code. This makes it quite easy to insert processor instructions to enable and disable interrupts. Other compilers actually contain language extensions to enable and disable interrupts directly from C. To hide the implementation method chosen by the compiler manufacturer, µC/OS-II defines two *macros* to disable and enable interrupts: OS_ENTER_CRITICAL() and OS_EXIT_CRITICAL(), respectively [L8.1(3)], which wrap critical sections.

```
{
    OS_ENTER_CRITICAL();
    /* µC/OS-II critical code section */
    OS_EXIT_CRITICAL();
}
```

Method 1

The first and simplest way to implement these two macros is to invoke the processor instruction to disable interrupts for OS_ENTER_CRITICAL() and the enable interrupts instruction for OS_EXIT_CRITICAL(). However, there is a little problem with this scenario. If you call the µC/OS-II function with interrupts disabled, on return from µC/OS-II, interrupts would be enabled! If you disable interrupts, you may want them to be disabled on return from the µC/OS-II function. In this case, this implementation would not be adequate.

Method 2

The second way to implement OS_ENTER_CRITICAL() is to save the interrupt disable status onto the stack and then disable interrupts. OS_EXIT_CRITICAL() is simply implemented by restoring the interrupt status from the stack. Using this scheme, if you call a µC/OS-II service with interrupts either enabled or disabled, the status is preserved across the call. If you call a μC/OS-II service with interrupts disabled, you are potentially extending the interrupt latency of your application. Your application can use OS_ENTER_CRITICAL() and OS_EXIT_CRITICAL() to protect critical sections of code as well. Be careful, however, because your application will crash if you disable interrupts before calling a service such as OSTimeDly(). This happens because the task is suspended until time expires, but because interrupts are disabled, you never service the tick interrupt! Obviously, all the PEND calls are also subject to this problem, so be careful. As a general rule, you should always call μC/OS-II services with interrupts enabled!

The question is: which method is better? Well, that all depends on what you are willing to sacrifice. If you don't care whether interrupts are enabled in your application after calling a μC/OS-II service, you should opt for the first method for performance. If you want to preserve the interrupt disable status across μC/OS-II service calls, then obviously the second method is for you.

Just to give you an example, disabling interrupts on an Intel 80186 is done by executing the STI instruction, and enabling interrupts is done by executing the CLI instruction. You can thus implement the macros as follows:

```
#define OS_ENTER_CRITICAL()    asm CLI
#define OS_EXIT_CRITICAL()     asm STI
```

Both the CLI and STI instructions execute in less that two clock cycles each on this processor (i.e., a total of four cycles). To preserve the interrupt status, you need to implement the macros as follows:

8

```
#define OS_ENTER_CRITICAL()    asm PUSHF; CLI
#define OS_EXIT_CRITICAL()     asm POPF
```

In this case, OS_ENTER_CRITICAL() consumes 12 clock cycles while OS_EXIT_CRITICAL() uses up another eight clock cycles (a total of 20 cycles). Preserving the state of the interrupt disable status would thus take 16 clock cycles longer than simply disabling/enabling interrupts (at least on the 80186). Obviously, if you have a faster processor, such as an Intel Pentium II, then the difference would be minimal.

8.03.03 OS_STK_GROWTH

The stack on most microprocessors and microcontrollers grows from high to low memory. However, some processors work the other way around. μC/OS-II has been designed to be able to handle either flavor by specifying which way the stack grows through the configuration constant OS_STK_GROWTH [L8.1(4)], as shown below.

Set OS_STK_GROWTH to 0 for low to high memory stack growth.
Set OS_STK_GROWTH to 1 for high to low memory stack growth.

8.03.04 OS_TASK_SW()   *Pg 85*

OS_TASK_SW() [L8.1(5)] is a macro that is invoked when μC/OS-II switches from a low-priority task to the highest priority task. OS_TASK_SW() is always called from task-level code. Another mechanism, OSIntExit(), is used to perform a context switch when an ISR makes a higher priority task ready for

Pg 94

execution. A context switch simply consists of saving the processor registers on the stack of the task being suspended and restoring the registers of the higher priority task from its stack.

In µC/OS-II, the stack frame for a ready task always looks as if an interrupt has just occurred and all processor registers were saved onto it. In other words, all that µC/OS-II has to do to run a ready task is to restore all processor registers from the task's stack and execute a return from interrupt. To switch context, implement OS_TASK_SW() to simulate an interrupt. Most processors provide either software interrupt or TRAP instructions to accomplish this. The ISR or trap handler (also called the exception handler) must vector to the assembly language function OSCtxSw() (see section 8.04.02).

For example, a port for an Intel or AMD 80x86 processor would use an INT instruction. The interrupt handler needs to vector to OSCtxSw(). A port for the Motorola 68HC11 processor would most likely uses the SWI instruction. Again, the SWI handler is OSCtxSw(). Finally, a port for a Motorola 680x0/CPU32 processor probably uses one of the 16 TRAP instructions. Of course, the selected TRAP handler is none other than OSCtxSw().

Some processors, like the Zilog Z80, do not provide a software interrupt mechanism. In this case, you need to simulate the stack frame as closely to an interrupt stack frame as you can. OS_TASK_SW() would simply call OSCtxSw() instead of vectoring to it. The Z80 is a processor that has been ported to µC/OS and is portable to µC/OS-II.

8.04 OS_CPU_A.ASM

A µC/OS-II port requires that you write four fairly simple assembly language functions:

```
OSStartHighRdy()
OSCtxSw()
OSIntCtxSw()
OSTickISR()
```

If your compiler supports in-line assembly language code, you could actually place all the processor-specific code into OS_CPU_C.C instead of having a separate assembly language file.

8.04.01 OSStartHighRdy()

The function that starts the highest priority task ready to run is called by OSStart() and is shown below. Before you can call OSStart(), however, you must have created at least one of your tasks [see OSTaskCreate() and OSTaskCreateExt()]. OSStartHighRdy() assumes that OSTCBHighRdy points to the task control block of the task with the highest priority. As mentioned previously, in µC/OS-II, the stack frame for a ready task always looks as if an interrupt has just occurred and all processor registers were saved onto it. To run the highest priority task, all you need to do is restore all processor registers from the task's stack in the proper order and execute a return from interrupt. To simplify things, the stack pointer is always stored at the beginning of the task control block (i.e., its OS_TCB). In other words, the stack pointer of the task to resume is always stored at offset 0 in the OS_TCB.

```
void OSStartHighRdy (void)
{
    Call user definable OSTaskSwHook();
    Get the stack pointer of the task to resume:
        Stack pointer = OSTCBHighRdy->OSTCBStkPtr;
```

```
        OSRunning = TRUE;
        Restore all processor registers from the new task's stack;
        Execute a return from interrupt instruction;
}
```

Note that OSStartHighRdy() must call OSTaskSwHook() because you are basically doing a "half" context switch — you are restoring the registers of the highest priority task. OSTaskSwHook() can examine OSRunning to tell it whether OSTaskSwHook() was called from OSStartHighRdy() (OSRunning is FALSE) or from a regular context switch (OSRunning is TRUE).

OSStartHighRdy() must also set OSRunning to TRUE before the highest priority task is restored, but after calling OSTaskSwHook().

8.04.02   OSCtxSw()

As previously mentioned, a task-level context switch is accomplished by issuing a software interrupt instruction or, depending on the processor, executing a TRAP instruction. The interrupt service routine, trap, or exception handler must vector to OSCtxSw().

The sequence of events that leads µC/OS-II to vector to OSCtxSw() begins when the current task calls a service provided by µC/OS-II, which causes a higher priority task to be ready to run. At the end of the service call, µC/OS-II calls OSSched(), which concludes that the current task is no longer the most important task to run. OSSched() loads the address of the highest priority task into OSTCBHigh-Rdy then executes the software interrupt or trap instruction by invoking the macro OS_TASK_SW(). Note that the variable OSTCBCur already contains a pointer to the current task's task control block, OS_TCB. The software interrupt instruction (or trap) forces some of the processor registers (most likely the return address and the processor's status word) onto the current task's stack, then the processor vectors to OSCtxSw(). The pseudocode for OSCtxSw() is shown in Listing 8.2. This code must be written in assembly language because you cannot access CPU registers directly from C. Note that interrupts are disabled during OSCtxSw() and also during execution of the user-definable function OSTaskSwHook().

Listing 8.2   Pseudocode for OSCtxSw().

```
void OSCtxSw(void)
{
    Save processor registers;
    Save the current task's stack pointer into the current task's OS_TCB:
        OSTCBCur->OSTCBStkPtr = Stack pointer;
    Call user definable OSTaskSwHook();
    OSTCBCur  = OSTCBHighRdy;
    OSPrioCur = OSPrioHighRdy;
    Get the stack pointer of the task to resume:
        Stack pointer = OSTCBHighRdy->OSTCBStkPtr;
    Restore all processor registers from the new task's stack;
    Execute a return from interrupt instruction;
}
```

8.04.03 *OSIntCtxSw()*

OSIntCtxSw() is called by OSIntExit() to perform a context switch from an ISR. Because OSInt-CtxSw() is called from an ISR, it is assumed that all the processor registers are properly saved onto the interrupted task's stack. In fact, there are more things on the stack frame than we need. OSIntCtxSw() has to clean up the stack so that the interrupted task is left with just the proper stack frame content.

To understand OSIntCtxSw(), look at the sequence of events that leads µC/OS-II to call the function. You may want to refer to Figure 8.2 to help understand the following description. Assume that interrupts are not nested (i.e., an ISR will not be interrupted), interrupts are enabled, and the processor is executing task-level code. When an interrupt arrives, the processor completes the current instruction, recognizes the interrupt, and initiates an interrupt-handling procedure. This generally consist of pushing the processor status register and the return address of the interrupted task onto the stack [F8.2(1)]. *Which* registers and the *order* in which they are pushed onto the stack is irrelevant.

Figure 8.2   *Stack contents during an ISR.*

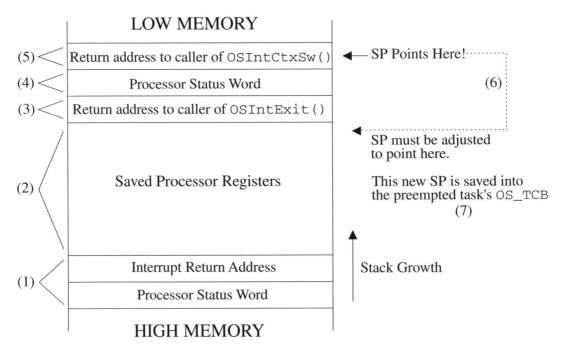

The CPU then vectors to the proper ISR. µC/OS-II requires that your ISR begins by saving the rest of the processor registers [F8.2(2)]. Once the registers are saved, µC/OS-II requires you to either call OSIntEnter() or increment the global variable OSIntNesting by one. At this point, the interrupted task's stack frame only contains the register contents of the interrupted task. The ISR can now start servicing the interrupting device and possibly make a higher priority task ready. This occurs if the ISR sends a message to a task [by calling OSMboxPost() or OSQPost()], resumes a task [by calling OSTaskResume()], or invokes OSTimeTick() or OSTimeDlyResume().

Assume that a higher priority task is made ready to run. µC/OS-II requires that your ISR calls OSIntExit() when the ISR completes servicing the interrupting device. OSIntExit() basically tell µC/OS-II that it's time to return to task-level code. The call to OSIntExit() causes the return address of the caller to be pushed onto the interrupted task's stack [F8.2(3)].

OSIntExit() starts by disabling interrupts because it needs to execute critical code. Depending on how OS_ENTER_CRITICAL() is implemented (see section 8.03.02), the processor's status register could be pushed onto the interrupted task's stack [F8.2(4)]. OSIntExit() notices that the interrupted task is no longer the task that needs to run because a higher priority task is now ready. In this case, the pointer OSTCBHighRdy is made to point to the new task's OS_TCB, and OSIntExit() calls OSIntCtxSw() to perform the context switch. Calling OSIntCtxSw() causes the return address to be pushed onto the interrupted task's stack [F8.2(5)].

As you switch context, you only want to leave items [F8.2(1)] and [F8.2(2)] on the stack and ignore items F8.2(3), (4), and (5). This is accomplished by adding a constant to the stack pointer [F8.2(6)]. The *exact* amount of stack adjustment *must* be known and this value greatly depends on the processor being ported (an address can be 16, 32, or 64 bits), the compiler being used, compiler options, memory model, and so on. Also, the processor status word could be 8, 16, 32, or even 64 bits wide, and OSIntExit() may allocate local variables. Some processors allow you to add a constant to the stack pointer directly; others don't. In the latter case, simply execute the appropriate number of pop instructions to one of the processor registers to accomplish the same thing. Once the stack is adjusted, the new stack pointer can be saved into the OS_TCB of the task being switched-out [F8.2(7)].

OSIntCtxSw() is the only function in µC/OS-II (and also µC/OS) that is compiler specific; it has generated more e-mail than any other aspect of µC/OS. If your port crashes after a few context switches, you should suspect that the stack is not being properly adjusted in OSIntCtxSw().

8

The pseudocode for OSIntCtxSw() is shown in Listing 8.3. This code must be written in assembly language because you cannot access CPU registers directly from C. If your C compiler supports in-line assembly, put the code for OSIntCtxSw() in OS_CPU_C.C instead of OS_CPU_A.ASM. As you can see, except for the first line, the code is identical to OSCtxSw(). You can thus reduce the amount of code in the port by "jumping" to the appropriate section of code in OSCtxSw().

Listing 8.3   Pseudocode for OSIntCtxSw().

```
void OSIntCtxSw(void)
{
    Adjust the stack pointer to remove calls to:
        OSIntExit(),
        OSIntCtxSw(), and possibly the push of the processor status word;
    Save the current task's stack pointer into the current task's OS_TCB:
        OSTCBCur->OSTCBStkPtr = Stack pointer;
    Call user-definable OSTaskSwHook();
    OSTCBCur  = OSTCBHighRdy;
    OSPrioCur = OSPrioHighRdy;
```

Listing 8.3   Pseudocode for OSIntCtxSw(). (Continued)

```
    Get the stack pointer of the task to resume:
        Stack pointer = OSTCBHighRdy->OSTCBStkPtr;
    Restore all processor registers from the new task's stack;
    Execute a return from interrupt instruction;
}
```

8.04.04 *OSTickISR()*

µC/OS-II requires you to provide a periodic time source to keep track of time delays and timeouts. A tick should occur between 10 and 100 times per second, or Hertz. To accomplish this, either dedicate a hardware timer or obtain 50/60Hz from an AC power line.

You must enable ticker interrupts after multitasking has started; that is, after calling OSStart(). In other words, you should initialize and tick interrupts in the first task that executes following a call to OSStart(). A common mistake is to enable ticker interrupts between calling OSInit() and OSStart(), as shown in Listing 8.4:

Listing 8.4   Incorrect place to start the tick interrupt.

```
void main(void)
{
    .
    .
    OSInit();                   /* Initialize µC/OS-II                 */
    .
    .
    /* Application initialization code ...                             */
    /* ... Create at least on task by calling OSTaskCreate()          */
    .
    .
    Enable TICKER interrupts; /* DO NOT DO THIS HERE!!!                */
    .
    .
    OSStart();                  /* Start multitasking                  */
}
```

Potentially, the tick interrupt could be serviced before µC/OS-II starts the first task. At that point, µC/OS-II is in an unknown state and your application will crash.

The pseudocode for the tick ISR is shown in Listing 8.5. This code must be written in assembly language because you cannot access CPU registers directly from C. If your processor is able to increment OSIntNesting with a single instruction, there is no need for you to call OSIntEnter(). Incrementing OSIntNesting is much quicker than going through the overhead of the function call and return. OSIntEnter() only increments OSIntNesting while protecting that increment in a critical section.

Listing 8.5   Pseudocode for tick ISR.

```
void OSTickISR(void)
{
    Save processor registers;
    Call OSIntEnter() or increment OSIntNesting;

    Call OSTimeTick();

    Call OSIntExit();
    Restore processor registers;
    Execute a return from interrupt instruction;
}
```

8.05   OS_CPU_C.C

A µC/OS-II port requires that you write six fairly simple C functions:

OSTaskStkInit()
OSTaskCreateHook()
OSTaskDelHook()
OSTaskSwHook()
OSTaskStatHook()
OSTimeTickHook()

[handwritten: ? Pg 198-199 · "...must call OSTaskSwHook()?]

The only necessary function is OSTaskStkInit(). The other five functions must be declared but don't need to contain code.

8.05.01   OSTaskStkInit()   *[handwritten: Pg 106]*

This function is called by OSTaskCreate() and OSTaskCreateExt() to initialize the stack frame of a task so that the stack looks as if an interrupt just occurred and all the processor registers were pushed onto that stack. Figure 8.3 shows what OSTaskStkInit() puts on the stack of the task being created. Note that I assume a stack grows from high to low memory. The discussion that follows applies just as well for a stack growing in the opposite direction.

When you create a task, you pass the start address of the task, a pointer called pdata, the task's top-of-stack, and the task's priority to OSTaskCreate() or OSTaskCreateExt(). OSTaskCreate-Ext() requires additional arguments, but they are irrelevant in discussing OSTaskStkInit(). To properly initialize the stack frame, OSTaskStkInit() requires only the first three arguments just mentioned in addition to an option value, which is only available in OSTaskCreateExt().

8

Figure 8.3   Stack frame initialization with pdata passed on the stack.

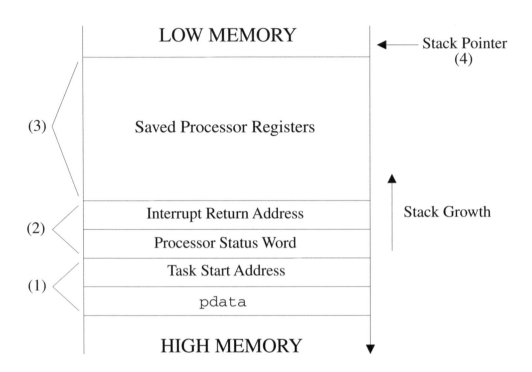

Recall that under µC/OS-II, a task is an infinite loop but otherwise looks just like any other C function. When the task is started by µC/OS-II, it receives an argument just as if it was called by another function:

```
void MyTask (void *pdata)
{
    /* Do something with argument 'pdata' */
    for (;;) {
        /* Task code                       */
    }
}
```

If I were to call MyTask() from another function, the C compiler would push the argument onto the stack followed by the return address of the function calling MyTask(). Some compilers actually pass pdata in one or more registers. I'll discuss this situation later. Assuming pdata is pushed onto the stack, OSTaskStkInit() simply simulates this scenario and loads the stack accordingly [F8.3(1)]. However, it turns out that, unlike a C function call, the return address of the caller is unknown. All you have is the start address of the task, not the return address of the function that called this function (task)! It turns out that you don't really care because a task is not supposed to return to another function anyway.

At this point, you need to put on the stack the registers that are automatically pushed by the processor when it recognizes and starts servicing an interrupt. Some processors stack all of its registers; others stack just a few. Generally speaking, a processor stacks at least the value of the program counter for the instruction to return to upon returning from an interrupt and the processor status word [F8.3(2)]. Obviously, you must match the order exactly.

Next, you need to put the rest of the processor registers on the stack [F8.3(3)]. The stacking order depends on whether your processor gives you a choice or not. Some processors have one or more instructions that push many registers at once. You would have to emulate the stacking order of such instructions. For example, the Intel 80x86 has the PUSHA instruction, which pushes eight registers onto the stack. On the Motorola 68HC11 processor, all the registers are automatically pushed onto the stack during an interrupt response, so you also need to match the stacking order.

Now it's time to come back to the issue of what to do if your C compiler passes the pdata argument in registers instead of on the stack. You need to find out from the compiler documentation the register in which pdata is stored. pdata is placed on the stack (Figure 8.4) in the same area you save the corresponding register.

Figure 8.4   Stack frame initialization with **pdata** passed in register.

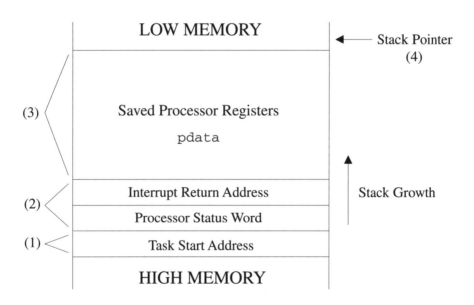

Once you've initialized the stack, OSTaskStkInit() needs to return the address where the stack pointer points after the stacking is complete [F8.3(4)]. OSTaskCreate() or OSTaskCreateExt() takes this address and saves it in the task control block (OS_TCB). The processor documentation tells you whether the stack pointer should point to the next free location on the stack or the location of the last stored value. For example, on an Intel 80x86 processor, the stack pointer points to the last stored data, whereas on a Motorola 68HC11 processor, it points at the next free location.

8.05.02 *OSTaskCreateHook()*

OSTaskCreateHook() is called whenever a task is created by either OSTaskCreate() or OSTask-CreateExt(). This allows you or the user of your port to extend the functionality of µC/OS-II. OSTaskCreateHook() is called when µC/OS-II is done setting up its internal structures but before the scheduler is called. Interrupts are disabled when this function is called. Because of this, you should keep the code in this function to a minimum because it directly affects interrupt latency.

When called, OSTaskCreateHook() receives a pointer to the OS_TCB of the task created and can thus access all of the structure elements. OSTaskCreateHook() has limited capability when the task is created with OSTaskCreate(). However, with OSTaskCreateExt(), you get access to a TCB extension pointer (OSTCBExtPtr) in OS_TCB that can be used to access additional data about the task, such as the contents of floating-point registers, MMU (Memory Management Unit) registers, task counters, and debug information.

The code for OSTaskCreateHook() is generated only if OS_CPU_HOOKS_EN is set to 1 in OS_CFG.H. This allows the user of your port to redefine all the hook functions in a different file. Obviously, users of your port need access to the source to compile it with OS_CPU_HOOKS_EN set to 0 in order to prevent multiply defined symbols at link time.

8.05.03 *OSTaskDelHook()*

OSTaskDelHook() is called whenever a task is deleted. It is called before unlinking the task from µC/OS-II's internal linked list of active tasks. When called, OSTaskDelHook() receives a pointer to the task control block (OS_TCB) of the task being deleted and can thus access all of the structure elements. OSTaskDelHook() can see if a TCB extension has been created (a non-NULL pointer) and is thus responsible for performing cleanup operations. OSTaskDelHook() is not expected to return anything.

The code for OSTaskDelHook() is generated only if OS_CPU_HOOKS_EN is set to 1 in OS_CFG.H.

8.05.04 *OSTaskSwHook()*

OSTaskSwHook() is called whenever a task switch occurs. This happens whether the task switch is performed by OSCtxSw() or OSIntCtxSw(). OSTaskSwHook() can access OSTCBCur and OSTCB-HighRdy directly because they are global variables. OSTCBCur points to the OS_TCB of the task being switched out, and OSTCBHighRdy points to the OS_TCB of the new task. Note that interrupts are always disabled during the call to OSTaskSwHook(), so you should keep additional code to a minimum since it will affect interrupt latency. OSTaskSwHook() has no arguments and is not expected to return anything.

The code for OSTaskSwHook() is generated only if OS_CPU_HOOKS_EN is set to 1 in OS_CFG.H.

8.05.05 *OSTaskStatHook()*

OSTaskStatHook() is called once every second by OSTaskStat(). You can extend the statistics capability with OSTaskStatHook(). For instance, you can keep track of and display the execution time of each task, the percentage of the CPU that is used by each task, how often each task executes, and more. OSTaskStatHook() has no arguments and is not expected to return anything.

The code for OSTaskStatHook() is generated only if OS_CPU_HOOKS_EN is set to 1 in OS_CFG.H.

8.05.06 *OSTimeTickHook()*

OSTaskTimeHook() is called by OSTimeTick() at every system tick. In fact, OSTimeTickHook() is called before a tick is actually processed by µC/OS-II to give your port or application first claim on the tick. OSTimeTickHook() has no arguments and is not expected to return anything.

The code for OSTimeTickHook() is generated only if OS_CPU_HOOKS_EN is set to 1 in OC_CFG.H.

OSTaskCreateHook()

void OSTaskCreateHook(OS_TCB *ptcb)

File	Called from	Code enabled by
OS_CPU_C.C	OSTaskCreate() and OSTaskCreateExt()	OS_CPU_HOOKS_EN

This function is called whenever a task is created, after a TCB has been allocated and initialized; the stack frame of the task is also initialized. OSTaskCreateHook() allows you to extend the functionality of the task creation function with your own features. For example, you can initialize and store the contents of floating-point registers, MMU registers or anything else that can be associated with a task. Typically, you would store this additional information in memory allocated by your application. You could also use OSTaskCreateHook() to trigger an oscilloscope or a logic analyzer or to set a breakpoint.

Arguments

ptcb is a pointer to the task control block of the task created.

Return Value

NONE

Notes/Warnings

Interrupts are disabled when this function is called. Because of this, you should keep the code in this function to a minimum because it directly affects interrupt latency.

Example

This example assumes that you created a task using OSTaskCreateExt() because it expects to have the .OSTCBExtPtr field in the task's OS_TCB contain a pointer to storage for floating-point registers.

```
void OSTaskCreateHook (OS_TCB *ptcb)
{
    if (ptcb->OSTCBExtPtr != (void *)0) {
        /* Save contents of floating-point registers in .. */
        /* .. the TCB extension                            */
    }
}
```

8

OSTaskDelHook()

void OSTaskDelHook(OS_TCB *ptcb)

File	Called from	Code enabled by
OS_CPU_C.C	OSTaskDel()	OS_CPU_HOOKS_EN

This function is called whenever you delete a task by calling OSTaskDel(). You can thus dispose of memory you have allocated through the task create hook, OSTaskCreateHook(). OSTaskDelHook() is called just before the TCB is removed from the TCB chain. You can also use OSTaskCreateHook() to trigger an oscilloscope or a logic analyzer or to set a breakpoint.

Arguments

ptcb is a pointer to the task control block of the task being deleted.

Return Value

NONE

Notes/Warnings

Interrupts are disabled when this function is called. Because of this, you should keep the code in this function to a minimum because it directly affects interrupt latency.

Example

```
void OSTaskDelHook (OS_TCB *ptcb)
{
    /* Output signal to trigger an oscilloscope          */
}
```

OSTaskSwHook()

void OSTaskSwHook(void)

File	*Called from*	*Code enabled by*
OS_CPU_C.C	OSCtxSw() and OSIntCtxSw()	OS_CPU_HOOKS_EN

This function is called whenever a context switch is performed. The global variable OSTCBHighRdy points to the TCB of the task that will get the CPU, and OSTCBCur points to the TCB of the task being switched out. OSTaskSwHook() is called just after saving the task's registers and after saving the stack pointer into the current task's TCB. You can use this function to save/restore the contents of floating-point registers or MMU registers, to keep track of task execution time and of how many times the task has been switched-in, and more.

Arguments

NONE

Return Value

NONE

Notes/Warnings

Interrupts are disabled when this function is called. Because of this, you should keep the code in this function to a minimum because it directly affects interrupt latency.

Example

```
void OSTaskSwHook (void)
{
    /* Save    floating-point registers in current task's TCB ext. */
    /* Restore floating-point registers from new task's TCB ext.   */
}
```

8

OSTaskStatHook()

void OSTaskStatHook(void)

File	*Called from*	*Code enabled by*
OS_CPU_C.C	OSTaskStat()	OS_CPU_HOOKS_EN

This function is called every second by µC/OS-II's statistic task. OSTaskStatHook() allows you to add your own statistics.

Arguments

NONE

Return Value

NONE

Notes/Warnings

The statistic task starts executing about five seconds after calling OSStart(). Note that this function is not called if either OS_TASK_STAT_EN or OS_TASK_CREATE_EXT_EN is set to 0.

Example

```
void OSTaskStatHook (void)
{
    /* Compute the total execution time of all the tasks    */
    /* Compute the percentage of execution of each task      */
}
```

OSTimeTickHook()

void OSTimeTickHook(void)

File	Called from	Code enabled by
OS_CPU_C.C	OSTimeTick()	OS_CPU_HOOKS_EN

This function is called by OSTimeTick(), which in turn is called whenever a clock tick occurs. OSTimeTickHook() is called immediately upon entering OSTimeTick(), to allow execution of time-critical code in your application. You can also use this function to trigger an oscilloscope for debugging, trigger a logic analyzer, or establish a breakpoint for an emulator.

Arguments

NONE

Return Value

NONE

Notes/Warnings

OSTimeTick() is generally called by an ISR, so the execution time of the tick ISR is increased by the code you provide in this function. Interrupts may or may not be enabled when OSTimeTickHook() is called, depending on how the processor port has been implemented. If interrupts are disabled, this function affects interrupt latency.

Example

```
void OSTimeTickHook (void)
{
    /* Trigger an oscilloscope                          */
}
```

8

Chapter 9

80x86, Large Model Port

This chapter describes how μC/OS-II has been ported to the Intel 80x86 series of processors running in *real mode* and for the *large model*. This port applies to the following CPUs:

80186
80286
80386
80486
Pentium
Pentium II

It turns out that the port can run on most 80x86-compatible CPUs manufactured by AMD, Cyrix, NEC (V-series), and others. I use Intel here in a generic fashion. Literally millions of 80x86 CPUs are sold each year. Most of these end up in desktop computers, but a growing number of processors are making their way into embedded systems. The fastest processors (the Pentium IIs) should reach 1,000MHz by the year 2000.

Most C compilers that support 80x86 processors running in real mode offer different memory models, each suited for a different program and data size. Each model uses memory differently. The *large model* allows your application (code and data) to reside in a 1Mb memory space. Pointers in this model require 32 bits, although they only address up to 1Mb. The next section shows why a 32-bit pointer in this model can only address 20 bits worth of memory.

This port can also be adapted to run on the 8086 processor but requires that you replace the use of the PUSHA instruction with the proper number of PUSH instructions.

Figure 9.1 shows the programming model of an 80x86 processor running in real mode. All registers are 16 bits wide, and they all need to be saved during a context switch.

9

Figure 9.1   80x86 real-mode register map.

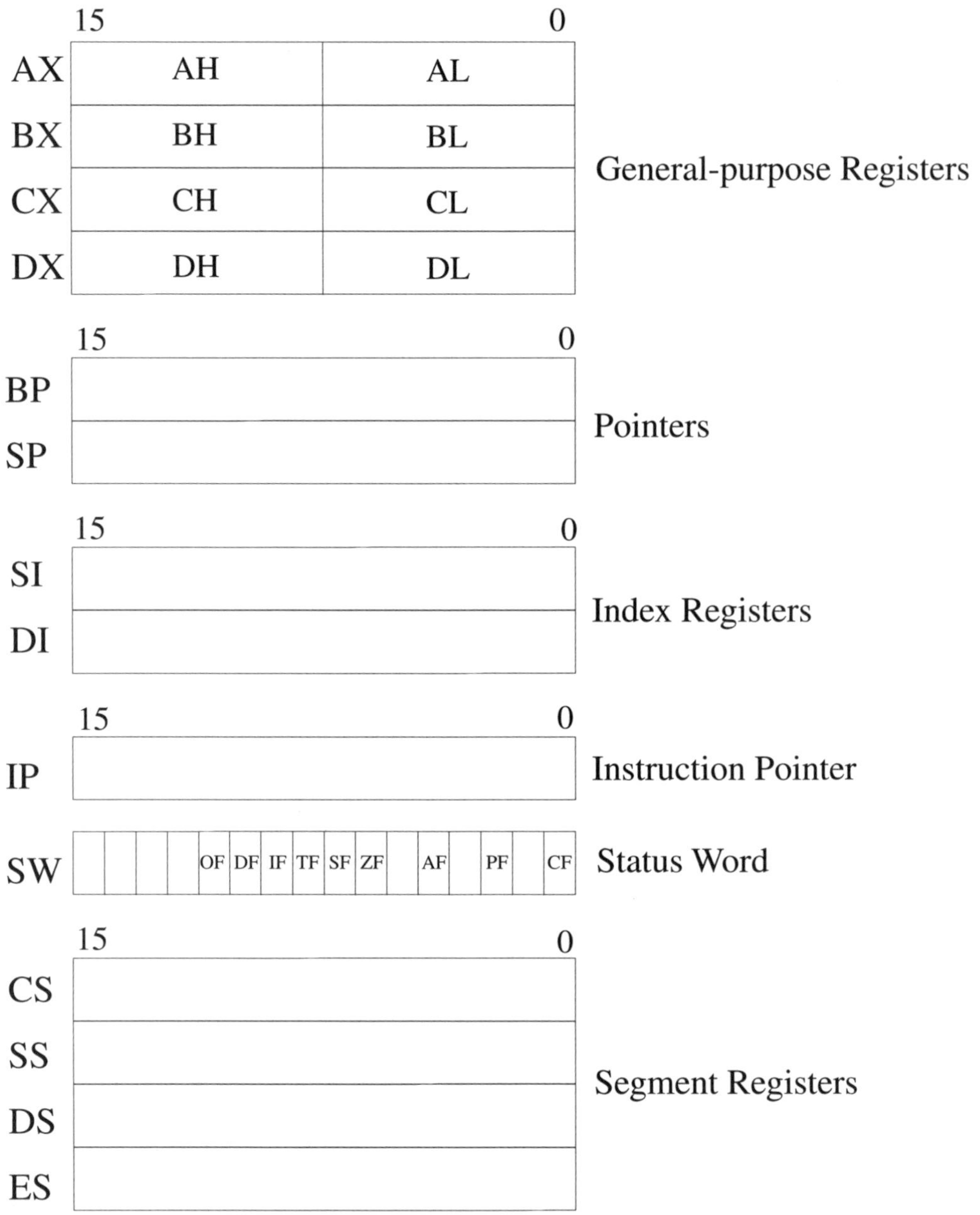

The 80x86 provides a clever mechanism to access up to 1Mb of memory with its 16-bit registers. Memory addressing relies on using a *segment* and an *offset* register. Physical address calculation is done by shifting a segment register by four (multiplying it by 16) and adding one of six other registers (AX, BP, SP, SI, DI, or IP). The result is a 20-bit address that can access up to 1Mb. Figure 9.2 shows how the registers are combined. Each segment points to a block of 16 memory locations called a *paragraph*.

A 16-bit segment register can point to any of 65,536 different paragraphs of 16 bytes and thus address 1,048,576 bytes. Because the offset is also 16 bits, a single segment of code cannot exceed 64Kb. In practice, however, programs are made up of many smaller segments.

Figure 9.2   Addressing with a segment and an offset.

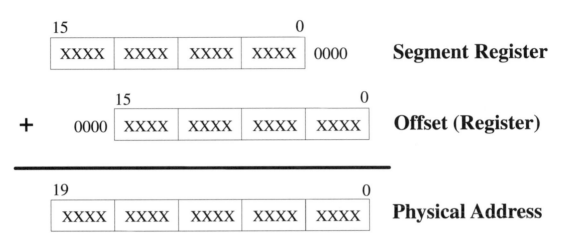

The *code segment* register (CS) points to the base of the program currently executing, the *stack segment* register (SS) points to the base of the stack, the *data segment* register (DS) points to the base of one data area, and the *extra segment* register (ES) points to the base of another area where data may be stored. Each time the CPU needs to generate a memory address, one of the segment registers is automatically chosen and its contents is added to an offset. It is common to find the segment-colon-offset notation in literature to reference a memory location. For example, `1000:00FF` represents physical memory location `0x100FF`.

9.00   Development Tools

I used the Borland C/C++ V3.1 compiler along with the Borland Turbo Assembler to port and test the 80x86 port. The compiler generates reentrant code and provides in-line assembly language instructions to be inserted in C code. Once compiled, the code is executed on a PC. I tested the code on a Pentium-II-based computer running the Microsoft Windows 95 operating system. In fact, I configured the compiler to generate a DOS executable which was run in a DOS window.

This port will run on most C compilers as long as the compiler can generate real-mode code. You will most likely have to change some of the compiler options and assembler directives if you use a different development environment.

9.01   Directories and Files

The installation program provided on the distribution diskette installs the port for the Intel 80x86 (real mode, large model) on your hard disk. The port is found under the `\SOFTWARE\uCOS-II\Ix86L`

9

directory. The directory name stands for **I**ntel 80**x86** real mode, **L**arge model. The source code for the port is found in the following files: OS_CPU.H, OS_CPU_C.C, and OS_CPU_A.ASM.

9.02 *INCLUDES.H*

INCLUDES.H is a *master* include file and is found at the top of all .C files. INCLUDES.H allows every .C file in your project to be written without concern about which header file is actually needed. The only drawback to having a master include file is that INCLUDES.H may include header files that are not pertinent to the actual .C file being compiled. This means that each file will require extra time to compile. This inconvenience is offset by code portability. You can edit INCLUDES.H to add your own header files, but your header files should be added at the end of the list. Listing 9.1 shows the contents of INCLUDES.H for the 80x86 port.

Listing 9.1 *INCLUDES.H*

```
#include    <stdio.h>
#include    <string.h>
#include    <ctype.h>
#include    <stdlib.h>
#include    <conio.h>
#include    <dos.h>
#include    <setjmp.h>

#include    "\software\ucos-ii\ix86l\os_cpu.h"
#include    "os_cfg.h"
#include    "\software\blocks\pc\source\pc.h"
#include    "\software\ucos-ii\source\ucos_ii.h"
```

9.03 *OS_CPU.H*

OS_CPU.H contains processor- and implementation-specific #defines constants, macros, and type-defs. OS_CPU.H for the 80x86 port is shown in Listing 9.2.

Listing 9.2 *OS_CPU.H*

```
#ifdef   OS_CPU_GLOBALS
#define OS_CPU_EXT
#else
#define OS_CPU_EXT   extern
#endif
```

9.03.01 Data Types

Because different microprocessors have different word lengths, the port of µC/OS-II includes a series of type definitions that ensures portability [L9.2(1)]. With the Borland C/C++ compiler, an `int` is 16 bits and a `long` is 32 bits. Also, for your convenience, I included floating-point data types even though µC/OS-II doesn't make use of floating-point numbers.

A stack entry for the 80x86 processor running in real mode is 16 bits wide; thus, OS_STK is declared accordingly for the Borland C/C++ compiler. All task stacks must be declared using OS_STK as its data type.

Listing 9.2   OS_CPU.H (Continued)

```
/*
*********************************************************************************
*                                  DATA TYPES
*                               (Compiler Specific)
*********************************************************************************
*/

typedef unsigned char BOOLEAN;
typedef unsigned char INT8U;             /* Unsigned  8 bit quantity      (1)*/
typedef signed   char INT8S;             /* Signed    8 bit quantity         */
typedef unsigned int  INT16U;            /* Unsigned 16 bit quantity         */
typedef signed   int  INT16S;            /* Signed   16 bit quantity         */
typedef unsigned long INT32U;            /* Unsigned 32 bit quantity         */
typedef signed   long INT32S;            /* Signed   32 bit quantity         */
typedef float         FP32;        /* Single precision floating point        */
typedef double        FP64;        /* Double precision floating point        */


typedef unsigned int  OS_STK;      /* Each stack entry is 16-bit wide        */

#define BYTE    INT8S     /* Define data types for backward compatibility ... */
#define UBYTE   INT8U     /* ... to uC/OS V1.xx.  Not actually needed for ... */
#define WORD    INT16S    /* ... uC/OS-II.                                    */
#define UWORD   INT16U
#define LONG    INT32S
#define ULONG   INT32U
```

9

9.03.02 Critical Sections

µC/OS-II, as with all real-time kernels, needs to disable interrupts in order to access critical sections of code and re-enable interrupts when done. This allows µC/OS-II to protect critical code from being entered simultaneously from either multiple tasks or ISRs. Because the Borland C/C++ compiler supports in-line assembly language, it's quite easy to specify the instructions to disable and enable interrupts. µC/OS-II defines two *macros* to disable and enable interrupts: OS_ENTER_CRITICAL() and OS_EXIT_CRITICAL(), respectively. I actually provide you with two methods of disabling and enabling interrupts [L9.2(2)]. The method used is established by the #define macro OS_CRITICAL_METHOD, which can be set either to 1 or 2. For the tests, I chose method 2, but it's up to you to decide which one is best for your application.

Listing 9.2   OS_CPU.H (Continued)

```
/*
*******************************************************************************
*                     Intel 80x86 (Real-Mode, Large Model)
*
* Method #1: Disable/Enable interrupts using simple instructions.
*            After critical section, interrupts will be enabled even if they
*            were disabled before entering the critical section.  You MUST
*            change the constant in OS_CPU_A.ASM, function OSIntCtxSw()
*            from 10 to 8.

* Method #2: Disable/Enable interrupts by preserving the state of interrupts.
*            In other words, if nterrupts were disabled before entering the
*            critiical section, they will be disabled when leaving the
*            critical section. You MUST change the constant in OS_CPU_A.ASM,
*             function, OSIntCtxSw() from 8 to 10.
*******************************************************************************
*/
#define  OS_CRITICAL_METHOD    2


#if      OS_CRITICAL_METHOD == 1
#define  OS_ENTER_CRITICAL()   asm  CLI           /* Disable interrupts     (2)*/
#define  OS_EXIT_CRITICAL()    asm  STI           /* Enable  interrupts        */
#endif


#if      OS_CRITICAL_METHOD == 2
#define  OS_ENTER_CRITICAL()   asm {PUSHF; CLI}   /* Disable interrupts        */
#define  OS_EXIT_CRITICAL()    asm  POPF          /* Enable  interrupts        */
#endif
```

Listing 9.2   OS_CPU.H *(Continued)*

```
/*
********************************************************************************
*              Intel 80x86 (Real-Mode, Large Model) Miscellaneous
********************************************************************************
*/

#define  OS_STK_GROWTH   1 /* Stack grows from HIGH to LOW memory on 80x86 (3)*/

#define  uCOS            0x80 /* Interrupt vector # used for context switch   (4)*/

#define  OS_TASK_SW() asm   INT   uCOS                                        (5)

/*
********************************************************************************
*                              GLOBAL VARIABLES
********************************************************************************
*/

OS_CPU_EXT  INT8U OSTickDOSCtr;   /* Counter used to invoke DOS's tick        */
                                  /* handler every 'n' ticks               (6)*/
```

Method 1

The first and simplest way to implement these two macros is to invoke the processor instruction to disable interrupts (CLI) for OS_ENTER_CRITICAL() and the enable interrupts instruction (STI) for OS_EXIT_CRITICAL(). There is, however, a little problem with this scenario. If you call the µC/OS-II function with interrupts disabled, on return from µC/OS-II, interrupts would be enabled! If you disable interrupts, you may want them to be disabled on return from the µC/OS-II function. In this case, the above implementation would not be adequate.   If you don't care in your application whether interrupts are enabled after calling a µC/OS-II service, you should opt for this method because of performance. If you chose this method, you need to change the constant in OSIntCtxSw() from 10 to 8 (see OS_CPU_A.ASM).

Method 2

The second way to implement OS_ENTER_CRITICAL() is to save the interrupt disable status onto the stack and then disable interrupts. This is accomplished on the 80x86 by executing the PUSHF instruction followed by the CLI instruction. OS_EXIT_CRITICAL() simply needs to execute a POPF instruction to restore the original contents of the processor's SW register. Using this scheme, if you call a µC/OS-II service with interrupts either enabled or disabled, the status would be preserved across the call. A few words of caution, however: if you call a µC/OS-II service with interrupts disabled, you are potentially extending the interrupt latency of your application. Also, your application will crash if you have interrupts disabled before calling a service such as OSTimeDly(). This happens because the task is suspended until time expires, but because interrupts are disabled, you never service the tick interrupt! Obviously, all PEND calls are also subject to this problem, so be careful. As a general rule, you should always call µC/OS-II services with interrupts enabled. If you want to preserve the interrupt disable status across µC/OS-II service calls, then obviously this method is for you, but be careful.

9.03.03 Stack Growth

The stack on an 80x86 processor grows from high to low memory, which means that OS_STK_GROWTH must be set to 1 [L9.2(3)].

9.03.04 OS_TASK_SW()

In µC/OS-II, the stack frame for a ready task always looks as if an interrupt has just occurred and all processor registers were saved onto it. To switch context, OS_TASK_SW() thus needs to simulate an interrupt [L9.2(5)]. The 80x86 provides 256 software interrupts to accomplish this. The interrupt service routine (ISR) (also called the exception handler) must vector to the assembly language function OSCtxSw() (see OS_CPU_A.ASM).

Because I tested the code on a PC, I decided to use interrupt number 128 (0x80) because I found it to be available [L9.2(4)]. Actually, the original PC used interrupts 0x80 through 0xF0 for the BASIC interpreter. Few if any PCs come with a BASIC interpreter built in anymore so it should be safe to use these vectors. Optionally, you can also use vectors 0x4B to 0x5B, 0x5D to 0x66, or 0x68 to 0x6F. If you use this port on an embedded processor such as the 80186 processor, you will most likely not be as restricted in your choice of vectors.

9.03.05 Tick Rate

The tick rate for an RTOS should generally be set between 10 and 100Hz. It is always preferable (but not necessary) to set the tick rate to a round number. Unfortunately, on the PC, the default tick rate is 18.20648Hz, which is not what I would call a nice round number. For this port, I decided to change the tick rate of the PC from the standard 18.20648Hz to 200Hz (i.e., 5ms between ticks). There are two reasons to do this. First, 200Hz happens to be about 11 times faster than 18.20648Hz. This allows you to "chain" into DOS once every 11 ticks. In DOS, the tick handler is responsible for some system maintenance that is expected to happen every 54.93ms. The second reason is to have a 5.00ms time resolution for time delays and timeouts. If you are running the example code on an 80386 PC, you may find the overhead of 200Hz is unacceptable. However, on a Pentium II processor, 200Hz is not likely to be a problem.

The last statement in OS_CPU.H declares an 8-bit variable (OSTickDOSCtr) that keeps track of the number of times the ticker is called [L9.2(6)]. Every 11th time, the DOS tick handler is called. OSTick-DOSCtr is used in OS_CPU_A.ASM and really only applies to a PC environment. You most likely would not use this scheme if you design an embedded system around a non-PC architecture because you would set the tick rate to the proper value in the first place.

9.04 OS_CPU_A.ASM

A µC/OS-II port requires that you write four fairly simple assembly language functions:

```
OSStartHighRdy()
OSCtxSw()
OSIntCtxSw()
OSTickISR()
```

9.04.01 *OSStartHighRdy()*

This function is called by OSStart() to start the highest priority task ready to run. However, before you can call OSStart(), you must have called OSInit() and created at least one task [see OSTaskCreate() and OSTaskCreateExt()]. OSStartHighRdy() assumes that OSTCBHighRdy points to the task control block of the task with the highest priority [OSTCBHighRdy is set up properly in OSStart() so you don't have to worry about it in OSStartHighRdy()]. Figure 9.3 shows the stack frame for an 80x86 real-mode task created by either OSTaskCreate() or OSTaskCreateExt(). As can be seen, OSTCBHighRdy->OSTCBStkPtr points to the task's top-of-stack.

The code for OSStartHighRdy() is shown in Listing 9.3.

Figure 9.3   80x86 stack frame when task is created.

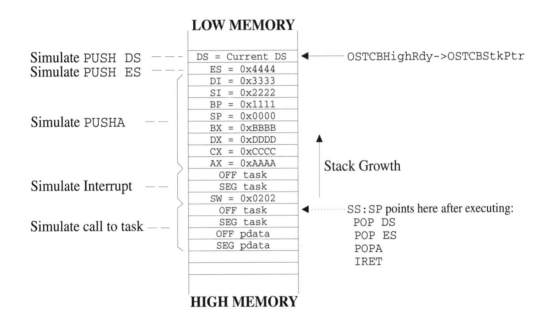

To start the task, OSStartHighRdy() simply retrieves and loads the stack pointer from the task's OS_TCB [L9.3(1)] and executes POP DS [L9.3(2)], POP ES [L9.3(3)], POPA [L9.3(4)], and IRET [L9.3(5)] instructions. I decided to store the stack pointer at the beginning of the task control block (i.e., its OS_TCB) to make it easier to access from assembly language.

Upon executing the IRET instruction, the task code resumes and the stack pointer (SS:SP) points to the return address of the task as if the task was called by a normal function. SS:SP+4 points to the argument pdata, which is passed to the task.

Listing 9.3   OSStartHighRdy().

```
_OSStartHighRdy   PROC FAR


    MOV     AX, SEG _OSTCBHighRdy            ; Reload DS
    MOV     DS, AX                          ;


    LES     BX, DWORD PTR DS:_OSTCBHighRdy  ; SS:SP = OSTCBHighRdy->OSTCBStkPtr  (1)
    MOV     SS, ES:[BX+2]                   ;
    MOV     SP, ES:[BX+0]                   ;
;
    POP     DS                             ; Load task's context                (2)
    POP     ES                             ;                                    (3)
    POPA                                   ;                                    (4)
;
    IRET                                   ; Run task                           (5)


_OSStartHighRdy   ENDP
```

9.04.02   OSCtxSw()

A task-level context switch is accomplished on the 80x86 processor by executing a software interrupt instruction. The interrupt service routine must vector to OSCtxSw(). The sequence of events that leads μC/OS-II to vector to OSCtxSw() begins when the current task calls a service provided by μC/OS-II, which causes a higher priority task to be ready to run. At the end of the service call, μC/OS-II calls the function OSSched(), which concludes that the current task is no longer the most important task to run. OSSched() loads the address of the highest priority task into OSTCBHighRdy, then executes the software interrupt instruction by invoking the macro OS_TASK_SW(). Note that the variable OSTCBCur already contains a pointer to the current task's task control block, OS_TCB. The code for OSCtxSw() is shown in Listing 9.4.

Figure 9.4 shows the stack frames of the task being suspended and the task being resumed. On the 80x86 processor, the software interrupt instruction forces the SW register to be pushed onto the current task's stack followed by the return address (segment and offset) of the task that executed the INT instruction [F9.4/L9.4(1)] [i.e., the task that invoked OS_TASK_SW()]. To save the rest of the task's context, the PUSHA [F9.4/L9.4(2)], PUSH ES [F9.4/L9.4(3)], and PUSH DS [F9.4/L9.4(4)] instructions are executed. To finish saving the context of the task being suspended, OSCtxSw() saves the SS and SP registers in its OS_TCB [F9.4/L9.4(5)].

The user-definable task switch hook OSTaskSwHook() is then called [L9.4(6)]. Note that when OSTaskSwHook() is called, OSTCBCur points to the current task's OS_TCB, while OSTCBHighRdy points to the new task's OS_TCB. You can thus access each task's OS_TCB from OSTaskSwHook(). If you never intend to use the context switch hook, comment out the call and save yourself a few clock cycles during the context switch.

Listing 9.4   OSCtxSw().

```
_OSCtxSw      PROC    FAR                                                      (1)
;
    PUSHA                                   ; Save current task's context      (2)
    PUSH ES                                                                    (3)
    PUSH DS                                                                    (4)
;
    MOV  AX, SEG _OSTCBCur                   ; Reload DS in case it was altered
    MOV  DS, AX
;
    LES  BX, DWORD PTR DS:_OSTCBCur         ; OSTCBCur->OSTCBStkPtr = SS:S     (5)
    MOV  ES:[BX+2], SS
    MOV  ES:[BX+0], SP
;
    CALL FAR PTR _OSTaskSwHook                                                 (6)
;
    MOV  AX, WORD PTR DS:_OSTCBHighRdy+2    ; OSTCBCur = OSTCBHighRdy          (7)
    MOV  DX, WORD PTR DS:_OSTCBHighRdy
    MOV  WORD PTR DS:_OSTCBCur+2, AX
    MOV  WORD PTR DS:_OSTCBCur, DX
;
    MOV  AL, BYTE PTR DS:_OSPrioHighRdy     ; OSPrioCur = OSPrioHighRdy        (8)
    MOV  BYTE PTR DS:_OSPrioCur, AL
;
    LES  BX, DWORD PTR DS:_OSTCBHighRdy     ; SS:SP = OSTCBHighRdy->OSTCBStkPtr(9)
    MOV  SS, ES:[BX+2]
    MOV  SP, ES:[BX]
;
    POP  DS                                  ; Load new task's context         (10)
    POP  ES                                                                    (11)
    POPA                                                                       (12)
;
    IRET                                     ; Return to new task              (13)
;
_OSCtxSw      ENDP
```

9

Upon return from OSTaskSwHook(), OSTCBHighRdy is copied to OSTCBCur because the new task will now also be the current task [L9.4(7)]. Also, OSPrioHighRdy is copied to OSPrioCur for the same reason [L9.4(8)]. At this point, OSCtxSw() can load the processor's registers with the new task's context. This is done by first retrieving the SS and SP registers from the new task's OS_TCB [F9.4(6)/L9.4(9)]. The other registers are pulled from the stack by executing the POP DS [F9.4(7)/L9.4(10)], POP ES [F9.4(8)/L9.4(11)], POPA [F9.4(9)/L9.4(12)], and IRET [F9.4(10)/ L9.4(13)] instructions. The task code resumes once the IRET instruction completes.

Note that interrupts are disabled during OSCtxSw() and also during execution of the user-definable function OSTaskSwHook().

9.04.03 *OSIntCtxSw()*

OSIntCtxSw() is called by OSIntExit() to perform a context switch from an ISR (Interrupt Service Routine). Because OSIntCtxSw() is called from an ISR, it is assumed that all the processor registers are already properly saved onto the interrupted task's stack. In fact, there are more things on the stack frame than are needed. OSIntCtxSw() cleans up the stack so that the interrupted task is left with just the proper stack frame content.

Figure 9.4   80x86 stack frames during a task-level context switch.

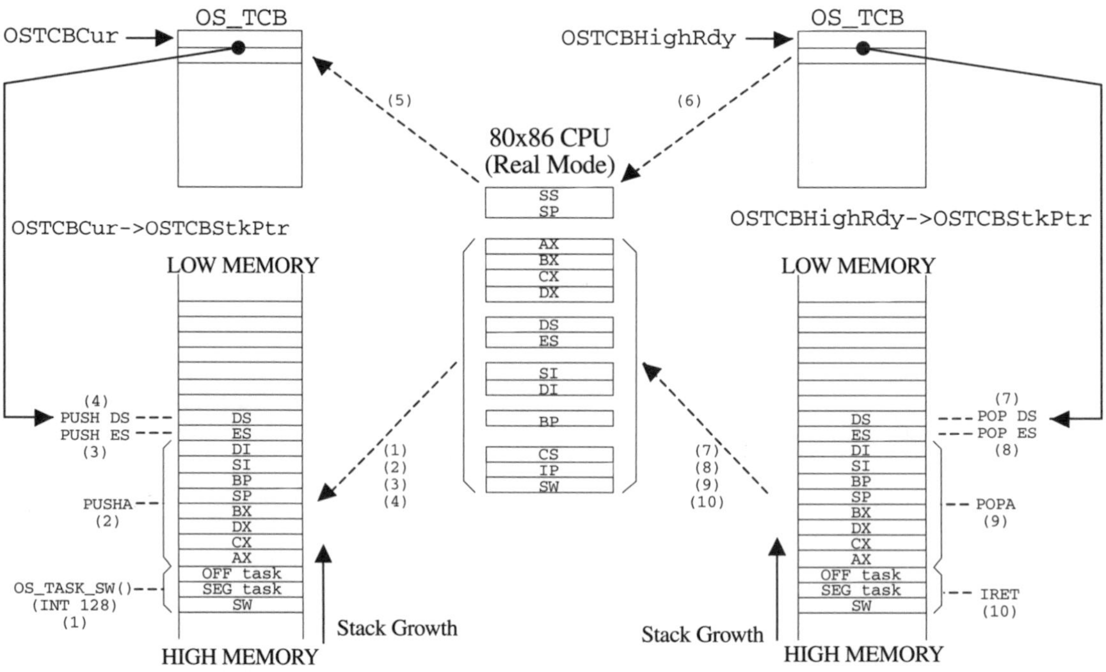

The code shown in Listing 9.5 is identical to OSCtxSw(), except for two things. First, there is no need to save the registers (i.e., no PUSHA, PUSH ES, or PUSH DS) onto the stack because it is assumed that the beginning of the ISR has done that. Second, OSIntCtxSw() needs to adjust the stack pointer so that the stack frame contains only the task's context. To understand what is happening, refer also to Figure 9.5.

Listing 9.5 *OSIntCtxSw()*.

```
_OSIntCtxSw PROC   FAR
;                  ; Ignore calls to OSIntExit and OSIntCtxSw
;   ADD  SP,8    ; (Uncomment if OS_CRITICAL_METHOD is 1, see OS_CPU.H)        (1)
    ADD  SP,10   ; (Uncomment if OS_CRITICAL_METHOD is 2, see OS_CPU.H)
;
    MOV  AX, SEG _OSTCBCur              ; Reload DS in case it was altered
    MOV  DS, AX
;
    LES  BX, DWORD PTR DS:_OSTCBCur     ; OSTCBCur->OSTCBStkPtr = SS:SP        (2)
    MOV  ES:[BX+2], SS
    MOV  ES:[BX+0], SP
;
    CALL FAR PTR _OSTaskSwHook                                                 (3)
;
    MOV  AX, WORD PTR DS:_OSTCBHighRdy+2 ; OSTCBCur = OSTCBHighRdy             (4)
    MOV  DX, WORD PTR DS:_OSTCBHighRdy
    MOV  WORD PTR DS:_OSTCBCur+2, AX
    MOV  WORD PTR DS:_OSTCBCur, DX
;
    MOV  AL, BYTE PTR DS:_OSPrioHighRdy  ; OSPrioCur = OSPrioHighRdy           (5)
    MOV  BYTE PTR DS:_OSPrioCur, AL
;
    LES  BX, DWORD PTR DS:_OSTCBHighRdy  ; SS:SP = OSTCBHighRdy->OSTCBStkPtr (6)
    MOV  SS, ES:[BX+2]
    MOV  SP, ES:[BX]
;
    POP  DS                             ; Load new task's context             (7)
    POP  ES                                                                   (8)
    POPA                                                                      (9)
;
    IRET                               ; Return to new task                  (10)
;
_OSIntCtxSw ENDP
```

9

Figure 9.5 80x86 stack frames during an interrupt-level context switch.

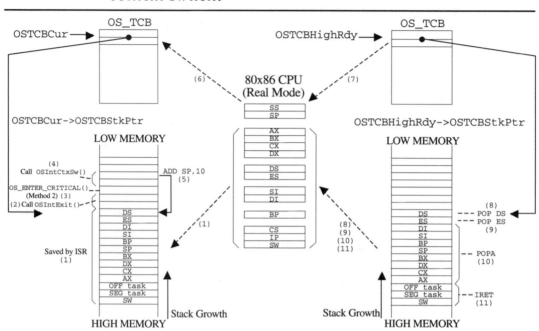

Assuming that the processor recognizes an interrupt, the processor completes the current instruction and initiates an interrupt handling procedure. This consist of automatically pushing the processor status register followed by the return address of the interrupted task onto the stack.

The CPU then vectors to the proper ISR. µC/OS-II requires that your ISR begins by saving the rest of the processor registers [F9.5(1)]. Once the registers are saved, µC/OS-II requires that you either call OSIntEnter() or that you increment the global variable OSIntNesting by one. At this point, the interrupted task's stack frame only contains the register contents of the interrupted task. The ISR can now start servicing the interrupting device and, possibly, make a higher priority task ready. This occurs if the ISR sends a message to a task by calling OSMboxPost(), OSQPostFront(), or OSQPost(), resumes a task by calling OSTaskResume(), or invokes OSTimeTick() or OSTimeDlyResume().

Assume that a higher priority task is made ready to run. µC/OS-II requires that an ISR calls OSInt-Exit() when it has finished servicing the interrupting device. OSIntExit() basically tell µC/OS-II that it's time to return back to task-level code. The call to OSIntExit() causes the return address of the caller to be pushed onto the interrupted task's stack [F9.5(2)].

OSIntExit() starts by disabling interrupts because it needs to execute critical code. De\pending on how OS_ENTER_CRITICAL() is implemented (see section 9.03.02), the processor's status register (SW) could be pushed onto the interrupted task's stack [F9.5(3)]. OSIntExit() notices that the interrupted task is no longer the task that needs to run because a higher priority task is now ready. In this case, the pointer OSTCBHighRdy is made to point to the new task's OS_TCB, and OSIntExit() calls OSIntCtxSw() to perform the context switch. Calling OSIntCtxSw() causes the return address to be pushed onto the interrupted task's stack [F9.5(4)].

Because you are switching context, you only want to leave the registers in Figure 9.5(1) on the stack and ignore the stack content in Figure 9.5(2), (3), and (4). This is accomplished by adding a constant to the stack pointer [F9.5(5)/L9.5(1)]. When using Method 2 for OS_ENTER_CRITICAL(), this constant needs to be 10. If you decide to use Method 1, you need to change the constant to 8. The actual value of this constant depends on the compiler and compiler options. Specifically, a different compiler may allocate variables for OSIntExit().

Once the stack pointer is adjusted, it can be saved into the OS_TCB of the task being switched-out [F9.5(6)/L9.5(2)]. OSIntCtxSw() is the only function in μC/OS-II (and also μC/OS) that is compiler specific and has generated more e-mail than any other aspect of μC/OS. If your port appears to crash after a few context switches, you should suspect that the stack is not being properly adjusted in OSIntCtxSw().

The user-definable task switch hook OSTaskSwHook() is called next [L9.5(3)]. Note that OSTCB-Cur points to the current task's OS_TCB, while OSTCBHighRdy points to the new task's OS_TCB. You can thus access each task's OS_TCB from OSTaskSwHook(). If you never intend to use the context switch hook, comment out the call and save yourself a few clock cycles during the context switch.

Upon return from OSTaskSwHook(), OSTCBHighRdy is copied to OSTCBCur because the new task is now also the current task [L9.5(4)]. Also, OSPrioHighRdy is copied to OSPrioCur for the same reason [L9.5(5)]. At this point, OSIntCtxSw() can load the processor's registers with the new task's context. This is done by first retrieving the SS and SP registers from the new task's OS_TCB [F9.5(7)/L9.5(6)]. The other registers are pulled from the stack by executing the POP DS [F9.5(8)/L9.5(7)], POP ES [F9.5(9)/L9.5(8)], POPA [F9.5(10)/L9.5(9)], and IRET [F9.5(11)/L9.5(10)] instructions. The task code resumes once the IRET instruction completes.

Note that interrupts are disabled during OSIntCtxSw() and also during execution of the user-definable function OSTaskSwHook().

9.04.04 OSTickISR()

As mentioned in section 9.03.05, Tick Rate, the tick rate of an RTOS should be set between 10 and 100Hz. On the PC, the ticker occurs every 54.93ms (18.20648Hz) and is obtained by a hardware timer that interrupts the CPU. Recall that I reprogrammed the tick rate to 200Hz. The ticker on the PC is assigned to vector 0x08 but μC/OS-II redefined it so that it vectors to OSTickISR() instead. Because of this, the PC's tick handler is saved [see PC.C, PC_DOSSaveReturn()] in vector 129 (0x81). To satisfy DOS, however, the PC's handler is called every 54.93ms (described shortly). Figure 9.6 shows the contents of the interrupt vector table (IVT) before and after installing μC/OS-II.

With μC/OS-II, it is very important that you enable ticker interrupts after multitasking has started; that is, after calling OSStart(). In the case of the PC, however, ticker interrupts are already occurring before you actually execute your μC/OS-II application. To prevent the ISR from invoking OSTick-ISR() until μC/OS-II is ready, do the following.

PC_DOSSaveReturn() (see PC.C), which is called by main(), needs to:
> Get the address of the interrupt handler for the DOS ticker
> Relocate the DOS ticker at location 0x81

main() needs to:
> Install the context switch vector OSCtxSw() at vector 0x80
> Create at least one application task
> Call OSStart() when ready to multitask

The first task to execute needs to:
> Install OSTickISR() at vector 0x08
> Change the tick rate from 18.20648 to 200Hz

9

Figure 9.6   The PC interrupt vector table (IVT).

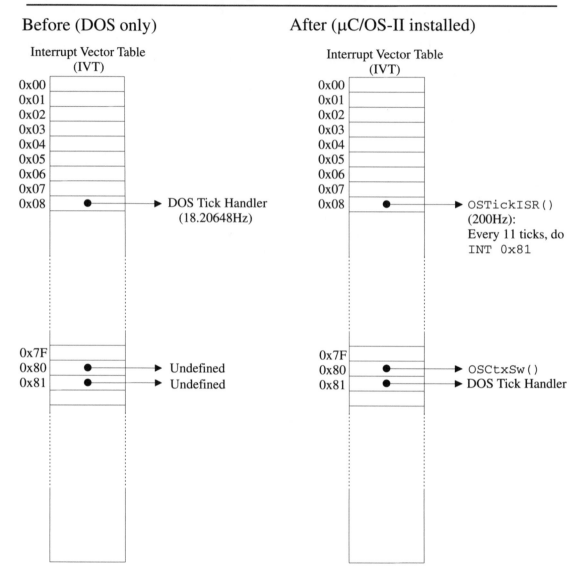

The tick handler on the PC is somewhat tricky, so I explain it using the pseudocode shown in Listing 9.6. Like all μC/OS-II ISRs, all registers need to be saved onto the current task's stack [L9.6(1)]. Upon entering an ISR, you need to tell μC/OS-II that you are starting an ISR by either calling OSIntEnter() or directly incrementing OSIntNesting [L9.6(2)]. You can directly increment this variable because the 80x86 processor can perform this operation indivisibly. Next, the counter OSTickDOSCtr is decremented [L9.6(3)] and when it reaches 0, the DOS ticker handler is called [L9.6(4)]. This happens every 54.93ms. Ten times out of 11, however, a command is sent to the Priority Interrupt Controller (PIC) to clear the interrupt [L9.6(5)]. Note that there is no need to do this when the DOS ticker is called because it directly clears the interrupt source. Next, OSTickISR() calls OSTimeTick() so that μC/OS-II can update all tasks waiting for time to expire or pending for some event to occur, with a timeout [L9.6(6)]. At the completion of all ISRs, OSIntExit() is called [L9.6(7)]. If a higher priority task has been made ready by this ISR (or any other nested ISRs) and this is the last nested ISR, then OSIntExit() will not return to OSTickISR()! Instead, OSIntCtxSw() restores the processor's context of the new task and issues an IRET. If the ISR is not the last nested ISR or the ISR did not cause a higher priority task to be ready, then OSIntExit() returns back to OSTickISR(). At this point, the processor registers are restored [L9.6(8)], and the ISR returns to the interrupted source by executing an IRET instruction [L9.6(9)].

The actual code for OSTickISR() is shown in Listing 9.7 for reference.

Listing 9.6   Pseudocode for *OSTickISR()*.

```
void OSTickISR (void)
{
    Save processor registers;                                              (1)
    OSIntNesting++;                                                        (2)
    OSTickDOSCtr--;                                                        (3)
    if (OSTickDOSCtr == 0) {
        Chain into DOS by executing an 'INT 81H' instruction;             (4)
    } else {
        Send EOI command to PIC (Priority Interrupt Controller);          (5)
    }
    OSTimeTick();                                                          (6)
    OSIntExit();                                                           (7)
    Restore processor registers;                                          (8)
    Execute a return from interrupt instruction (IRET);                   (9)
}
```

9

Listing 9.7   OSTickISR().

```
_OSTickISR  PROC    FAR
;
    PUSHA                           ; Save interrupted task's context
    PUSH ES
    PUSH DS
;
    MOV  AX, SEG _OSTickDOSCtr       ; Reload DS
    MOV  DS, AX
;
    INC  BYTE PTR _OSIntNesting      ; Notify uC/OS-II of ISR
;
    DEC  BYTE PTR DS:_OSTickDOSCtr
    CMP  BYTE PTR DS:_OSTickDOSCtr, 0
    JNE  SHORT _OSTickISR1           ; Every 11 ticks (18.206 Hz), chain into DOS
;
    MOV  BYTE PTR DS:_OSTickDOSCtr, 11
    INT  081H                        ; Chain into DOS's tick ISR
    JMP  SHORT _OSTickISR2

_OSTickISR1:
    MOV  AL, 20H                     ; Move EOI code into AL.
    MOV  DX, 20H                     ; Address of 8259 PIC in DX.
    OUT  DX, AL                      ; Send EOI to PIC if not processing DOS timer.
;
_OSTickISR2:
    CALL FAR PTR _OSTimeTick         ; Process system tick
;
    CALL FAR PTR _OSIntExit          ; Notify uC/OS-II of end of ISR
;
    POP  DS                          ; Restore interrupted task's context
    POP  ES
    POPA
;
    IRET                             ; Return to interrupted task
;
_OSTickISR  ENDP
```

You can simplify OSTickISR() by not increasing the tick rate from 18.20648 to 200Hz, as shown in the pseudocode in Listing 9.8. The ISR still needs to save all the registers onto the current task's stack [L9.8(1)] and increment OSIntNesting [L9.8(2)]. Next, the DOS tick handler is called [L9.8(3)]. Note that you do not need to clear the interrupt because this is handled by the DOS ticker. Call OSTimeTick() so that μC/OS-II can update all tasks waiting for time to expire or pending on some event to occur with a timeout [L9.8(4)]. When you are done servicing the ISR, call OSIntExit() [L9.8(5)]. Finally, the processor registers are restored [L9.8(6)] and the ISR returns to the interrupted source by executing an IRET instruction [L9.8(7)]. Note that you must not change the tick rate by calling PC_SetTickRate() if you are to use this version of the code. You also have to change the configuration constant OS_TICKS_PER_SEC (see OS_CFG.H) from 200 to 18.

The new code for OSTickISR() is shown in Listing 9.9.

Listing 9.8   *Pseudocode for 18.2Hz* **OSTickISR()**.

```
void OSTickISR (void)
{
    Save processor registers;                                      (1)
    OSIntNesting++;                                                (2)
    Chain into DOS by executing an 'INT 81H' instruction;          (3)
    OSTimeTick();                                                  (4)
    OSIntExit();                                                   (5)
    Restore processor registers;                                  (6)
    Execute a return from interrupt instruction (IRET);           (7)
}
```

9.05 *OS_CPU_C.C*

A μC/OS-II port requires that you write six fairly simple C functions:

```
OSTaskStkInit()
OSTaskCreateHook()
OSTaskDelHook()
OSTaskSwHook()
OSTaskStatHook()
OSTimeTickHook()
```

The only necessary function is OSTaskStkInit(). The other five functions must be declared but don't need to contain code. I didn't put code in these five functions in OS_CPU_C.C because I assumed they would be defined by the user. To that end, the #define constant OS_CPU_HOOKS_EN (see OS_CFG.H) is set to 0. To define the code in OS_CPU_C.C, you need to set OS_CPU_HOOKS_EN to 1.

9

Listing 9.9   18.2Hz version of OSTickISR().

```
_OSTickISR  PROC    FAR
;
        PUSHA                           ; Save interrupted task's context
        PUSH    ES
        PUSH    DS
;
        MOV     AX, SEG _OSIntNesting   ; Reload DS
        MOV     DS, AX
;
        INC     BYTE PTR _OSIntNesting  ; Notify uC/OS-II of ISR
;
        INT     081H                    ; Chain into DOS's tick ISR
;
        CALL    FAR PTR _OSTimeTick     ; Process system tick
;
        CALL    FAR PTR _OSIntExit      ; Notify uC/OS-II of end of ISR
;
        POP     DS                      ; Restore interrupted task's context
        POP     ES
        POPA
;
        IRET                            ; Return to interrupted task
;
_OSTickISR  ENDP
```

Figure 9.7   Stack frame initialization with **pdata** *passed on the stack.*

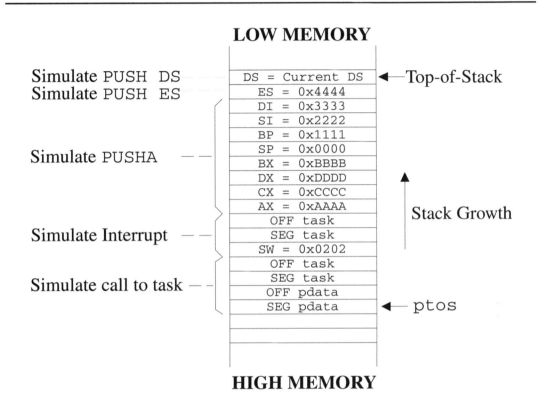

LOW MEMORY

Simulate PUSH DS	DS = Current DS ◄—Top-of-Stack
Simulate PUSH ES	ES = 0x4444
	DI = 0x3333
	SI = 0x2222
	BP = 0x1111
Simulate PUSHA	SP = 0x0000
	BX = 0xBBBB
	DX = 0xDDDD
	CX = 0xCCCC
	AX = 0xAAAA
	OFF task
Simulate Interrupt	SEG task
	SW = 0x0202
	OFF task
Simulate call to task	SEG task
	OFF pdata
	SEG pdata ◄— ptos

Stack Growth

HIGH MEMORY

9.05.01 *OSTaskStkInit()*

This function is called by OSTaskCreate() and OSTaskCreateExt() to initialize the stack frame of a task so that it looks as if an interrupt has just occurred and all processor registers were pushed onto it. Figure 9.7 shows what OSTaskStkInit() puts on the stack of the task being created. Note that the diagram doesn't show the stack frame of the code calling OSTaskStkInit() but, rather, the stack frame of the task being created.

When you create a task, you pass the start address of the task (task), a pointer (pdata), the task's top-of-stack (ptos), and the task's priority (prio) to OSTaskCreate() or OSTaskCreateExt(). OSTaskCreateExt() requires additional arguments, but these are irrelevant in discussing OSTask-StkInit(). To properly initialize the stack frame, OSTaskStkInit() (Listing 9.10) requires only the first three arguments just mentioned (i.e., task, pdata, and ptos).

9

Listing 9.10 *OSTaskStkInit()*.

```
void *OSTaskStkInit (void (*task)(void *pd), void *pdata, void *ptos, INT16U opt)
{
    INT16U *stk;


    opt     = opt;                      /* 'opt' is not used, prevent warning      */
    stk     = (INT16U *)ptos;           /* Load stack pointer                  (1) */
    *stk--  = (INT16U)FP_SEG(pdata);    /* Simulate call to function with argument (2) */
    *stk--  = (INT16U)FP_OFF(pdata);
    *stk--  = (INT16U)FP_SEG(task);     /* Place return address of function call   (3) */
    *stk--  = (INT16U)FP_OFF(task);
    *stk--  = (INT16U)0x0202;           /* SW = Interrupts enabled             (4) */
    *stk--  = (INT16U)FP_SEG(task);     /* Put pointer to task   on top of stack   */
    *stk--  = (INT16U)FP_OFF(task);
    *stk--  = (INT16U)0xAAAA;           /* AX = 0xAAAA                         (5) */
    *stk--  = (INT16U)0xCCCC;           /* CX = 0xCCCC                             */
    *stk--  = (INT16U)0xDDDD;           /* DX = 0xDDDD                             */
    *stk--  = (INT16U)0xBBBB;           /* BX = 0xBBBB                             */
    *stk--  = (INT16U)0x0000;           /* SP = 0x0000                             */
    *stk--  = (INT16U)0x1111;           /* BP = 0x1111                             */
    *stk--  = (INT16U)0x2222;           /* SI = 0x2222                             */
    *stk--  = (INT16U)0x3333;           /* DI = 0x3333                             */
    *stk--  = (INT16U)0x4444;           /* ES = 0x4444                             */
    *stk     = _DS;                     /* DS = Current value of DS            (6) */
    return ((void *)stk);
}
```

OSTaskStkInit() creates and initializes a local pointer to 16-bit elements because stack entries are 16 bits wide on the 80x86 [L9.10(1)]. Note that µC/OS-II requires that the pointer ptos points to an empty stack entry.

The Borland C/C++ compiler passes the argument pdata on the stack instead of registers (at least with the compiler options I selected). Because of this, pdata is placed on the stack frame with the offset and segment in the order shown [L9.10(2)].

The address of your task is placed on the stack next [L9.10(3)]. In theory, this should be the return address of your task. However, in µC/OS-II, a task must never return, so what is placed here is not really critical.

The status word (SW) along with the task address are placed on the stack [L9.10(4)] to simulate the behavior of the processor in response to an interrupt. The SW register is initialized to 0x0202. This allows the task to have interrupts enabled when it starts. You can in fact start all your tasks with interrupts disabled by forcing SW to 0x0002 instead. There are no options in µC/OS-II to selectively enable interrupts upon startup for some tasks and disable interrupts upon task startup for others. In other words, either all tasks have interrupts disabled upon startup or all tasks have them disabled. You could, however, overcome this limitation by passing the desired interrupt startup state of a task by using pdata. If you chose to have interrupts disabled, each task needs to enable them when they execute. You also have to modify OSTaskIdle() and OSTaskStat() to enable interrupts in those functions. If you don't, your application will crash! I would thus recommend that you leave SW initialized to 0x0202 and have interrupts enabled when the task starts.

Next, the remaining registers are placed on the stack to simulate the PUSHA, PUSH ES, and PUSH DS instructions, which are assumed to be found at the beginning of every ISR [L9.10(5)]. Note that the AX, BX, CX, DX, SP, BP, SI, and DI registers are placed to satisfy the order of the PUSHA instruction. If you port this code to a "plain" 8086 processor, you may want to simulate the PUSHA instruction or place the registers in a neater order. You should also note that each register has a unique value instead of all zeros. This can be useful for debugging. Also, the Borland compiler supports "pseudoregisters" (i.e., the _DS keyword notifies the compiler to obtain the value of the DS register), which in this case is used to copy the current value of the DS register to the simulated stack frame [L9.10(6)].

Once completed, OSTaskStkInit() returns the address of the new top-of-stack. OSTaskCreate() or OSTaskCreateExt() takes this address and saves it in the task's OS_TCB.

9.05.02   *OSTaskCreateHook()*

As previously mentioned, OS_CPU_C.C does not define code for this function.

9.05.03   *OSTaskDelHook()*

As previously mentioned, OS_CPU_C.C does not define code for this function.

9.05.04   *OSTaskSwHook()*

As previously mentioned, OS_CPU_C.C does not define code for this function. See Example 3 on how to use this function.

9.05.05   *OSTaskStatHook()*

As previously mentioned, OS_CPU_C.C does not define code for this function. See Example 3 for an example on how to use this function.

9.05.06   *OSTimeTickHook()*

As previously mentioned, OS_CPU_C.C does not define code for this function.

9

9.06 Memory Requirements

Table 9.1 shows the amount of memory (both code and data space) used by μC/OS-II based on the value of configuration constants. *Data* in this case means RAM and *code* means ROM if μC/OS-II is used in an embedded system. The spreadsheet is provided on the companion diskette (\SOFT-WARE\uCOS-II\Ix86L\DOC\ROM-RAM.XLS). You need Microsoft Excel for Office 97 (or higher) to use this file. The spreadsheet allows you to do "what-if" scenarios based on the options you select.

The number of bytes in the Code column have been rounded up to the nearest 25 bytes. I used the Borland C/C++ compiler V3.1, and the options were set to generate the fastest code. The number of bytes shown are not meant to be accurate but are simply provided to give you a relative idea of how much code space each of the μC/OS-II group of services require. For example, if you don't need message queue services (OS_Q_EN is set to 0), then you will save about 1,475 bytes of code space. In this case, μC/OS-II would only use 6,875 bytes of code space.

The Data column is not as straightforward. Notice that the stacks for both the idle task and the statistics task have been set to 1,024 bytes (1Kb) each. Based on your own requirements, these number may be higher or lower. As a minimum, μC/OS-II requires 35 bytes of RAM (μC/OS-II Internals) for internal data structures.

Table 9.2 shows how μC/OS-II can scale down the amount of memory required for smaller applications. In this case, I allowed only 16 tasks with 64 priority levels (0 to 63), so applications will not have access to:

- Message mailbox services (OS_MBOX_EN set to 0)
- Memory partition services (OS_MEM_EN set to 0)
- Changing task priorities (OS_TASK_CHANGE_PRIO_EN set to 0)
- The old task creation function OSTaskCreate() (OS_TASK_CREATE_EN set to 0)
- Deleting tasks (OS_TASK_DEL_EN set to 0)
- Suspending and resuming tasks (OS_TASK_SUSPEND_EN set to 0)

Notice that the Code space was reduced by about 3Kb and the Data space was reduced by over 2,200 bytes! Most of the Data savings come from the reduced number of OS_TCBs needed because only 16 tasks are available. For the 80x86 large model port, each OS_TCB eats up 45 bytes of RAM.

9.07 Execution Times

Tables 9.3 through 9.5 show the execution time for most μC/OS-II functions. The values were obtained by having the compiler generate assembly language code for the 80186 processor with the C source interleaved as comments. The assembly code was then passed through the Microsoft MASM 6.11 assembler with the option that includes the number of cycles for each instruction set. I then added the number of instructions (the **I** column) and clock cycles (the **C** column) for the code to obtain three values: the maximum amount of time interrupts are disabled for the service and the minimum and maximum execution times of the service. As you can imagine, this is a very tedious job, but worth the effort. This information allows you to see the cost of each function in terms of execution time. Obviously, this information has very little use unless you are using a 80186 processor, except that it gives you an idea of the relative cost for each function.

Table 9.1   *µC/OS-II memory requirements for 80186.*

Configuration Parameters	Value	Code (bytes)	Data (bytes)
OS_MAX_EVENTS	10		164
OS_MAX_MEM_PART	5		104
OS_MAX_QS	5		124
OS_MAX_TASKS	63		2,925
OS_LOWEST_PRIO	63		264
OS_TASK_IDLE_STK_SIZE	512		1,024
OS_TASK_STAT_EN	1	325	10
OS_TASK_STAT_STK_SIZE	512		1,024
OS_CPU_HOOKS_EN	1		0
OS_MBOX_EN	1	600	(see OS_MAX_EVENTS)
OS_MEM_EN	1	725	(see OS_MAX_MEM_PART)
OS_Q_EN	1	1,475	(see OS_MAX_QS)
OS_SEM_EN	1	475	(see OS_MAX_EVENTS)
OS_TASK_CHANGE_PRIO_EN	1	450	0
OS_TASK_CREATE_EN	1	225	1
OS_TASK_CREATE_EXT_EN	1	300	0
OS_TASK_DEL_EN	1	550	0
OS_TASK_SUSPEND_EN	1	525	0
µC/OS-II Internals		2,700	35
Total Application Stacks	0		0
Total Application RAM	0		0
Total		8,350	5,675

9

Table 9.2   A scaled-down µC/OS-II configuration.

Configuration Parameters	Value	Code (bytes)	Data (bytes)
OS_MAX_EVENTS	10		164
OS_MAX_MEM_PART	5		0
OS_MAX_QS	5		124
OS_MAX_TASKS	16		792
OS_LOWEST_PRIO	63		264
OS_TASK_IDLE_STK_SIZE	512		1,024
OS_TASK_STAT_EN	1	325	10
OS_TASK_STAT_STK_SIZE	512		1,024
OS_CPU_HOOKS_EN	1		0
OS_MBOX_EN	0	0	(see OS_MAX_EVENTS)
OS_MEM_EN	0	0	(see OS_MAX_MEM_PART)
OS_Q_EN	1	1,475	(see OS_MAX_QS)
OS_SEM_EN	1	475	(see OS_MAX_EVENTS)
OS_TASK_CHANGE_PRIO_EN	0	0	0
OS_TASK_CREATE_EN	0	0	1
OS_TASK_CREATE_EXT_EN	1	300	0
OS_TASK_DEL_EN	0	0	0
OS_TASK_SUSPEND_EN	0	0	0
µC/OS-II Internals		2,700	35
Total Application Stacks	0		0
Total Application RAM	0		0
Total		5,275	3,438

The number of clock cycles were divided by 33 (i.e., I assumed a 33MHz clock) to obtain the execution time of the service in microseconds (the **μs** column). For the minimum and maximum execution times, I always assumed that the intended function of the service was performed successfully. I further assumed that the processor was able to run at the full bus speed (without wait states). On average, I determined that the 80186 requires 10 clock cycles per instruction!

For the 80186, maximum interrupt disable time is 33.3μs (or 1,100 clock cycles).

N/A means that the execution time for the function was not determined because I didn't believe it was critical.

I provided the column listing the number of instructions because you can determine the execution time of the functions for other x86 processors if you have an idea of the number of cycles per instruction. For example, you could assume that a 80486 executes (on average) one instruction every two clock cycles (five times faster than an 80186). Also, if your 80486 runs at 66MHz instead of 33MHz (two times faster), you could take the execution times listed in the tables and divide by 10.

Table 9.3 Execution times of μC/OS-II services on 33MHz 80186.

Service	Interrupts Disabled			Minimum			Maximum		
	I	*C*	*μs*	*I*	*C*	*μs*	*I*	*C*	*μs*
Miscellaneous									
OSInit()	N/A	N/A	N/A	N/A	N/A	N/A	N/A	N/A	N/A
OSSchedLock()	4	34	1.0	7	87	2.6	7	87	2.6
OSSchedUnlock()	57	567	17.2	13	130	3.9	73	782	23.7
OSStart()	0	0	0.0	35	278	8.4	35	278	8.4
OSStatInit()	N/A	N/A	N/A	N/A	N/A	N/A	N/A	N/A	N/A
OSVersion()	0	0	0.0	2	19	0.6	2	19	0.6
Interrupt Management									
OSIntEnter()	4	42	1.3	4	42	1.3	4	42	1.3
OSIntExit()	56	558	16.9	27	207	6.3	57	574	17.4
OSTickISR()	30	310	9.4	948	10,803	327.4	2,304	20,620	624.8
Message Mailboxes									
OSMboxAccept()	15	161	4.9	13	257	7.8	13	257	7.8
OSMboxCreate()	15	148	4.5	115	939	28.5	115	939	28.5
OSMboxPend()	68	567	17.2	28	317	9.6	184	1,912	57.9
OSMboxPost()	84	747	22.6	24	305	9.2	152	1,484	45.0
OSMboxQuery()	120	988	29.9	128	1,257	38.1	128	1,257	38.1

9

Table 9.3   Execution times of µC/OS-II services on 33MHz 80186. (Continued)

Service	Interrupts Disabled			Minimum			Maximum		
	I	C	µs	I	C	µs	I	C	µs
Memory Partition Management									
OSMemCreate()	21	181	5.5	72	766	23.2	72	766	23.2
OSMemGet()	19	247	7.5	18	172	5.2	33	350	10.6
OSMemPut()	23	282	8.5	12	161	4.9	29	321	9.7
OSMemQuery()	40	400	12.1	45	450	13.6	45	450	13.6
Message Queues									
OSQAccept()	34	387	11.7	25	269	8.2	44	479	14.5
OSQCreate()	14	150	4.5	154	1,291	39.1	154	1,291	39.1
OSQFlush()	18	202	6.1	25	253	7.7	25	253	7.7
OSQPend()	64	620	18.8	45	495	15.0	186	1,938	58.7
OSQPost()	98	873	26.5	51	547	16.6	155	1,493	45.2
OSQPostFront()	87	788	23.9	44	412	12.5	153	1,483	44.9
OSQQuery()	128	1,100	33.3	137	1,171	35.5	137	1,171	35.5
Semaphore Management									
OSSemAccept()	10	113	3.4	16	161	4.9	16	161	4.9
OSSemCreate()	14	140	4.2	98	768	23.3	98	768	23.3
OSSemPend()	58	567	17.2	17	184	5.6	164	1,690	51.2
OSSemPost()	87	776	23.5	18	198	6.0	151	1,469	44.5
OSSemQuery()	110	882	26.7	116	931	28.2	116	931	28.2
Task Management									
OSTaskChangePrio()	63	567	17.2	178	981	29.7	166	1,532	46.4
OSTaskCreate()	57	567	17.2	217	2,388	72.4	266	2,939	89.1
OSTaskCreateExt()	57	567	17.2	235	2,606	79.0	284	3,157	95.7
OSTaskDel()	62	620	18.8	116	1,206	36.5	165	1,757	53.2
OSTaskDelReq()	23	199	6.0	39	330	10.0	39	330	10.0
OSTaskQuery()	84	1,025	31.1	95	1,122	34.0	95	1,122	34.0
OSTaskResume()	27	242	7.3	48	430	13.0	97	981	29.7
OSTaskStkChk()	31	316	9.6	62	599	18.2	62	599	18.2
OSTaskSuspend()	37	352	10.7	63	579	17.5	112	1,130	34.2

Table 9.3 Execution times of µC/OS-II services on 33MHz 80186. (Continued)

Service	Interrupts Disabled			Minimum			Maximum		
	I	C	µs	I	C	µs	I	C	µs
Time Management									
OSTimeDly()	57	567	17.2	81	844	25.6	85	871	26.4
OSTimeDlyHMSM()	57	567	17.2	216	2,184	66.2	220	2,211	67.0
OSTimeDlyResume()	57	567	17.2	23	181	5.5	98	989	30.0
OSTimeGet()	7	57	1.7	14	117	3.5	14	117	3.5
OSTimeSet()	7	61	1.8	11	99	3.0	11	99	3.0
OSTimeTick()	30	310	9.4	900	10,257	310.8	1,908	19,707	597.2
User-Defined Functions									
OSTaskCreateHook()	0	0	0.0	4	38	1.2	4	38	1.2
OSTaskDelHook()	0	0	0.0	4	38	1.2	4	38	1.2
OSTaskStatHook()	0	0	0.0	1	16	0.5	1	16	0.5
OSTaskSwHook()	0	0	0.0	1	16	0.5	1	16	0.5
OSTimeTickHook()	0	0	0.0	1	16	0.5	1	16	0.5

Below is a list of assumptions about how the minimum, maximum, and interrupt disable times were determined and the conditions that lead to these values.

OSSchedUnlock()

Minimum assumes that OSLockNesting is decremented to 0 but there are no higher priority tasks ready to run, so OSSchedUnlock() returns to the caller.

Maximum also decrements OSLockNesting to 0, but this time, a higher priority task is ready to run. This means that a context switch occurs.

OSIntExit()

Minimum assumes that OSIntNesting is decremented to 0 but there are no higher priority tasks ready to run, so OSIntExit() returns to the interrupted task.

Maximum also decrements OSIntNesting to 0, but this time the ISR has made a higher priority task ready to run. This means that OSIntExit() does not return to the interrupted task but to the higher priority task that is ready to run instead.

9

OSTickISR()

For this function, I assume that your application has the maximum number of tasks allowed by µC/OS-II (64).

Minimum assumes that none of the 64 tasks are waiting either for time to expire or for a timeout on an event.

Maximum assumes that all 63 tasks (the idle task is never waiting) are waiting for time to expire. About 625µs may seem like a lot of time, but if you consider that all the tasks are waiting for time to expire, the CPU has nothing else to do anyway! On average, though, you can assume that OSTickISR() takes about 500µs (i.e., 5% overhead if your tick interrupt occurs every 10ms).

OSMboxPend()

Minimum assumes that a message is available at the mailbox.

Maximum occurs when a message is not available and the task has to wait. In this case, a context switch occurs. The maximum time is as seen by the calling task. This is the time it takes to look at the mailbox, determine that there is no message, call the scheduler, context switch to the new task, context switch back from whatever task was running, determine that a timeout occurred, and return to the caller.

OSMboxPost()

Minimum assumes that the mailbox is empty and no task is waiting for the mailbox to contain a message.

Maximum occurs when one or more tasks are waiting on the mailbox for a message. In this case, the message is given to the highest priority task waiting and a context switch is performed to resume that task. Again, the maximum time is as seen by the calling task. This is the time it takes to wake up the waiting task, pass it the message, call the scheduler, context switch to the task, context switch back from whatever task was running, determine that a timeout occurred, and return to the caller.

OSMemGet()

Minimum assumes that a memory block is not available.

Maximum assumes that a memory block is available and is returned to the caller.

OSMemPut()

Minimum assumes that you are returning a memory block to an already-full partition.

Maximum assumes that your are returning the memory block to the partition.

OSQPend()

Minimum assumes that a message is available at the queue.

Maximum occurs when a message is not available and the task has to wait. In this case, a context switch occurs. The maximum time is as seen by the calling task. This is the time it takes to look at the queue, determine that there is no message, call the scheduler, context switch to the new task, context switch back from whatever task was running, determine that a timeout occurred, and return to the caller.

OSQPost()

Minimum assumes that the queue is empty and that no task is waiting on the queue for a message.

Maximum occurs when one or more tasks are waiting on the queue for a message. In this case, the message is given to the highest priority task waiting, and a context switch is performed to resume that task. Again, the maximum time is as seen by the calling task. This is the time it takes to wake up the waiting task, pass it the message, call the scheduler, context switch to the task, context switch back from whatever task was running, determine that a timeout occurred, and return to the caller.

OSQPostFront()

This function is virtually the same as OSQPost().

OSSemPend()

Minimum assumes that the semaphore is available (i.e., has a count greater than 0).

Maximum occurs when the semaphore is not available and the task has to wait. In this case, a context switch occurs. As usual, the maximum time is as seen by the calling task. This is the time it takes to look at the semaphore value, determine that it's 0, call the scheduler, context switch to the new task, context switch back from whatever task was running, determine that a timeout occurred, and return to the caller.

OSSemPost()

Minimum assumes that there are no tasks waiting on the semaphore.

Maximum occurs when one or more tasks are waiting for the semaphore. In this case, the highest priority task waiting is readied and a context switch is performed to resume that task. Again, the maximum time is as seen by the calling task. This is the time it takes to wake up the waiting task, call the scheduler, context switch to the task, context switch back from whatever task was running, determine that a timeout occurred, and return to the caller.

OSTaskChangePrio()

Minimum assumes that you are changing the priority of a task that does not have a priority higher than the current task.

Maximum assumes that you are changing the priority of a task that has a higher priority than the current task. In this case, a context switch occurs.

9

OSTaskCreate()

Minimum assumes that OSTaskCreate() is not creating a higher priority task, so no context switch is involved.

Maximum assumes that OSTaskCreate() is creating a higher priority task, so a context switch will result.

In both cases, the execution times assumed that OSTaskCreateHook() didn't do anything.

OSTaskCreateExt()

Minimum assumes that OSTaskCreateExt() does not need to initialize the stack with zeros in order to do stack checking.

Maximum assumes that OSTaskCreateExt() has to initialize the stack of the task. However, the execution time greatly depends on the number of elements to initialize. I determined that it takes 100 clock cycles (3µs) to clear each element. A 1,000-byte stack would require: 1,000 bytes divided by 2 bytes/element (16-bit wide stack) times 3µs per element, or an additional 1,500µs. Note that interrupts are enabled while the stack is being cleared to allow your application to respond to interrupts.

In both cases, the execution times assumed that OSTaskCreateHook() didn't do anything.

OSTaskDel()

Minimum assumes that the task being deleted is not the current task.

Maximum assumes that the task being deleted is the current task. In this case, a context switch occurs.

OSTaskDelReq()

Both *minimum* and *maximum* assume that the call returns with an indication that the task is deleted. This function is so short that it doesn't make much difference anyway.

OSTaskResume()

Minimum assumes that a task is being resumed but has a lower priority than the current task. In this case, a context switch does not occur.

Maximum assumes that the task being resumed is ready to run and has a higher priority than the current task. In this case, a context switch occurs.

OSTaskStkChk()

Minimum assumes that OSTaskStkChk() is checking a full stack. Obviously, this is hardly possible since the task being checked most likely would have crashed. However, this does establish the absolute minimum execution time, however unlikely.

Maximum also assumes that OSTaskStkChk() is checking a full stack, but you need to add the amount of time it takes to check each zero stack element. I was able to determine that each element takes 80 clock cycles (2.4µs) to check. A 1,000-byte stack would require: 1,000 bytes divided by 2 bytes/element (16-bit wide stack) times 2.4µs per element, or an additional 1,200µs. Total execution time would be 1,218µs. Note that interrupts are enabled while the stack is being checked.

OSTaskSuspend()

Minimum assumes that the task being suspended is not the current task.

Maximum assumes that the current task is being suspended, and a context switch occurs.

OSTaskQuery()

Minimum and *maximum* are the same, and it is assumed that all the options are included so that an OS_ TCB contains all the fields. In this case, an OS_TCB for the large model port requires 45 bytes.

OSTimeDly()

Both *minimum* and *maximum* assume that the time delay is greater than 0 ticks. In this case, a context switch always occurs.

Minimum is the case where the bit in OSRdyGrp doesn't need to be cleared.

OSTimeDlyHMSM()

Both *minimum* and *maximum* assume that the time delay is greater than 0. In this case, a context switch occurs. Furthermore, the time specified must result in a delay of fewer than 65,536 ticks. In other words, if a tick interrupt occurs every 10ms (100Hz), the maximum value that you can specify is 10 minutes, 55 seconds, 350ms in order for the execution times shown to be valid. Obviously, you can specify longer delays using this function call.

OSTimeDlyResume()

Minimum assumes that the delayed task is made ready to run but has a lower priority than the current task. In this case, µC/OS-II does not perform a context switch.

Maximum assumes that the delayed task is made ready to run and has a higher priority than the current task. This, of course, results in a context switch.

OSTimeTick()

This function is almost identical to OSTickISR(), except that OSTickISR() accounted for OSIntEnter() and OSIntExit(). I assume that your application can have the maximum number of tasks allowed by µC/OS-II (64).

Minimum assumes that none of the 64 tasks are waiting either for time to expire or for a timeout on an event.

Maximum assumed that all 63 tasks (the idle task is never waiting) are waiting for time to expire. Although 600µs may seem like a lot of time, if you consider that all the tasks are waiting for time to expire, then the CPU has nothing else to do anyway! On average, though, you can assume that OSTimeTick() takes about 450µs (i.e., 4.5% overhead if your tick interrupt occurs every 10ms).

9

Table 9.4 Execution times sorted by interrupt disable time.

Service	Interrupts Disabled			Minimum			Maximum		
	I	C	µs	I	C	µs	I	C	µs
OSVersion()	0	0	0.0	2	19	0.6	2	19	0.6
OSStart()	0	0	0.0	35	278	8.4	35	278	8.4
OSSchedLock()	4	34	1.0	7	87	2.6	7	87	2.6
OSIntEnter()	4	42	1.3	4	42	1.3	4	42	1.3
OSTimeGet()	7	57	1.7	14	117	3.5	14	117	3.5
OSTimeSet()	7	61	1.8	11	99	3.0	11	99	3.0
OSSemAccept()	10	113	3.4	16	161	4.9	16	161	4.9
OSSemCreate()	14	140	4.2	98	768	23.3	98	768	23.3
OSMboxCreate()	15	148	4.5	115	939	28.5	115	939	28.5
OSQCreate()	14	150	4.5	154	1,291	39.1	154	1,291	39.1
OSMboxAccept()	15	161	4.9	13	257	7.8	13	257	7.8
OSMemCreate()	21	181	5.5	72	766	23.2	72	766	23.2
OSTaskDelReq()	23	199	6.0	39	330	10.0	39	330	10.0
OSQFlush()	18	202	6.1	25	253	7.7	25	253	7.7
OSTaskResume()	27	242	7.3	48	430	13.0	97	981	29.7
OSMemGet()	19	247	7.5	18	172	5.2	33	350	10.6
OSMemPut()	23	282	8.5	12	161	4.9	29	321	9.7
OSTimeTick()	30	310	9.4	900	10,257	310.8	1,908	19,707	597.2
OSTickISR()	30	310	9.4	948	10,803	327.4	2,304	20,620	624.8
OSTaskStkChk()	31	316	9.6	62	599	18.2	62	599	18.2
OSTaskSuspend()	37	352	10.7	63	579	17.5	112	1,130	34.2
OSQAccept()	34	387	11.7	25	269	8.2	44	479	14.5
OSMemQuery()	40	400	12.1	45	450	13.6	45	450	13.6
OSIntExit()	56	558	16.9	27	207	6.3	57	574	17.4
OSSchedUnlock()	57	567	17.2	13	130	3.9	73	782	23.7
OSTimeDly()	57	567	17.2	81	844	25.6	85	871	26.4
OSTimeDlyResume()	57	567	17.2	23	181	5.5	98	989	30.0
OSTaskChangePrio()	63	567	17.2	178	981	29.7	166	1,532	46.4
OSSemPend()	58	567	17.2	17	184	5.6	164	1,690	51.2
OSMboxPend()	68	567	17.2	28	317	9.6	184	1,912	57.9
OSTimeDlyHMSM()	57	567	17.2	216	2,184	66.2	220	2,211	67.0
OSTaskCreate()	57	567	17.2	217	2,388	72.4	266	2,939	89.1
OSTaskCreateExt()	57	567	17.2	235	2,606	79.0	284	3,157	95.7

Table 9.4 Execution times sorted by interrupt disable time. (Continued)

Service	Interrupts Disabled			Minimum			Maximum		
	I	C	μs	I	C	μs	I	C	μs
OSTaskDel()	62	620	18.8	116	1,206	36.5	165	1,757	53.2
OSQPend()	64	620	18.8	45	495	15.0	186	1,938	58.7
OSMboxPost()	84	747	22.6	24	305	9.2	152	1,484	45.0
OSSemPost()	87	776	23.5	18	198	6.0	151	1,469	44.5
OSQPostFront()	87	788	23.9	44	412	12.5	153	1,483	44.9
OSQPost()	98	873	26.5	51	547	16.6	155	1,493	45.2
OSSemQuery()	110	882	26.7	116	931	28.2	116	931	28.2
OSMboxQuery()	120	988	29.9	128	1,257	38.1	128	1,257	38.1
OSTaskQuery()	84	1,025	31.1	95	1,122	34.0	95	1,122	34.0
OSQQuery()	128	1,100	33.3	137	1,171	35.5	137	1,171	35.5
OSStatInit()	N/A	N/A	N/A	N/A	N/A	N/A	N/A	N/A	N/A
OSInit()	N/A	N/A	N/A	N/A	N/A	N/A	N/A	N/A	N/A

9

Table 9.5   Execution times sorted by maximum execution time.

Service	Interrupts Disabled			Minimum			Maximum		
	I	C	µs	I	C	µs	I	C	µs
OSVersion()	0	0	0.0	2	19	0.6	2	19	0.6
OSIntEnter()	4	42	1.3	4	42	1.3	4	42	1.3
OSSchedLock()	4	34	1.0	7	87	2.6	7	87	2.6
OSTimeSet()	7	61	1.8	11	99	3.0	11	99	3.0
OSTimeGet()	7	57	1.7	14	117	3.5	14	117	3.5
OSSemAccept()	10	113	3.4	16	161	4.9	16	161	4.9
OSQFlush()	18	202	6.1	25	253	7.7	25	253	7.7
OSMboxAccept()	15	161	4.9	13	257	7.8	13	257	7.8
OSStart()	0	0	0.0	35	278	8.4	35	278	8.4
OSMemPut()	23	282	8.5	12	161	4.9	29	321	9.7
OSTaskDelReq()	23	199	6.0	39	330	10.0	39	330	10.0
OSMemGet()	19	247	7.5	18	172	5.2	33	350	10.6
OSMemQuery()	40	400	12.1	45	450	13.6	45	450	13.6
OSQAccept()	34	387	11.7	25	269	8.2	44	479	14.5
OSIntExit()	56	558	16.9	27	207	6.3	57	574	17.4
OSTaskStkChk()	31	316	9.6	62	599	18.2	62	599	18.2
OSMemCreate()	21	181	5.5	72	766	23.2	72	766	23.2
OSSemCreate()	14	140	4.2	98	768	23.3	98	768	23.3
OSSchedUnlock()	57	567	17.2	13	130	3.9	73	782	23.7
OSTimeDly()	57	567	17.2	81	844	25.6	85	871	26.4
OSSemQuery()	110	882	26.7	116	931	28.2	116	931	28.2
OSMboxCreate()	15	148	4.5	115	939	28.5	115	939	28.5
OSTaskResume()	27	242	7.3	48	430	13.0	97	981	29.7
OSTimeDlyResume()	57	567	17.2	23	181	5.5	98	989	30.0
OSTaskQuery()	84	1,025	31.1	95	1,122	34.0	95	1,122	34.0
OSTaskSuspend()	37	352	10.7	63	579	17.5	112	1,130	34.2
OSQQuery()	128	1,100	33.3	137	1,171	35.5	137	1,171	35.5
OSMboxQuery()	120	988	29.9	128	1,257	38.1	128	1,257	38.1
OSQCreate()	14	150	4.5	154	1,291	39.1	154	1,291	39.1
OSSemPost()	87	776	23.5	18	198	6.0	151	1,469	44.5
OSQPostFront()	87	788	23.9	44	412	12.5	153	1,483	44.9
OSMboxPost()	84	747	22.6	24	305	9.2	152	1,484	45.0
OSQPost()	98	873	26.5	51	547	16.6	155	1,493	45.2

Table 9.5   Execution times sorted by maximum execution time. (Continued)

Service	Interrupts Disabled			Minimum			Maximum		
	I	*C*	*μs*	*I*	*C*	*μs*	*I*	*C*	*μs*
OSTaskChangePrio()	63	567	17.2	178	981	29.7	166	1,532	46.4
OSSemPend()	58	567	17.2	17	184	5.6	164	1,690	51.2
OSTaskDel()	62	620	18.8	116	1,206	36.5	165	1,757	53.2
OSMboxPend()	68	567	17.2	28	317	9.6	184	1,912	57.9
OSQPend()	64	620	18.8	45	495	15.0	186	1,938	58.7
OSTimeDlyHMSM()	57	567	17.2	216	2,184	66.2	220	2,211	67.0
OSTaskCreate()	57	567	17.2	217	2,388	72.4	266	2,939	89.1
OSTaskCreateExt()	57	567	17.2	235	2,606	79.0	284	3,157	95.7
OSTimeTicK()	30	310	9.4	900	10,257	310.8	1,908	19,707	597.2
OSTickISR()	30	310	9.4	948	10,803	327.4	2,304	20,620	624.8
OSInit()	N/A	N/A	N/A	N/A	N/A	N/A	N/A	N/A	N/A
OSStatInit()	N/A	N/A	N/A	N/A	N/A	N/A	N/A	N/A	N/A

9

Chapter 10

Upgrading from µC/OS to µC/OS-II

This chapter describes how to migrate a µC/OS port to µC/OS-II. If you have ported µC/OS to a processor, the effort required to migrate to µC/OS-II should be minimal. In most cases, you should be able to do this in about an hour. If you are familiar with the µC/OS port, you may want to go to the summary in section 10.05.

10.00 Directories and Files

The first similarity you will notice is the directory structure, except that the main directory is called \SOFTWARE\uCOS-II instead of \SOFTWARE\uCOS.

All µC/OS-II ports should be placed under the \SOFTWARE\uCOS-II directory on your hard drive. The source code for each microprocessor or microcontroller port must be found in either two or three files: OS_CPU.H, OS_CPU_C.C, and, optionally, OS_CPU_A.ASM. The assembly language file is optional because some compilers allow you to have in-line assembly code, which you can place directly in OS_CPU_C.C.

The processor-specific code (i.e., the port) for µC/OS is placed in files having the processor name as part of the filenames. For example, the Intel 80x86 real mode, large model has files called Ix86L.H, Ix86L_C.C, and Ix86L_A.ASM. Table 10.1 shows the correspondence between the new filenames and directories and the old ones.

Table 10.1 Renaming files for µC/OS-II.

\SOFTWARE\uCOS\Ix86L	\SOFTWARE\uCOS-II\Ix86L
Ix86L.H	OS_CPU.H
Ix86L_A.ASM	OS_CPU_A.ASM
Ix86L_C.C	OS_CPU_C.C

10

As a starting point, all you have to do is copy the old filenames (from the µC/OS directory) to the new names in the equivalent µC/OS-II directory. It will be easier to modify these files than to create them from scratch. Table 10.2 shows a few more examples of µC/OS port file translations.

Table 10.2   *Renaming files from µC/OS to µC/OS-II.*

\SOFTWARE\uCOS\I80251	\SOFTWARE\uCOS-II\I80251
I80251.H	OS_CPU.H
I80251.C	OS_CPU_C.C
\SOFTWARE\uCOS\M680x0	\SOFTWARE\uCOS-II\M680x0
M680x0.H	OS_CPU.H
M680x0.C	OS_CPU_C.C
\SOFTWARE\uCOS\M68HC11	\SOFTWARE\uCOS-II\M68HC11
M68HC11.H	OS_CPU.H
M68HC11.C	OS_CPU_C.C
\SOFTWARE\uCOS\Z80	\SOFTWARE\uCOS-II\Z80
Z80.H	OS_CPU.H
Z80_A.ASM	OS_CPU_A.ASM
Z80_C.C	OS_CPU_C.C

10.01   `INCLUDES.H`

You need to modify the `INCLUDES.H` file of your application. For example, the µC/OS `INCLUDES.H` file for the Intel 80x86 real mode, large model is shown in Listing 10.1. You should change

- the directory name `UCOS` to `uCOS-II`
- the filename `IX86L.H` to `OS_CPU.H`
- the filename `UCOS.H` to `uCOS_II.H`

The new file is shown in Listing 10.2.

10.02   `OS_CPU.H`

`OS_CPU.H` contains processor- and implementation-specific `#define` constants, macros, and `typedefs`.

10.02.01   *Compiler-Specific Data Types*

To satisfy µC/OS-II, you need to create six new data types: `INT8U`, `INT8S`, `INT16U`, `INT16S`, `INT32U`, and `INT32S`. These correspond to unsigned and signed 8-, 16-, and 32-bit integers, respectively. In µC/OS, I declared the equivalent data types: `UBYTE`, `BYTE`, `UWORD`, `WORD`, `ULONG`, and `LONG`. All you have to do is copy the µC/OS data types and change `UBYTE` to `INT8U`, `BYTE` to `INT8S`, `UWORD` to `INT16U`, …, as shown in Listing 10.2.

Listing 10.1   µC/OS **INCLUDES.H**

```
/*
****************************************************************
*                        INCLUDES.H
****************************************************************
*/

#include      <STDIO.H>
#include      <STRING.H>
#include      <CTYPE.H>
#include      <STDLIB.H>
#include      <CONIO.H>
#include      <DOS.H>

#include      "\SOFTWARE\UCOS\IX86L\IX86L.H"
#include      "OS_CFG.H"
#include      "\SOFTWARE\UCOS\SOURCE\UCOS.H"
```

Listing 10.2   µC/OS-II **INCLUDES.H**.

```
/*
****************************************************************
*                        INCLUDES.H
****************************************************************
*/

#include      <STDIO.H>
#include      <STRING.H>
#include      <CTYPE.H>
#include      <STDLIB.H>
#include      <CONIO.H>
#include      <DOS.H>

#include      "\SOFTWARE\uCOS-II\IX86L\OS_CPU.H"
#include      "OS_CFG.H"
#include      "\SOFTWARE\uCOS-II\SOURCE\uCOS_II.H"
```

10

Listing 10.3   µC/OS to µC/OS-II data types.

```
/* uC/OS data types:                                                        */
typedef unsigned char   UBYTE;      /* Unsigned  8 bit quantity             */
typedef signed   char   BYTE;       /* Signed    8 bit quantity             */
typedef unsigned int    UWORD;      /* Unsigned 16 bit quantity             */
typedef signed   int    WORD;       /* Signed   16 bit quantity             */
typedef unsigned long   ULONG;      /* Unsigned 32 bit quantity             */
typedef signed   long   LONG;       /* Signed   32 bit quantity             */


/* uC/OS-II data types                                                      */
typedef unsigned char   INT8U;      /* Unsigned  8 bit quantity             */
typedef signed   char   INT8S;      /* Signed    8 bit quantity             */
typedef unsigned int    INT16U;     /* Unsigned 16 bit quantity             */
typedef signed   int    INT16S;     /* Signed   16 bit quantity             */
typedef unsigned long   INT32U;     /* Unsigned 32 bit quantity             */
typedef signed   long   INT32S;     /* Signed   32 bit quantity             */
```

In µC/OS, a task stack was declared as being of type OS_STK_TYPE. A stack in µC/OS-II must be declared as type OS_STK. To avoid editing all your application files, simply create the two data types in OS_CPU.H, as shown in Listing 10.4 (Intel 80x86 given as an example).

Listing 10.4   µC/OS and µC/OS-II task stack data types.

```
#define OS_STK_TYPE   UWORD      /* Satisfy uC/OS                           */
#define OS_STK        INT16U     /* Satisfy uC/OS-II                        */
```

10.02.02   OS_ENTER_CRITICAL(), and OS_EXIT_CRITICAL()

µC/OS-II (as did µC/OS) defines two macros to disable and enable interrupts: OS_ENTER_CRITICAL() and OS_EXIT_CRITICAL(), respectively. You shouldn't have to change these macros when migrating from µC/OS to µC/OS-II.

10.02.03   OS_STK_GROWTH

The stack on most microprocessors and microcontrollers grows from high to low memory. However, some processors work the other way around. µC/OS-II has been designed to handle either flavor by specifying which way the stack grows through the configuration constant OS_STK_GROWTH, as shown below.

Set OS_STK_GROWTH to 0 for low to high memory stack growth.
Set OS_STK_GROWTH to 1 for high to low memory stack growth.

These are new #define constants from µC/OS, so you need to include them in OS_CPU.H.

10.02.04 OS_TASK_SW()

OS_TASK_SW() is a macro that is invoked when μC/OS-II switches from a low-priority task to the highest priority task. OS_TASK_SW() is always called from task-level code. This macro doesn't need to be changed from μC/OS to μC/OS-II.

10.02.05 OS_FAR

OS_FAR was used in μC/OS because of the Intel 80x86 architecture. This #define has been removed in μC/OS-II because it made the code less portable. It turns out that if you specify the large model (for the Intel 80x86), all memory references assumed the far attribute anyway.

All tasks in μC/OS were declared as shown in Listing 10.5. You can either edit all the files that make references to OS_FAR or simply create a macro in OS_CPU.H to equate OS_FAR to nothing in order to satisfy μC/OS-II.

Listing 10.5 Declaration of a task in μC/OS.

```
void OS_FAR task (void *pdata)
{
    pdata = pdata;
    while (1) {

        .

        .

    }
}
```

10.03 OS_CPU_A.ASM

A μC/OS and μC/OS-II port requires that you write four fairly simple assembly language functions:

```
OSStartHighRdy()
OSCtxSw()
OSIntCtxSw()
OSTickISR()
```

10.03.01 OSStartHighRdy()

In μC/OS-II, OSStartHighRdy() must call OSTaskSwHook(). OSTaskSwHook() does not exist in μC/OS. OSStartHighRdy() needs to call OSTaskSwHook() before you load the stack pointer of the highest priority task. Also, OSStartHighRdy() needs to set OSRunning to 1 immediately after calling OSTaskSwHook(). Listing 10.6 shows the pseudocode of OSStartHighRdy(). μC/OS only had the last three steps.

10

Listing 10.6 Pseudocode for *OSStartHighRdy()*.

```
OSStartHighRdy:
    Call OSTaskSwHook();
    Set OSRunning to 1;
    Load the processor stack pointer with OSTCBHighRdy->OSTCBStkPtr;
    POP all the processor registers from the stack;
    Execute a Return from Interrupt instruction;
```

10.03.02 *OSCtxSw()*

Two things have been added in µC/OS-II during a context switch. First, you must call OSTaskSwHook() immediately after saving the current task's stack pointer into the current task's TCB. Second, you must set OSPrioCur to OSPrioHighRdy before you load the new task's stack pointer.

Listing 10.7 shows the pseudocode of OSCtxSw(). µC/OS-II adds steps L10.7(1) and (2).

Listing 10.7 Pseudocode for *OSCtxSw()*.

```
OSCtxSw:
    PUSH processor registers onto the current task's stack;
    Save the stack pointer at OSTCBCur->OSTCBStkPtr;
    Call OSTaskSwHook();                                              (1)
    OSTCBCur  = OSTCBHighRdy;
    OSPrioCur = OSPrioHighRdy;                                        (2)
    Load the processor stack pointer with OSTCBHighRdy->OSTCBStkPtr;
    POP all the processor registers from the stack;
    Execute a Return from Interrupt instruction;
```

10.03.03 *OSIntCtxSw()*

Like OSCtxSw(), two things have been added in OSIntCtxSw() for µC/OS-II. First, you must call OSTaskSwHook() immediately after saving the current task's stack pointer into the current task's TCB. Second, you must set OSPrioCur to OSPrioHighRdy before you load the new task's stack pointer.

Listing 10.8 shows the pseudocode of OSIntCtxSw(). µC/OS-II adds steps L10.8(1) and (2).

Listing 10.8 Pseudocode for *OSIntCtxSw()*.

```
OSIntCtxSw():
    Adjust the stack pointer to remove call to OSIntExit(), locals in OSIntExit()
        and the call to OSIntCtxSw();
    Save the stack pointer at OSTCBCur->OSTCBStkPtr;
    Call OSTaskSwHook();                                              (1)
    OSTCBCur  = OSTCBHighRdy;
```

Listing 10.8   Pseudocode for *OSIntCtxSw()*. (Continued)

```
OSPrioCur = OSPrioHighRdy;                                          (2)
Load the processor stack pointer with OSTCBHighRdy->OSTCBStkPtr;
POP all the processor registers from the stack;
Execute a Return from Interrupt instruction;
```

10.03.04   *OSTickISR()*

The code for this function in µC/OS-II is identical to µC/OS and shouldn't be altered.

10.04   *OS_CPU_C.C*

A µC/OS-II port requires that you write six fairly simple C functions:

```
OSTaskStkInit()
OSTaskCreateHook()
OSTaskDelHook()
OSTaskSwHook()
OSTaskStatHook()
OSTimeTickHook()
```

The only necessary function is OSTaskStkInit(). The other five functions must be declared but don't need to contain code.

10.04.01   *OSTaskStkInit()*

In µC/OS, OSTaskCreate() was considered a processor-specific function. It turned out that only a portion of OSTaskCreate() was actually processor specific. This portion has been extracted out of OSTaskCreate() and placed in a new function called OSTaskStkInit().

OSTaskStkInit() is only responsible for setting up the task's stack to look as if an interrupt has just occurred and all the processor registers were pushed onto the task's stack. To give you an example, Listing 10.9 shows the µC/OS code for OSTaskCreate() for the Intel 80x86 real mode, large model. Listing 10.10 shows the µC/OS-II code for OSTaskStkInit() for the same processor. As you can see by comparing the two listings, everything between OS_EXIT_CRITICAL() [L10.9(1)] and the call to OSTCBInit() [L10.9(2)] has been moved to OSTaskStkInit().

Notice that the code for µC/OS-II uses the new data types (see section 10.02.01, Compiler-Specific Data Types). Also, instead of initializing all the processor registers to 0x0000, I decided to initialize them with a value that would make debugging a little easier. Note that the initial value of a register when a task is created is not critical.

10

Listing 10.9   *OSTaskCreate()* for *µC/OS*.

```
UBYTE OSTaskCreate(void (*task)(void *pd), void *pdata, void *pstk, UBYTE p)
{
    UWORD OS_FAR *stk;
    UBYTE        err;
```

Listing 10.9 *OSTaskCreate()* for µC/OS. *(Continued)*

```
OS_ENTER_CRITICAL();
if (OSTCBPrioTbl[p] == (OS_TCB *)0) {
    OSTCBPrioTbl[p] = (OS_TCB *)1;
    OS_EXIT_CRITICAL();                                     (1)
    stk   = (UWORD OS_FAR *)pstk;
    *--stk = (UWORD)FP_OFF(pdata);
    *--stk = (UWORD)FP_SEG(task);
    *--stk = (UWORD)FP_OFF(task);
    *--stk = (UWORD)0x0202;
    *--stk = (UWORD)FP_SEG(task);
    *--stk = (UWORD)FP_OFF(task);
    *--stk = (UWORD)0x0000;
    *--stk = (UWORD)0x0000;
    *--stk = (UWORD)0x0000;
    *--stk = (UWORD)0x0000;
    *--stk = (UWORD)0x0000;
    *--stk = (UWORD)0x0000;
    *--stk = (UWORD)0x0000;
    *--stk = (UWORD)0x0000;
    *--stk = (UWORD)0x0000;
    *--stk = _DS;
    err   = OSTCBInit(p, (void far *)stk);                  (2)
    if (err == OS_NO_ERR) {
        if (OSRunning) {
            OSSched();
        }
    } else {
        OSTCBPrioTbl[p] = (OS_TCB *)0;
    }
    return (err);
} else {
    OS_EXIT_CRITICAL();
    return (OS_PRIO_EXIST);
}
}
```

Listing 10.10 *OSTaskStkInit() for μC/OS-II.*

```
void *OSTaskStkInit (void (*task)(void *pd), void *pdata, void *ptos, INT16U opt)
{
    INT16U *stk;


    opt   = opt;
    stk   = (INT16U *)ptos;
    *stk-- = (INT16U)FP_SEG(pdata);
    *stk-- = (INT16U)FP_OFF(pdata);
    *stk-- = (INT16U)FP_SEG(task);
    *stk-- = (INT16U)FP_OFF(task);
    *stk-- = (INT16U)0x0202;
    *stk-- = (INT16U)FP_SEG(task);
    *stk-- = (INT16U)FP_OFF(task);
    *stk-- = (INT16U)0xAAAA;
    *stk-- = (INT16U)0xCCCC;
    *stk-- = (INT16U)0xDDDD;
    *stk-- = (INT16U)0xBBBB;
    *stk-- = (INT16U)0x0000;
    *stk-- = (INT16U)0x1111;
    *stk-- = (INT16U)0x2222;
    *stk-- = (INT16U)0x3333;
    *stk-- = (INT16U)0x4444;
    *stk   = _DS;
    return ((void *)stk);
}
```

10.04.02 *OSTaskCreateHook()*

OSTaskCreateHook() does not exist in μC/OS. When migrating from μC/OS to μC/OS-II, simply declare an empty function, as shown in Listing 10.11. Note that if I didn't assign ptcb to ptcb, some compilers would generate a warning indicating that the argument ptcb is not used.

Listing 10.11 *OSTaskCreateHook() for μC/OS-II.*

```
#if OS_CPU_HOOKS_EN
OSTaskCreateHook(OS_TCB *ptcb)
{
    ptcb = ptcb;
}
#endif
```

10

You should also wrap the function declaration with the conditional compilation directive. The code for OSTaskCreateHook() is generated only if OS_CPU_HOOKS_EN is set to 1 in OS_CFG.H. This allows the user of your port to redefine all the hook functions in a different file.

10.04.03   OSTaskDelHook()

OSTaskDelHook() does not exist in μC/OS. Again, to migrate from μC/OS to μC/OS-II, simply declare an empty function, as shown in Listing 10.12. Note that if I didn't assign ptcb to ptcb, some compilers would generate a warning indicating that the argument ptcb is not used.

Listing 10.12 *OSTaskDelHook() for μC/OS-II.*

```
#if OS_CPU_HOOKS_EN
OSTaskDelHook(OS_TCB *ptcb)
{
    ptcb = ptcb;
}
#endif
```

You should also wrap the function declaration with the conditional compilation directive. The code for OSTaskDelHook() is generated only if OS_CPU_HOOKS_EN is set to 1 in OS_CFG.H. This allows the user of your port to redefine all the hook functions in a different file.

10.04.04   OSTaskSwHook()

OSTaskSwHook() also does not exist in μC/OS. To migrate from μC/OS to μC/OS-II, simply declare an empty function, as shown in Listing 10.13.

Listing 10.13 *OSTaskSwHook() for μC/OS-II.*

```
#if OS_CPU_HOOKS_EN
OSTaskSwHook(void)
{
}
#endif
```

You should also wrap the function declaration with the conditional compilation directive. The code for OSTaskSwHook() is generated only if OS_CPU_HOOKS_EN is set to 1 in OS_CFG.H.

10.04.05 `OSTaskStatHook()`

`OSTaskStatHook()` also does not exist in µC/OS. Simply declare an empty function, as shown in Listing 10.14.

Listing 10.14 `OSTaskStatHook()` *for µC/OS-II.*

```
#if OS_CPU_HOOKS_EN
OSTaskStatHook(void)
{
}
#endif
```

You should also wrap the function declaration with the conditional compilation directive. The code for `OSTaskStatHook()` is generated only if `OS_CPU_HOOKS_EN` is set to 1 in `OS_CFG.H`.

10.04.06 `OSTimeTickHook()`

`OSTimeTickHook()` also does not exist in µC/OS. Simply declare an empty function, as shown in Listing 10.15.

Listing 10.15 `OSTimeTickHook()` *for µC/OS-II.*

```
#if OS_CPU_HOOKS_EN
OSTimeTickHook(void)
{
}
#endif
```

You should also wrap the function declaration with the conditional compilation directive. The code for `OSTimeTickHook()` is generated only if `OS_CPU_HOOKS_EN` is set to 1 in `OS_CFG.H`.

10.05 Summary

Table 10.3 provides a summary of the changes needed to migrate a µC/OS port to µC/OS-II. Note that *processor_name.?* is the name of the µC/OS file containing the port.

10

Table 10.3 Summary of changes when migrating a µC/OS port to µC/OS-II.

µC/OS	µC/OS-II
Processor_name.H	OS_CPU.H

Data types
  UBYTE
  BYTE
  UWORD
  WORD
  ULONG
  LONG
	Data types
	  INT8U
	  INT8S
	  INT16U
	  INT16S
	  INT32U
	  INT32S

OS_STK_TYPE	OS_STK
OS_ENTER_CRITICAL()	No change
OS_EXIT_CRITICAL()	No change
—	Add OS_STK_GROWTH
OS_TASK_SW()	No change
OS_FAR	Define OS_FAR to nothing or remove all references to OS_FAR
Processor_name.ASM	OS_CPU_A.ASM
OSStartHighRdy()	Add call to OSTaskSwHook(); set OSRunning to 1 (8 bits)
OSCtxSw()	Add call to OSTaskSwHook(); copy OSPrioHighRdy to OSPrioCur (8 bits)
OSIntCtxSw()	Add call to OSTaskSwHook(); copy OSPrioHighRdy to OSPrioCur (8 bits)
OSTickISR()	No change
Processor_name.C	OS_CPU_C.C
OSTaskCreate()	Extract stack initialization code and put it in OSTaskStkInit()
—	Add the empty function OSTaskCreateHook()
—	Add the empty function OSTaskDelHook()
—	Add the empty function OSTaskSwHook()
—	Add the empty function OSTaskStatHook()
—	Add the empty function OSTimeTickHook()

Chapter 11

Reference Manual

This chapter provides a user's guide to μC/OS-II services. Each of the user-accessible kernel services is presented in alphabetical order and the following information is provided for each of the services.

- A brief description
- The function prototype
- The filename of the source code
- The #define constant needed to enable the code for the service
- A description of the arguments passed to the function
- A description of the return value(s)
- Specific notes and warnings on using the service
- One or two examples of how to use the function

OSInit()

`void OSInit(void);`

File	Called from	Code enabled by
OS_CORE.C	Startup code only	N/A

OSInit() initializes µC/OS-II and must be called prior to calling OSStart(), which actually starts multitasking.

Arguments

None

Return Value

None

Notes/Warnings

OSInit() must be called before OSStart().

Example

```
void main (void)
{
    .

    .

    OSInit();       /* Initialize uC/OS-II */

    .

    .

    OSStart();      /* Start Multitasking  */
}
```

11

OSIntEnter()

`void OSIntEnter(void);`

File	*Called from*	*Code enabled by*
OS_CORE.C	ISR only	N/A

OSIntEnter() notifies µC/OS-II that an ISR is being processed. This allows µC/OS-II to keep track of interrupt nesting. OSIntEnter() is used in conjunction with OSIntExit().

Arguments

None

Return Value

None

Notes/Warnings

This function must not be called by task-level code.

You can increment the interrupt nesting counter (OSIntNesting) directly if your processor can perform this operation indivisibly; that is, if your processor can perform a read-modify-write as an atomic operation, you don't need to call OSIntEnter() — you can increment OSIntNesting directly. This avoids the overhead associated with calling a function.

Example 1
(Intel 80x86, real mode, large model)

Use OSIntEnter() for backward compatibility with µC/OS. Also, follow this example if the processor you are using does not allow you to increment OSIntNesting using a single instruction.

```
    ISRx PROC    FAR
         PUSHA                        ; Save interrupted task's context
         PUSH    ES
         PUSH    DS
;
         MOV     AX, DGROUP           ; Reload DS
         MOV     DS, AX
;
         CALL    FAR PTR _OSIntEnter  ; Notify µC/OS-II of start of ISR
          .
          .
         POP     DS                   ; Restore processor registers
```

```
        POP    ES
        POPA
        IRET                            ; Return from interrupt
    ISRx ENDP
```

Example 2
(Intel 80x86, real mode, large model)

You can increment OSIntNesting because the 80x86 allows you to perform this operation indivisibly.

```
    ISRx    PROC    FAR
            PUSHA                           ; Save interrupted task's context
            PUSH    ES
            PUSH    DS
;
            MOV     AX, DGROUP              ; Reload DS
            MOV     DS, AX
;
            INC     BYTE PTR _OSIntNesting  ; Notify µC/OS-II of start of ISR
              .
              .
              .
            POP     DS                      ; Restore processor registers
            POP     ES
            POPA
            IRET                            ; Return from interrupt
    ISRx    ENDP
```

11

OSIntExit()

```
void OSIntExit(void);
```

File	Called from	Code enabled by
OS_CORE.C	ISR only	N/A

OSIntExit() notifies µC/OS-II that an ISR has completed. This allows µC/OS-II to keep track of interrupt nesting. OSIntExit() is used in conjunction with OSIntEnter(). When the last nested interrupt completes, µC/OS-II calls the scheduler to determine if a higher priority task has been made ready to run, in which case, the interrupt returns to the higher priority task instead of the interrupted task.

Arguments

None

Return Value

None

Notes/Warnings

This function must not be called by task-level code. Also, if you decided to increment OSIntNesting, you still need to call OSIntExit().

Example
(Intel 80x86, real mode, large model)

```
        ISRx    PROC    FAR
                PUSHA                       ; Save processor registers
                PUSH    ES
                PUSH    DS
                .
                .
                CALL    FAR PTR _OSIntExit  ; Notify µC/OS-II of end of ISR
                POP     DS                  ; Restore processor registers
                POP     ES
                POPA
                IRET                        ; Return to interrupted task
        ISRx    ENDP
```

11

OSMboxAccept ()

void *OSMboxAccept(OS_EVENT *pevent);

File	*Called from*	*Code enabled by*
OS_MBOX.C	Task or ISR	OS_MBOX_EN

OSMboxAccept () allows you to see if a message is available from the desired mailbox. Unlike OSMboxPend (), OSMboxAccept () does not suspend the calling task if a message is not available. If a message is available, the message is returned to your application and the content of the mailbox is cleared. This call is typically used by ISRs because an ISR is not allowed to wait for a message at a mailbox.

Arguments

pevent is a pointer to the mailbox from which the message is received. This pointer is returned to your application when the mailbox is created [see OSMboxCreate ()].

Return Value

A pointer to the message if one is available; NULL if the mailbox does not contain a message.

Notes/Warnings

Mailboxes must be created before they are used.

Example

```
OS_EVENT *CommMbox;



void Task (void *pdata)
{
    void *msg;



    pdata = pdata;
    for (;;) {
        msg = OSMboxAccept(CommMbox); /* Check mailbox for a message        */
        if (msg != (void *)0) {
                                      /* Message received, process          */
            .
            .
        } else {
                                      /* Message not received, do ..        */
            .                         /* .. something else                  */
        }
        .
        .

    }
}
```

11

OSMboxCreate()

`OS_EVENT *OSMboxCreate(void *msg);`

File	*Called from*	*Code enabled by*
OS_MBOX.C	Task or startup code	OS_MBOX_EN

OSMboxCreate() creates and initializes a mailbox. A mailbox allows tasks or ISRs to send a pointer-sized variable (message) to one or more tasks.

Arguments

msg is used to initialize the contents of the mailbox. The mailbox is empty when msg is a NULL pointer. The mailbox initially contains a message when msg is non-NULL.

Return Value

A pointer to the event control block allocated to the mailbox. If no event control block is available, OSMboxCreate() returns a NULL pointer.

Notes/Warnings

Mailboxes must be created before they are used.

Example

```
OS_EVENT *CommMbox;


    void main(void)
    {
        .
        .
        OSInit();                               /* Initialize μC/OS-II  */
        .
        .
        CommMbox = OSMboxCreate((void *)0);     /* Create COMM mailbox  */
        OSStart();                              /* Start Multitasking   */
    }
```

11

OSMboxPend()

```
void *OSMboxPend(OS_EVENT *pevent, INT16U timeout, INT8U *err);
```

File	Called from	Code enabled by
OS_MBOX.C	Task only	OS_MBOX_EN

OSMboxPend() is used when a task expects to receive a message. The message is sent to the task either by an ISR or by another task. The message received is a pointer-sized variable and its use is application specific. If a message is present in the mailbox when OSMboxPend() is called, the message is retrieved, the mailbox is emptied, and the retrieved message is returned to the caller. If no message is present in the mailbox, OSMboxPend() suspends the current task until either a message is received or a user-specified timeout expires. If a message is sent to the mailbox and multiple tasks are waiting for the message, µC/OS-II resumes the highest priority task waiting to run. A pended task that has been suspended with OSTaskSuspend() can receive a message. However, the task remains suspended until it is resumed by calling OSTaskResume().

Arguments

pevent is a pointer to the mailbox from which the message is received. This pointer is returned to your application when the mailbox is created [see OSMboxCreate()].

timeout allows the task to resume execution if a message is not received from the mailbox within the specified number of clock ticks. A timeout value of 0 indicates that the task wants to wait forever for the message. The maximum timeout is 65,535 clock ticks. The timeout value is not synchronized with the clock tick. The timeout count begins decrementing on the next clock tick, which could potentially occur immediately.

err is a pointer to a variable that holds an error code. OSMboxPend() sets *err to one of the following:

- OS_NO_ERR if a message was received.
- OS_TIMEOUT if a message was not received within the specified timeout period.
- OS_ERR_PEND_ISR if you called this function from an ISR and µC/OS-II has to suspend it. In general, you should not call OSMboxPend() from an ISR, but µC/OS-II checks for this situation anyway.
- OS_ERR_EVENT_TYPE pevent is not pointing to a mailbox.

Return Value

OSMboxPend() returns the message sent by either a task or an ISR and *err is set to OS_NO_ERR. If a message is not received within the specified timeout period, the returned message is a NULL pointer and *err is set to OS_TIMEOUT.

Notes/Warnings

Mailboxes must be created before they are used.

You should not call OSMboxPend() from an ISR.

Example

```
OS_EVENT  *CommMbox;


void CommTask(void *pdata)
{
     INT8U  err;
     void  *msg;


     pdata = pdata;
     for (;;) {
        .
        .
       msg = OSMboxPend(CommMbox, 10, &err);
       if (err == OS_NO_ERR) {
           .
           .  /* Code for received message                 */
           .
       } else {
           .
           .  /* Code for message not received within timeout */
           .
       }
        .
        .
     }
}
```

OSMboxPost()

INT8U OSMboxPost(OS_EVENT *pevent, void *msg);

File	Called from	Code enabled by
OS_MBOX.C	Task or ISR	OS_MBOX_EN

OSMboxPost() sends a message to a task through a mailbox. A message is a pointer-sized variable and its use is application specific. If a message is already in the mailbox, an error code is returned indicating that the mailbox is full. OSMboxPost() then immediately returns to its caller and the message is not placed in the mailbox. If any task is waiting for a message at the mailbox, the highest priority task waiting receives the message. If the task waiting for the message has a higher priority than the task sending the message, the higher priority task is resumed and the task sending the message is suspended. In other words, a context switch occurs.

Arguments

pevent is a pointer to the mailbox into which the message is deposited. This pointer is returned to your application when the mailbox is created [see OSMboxCreate()].

msg is the actual message sent to the task. msg is a pointer-sized variable and is application specific. You must never post a NULL pointer because this indicates that the mailbox is empty.

Return Value

OSMboxPost() returns one of two error codes:

- OS_NO_ERR if the message was deposited in the mailbox.
- OS_MBOX_FULL if the mailbox already contained a message.
- OS_ERR_EVENT_TYPE pevent is not pointing to a mailbox.

Notes/Warnings

Mailboxes must be created before they are used.

You must never post a NULL pointer because this indicates that the mailbox is empty.

Example

```
OS_EVENT *CommMbox;
INT8U    CommRxBuf[100];



void CommTaskRx(void *pdata)
{
    INT8U  err;



    pdata = pdata;
    for (;;) {
        .
        .
        err = OSMboxPost(CommMbox, (void *)&CommRxBuf[0]);
        .
        .
    }
}
```

OSMboxQuery()

```
INT8U OSMboxQuery(OS_EVENT *pevent, OS_MBOX_DATA *pdata);
```

File	Called from	Code enabled by
OS_MBOX.C	Task or ISR	OS_MBOX_EN

OSMboxQuery() obtains information about a message mailbox. Your application must allocate an OS_MBOX_DATA data structure, which is used to receive data from the event control block of the message mailbox. OSMboxQuery() allows you to determine whether any tasks are waiting for a message at the mailbox and how many tasks are waiting (by counting the number of 1s in the .OSEventTbl[] field). You can also examine the current content of the mailbox. Note that the size of .OSEventTbl[] is established by the #define constant OS_EVENT_TBL_SIZE (see uCOS_II.H).

Arguments

pevent is a pointer to the mailbox. This pointer is returned to your application when the mailbox is created [see OSMboxCreate()].

pdata is a pointer to a data structure of type OS_MBOX_DATA, which contains the following fields:

```
void    *OSMsg;                    /* Copy of the message stored in the mailbox */
INT8U   OSEventTbl[OS_EVENT_TBL_SIZE];     /* Copy of the mailbox wait list  */
INT8U   OSEventGrp;
```

Return Value

OSMboxQuery() returns one of two error codes:

- OS_NO_ERR if the call was successful.
- OS_ERR_EVENT_TYPE if you didn't pass a pointer to a message mailbox.

Notes/Warnings

Message mailboxes must be created before they are used.

Example

```
OS_EVENT *CommMbox;


void Task (void *pdata)
{
    OS_MBOXDATA mbox_data;
    INT8U       err;


    pdata = pdata;
    for (;;) {
        .
        .
        err = OSMboxQuery(CommMbox, &mbox_data);
        if (err == OS_NO_ERR) {
            .  /* Mailbox contains a message if mbox_data.OSMsg is not NULL   */
        }
        .
        .
    }
}
```

11

OSMemCreate()

`OS_MEM *OSMemCreate(void *addr, INT32U nblks, INT32U blksize, INT8U *err);`

File	Called from	Code enabled by
OS_MEM.C	Task or startup code	OS_MEM_EN

OSMemCreate() creates and initializes a memory partition. A memory partition contains a user-specified number of fixed-size memory blocks. Your application can obtain one of these memory blocks and, when done, release the block back to the partition.

Arguments

addr is the address of the start of a memory area that is used to create fixed-size memory blocks. Memory partitions can be created either using static arrays or malloc() during startup.

nblks contains the number of memory blocks available from the specified partition. You must specify at least two memory blocks per partition.

blksize specifies the size (in bytes) of each memory block within a partition. A memory block must be large enough to hold at least a pointer.

err is a pointer to a variable that holds an error code. OSMemCreate() sets *err to

- OS_NO_ERR if the memory partition was created successfully,
- OS_MEM_INVALID_PART if a free memory partition was not available,
- OS_MEM_INVALID_BLKS if you didn't specify at least two memory blocks per partition, or
- OS_MEM_INVALID_SIZE if you didn't specify a block size that can contain at least a pointer variable.

Return Value

OSMemCreate() returns a pointer to the created memory partition control block if one is available. If no memory partition control block is available, OSMemCreate() returns a NULL pointer.

Notes/Warnings

Memory partitions must be created before they are used.

Example

```
OS_MEM  *CommMem;
INT8U   CommBuf[16][128];



void main(void)
{
    INT8U err;


    OSInit();                       /* Initialize µC/OS-II      */
    .

    .
    CommMem = OSMemCreate(&CommBuf[0][0], 16, 128, &err);
    .

    .
    OSStart();                      /* Start Multitasking       */
}
```

11

OSMemGet()

```
void *OSMemGet(OS_MEM *pmem, INT8U *err);
```

File	Called from	Code enabled by
OS_MEM.C	Task or ISR	OS_MEM_EN

OSMemGet obtains a memory block from a memory partition. It is assumed that your application knows the size of each memory block obtained. Also, your application must return the memory block [using OSMemPut()] when it no longer needs it. You can call OSMemGet() more than once until all memory blocks are allocated.

Arguments

pmem is a pointer to the memory partition control block that is returned to your application from the OSMemCreate() call.

err is a pointer to a variable that holds an error code. OSMemGet() sets *err to one of the following:

- OS_NO_ERR if a memory block was available and returned to your application.
- OS_MEM_NO_FREE_BLKS if the memory partition didn't contain any more memory blocks to allocate.

Return Value

OSMemGet() returns a pointer to the allocated memory block if one is available. If no memory block is available from the memory partition, OSMemGet() returns a NULL pointer.

Notes/Warnings

Memory partitions must be created before they are used.

Example

```
OS_MEM  *CommMem;


void Task (void *pdata)
{
     INT8U *msg;


     pdata = pdata;
     for (;;) {
        msg = OSMemGet(CommMem, &err);
        if (msg != (INT8U *)0) {
           .                          /* Memory block allocated, use it. */
           .
        }
        .
        .
     }
}
```

11

OSMemPut()

INT8U OSMemPut(OS_MEM *pmem, void *pblk);

File	Called from	Code enabled by
OS_MEM.C	Task or ISR	OS_MEM_EN

OSMemPut() returns a memory block to a memory partition. It is assumed that you will return the memory block to the appropriate memory partition.

Arguments

pmem is a pointer to the memory partition control block that is returned to your application from the OSMemCreate() call.

pblk is a pointer to the memory block to be returned to the memory partition.

Return Value

OSMemPut() returns one of the following error codes:

- OS_NO_ERR if a memory block was available and returned to your application.
- OS_MEM_FULL if the memory partition could not accept more memory blocks. This is surely an indication that something is wrong because you are returning more memory blocks than you obtained using OSMemGet().

Notes/Warnings

Memory partitions must be created before they are used.

You must return a memory block to the proper memory partition.

Example

```
OS_MEM *CommMem;
INT8U  *CommMsg;


void Task (void *pdata)
{
    INT8U err;


    pdata = pdata;
    for (;;) {
        err = OSMemPut(CommMem, (void *)CommMsg);
        if (err == OS_NO_ERR) {
            .                              /* Memory block released       */
            .
            .
        }
        .
        .
    }
}
```

11

OSMemQuery()

INT8U OSMemQuery(OS_MEM *pmem, OS_MEM_DATA *pdata);

File	Called from	Code enabled by
OS_MEM.C	Task or ISR	OS_MEM_EN

OSMemQuery() obtains information about a memory partition. Basically, this function returns the same information found in the OS_MEM data structure, but in a new data structure called OS_MEM_DATA. OS_MEM_DATA also contains an additional field that indicates the number of memory blocks in use.

Arguments

pmem is a pointer to the memory partition control block that is returned to your application from the OSMemCreate() call.

pdata is a pointer to a data structure of type OS_MEM_DATA, which contains the following fields:

```
void    *OSAddr;      /* Points to beginning address of the memory partition    */
void    *OSFreeList;  /* Points to beginning of the free list of memory blocks   */
INT32U  OSBlkSize;    /* Size (in bytes) of each memory block                    */
INT32U  OSNBlks;      /* Total number of blocks in the partition                 */
INT32U  OSNFree;      /* Number of memory blocks free                            */
INT32U  OSNUsed;      /* Number of memory blocks used                            */
```

Return Value

OSMemQuery() always returns OS_NO_ERR.

Notes/Warnings

Memory partitions must be created before they are used.

Example

```
OS_MEM        *CommMem;


void Task (void *pdata)
{
    INT8U        err;
    OS_MEM_DATA   mem_data;


    pdata = pdata;
    for (;;) {
        .
        .
        err = OSMemQuery(CommMem, &mem_data);
        .
        .
    }
}
```

11

OSQAccept()

```
void *OSQAccept(OS_EVENT *pevent);
```

File	Called from	Code enabled by
OS_Q.C	Task or ISR	OS_Q_EN

OSQAccept() checks to see if a message is available in the desired message queue. Unlike OSQPend(), OSQAccept() does not suspend the calling task if a message is not available. If a message is available, it is extracted from the queue and returned to your application. This call is typically used by ISRs because an ISR is not allowed to wait for messages at a queue.

Arguments

pevent is a pointer to the message queue from which the message is received. This pointer is returned to your application when the message queue is created [see OSQCreate()].

Return Value

A pointer to the message if one is available; NULL if the message queue does not contain a message.

Notes/Warnings

Message queues must be created before they are used.

Example

```
OS_EVENT *CommQ;


void Task (void *pdata)
{
    void *msg;


    pdata = pdata;
    for (;;) {
        msg = OSQAccept(CommQ);         /* Check queue for a message    */
        if (msg != (void *)0) {
                                        /* Message received, process    */
            .
            .
        } else {
            .                           /* Message not received, do .. */
            .                           /* .. something else            */
        }
        .
        .
    }
}
```

11

OSQCreate()

`OS_EVENT *OSQCreate(void **start, INT8U size);`

File	*Called from*	*Code enabled by*
OS_Q.C	Task or startup code	OS_Q_EN

OSQCreate() creates a message queue. A message queue allows tasks or ISRs to send pointer-sized variables (messages) to one or more tasks. The meaning of the messages sent are application specific.

Arguments

start is the base address of the message storage area. A message storage area is declared as an array of pointers to voids.

size is the size (in number of entries) of the message storage area.

Return Value

OSQCreate() returns a pointer to the event control block allocated to the queue. If no event control block is available, OSQCreate() returns a NULL pointer.

Notes/Warnings

Queues must be created before they are used.

Example

```
OS_EVENT  *CommQ;
void      *CommMsg[10];



void main(void)
{
     OSInit();                              /* Initialize μC/OS-II   */
     .

     .

     CommQ = OSQCreate(&CommMsg[0], 10);    /* Create COMM Q         */
     .

     .

     OSStart();                             /* Start Multitasking    */
}
```

OSQFlush()

`INT8U *OSQFlush(OS_EVENT *pevent);`

File	Called from	Code enabled by
OS_Q.C	Task or ISR	OS_Q_EN

OSQFlush() empties the contents of the message queue and eliminates all the messages sent to the queue. This function takes the same amount of time to execute whether tasks are waiting on the queue (and thus no messages are present) or the queue contains one or more messages.

Arguments

pevent is a pointer to the message queue. This pointer is returned to your application when the message queue is created [see OSQCreate()].

Return Value

OSQFlush() returns one of the following codes:

- OS_NO_ERR if the message queue was flushed.
- OS_ERR_EVENT_TYPE if you attempted to flush an object other than a message queue.

Notes/Warnings

Queues must be created before they are used.

Example

```
OS_EVENT *CommQ;


void main(void)
{
      INT8U err;

      OSInit();                         /* Initialize µC/OS-II   */
      .

      .
      err = OSQFlush(CommQ);

      .

      .
      OSStart();                        /* Start Multitasking    */
}
```

11

OSQPend()

```
void *OSQPend(OS_EVENT *pevent, INT16U timeout, INT8U *err);
```

File	*Called from*	*Code enabled by*
OS_Q.C	Task only	OS_Q_EN

OSQPend() is used when a task wants to receive messages from a queue. The messages are sent to the task either by an ISR or by another task. The messages received are pointer-sized variables, and their use is application specific. If a at least one message is present at the queue when OSQPend() is called, the message is retrieved and returned to the caller. If no message is present at the queue, OSQPend() suspends the current task until either a message is received or a user-specified timeout expires. If a message is sent to the queue and multiple tasks are waiting for such a message, then µC/OS-II resumes the highest priority task that is waiting. A pended task that has been suspended with OSTaskSuspend() can receive a message. However, the task remains suspended until it is resumed by calling OSTaskResume().

Arguments

pevent is a pointer to the queue from which the messages are received. This pointer is returned to your application when the queue is created [see OSQCreate()].

timeout allows the task to resume execution if a message is not received from the mailbox within the specified number of clock ticks. A timeout value of 0 indicates that the task wants to wait forever for the message. The maximum timeout is 65,535 clock ticks. The timeout value is not synchronized with the clock tick. The timeout count starts decrementing on the next clock tick, which could potentially occur immediately.

err is a pointer to a variable used to hold an error code. OSQPend() sets *err to one of the following:

- OS_NO_ERR if a message was received.
- OS_TIMEOUT if a message was not received within the specified timeout.
- OS_ERR_PEND_ISR if you called this function from an ISR and µC/OS-II would have to suspend it. In general, you should not call OSQPend() from an ISR. µC/OS-II checks for this situation anyway.
- OS_ERR_EVENT_TYPE pevent is not pointing to a message queue.

Return Value

OSQPend() returns a message sent by either a task or an ISR, and *err is set to OS_NO_ERR. If a timeout occurs, OSQPend() returns a NULL pointer and sets *err to OS_TIMEOUT.

Notes/Warnings

Queues must be created before they are used.

You should not call OSQPend() from an ISR.

Example

```
OS_EVENT *CommQ;


void CommTask(void *data)
{
      INT8U  err;
      void  *msg;


      pdata = pdata;
      for (;;) {
        .
        .
        msg = OSQPend(CommQ, 100, &err);
        if (err == OS_NO_ERR) {
          .
          .                     /* Message received within 100 ticks!     */
          .
        } else {
          .
          .                     /* Message not received, must have timed out  */
          .
        }
        .
        .
      }
}
```

11

OSQPost()

INT8U OSQPost(OS_EVENT *pevent, void *msg);

File	*Called from*	*Code enabled by*
OS_Q.C	Task or ISR	OS_Q_EN

OSQPost() sends a message to a task through a queue. A message is a pointer-sized variable, and its use is application specific. If the message queue is full, an error code is returned to the caller. In this case, OSQPost() immediately returns to its caller, and the message is not placed in the queue. If any task is waiting for a message at the queue, the highest priority task receives the message. If the task waiting for the message has a higher priority than the task sending the message, the higher priority task resumes and the task sending the message is suspended; that is, a context switch occurs. Message queues are first-in-first-out (FIFO), which means that the first message sent is the first message received.

Arguments

pevent is a pointer to the queue into which the message is deposited. This pointer is returned to your application when the queue is created [see OSQCreate()].

msg is the actual message sent to the task. msg is a pointer-sized variable and is application specific. You must never post a NULL pointer.

Return Value

OSQPost() returns one of two error codes:

* OS_NO_ERR if the message was deposited in the queue.
* OS_Q_FULL if the queue was already full.
* OS_ERR_EVENT_TYPE pevent is not pointing to a message queue.

Notes/Warnings

Queues must be created before they are used.

You must never post a NULL pointer.

Example

```
OS_EVENT *CommQ;
INT8U    CommRxBuf[100];


void CommTaskRx(void *pdata)
{
    INT8U  err;


    pdata = pdata;
    for (;;) {
        .

        .

        err = OSQPost(CommQ, (void *)&CommRxBuf[0]);
        if (err == OS_NO_ERR) {
            .                       /* Message was deposited into queue   */

            .

        } else {
            .                       /* Queue is full                      */

            .

        }
        .

        .

    }
}
```

OSQPostFront()

`INT8U OSQPostFront(OS_EVENT *pevent, void *msg);`

File	Called from	Code enabled by
OS_Q.C	Task or ISR	OS_Q_EN

OSQPostFront() sends a message to a task through a queue. OSQPostFront() behaves very much like OSQPost(), except that the message is inserted at the front of the queue. This means that OSQPostFront() makes the message queue behave like a last-in-first-out (LIFO) queue instead of a first-in-first-out (FIFO) queue. The message is a pointer-sized variable, and its use is application specific. If the message queue is full, an error code is returned to the caller. OSQPostFront() immediately returns to its caller and the message is not placed in the queue. If any tasks are waiting for a message at the queue, the highest priority task receives the message. If the task waiting for the message has a higher priority than the task sending the message, the higher priority task is resumed and the task sending the message is suspended; that is, a context switch occurs.

Arguments

pevent is a pointer to the queue into which the message is deposited. This pointer is returned to your application when the queue is created [see OSQCreate()].

msg is the actual message sent to the task. msg is a pointer-sized variable and is application specific. You must never post a NULL pointer.

Return Value

OSQPostFront() returns one of two error codes:
- OS_NO_ERR if the message was deposited in the queue.
- OS_Q_FULL if the queue was already full.
- OS_ERR_EVENT_TYPE pevent is not pointing to a message queue.

Notes/Warnings

Queues must be created before they are used.

You must never post a NULL pointer.

Example

```
OS_EVENT *CommQ;
INT8U    CommRxBuf[100];


void CommTaskRx(void *pdata)
{
    INT8U  err;


    pdata = pdata;
    for (;;) {
        .
        .
        err = OSQPostFront(CommQ, (void *)&CommRxBuf[0]);
        if (err == OS_NO_ERR) {
            .                    /* Message was deposited into queue   */
            .
        } else {
            .                    /* Queue is full                      */
            .
        }
        .
        .
    }
}
```

11

OSQQuery()

INT8U OSQQuery(OS_EVENT *pevent, OS_Q_DATA *pdata);

File	Called from	Code enabled by
OS_Q.C	Task or ISR	OS_MBOX_EN

OSQQuery() obtains information about a message queue. Your application must allocate an OS_Q_DATA data structure used to receive data from the event control block of the message queue. OSQQuery() allows you to determine whether any tasks are waiting for messages at the queue, how many tasks are waiting (by counting the number of 1s in the .OSEventTbl[] field), how many messages are in the queue, and what the message queue size is. OSQQuery() also obtains the next message that would be returned if the queue is not empty. Note that the size of .OSEventTbl[] is established by the #define constant OS_EVENT_TBL_SIZE (see uCOS_II.H).

Arguments

pevent is a pointer to the message queue. This pointer is returned to your application when the queue is created [see OSQCreate()].

pdata is a pointer to a data structure of type OS_Q_DATA, which contains the following fields:

```
void   *OSMsg;                  /* Next message if one available      */
INT16U OSNMsgs;                 /* Number of messages in the queue    */
INT16U OSQSize;                 /* Size of the message queue          */
INT8U  OSEventTbl[OS_EVENT_TBL_SIZE];      /* Message queue wait list  */
INT8U  OSEventGrp;
```

Return Value

OSQQuery() returns one of two error codes:

- OS_NO_ERR if the call was successful.
- OS_ERR_EVENT_TYPE if you didn't pass a pointer to a message queue.

Notes/Warnings

Message queues must be created before they are used.

Example

```
OS_EVENT *CommQ;


void Task (void *pdata)
{
    OS_Q_DATA qdata;
    INT8U     err;


    pdata = pdata;
    for (;;) {
        .
        .
        err = OSQQuery(CommQ, &qdata);
        if (err == OS_NO_ERR) {
            .   /* 'qdata' can be examined! */
        }
        .
        .
    }
}
```

OSSchedLock()

void OSSchedLock(void);

File	Called from	Code enabled by
OS_CORE.C	Task or ISR	N/A

OSSchedLock() prevents task rescheduling until its counterpart, OSSchedUnlock(), is called. The task that calls OSSchedLock() keeps control of the CPU even though other higher priority tasks are ready to run. However, interrupts are still recognized and serviced (assuming interrupts are enabled). OSSchedLock() and OSSchedUnlock() must be used in pairs. µC/OS-II allows OSSchedLock() to be nested up to 254 levels deep. Scheduling is enabled when an equal number of OSSchedUnlock() calls have been made.

Arguments

None

Return Value

None

Notes/Warnings

After calling OSSchedLock(), your application must not make system calls that suspend execution of the current task; that is, your application cannot call OSTimeDly(), OSTimeDlyHMSM(), OSSem-Pend(), OSMboxPend(), or OSQPend(). Since the scheduler is locked out, no other task is allowed to run and your system will lock up.

Example

```
void TaskX(void *pdata)
{
    pdata = pdata;
    for (;;) {
        .
        OSSchedLock();          /* Prevent other tasks to run      */
        .
                                /* Code protected from context switch */
        .
        OSSchedUnlock();        /* Enable other tasks to run       */
        .
    }
}
```

OSSchedUnlock()

`void OSSchedUnlock(void);`

File	Called from	Code enabled by
OS_CORE.C	Task or ISR	N/A

OSSchedUnlock() re-enables task scheduling whenever it is paired with OSSchedLock().

Arguments

None

Return Value

None

Notes/Warnings

After calling OSSchedLock(), you application must not make a system call that suspends execution of the current task; that is, your application cannot call OSTimeDly(), OSTimeDlyHMSM(), OSSem-Pend(), OSMboxPend(), or OSQPend(). Since the scheduler is locked out, no other task is allowed to run and your system will lock up.

Example

```
void TaskX(void *pdata)
{
    pdata = pdata;
    for (;;) {
        .
        OSSchedLock();                  /* Prevent other tasks to run        */
        .
        .                               /* Code protected from context switch */
        .
        OSSchedUnlock();                /* Enable other tasks to run         */
        .
    }
}
```

11

OSSemAccept()

INT16U OSSemAccept(OS_EVENT *pevent);

File	Called from	Code enabled by
OS_SEM.C	Task or ISR	OS_SEM_EN

OSSemAccept() checks to see if a resource is available or an event has occurred. Unlike OSSem-Pend(), OSSemAccept() does not suspend the calling task if the resource is not available. Use OSSemAccept() from an ISR to obtain the semaphore.

Arguments

pevent is a pointer to the semaphore that guards the resource. This pointer is returned to your application when the semaphore is created [see OSSemCreate()].

Return Value

When OSSemAccept() is called and the semaphore value is greater than 0, the semaphore value is decremented and the value of the semaphore before the decrement is returned to your application. If the semaphore value is 0 when OSSemAccept() is called, the resource is not available and 0 is returned to your application.

Notes/Warnings

Semaphores must be created before they are used.

Example

```
OS_EVENT *DispSem;


void Task (void *pdata)
{
     INT16U value;


     pdata = pdata;
     for (;;) {
        value = OSSemAccept(DispSem);          /* Check resource availability */
        if (value > 0) {
           .                                   /* Resource available, process */
           .
        }
        .
        .
     }
}
```

11

OSSemCreate()

OS_EVENT *OSSemCreate(WORD value);

File	*Called from*	*Code enabled by*
OS_SEM.C	Task or startup code	OS_SEM_EN

OSSemCreate() creates and initializes a semaphore. A semaphore

- allows a task to synchronize with either an ISR or a task,
- gains exclusive access to a resource, and
- signals the occurrence of an event.

Arguments

value is the initial value of the semaphore and can be between 0 and 65535.

Return Value

OSSemCreate() returns a pointer to the event control block allocated to the semaphore. If no event control block is available, OSSemCreate() returns a NULL pointer.

Notes/Warnings

Semaphores must be created before they are used.

Example

```
OS_EVENT *DispSem;


void main(void)
{
    .
    .
    OSInit();                           /* Initialize µC/OS-II         */
    .
    .
    DispSem = OSSemCreate(1);           /* Create Display Semaphore     */
    .
    .
    OSStart();                          /* Start Multitasking          */
}
```

OSSemPend()

```
void OSSemPend(OS_EVENT *pevent, INT16U timeout, INT8U *err);
```

File	Called from	Code enabled by
OS_SEM.C	Task only	OS_SEM_EN

OSSemPend() is used when a task wants exclusive access to a resource, needs to synchronize its activities with an ISR or a task, or is waiting until an event occurs. If a task calls OSSemPend() and the value of the semaphore is greater than 0, OSSemPend() decrements the semaphore and returns to its caller. However, if the value of the semaphore is 0, OSSemPend() places the calling task in the waiting list for the semaphore. The task waits until a task or an ISR signals the semaphore or the specified timeout expires. If the semaphore is signaled before the timeout expires, µC/OS-II resumes the highest priority task waiting for the semaphore. A pended task that has been suspended with OSTaskSuspend() can obtain the semaphore. However, the task remains suspended until it is resumed by calling OSTaskResume().

Arguments

pevent is a pointer to the semaphore. This pointer is returned to your application when the semaphore is created [see OSSemCreate()].

timeout allows the task to resume execution if a message is not received from the mailbox within the specified number of clock ticks. A timeout value of 0 indicates that the task will wait forever for the message. The maximum timeout is 65,535 clock ticks. The timeout value is not synchronized with the clock tick. The timeout count begins decrementing on the next clock tick, which could potentially occur immediately.

err is a pointer to a variable used to hold an error code. OSSemPend() sets *err to one of the following:

- OS_NO_ERR if the semaphore was available.
- OS_TIMEOUT if the semaphore was not signaled within the specified timeout.
- OS_ERR_PEND_ISR if you called this function from an ISR and µC/OS-II would have to suspend it. In general, you should not call OSMboxPend() from an ISR. µC/OS-II checks for this situation.
- OS_ERR_EVENT_TYPE pevent is not pointing to a semaphore.

Return Value

None

Notes/Warnings

Semaphores must be created before they are used.

Example

```
OS_EVENT *DispSem;



void DispTask(void *pdata)
{
    INT8U  err;



    pdata = pdata;
    for (;;) {
       .

       .

       OSSemPend(DispSem, 0, &err);
       .                        /* The only way this task continues is if … */
       .                        /* … the semaphore is signaled!            */
    }
}
```

11

OSSemPost()

INT8U OSSemPost(OS_EVENT *pevent);

File	*Called from*	*Code enabled by*
OS_SEM.C	Task or ISR	OS_SEM_EN

A semaphore is signaled by calling OSSemPost(). If the semaphore value is 0 or more, it is incremented and OSSemPost() returns to its caller. If tasks are waiting for the semaphore to be signaled, OSSemPost() removes the highest priority task pending for the semaphore from the waiting list and makes this task ready to run. The scheduler is then called to determine if the awakened task is now the highest priority task ready to run.

Arguments

pevent is a pointer to the semaphore. This pointer is returned to your application when the semaphore is created [see OSSemCreate()].

Return Value

OSSemPost() returns one of two error codes:

- OS_NO_ERR if the semaphore was signaled successfully.
- OS_SEM_OVF if the semaphore count overflowed.
- OS_ERR_EVENT_TYPE pevent is not pointing to a semaphore.

Notes/Warnings

Semaphores must be created before they are used.

Example

```
OS_EVENT *DispSem;


void TaskX(void *pdata)
{
     INT8U  err;


     pdata = pdata;
     for (;;) {
       .

       .

       err = OSSemPost(DispSem);
       if (err == OS_NO_ERR) {
         .                                /* Semaphore signaled     */
         .

       } else {
         .                                /* Semaphore has overflowed */
         .

       }
       .

       .

     }
}
```

OSSemQuery()

INT8U OSSemQuery(OS_EVENT *pevent, OS_SEM_DATA *pdata);

File	Called from	Code enabled by
OS_SEM.C	Task or ISR	OS_SEM_EN

OSSemQuery() obtains information about a semaphore. Your application must allocate an OS_SEM_DATA data structure used to receive data from the event control block of the semaphore. OSSem-Query() allows you to determine whether any tasks are waiting on the semaphore and how many tasks are waiting (by counting the number of 1s in the .OSEventTbl[] field) and obtains the semaphore count. Note that the size of .OSEventTbl[] is established by the #define constant OS_EVENT_TBL_SIZE (see uCOS_II.H).

Arguments

pevent is a pointer to the semaphore. This pointer is returned to your application when the semaphore is created [see OSSemCreate()].

pdata is a pointer to a data structure of type OS_SEM_DATA, which contains the following fields:

```
INT16U OSCnt;                              /* Current semaphore count    */
INT8U  OSEventTbl[OS_EVENT_TBL_SIZE];      /* Semaphore wait list        */
INT8U  OSEventGrp;
```

Return Value

OSSemQuery() returns one of two error codes:
* OS_NO_ERR if the call was successful.
* OS_ERR_EVENT_TYPE if you didn't pass a pointer to a semaphore.

Notes/Warnings

Semaphores must be created before they are used.

Example

In this example, the contents of the semaphore is checked to determine the highest priority task waiting.

```
OS_EVENT *DispSem;


void Task (void *pdata)
{
    OS_SEM_DATA sem_data;
    INT8U       err;
    INT8U       highest;  /* Highest priority task waiting on semaphore */
    INT8U       x;
    INT8U       y;


    pdata = pdata;
    for (;;) {
        .
        .
        err = OSSemQuery(DispSem, &sem_data);
        if (err == OS_NO_ERR) {
            if (sem_data.OSEventGrp != 0x00) {
                y       = OSUnMapTbl[sem_data.OSEventGrp];
                x       = OSUnMapTbl[sem_data.OSEventTbl[y]];
                highest = (y << 3) + x;
                .
                .
            }
        }
        .
        .
    }
}
```

11

OSStart()

`void OSStart(void);`

File	*Called from*	*Code enabled by*
OS_CORE.C	Startup code only	N/A

OSStart() starts multitasking under µC/OS-II.

Arguments

None

Return Value

None

Notes/Warnings

OSInit() must be called prior to calling OSStart(). OSStart() should only be called once by your application code. If you do call OSStart() more than once, it will not do anything on the second and subsequent calls.

Example

```
void main(void)
{
        .                          /* User Code            */
        .
    OSInit();                      /* Initialize µC/OS-II  */
        .                          /* User Code            */
        .
    OSStart();                     /* Start Multitasking   */
}
```

OSStatInit()

`void OSStatInit(void);`

File	Called from	Code enabled by
OS_CORE.C	Startup code only	OS_TASK_STAT_EN && OS_TASK_CREATE_EXT__EN

`OSStatInit()` determines the maximum value that a 32-bit counter can reach when no other task is executing. This function must be called when only one task is created in your application and when multitasking has started; that is, this function must be called from the first, and only, task created.

Arguments

None

Return Value

None

Notes/Warnings

None

Example

```
void FirstAndOnlyTask (void *pdata)
{
    .
    .
    OSStatInit();              /* Compute CPU capacity with no task running */
    .
    OSTaskCreate(…);           /* Create the other tasks                    */
    OSTaskCreate(…);
    .
    for (;;) {
        .
        .
    }
}
```

11

OSTaskChangePrio()

INT8U OSTaskChangePrio(INT8U oldprio, INT8U newprio);

File	Called from	Code enabled by
OS_TASK.C	Task only	OS_TASK_CHANGE_PRIO_EN

OSTaskChangePrio() changes the priority of a task.

Arguments

oldprio is the priority number of the task to change.

newprio is the new task's priority.

Return Value

OSTaskChangePrio() returns one of the following error codes:

- OS_NO_ERR if the task's priority was changed.
- OS_PRIO_INVALID if either the old priority or the new priority is equal to or exceeds OS_LOWEST_PRIO.
- OS_PRIO_EXIST if newprio already exists.
- OS_PRIO_ERR if no task with the specified "old" priority exists (i.e., the task specified by oldprio does not exist).

Notes/Warnings

The desired priority must not already have been assigned; otherwise, an error code is returned. Also, OSTaskChangePrio() verifies that the task to change exists.

Example

```
void TaskX(void *data)
{
    INT8U  err;


    for (;;) {
        .
        .
        err = OSTaskChangePrio(10, 15);
        .
        .
    }
}
```

11

OSTaskCreate()

INT8U OSTaskCreate(void (*task)(void *pd), void *pdata, OS_STK *ptos, INT8U prio);

File	Called from	Code enabled by
OS_TASK.C	Task or startup code	N/A

OSTaskCreate() creates a task so it can be managed by µC/OS-II. Tasks can be created either prior to the start of multitasking or by a running task. A task cannot be created by an ISR. A task must be written as an infinite loop, as shown below, and must not return.

OSTaskCreate() is used for backward compatibility with µC/OS and when the added features of OSTaskCreateExt() are not needed.

Depending on how the stack frame was built, your task will have interrupts either enabled or disabled. You need to check with the processor-specific code for details.

Arguments

task is a pointer to the task's code.

pdata is a pointer to an optional data area used to pass parameters to the task when it is created. Where the task is concerned, it thinks it was invoked and passed the argument pdata as follows:

```
void Task (void *pdata)
{
    .                      /* Do something with 'pdata'          */
    for (;;) {             /* Task body, always an infinite loop. */
        .
        .

        /* Must call one of the following services:           */
        /*    OSMboxPend()                                    */
        /*    OSQPend()                                       */
        /*    OSSemPend()                                     */
        /*    OSTimeDly()                                     */
        /*    OSTimeDlyHMSM()                                 */
        /*    OSTaskSuspend()    (Suspend self)               */
        /*    OSTaskDel()        (Delete  self)               */
        .
        .
    }
}
```

ptos is a pointer to the task's top-of-stack. The stack is used to store local variables, function parameters, return addresses, and CPU registers during an interrupt. The size of the stack is determined by the task's requirements and the anticipated interrupt nesting. Determining the size of the stack involves knowing how many bytes are required for storage of local variables for the task itself and all nested functions, as well as requirements for interrupts (accounting for nesting). If the configuration constant OS_STK_GROWTH is set to 1, the stack is assumed to grow downward (i.e., from high to low memory). ptos thus needs to point to the highest *valid* memory location on the stack. If OS_STK_GROWTH is set to 0, the stack is assumed to grow in the opposite direction (i.e., from low to high memory).

prio is the task priority. A unique priority number must be assigned to each task and the lower the number, the higher the priority.

Return Value

OSTaskCreate() returns one of the following error codes:

- OS_NO_ERR if the function was successful.
- OS_PRIO_EXIST if the requested priority already exists.
- OS_PRIO_INVALID if prio is higher than OS_LOWEST_PRIO.
- OS_NO_MORE_TCB if µC/OS-II doesn't have any more OS_TCBs to assign.

Notes/Warnings

The stack for the task must be declared with the OS_STK type.

A task must always invoke one of the services provided by µC/OS-II to either wait for time to expire, suspend the task, or wait for an event to occur (wait on a mailbox, queue, or semaphore). This allows other tasks to gain control of the CPU.

You should not use task priorities 0, 1, 2, 3, OS_LOWEST_PRIO-3, OS_LOWEST_PRIO-2, OS_LOWEST_PRIO-1, and OS_LOWEST_PRIO because they are reserved for use by µC/OS-II. This leaves you with up to 56 application tasks.

11

Example 1

This example shows that the argument that Task1() receives is not used, so the pointer pdata is set to NULL. Note that I assume the stack grows from high to low memory because I pass the address of the highest valid memory location of the stack Task1Stk[]. If the stack grows in the opposite direction for the processor you are using, pass &Task1Stk[0] as the task's top-of-stack.

```
OS_STK   Task1Stk[1024];

void main(void)
{
    INT8U err;


        .

    OSInit();                    /* Initialize µC/OS-II          */
        .

    OSTaskCreate(Task1,
                (void *)0,
                &Task1Stk[1023],
                25);
        .

    OSStart();                   /* Start Multitasking           */
}



void Task1(void *pdata)
{
    pdata = pdata;
    for (;;) {
        .                        /* Task code                    */
        .
        .

    }
}
```

Example 2

You can create a generic task that can be instantiated more than once. For example, a task that handles a serial port could be passed the address of a data structure that characterizes the specific port (i.e., port address, baud rate).

```
OS_STK    *Comm1Stk[1024];
COMM_DATA  Comm1Data;           /* Data structure containing COMM port    */
                                /* Specific data for channel 1            */


OS_STK    *Comm2Stk[1024];
COMM_DATA  Comm2Data;           /* Data structure containing COMM port    */
                                /* Specific data for channel 2            */



void main(void)
{
    INT8U err;


    .
    OSInit();                   /* Initialize µC/OS-II                    */
    .
    OSTaskCreate(CommTask,
                 (void *)&Comm1Data,
                 &Comm1Stk[1023],
                 25);
    OSTaskCreate(CommTask,
                 (void *)&Comm2Data,
                 &Comm2Stk[1023],
                 26);
    .
    OSStart();                  /* Start Multitasking                     */
}



void CommTask(void *pdata)      /* Generic communication task             */
{
    for (;;) {
        .                       /* Task code                              */
        .
        .
    }
}
```

11

OSTaskCreateExt()

```
INT8U OSTaskCreateExt(void (*task)(void *pd), void *pdata, OS_STK *ptos, INT8U prio,
    INT16U, id, OS_STK *pbos, INT32U stk_size, void *pext, INT16U opt);
```

File	Called from	Code enabled by
OS_TASK.C	Task or startup code	N/A

OSTaskCreateExt() creates a task to be managed by µC/OS-II. This function serves the same purpose as OSTaskCreate(), except that it allows you to specify additional information about your task to µC/OS-II. Tasks can be created either prior to the start of multitasking or by a running task. A task cannot be created by an ISR. A task must be written as an infinite loop, as shown below, and must not return. Depending on how the stack frame was built, your task will have interrupts either enabled or disabled. You need to check with the processor-specific code for details. Note that the first four arguments are exactly the same as the ones for OSTaskCreate(). This was done to simplify the migration to this new and more powerful function.

Arguments

task is a pointer to the task's code.

pdata is a pointer to an optional data area, which is used to pass parameters to the task when it is created. Where the task is concerned, it thinks it was invoked and passed the argument pdata as follows:

```
void Task (void *pdata)
{
            .             /* Do something with 'pdata'                    */
    for (;;) {            /* Task body, always an infinite loop.          */
        .

        .

        /* Must call one of the following services:                       */
        /*      OSMboxPend()                                              */
        /*      OSQPend()                                                 */
        /*      OSSemPend()                                               */
        /*      OSTimeDly()                                               */
        /*      OSTimeDlyHMSM()                                           */
        /*      OSTaskSuspend()      (Suspend self)                       */
        /*      OSTaskDel()          (Delete  self)                       */
        .

        .
    }
}
```

ptos is a pointer to the task's top-of-stack. The stack is used to store local variables, function parameters, return addresses, and CPU registers during an interrupt. The size of this stack is determined by the task's requirements and the anticipated interrupt nesting. Determining the size of the stack involves knowing how many bytes are required for storage of local variables for the task itself and all nested functions, as well as requirements for interrupts (accounting for nesting). If the configuration constant OS_STK_GROWTH is set to 1, the stack is assumed to grow downward (i.e., from high to low memory). ptos thus needs to point to the highest *valid* memory location on the stack. If OS_STK_GROWTH is set to 0, the stack is assumed to grow in the opposite direction (i.e., from low to high memory).

prio is the task priority. A unique priority number must be assigned to each task: the lower the number, the higher the priority (i.e., the importance) of the task.

id is the task's ID number. At this time, the ID is not currently used in any other function and has simply been added in OSTaskCreateExt() for future expansion. You should set id to the same value as the task's priority.

pbos is a pointer to the task's bottom-of-stack. If the configuration constant OS_STK_GROWTH is set to 1, the stack is assumed to grow downward (i.e., from high to low memory); thus, pbos must point to the lowest *valid* stack location. If OS_STK_GROWTH is set to 0, the stack is assumed to grow in the opposite direction (i.e., from low to high memory); thus, pbos must point to the highest *valid* stack location. pbos is used by the stack-checking function OSTaskStkChk().

stk_size specifies the size of the task's stack in number of elements. If OS_STK is set to INT8U, then stk_size corresponds to the number of bytes available on the stack. If OS_STK is set to INT16U, then stk_size contains the number of 16-bit entries available on the stack. Finally, if OS_STK is set to INT32U, then stk_size contains the number of 32-bit entries available on the stack.

pext is a pointer to a user-supplied memory location (typically a data structure) used as a TCB extension. For example, this user memory can hold the contents of floating-point registers during a context switch, the time each task takes to execute, the number of times the task is switched-in, and so on.

opt contains task-specific options. The lower 8 bits are reserved by μC/OS-II, but you can use the upper 8 bits for application-specific options. Each option consists of one or more bits. The option is selected when the bit(s) is(are) set. The current version of μC/OS-II supports the following options:

- OS_TASK_OPT_STK_CHK specifies whether stack checking is allowed for the task.
- OS_TASK_OPT_STK_CLR specifies whether the stack needs to be cleared.
- OS_TASK_OPT_SAVE_FP specifies whether floating-point registers will be saved. This option is only valid if your processor has floating-point hardware and the processor-specific code saves the floating-point registers.

Refer to uCOS_II.H for other options.

Return Value

OSTaskCreateExt() returns one of the following error codes:

- OS_NO_ERR if the function was successful.
- OS_PRIO_EXIST if the requested priority already exist.
- OS_PRIO_INVALID if prio is higher than OS_LOWEST_PRIO.
- OS_NO_MORE_TCB if μC/OS-II doesn't have any more OS_TCBs to assign.

11

Notes/Warnings

The stack must be declared with the OS_STK type.

A task must always invoke one of the services provided by µC/OS-II either to wait for time to expire, suspend the task or, wait an event to occur (wait on a mailbox, queue, or semaphore). This allows other tasks to gain control of the CPU.

You should not use task priorities 0, 1, 2, 3, OS_LOWEST_PRIO-3, OS_LOWEST_PRIO-2, OS_LOWEST_PRIO-1, and OS_LOWEST_PRIO because they are reserved for use by µC/OS-II. This leaves you with up to 56 application tasks.

Example 1

The task control block is extended using a user-defined data structure called TASK_USER_DATA [Example 1(1)], which in this case contains the name of the task as well as other fields. The task name is initialized with the strcpy() standard library function [Example 1(2)]. Note that stack checking has been enabled [Example 1(4)] for this task, so you are allowed to call OSTaskStkChk(). Also, assume here that the stack grows downward Example 1(3) on the processor used (i.e., OS_STK_GROWTH is set to 1; TOS stands for Top-Of-Stack and BOS stands for Bottom-Of-Stack).

```c
typedef struct {                       /*  User defined data structure          (1)*/
    char    TaskName[20];
    INT16U  TaskCtr;
    INT16U  TaskExecTime;
    INT32U  TaskTotExecTime;
} TASK_USER_DATA;



OS_STK           TaskStk[1024];
TASK_USER_DATA   TaskUserData;



void main(void)
{
    INT8U err;


    .

    OSInit();                                  /* Initialize µC/OS-II           */

    .
    strcpy(TaskUserData.TaskName, "MyTaskName");   /*  Name of task          (2)*/
    err = OSTaskCreateExt(Task,
             (void *)0,
             &TaskStk[1023],                   /*  Stack grows down (TOS)     (3)*/
```

```
          10,
          &TaskStk[0],                  /*  Stack grows down (BOS)     (3)*/
          1024,
          (void *)&TaskUserData,        /* TCB Extension                 */
          OS_TASK_OPT_STK_CHK);         /*  Stack checking enabled     (4)*/
     .
     OSStart();                         /* Start Multitasking            */
}


void Task(void *pdata)
{
     pdata = pdata;            /* Avoid compiler warning                 */
     for (;;) {
         .                     /* Task code                              */
         .
     }
}
```

11

Example 2

Now create a task, but this time on a processor for which the stack grows upward [Example 2(1)]. The Intel MCS-251 is an example of such a processor. In this case, OS_STK_GROWTH is set to 0. Note that stack checking has been enabled Example 2(2) for this task so you are allowed to call OSTask-StkChk() (TOS stands for Top-Of-Stack and BOS stands for Bottom-Of-Stack).

```
OS_STK *TaskStk[1024];


void main(void)
{
    INT8U err;


    .
    OSInit();                              /* Initialize µC/OS-II        */
    .
    err = OSTaskCreateExt(Task,
            (void *)0,
            &TaskStk[0],                   /*  Stack grows up (TOS)    (1)*/
            10,
            10,
            &TaskStk[1023],                /*  Stack grows up (BOS)    (1)*/
            1024,
            (void *)0,
            OS_TASK_OPT_STK_CHK);          /*  Stack checking enabled  (2)*/
    .
    OSStart();                             /* Start Multitasking         */
}


void Task(void *pdata)
{
    pdata = pdata;              /* Avoid compiler warning          */
    for (;;) {
        .                       /* Task code                       */
        .
        .
    }
}
```

11

OSTaskDel()

INT8U OSTaskDel(INT8U prio);

File	*Called from*	*Code enabled by*
OS_TASK.C	Task only	OS_TASK_DEL_EN

OSTaskDel() deletes a task by specifying the priority number of the task to delete. The calling task can be deleted by specifying its own priority number or OS_PRIO_SELF (if the task doesn't know its own priority number). The deleted task is returned to the dormant state. The deleted task is created by calling either OSTaskCreate() or OSTaskCreateExt() to make the task active again.

Arguments

prio is the priority number of the task to delete. You can delete the calling task by passing OS_PRIO_SELF, in which case, the next highest priority task is executed.

Return Value

OSTaskDel() returns one of the following error codes:

- OS_NO_ERR if the task didn't delete itself.
- OS_TASK_DEL_IDLE if you tried to delete the idle task.
- OS_TASK_DEL_ERR if the task to delete does not exist.
- OS_PRIO_INVALID if you specified a task priority higher than OS_LOWEST_PRIO.
- OS_TASK_DEL_ISR if you tried to delete a task from an ISR.

Notes/Warnings

OSTaskDel() verifies that you are not attempting to delete the µC/OS-II idle task.

You must be careful when you delete a task that owns resources. Instead, consider using OSTaskDel-Req() as a safer approach.

Example

```
void TaskX(void *pdata)
{
    INT8U err;


    for (;;) {
        .
        .
        err = OSTaskDel(10);        /* Delete task with priority 10        */
        if (err == OS_NO_ERR) {
            .                       /* Task was deleted                    */
            .
        }
        .
        .
    }
}
```

OSTaskDelReq()

INT8U OSTaskDelReq(INT8U prio);

File	*Called from*	*Code enabled by*
OS_TASK.C	Task only	OS_TASK_DEL_EN

OSTaskDelReq() requests that a task delete itself. Basically, use OSTaskDelReq() when you need to delete a task that can potentially own resources (e.g., the task may own a semaphore). In this case, you don't want to delete the task until the resource is released. The requesting task calls OSTaskDelReq() to indicate that the task needs to be deleted. Deletion of the task is, however, deferred to the task being deleted. In other words, the task is actually deleted when it regains control of the CPU. For example, suppose Task 10 needs to be deleted. The task wanting to delete this task (example Task 5) would call OSTaskDelReq(10). When Task 10 executes, it calls OSTaskDelReq(OS_PRIO_SELF) and monitors the return value. If the return value is OS_TASK_DEL_REQ, then Task 10 is asked to delete itself. At this point, Task 10 calls OSTaskDel(OS_PRIO_SELF). Task 5 knows whether Task 10 has been deleted by calling OSTaskDelReq(10) and checking the return code. If the return code is OS_TASK_NOT_EXIST, then Task 5 knows that Task 10 has been deleted. Task 5 may have to check periodically until OS_TASK_NOT_EXIST is returned.

Arguments

prio is the task's priority number of the task to delete. If you specify OS_PRIO_SELF, you are asking whether another task wants the current task to be deleted.

Return Value

OSTaskDelReq() returns one of the following error codes:

- OS_NO_ERR if the task deletion has been registered.
- OS_TASK_NOT_EXIST if the task does not exist. The requesting task can monitor this return code to see if the task was actually deleted.
- OS_TASK_DEL_IDLE if you asked to delete the idle task (this is obviously not allowed).
- OS_PRIO_INVALID if you specified a task priority higher than OS_LOWEST_PRIO or you have not specified OS_PRIO_SELF.
- OS_TASK_DEL_REQ if a task (possibly another task) requested that the running task be deleted.

Notes/Warnings

OSTaskDelReq() verifies that you are not attempting to delete the µC/OS-II idle task.

Example

```
void TaskThatDeletes(void *pdata)          /* My priority is 5                    */
{
     INT8U err;


     for (;;) {
         .
         .
         err = OSTaskDelReq(10);       /* Request task #10 to delete itself   */
         if (err == OS_NO_ERR) {
             err = OSTaskDelReq(10);
             while (err != OS_TASK_NOT_EXIST) {
                 OSTimeDly(1);         /* Wait for task to be deleted         */
             }
             .                         /* Task #10 has been deleted           */
         }
         .
         .
     }
}


void TaskToBeDeleted(void *pdata)           /* My priority is 10                   */
{
   .
   .
   pdata = pdata;
   for (;;) {
      OSTimeDly(1);
      if (OSTaskDelReq(OS_PRIO_SELF) == OS_TASK_DEL_REQ) {
         /* Release any owned resources;                                       */
         /* De-allocate any dynamic memory;                                    */
         OSTaskDel(OS_PRIO_SELF);
      }
   }
}
```

11

OSTaskQuery()

INT8U OSTaskQuery(INT8U prio, OS_TCB *pdata);

File	*Called from*	*Code enabled by*
OS_TASK.C	Task or ISR	N/A

OSTaskQuery() obtains information about a task. Your application must allocate an OS_TCB data structure to receive a "snapshot" of the desired task's control block. Your copy will contain *every* field in the OS_TCB structure. You should be careful when accessing the contents of the OS_TCB structure, especially OSTCBNext and OSTCBPrev, because they point to the next and previous OS_TCB in the chain of created tasks, respectively.

Arguments

prio is the priority of the task you wish to obtain data from. You can obtain information about the calling task by specifying OS_PRIO_SELF.

pdata is a pointer to a structure of type OS_TCB, which contains a copy of the task's control block.

Return Value

OSTaskQuery() returns one of three error codes:
- OS_NO_ERR if the call was successful.
- OS_PRIO_ERR if you tried to obtain information from an invalid task.
- OS_PRIO_INVALID if you specified a priority higher than OS_LOWEST_PRIO.

Notes/Warnings

The fields in the task control block depend on the following configuration options (see OS_CFG.H):
- OS_TASK_CREATE_EN
- OS_Q_EN
- OS_MBOX_EN
- OS_SEM_EN
- OS_TASK_DEL_EN

Example

```
void Task (void *pdata)
{
    OS_TCB  task_data;
    INT8U   err;
    void    *pext;
    INT8U   status;


    pdata = pdata;
    for (;;) {
        .

        .
        err = OSTaskQuery(OS_PRIO_SELF, &task_data);
        if (err == OS_NO_ERR) {
            pext   = task_data.OSTCBExtPtr; /* Get TCB extension pointer  */
            status = task_data.OSTCBStat;   /* Get task status            */
            .

            .
        }
        .

        .
    }
}
```

OSTaskResume()

INT8U OSTaskResume(INT8U prio);

File	Called from	Code enabled by
OS_TASK.C	Task only	OS_TASK_SUSPEND_EN

OSTaskResume() resumes a task that was suspended through the OSTaskSuspend() function. In fact, OSTaskResume() is the only function that can "unsuspend" a suspended task.

Arguments

prio specifies the priority of the task to resume.

Return Value

OSTaskResume() returns one of the following error codes:

- OS_NO_ERR if the call was successful.
- OS_TASK_RESUME_PRIO if the task you are attempting to resume does not exist.
- OS_TASK_NOT_SUSPENDED if the task to resume has not been suspended.
- OS_PRIO_INVALID if prio is higher or equal to OS_LOWEST_PRIO.

Notes/Warnings

None

Example

```
void TaskX(void *pdata)
{
    INT8U err;


    for (;;) {
        .
        .
        err = OSTaskResume(10);        /* Resume task with priority 10   */
        if (err == OS_NO_ERR) {
            .                          /* Task was resumed               */
            .
        }
        .
        .
    }
}
```

OSTaskStkChk()

`INT8U OSTaskStkChk(INT8U prio, INT32U *pfree, INT32U *pused);`

File	Called from	Code enabled by
OS_TASK.C	Task code	OS_TASK_CREATE_EXT

OSTaskStkChk() determines a task's stack statistics. Specifically, it computes the amount of free stack space as well as the amount of stack space used by the specified task. This function requires that the task be created with OSTaskCreateExt() and that you specify OS_TASK_OPT_STK_CHK in the opt argument.

Stack sizing is done by walking from the bottom of the stack and counting the number of 0 entries on the stack until a nonzero value is found. Of course, this assumes that the stack is cleared when the task is created. For that purpose, you need to set OS_TASK_STK_CLR to 1 in your configuration. You could set OS_TASK_STK_CLR to 0 if your startup code clears all RAM and you never delete your tasks. This would reduce the execution time of OSTaskCreateExt().

Arguments

prio is the priority of the task you want to obtain stack information about. You can check the stack of the calling task by passing OS_PRIO_SELF.

pdata is a pointer to a variable of type OS_STK_DATA, which contains the following fields:

```
    INT32U OSFree;      /* Number of bytes free on the stack      */
    INT32U OSUsed;      /* Number of bytes used on the stack      */
```

Return Value

OSTaskStkChk() returns one of the following error codes:

- OS_NO_ERR if you specified valid arguments and the call was successful.
- OS_PRIO_INVALID if you specified a task priority higher than OS_LOWEST_PRIO, or you didn't specify OS_PRIO_SELF.
- OS_TASK_NOT_EXIST if the specified task does not exist.
- OS_TASK_OPT_ERR if you did not specify OS_TASK_OPT_STK_CHK when the task was created by OSTaskCreateExt() or if you created the task by using OSTaskCreate().

Notes/Warnings

Execution time of this task depends on the size of the task's stack and is thus nondeterministic.

Your application can determine the total task stack space (in number of bytes) by adding the two fields .OSFree and .OSUsed of the OS_STK_DATA data structure.

Technically, this function can be called by an ISR, but because of the possibly long execution time, it is not advisable.

Example

```
void Task (void *pdata)
{
    OS_STK_DATA stk_data;
    INT32U      stk_size;


    for (;;) {
        .

        .
      err = OSTaskStkChk(10, &stk_data);
      if (err == OS_NO_ERR) {
         stk_size = stk_data.OSFree + stk_data.OSUsed;
      }
        .

        .
    }
}
```

OSTaskSuspend()

INT8U OSTaskSuspend(INT8U prio);

File	*Called from*	*Code enabled by*
OS_TASK.C	Task only	OS_TASK_SUSPEND_EN

OSTaskSuspend() suspends (or blocks) execution of a task unconditionally. The calling task can be suspended by specifying its own priority number or OS_PRIO_SELF if the task doesn't know its own priority number. In this case, another task needs to resume the suspended task. If the current task is suspended, rescheduling occurs and µC/OS-II runs the next highest priority task ready to run. The only way to resume a suspended task is to call OSTaskResume().

Task suspension is additive. This means that if the task being suspended is delayed until *n* ticks expire, the task is resumed only when both the time expires and the suspension is removed. Also, if the suspended task is waiting for a semaphore and the semaphore is signaled, the task is removed from the semaphore wait list (if it is the highest priority task waiting for the semaphore) but execution is not resumed until the suspension is removed.

Arguments

prio specifies the priority of the task to suspend. You can suspend the calling task by passing OS_PRIO_SELF, in which case, the next highest priority task is executed.

Return Value

OSTaskSuspend() returns one of the following error codes:

- OS_NO_ERR if the call was successful.
- OS_TASK_SUSPEND_IDLE if you attempted to suspend the µC/OS-II idle task, which is not allowed.
- OS_PRIO_INVALID if you specified a priority higher than the maximum allowed (i.e., you specified a priority of OS_LOWEST_PRIO or more) or you didn't specify OS_PRIO_SELF.
- OS_TASK_SUSPEND_PRIO if the task you are attempting to suspend does not exist.

Notes/Warnings

OSTaskSuspend() and OSTaskResume() must be used in pairs.

A suspended task can only be resumed by OSTaskResume().

Example

```
void TaskX(void *pdata)
{
    INT8U err;


    for (;;) {
        .
        .
        err = OSTaskSuspend(OS_PRIO_SELF);      /* Suspend current task     */
        .                          /* Execution continues when ANOTHER task .. */
        .                          /* .. explicitly resumes this task.         */
        .
    }
}
```

11

OSTimeDly()

void OSTimeDly(INT16U ticks);

File	Called from	Code enabled by
OS_TIME.C	Task only	N/A

OSTimeDly() allows a task to delay itself for a number of clock ticks. Rescheduling always occurs when the number of clock ticks is greater than zero. Valid delays range from zero to 65,535 ticks. A delay of 0 means that the task is not delayed and OSTimeDly() returns immediately to the caller. The actual delay time depends on the tick rate (see OS_TICKS_PER_SEC in the configuration file OS_CFG.H).

Arguments

ticks is the number of clock ticks to delay the current task.

Return Value

None

Notes/Warnings

Note that calling this function with a value of 0 results in no delay, and the function returns immediately to the caller. To ensure that a task delays for the specified number of ticks, you should consider using a delay value that is one tick higher. For example, to delay a task for at least 10 ticks, you should specify a value of 11.

Example

```
void TaskX(void *pdata)
{
    for (;;) {
        .
        .
        OSTimeDly(10);                    /* Delay task for 10 clock ticks */
        .
        .
    }
}
```

11

OSTimeDlyHMSM()

`void OSTimeDlyHMSM(INT8U hours, INT8U minutes, INT8U seconds, INT8U milli);`

File	Called from	Code enabled by
OS_TIME.C	Task only	N/A

OSTimeDlyHMSM() allows a task to delay itself for a user-specified amount of time specified in hours, minutes, seconds, and milliseconds. This is a more convenient and natural format than ticks. Rescheduling always occurs when at least one of the parameters is nonzero.

Arguments

hours is the number of hours the task will be delayed. The valid range of values is 0 to 255.

minutes is the number of minutes the task will be delayed. The valid range of values is 0 to 59.

seconds is the number of seconds the task will be delayed. The valid range of values is 0 to 59.

milli is the number of milliseconds the task will be delayed. The valid range of values is 0 to 999. Note that the resolution of this argument is in multiples of the tick rate. For instance, if the tick rate is set to 10ms, a delay of 5ms results in no delay. The delay is rounded to the nearest tick. Thus, a delay of 15ms actually results in a delay of 20ms.

Return Value

OSTimeDlyHMSM() returns one of the following error codes:

- OS_NO_ERR if you specified valid arguments and the call was successful.
- OS_TIME_INVALID_MINUTES if the minutes argument is greater than 59.
- OS_TIME_INVALID_SECONDS if the seconds argument is greater than 59.
- OS_TIME_INVALID_MILLI if the milliseconds argument is greater than 999.
- OS_TIME_ZERO_DLY if all four arguments are 0.

Notes/Warnings

Note that OSTimeDlyHMSM(0,0,0,0) (i.e., hours, minutes, seconds, milli) results in no delay, and the function returns immediately to the caller. Also, if the total delay time is longer than 65,535 clock ticks, you will not be able to abort the delay and resume the task by calling OSTimeDlyResume().

Example

```
void TaskX(void *pdata)
{
    for (;;) {
        .
        .
        OSTimeDlyHMSM(0, 0, 1, 0);  /* Delay task for 1 second */
        .
        .
    }
}
```

11

OSTimeDlyResume()

INT8U OSTimeDlyResume(INT8U prio);

File	Called from	Code enabled by
OS_TIME.C	Task only	N/A

OSTimeDlyResume() resumes a task that has been delayed through a call to either OSTimeDly() or OSTimeDlyHMSM().

Arguments

prio specifies the priority of the task to resume.

Return Value

OSTimeDlyResume() returns one of the following error codes:

- OS_NO_ERR if the call was successful.
- OS_PRIO_INVALID if you specified a task priority greater than OS_LOWEST_PRIO.
- OS_TIME_NOT_DLY if the task is not waiting for time to expire.
- OS_TASK_NOT_EXIST if the task has not been created.

Notes/Warnings

Note that you must not call this function to resume a task that is waiting for an event with timeout. This situation would make the task look like a timeout occurred (unless you desire this effect).

You cannot resume a task that has called OSTimeDlyHMSM() with a combined time that exceeds 65,535 clock ticks. In other words, if the clock tick runs at 100Hz, you will not be able to resume a delayed task that called OSTimeDlyHMSM(0, 10, 55, 350) or higher.

$$[10 \text{ minutes} * 60 + (55 + 0.35) \text{ seconds}] * 100 \text{ ticks/second}$$

Example

```
void TaskX(void *pdata)
{
   INT8U err;


   pdata = pdata;
   for (;;) {
      .
      err = OSTimeDlyResume(10);          /* Resume task with priority 10    */
      if (err == OS_NO_ERR) {
         .                                /* Task was resumed                */
         .
      }
      .
   }
}
```

11

OSTimeGet()

`INT32U OSTimeGet(void);`

File	Called from	Code enabled by
OS_TIME.C	Task or ISR	N/A

OSTimeGet() obtains the current value of the system clock. The system clock is a 32-bit counter that counts the number of clock ticks since power was applied or since the system clock was last set.

Arguments

None

Return Value

The current system clock value (in number of ticks).

Notes/Warnings

None

Example

```
void TaskX(void *pdata)
{
    INT32U clk;


    for (;;) {
        .
        .
        clk = OSTimeGet();   /* Get current value of system clock */
        .
        .
    }
}
```

OSTimeSet()

void OSTimeSet(INT32U ticks);

File	Called from	Code enabled by
OS_TIME.C	Task or ISR	N/A

OSTimeSet() sets the system clock. The system clock is a 32-bit counter that counts the number of clock ticks since power was applied or since the system clock was last set.

Arguments

ticks is the desired value for the system clock, in ticks.

Return Value

None

Notes/Warnings

None

Example

```
void TaskX(void *pdata)
{
     for (;;) {
         .
         .
         OSTimeSet(0L);     /* Reset the system clock  */
         .
         .
     }
}
```

11

OSTimeTick()

void OSTimeTick(void);

File	*Called from*	*Code enabled by*
OS_TIME.C	Task or ISR	N/A

OSTimeTick() processes a clock tick. µC/OS-II checks all tasks to see if they are either waiting for time to expire [because they called OSTimeDly() or OSTimeDlyHMSM()] or waiting for events to occur until they timeout.

Arguments

None

Return Value

None

Notes/Warnings

The execution time of OSTimeTick() is directly proportional to the number of tasks created in an application. OSTimeTick() can be called by either an ISR or a task. If called by a task, the task priority should be very high (i.e., have a low priority number) because this function is responsible for updating delays and timeouts.

Example
(Intel 80x86, real mode, large model)

```
TickISRPROC    FAR
               PUSHA                           ; Save processor context
               PUSH ES
               PUSH DS
;
               INC  BYTE PTR _OSIntNesting     ; Notify µC/OS-II of start of ISR
               CALL FAR PTR _OSTimeTick        ; Process clock tick
               .                               ; User Code to clear interrupt
               .
               CALL FAR PTR _OSIntExit         ; Notify µC/OS-II of end of ISR
               POP  DS                         ; Restore processor registers
               POP  ES
               POPA
;
               IRET                            ; Return to interrupted task
TickISRENDP
```

11

OSVersion()

`INT16U OSVersion(void);`

File	Called from	Code enabled by
OS_CORE.C	Task or ISR	N/A

OSVersion() obtains the current version of µC/OS-II.

Arguments

None

Return Value

The version is returned as *x.yy* multiplied by 100. For example, version 2.00 is returned as 200.

Notes/Warnings

None

Example

```
void TaskX(void *pdata)
{
    INT16U os_version;


    for (;;) {
        .
        .
        os_version = OSVersion();  /* Obtain uC/OS-II's version   */
        .
        .
    }
}
```

OS_ENTER_CRITICAL()

OS_EXIT_CRITICAL()

File	Called from	Code enabled by
OS_CPU.H	Task or ISR	N/A

OS_ENTER_CRITICAL() and OS_EXIT_CRITICAL() are macros used to disable and enable, respectively, the processor's interrupts.

Arguments

None

Return Value

None

Notes/Warnings

These macros must be used in pairs.

Example

```
void TaskX(void *pdata)
{
    for (;;) {
        .
        .
        OS_ENTER_CRITICAL();    /* Disable interrupts    */
        .
                                /* Access critical code  */
        .
        OS_EXIT_CRITICAL();     /* Enable  interrupts    */
        .
        .
    }
}
```

11

Chapter 12

Configuration Manual

This chapter provides a description of the configurable elements of μC/OS-II. Because μC/OS-II is provided in source form, configuration is done through a number of #define constants, which are found in OS_CFG.H and should exist for each project/product that you make.

This section describes each of the #define constants in the order in which they are found in OS_CFG.H. Table 12.1 lists each μC/OS-II function by type (**Service**), indicates which variables enable the code (**Set to 1**), and lists other configuration constants that affect the function (**Other Constants**).

Of course, OS_CFG.H must be included when μC/OS-II is built, in order for the desired configuration to take effect.

Table 12.1 *μC/OS-II functions and #define configuration constants.*

Service	Set to 1	Other Constants
Miscellaneous		
OSInit()	N/A	OS_MAX_EVENTS
		OS_Q_EN and OS_MAX_QS
		OS_MEM_EN
		OS_TASK_IDLE_STK_SIZE
		OS_TASK_STAT_EN
		OS_TASK_STAT_STK_SIZE
OSSchedLock()	N/A	N/A
OSSchedUnlock()	N/A	N/A
OSStart()	N/A	N/A
OSStatInit()	OS_TASK_STAT_EN && OS_TASK_CREATE_EXT_EN	OS_TICKS_PER_SEC
OSVersion()	N/A	N/A

12

Table 12.1   μC/OS-II functions and #define configuration constants. (Continued)

Service	Set to 1	Other Constants
Interrupt Management		
OSIntEnter()	N/A	N/A
OSIntExit()	N/A	N/A
Message Mailboxes		
OSMboxAccept()	OS_MBOX_EN	N/A
OSMboxCreate()	OS_MBOX_EN	OS_MAX_EVENTS
OSMboxPend()	OS_MBOX_EN	N/A
OSMboxPost()	OS_MBOX_EN	N/A
OSMboxQuery()	OS_MBOX_EN	N/A
Memory Partition Management		
OSMemCreate()	OS_MEM_EN	OS_MAX_MEM_PART
OSMemGet()	OS_MEM_EN	N/A
OSMemPut()	OS_MEM_EN	N/A
OSMemQuery()	OS_MEM_EN	N/A
Message Queues		
OSQAccept()	OS_Q_EN	N/A
OSQCreate()	OS_Q_EN	OS_MAX_EVENTS OS_MAX_QS
OSQFlush()	OS_Q_EN	N/A
OSQPend()	OS_Q_EN	N/A
OSQPost()	OS_Q_EN	N/A
OSQPostFront()	OS_Q_EN	N/A
OSQQuery()	OS_Q_EN	N/A
Semaphore Management		
OSSemAccept()	OS_SEM_EN	N/A
OSSemCreate()	OS_SEM_EN	OS_MAX_EVENTS
OSSemPend()	OS_SEM_EN	N/A
OSSemPost()	OS_SEM_EN	N/A
OSSemQuery()	OS_SEM_EN	N/A

Table 12.1 *μC/OS-II functions and* **#define** *configuration constants. (Continued)*

Service	*Set to 1*	*Other Constants*
Task Management		
OSTaskChangePrio()	OS_TASK_CHANGE_PRIO_EN	OS_LOWEST_PRIO
OSTaskCreate()	OS_TASK_CREATE_EN	OS_MAX_TASKS OS_LOWEST_PRIO
OSTaskCreateExt()	OS_TASK_CREATE_EXT_EN	OS_MAX_TASKS OS_STK_GROWTH OS_LOWEST_PRIO
OSTaskDel()	OS_TASK_DEL_EN	OS_LOWEST_PRIO
OSTaskDelReq()	OS_TASK_DEL_EN	OS_LOWEST_PRIO
OSTaskResume()	OS_TASK_SUSPEND_EN	OS_LOWEST_PRIO
OSTaskStkChk()	OS_TASK_CREATE_EXT_EN	OS_LOWEST_PRIO
OSTaskSuspend()	OS_TASK_SUSPEND_EN	OS_LOWEST_PRIO
OSTaskQuery()		OS_LOWEST_PRIO
Time Management		
OSTimeDly()	N/A	N/A
OSTimeDlyHMSM()	N/A	OS_TICKS_PER_SEC
OSTimeDlyResume()	N/A	OS_LOWEST_PRIO
OSTimeGet()	N/A	N/A
OSTimeSet()	N/A	N/A
OSTimeTick()	N/A	N/A
User-Defined Functions		
OSTaskCreateHook()	OS_CPU_HOOKS_EN	N/A
OSTaskDelHook()	OS_CPU_HOOKS_EN	N/A
OSTaskStatHook()	OS_CPU_HOOKS_EN	N/A
OSTaskSwHook()	OS_CPU_HOOKS_EN	N/A
OSTimeTickHook()	OS_CPU_HOOKS_EN	N/A

12

OS_MAX_EVENTS

OS_MAX_EVENTS specifies the maximum number of event control blocks that will be allocated. An event control block is needed for every message mailbox, message queue, or semaphore object. For example, if you have 10 mailboxes, five queues, and three semaphores, you must set OS_MAX_EVENTS to at least 18. If you intend to use mailboxes, queues, or semaphores, you must set OS_MAX_EVENTS to 2 at least.

OS_MAX_MEM_PART

OS_MAX_MEM_PART specifies the maximum number of memory partitions that will be managed by the memory partition manager found in OS_MEM.C. To use a memory partition, however, you also need to set OS_MEM_EN to 1. If you intend to use memory partitions, you must set OS_MAX_MEM_PART to 2 at least.

OS_MAX_QS

OS_MAX_QS specifies the maximum number of message queues that your application will create. To use message queue services, you also need to set OS_Q_EN to 1. If you intend to use message queues, you must set OS_MAX_QS to 2 at least.

OS_MAX_TASKS

OS_MAX_TASKS specifies the maximum number of *application* tasks that can exist in your application. Note that OS_MAX_TASKS cannot be greater than 62 because µC/OS-II currently reserves two tasks for itself (see OS_N_SYS_TASKS in uCOS_II.H). If you set OS_MAX_TASKS to the exact number of tasks in your system, you need to make sure that you revise this value when you add additional tasks. Conversely, if you make OS_MAX_TASKS much higher than your current task requirements (for future expansion), you will be wasting valuable RAM.

OS_LOWEST_PRIO

OS_LOWEST_PRIO specifies the lowest task priority (i.e., highest number) that you intend to use in your application and is provided to reduce the amount of RAM needed by µC/OS-II. Remember that µC/OS-II priorities can go from 0 (highest priority) to a maximum of 63 (lowest possible priority). Setting OS_LOWEST_PRIO to a value less than 63 means that your application cannot create tasks with a priority number higher than OS_LOWEST_PRIO. In fact, µC/OS-II reserves priorities OS_LOWEST_PRIO and OS_LOWEST_PRIO-1 for itself: OS_LOWEST_PRIO is reserved for the idle task [OSTaskIdle()], and OS_LOWEST_PRIO-1 is reserved for the statistic task [OSTaskStat()]. The priorities of your application tasks can thus take a value between 0 and OS_LOWEST_PRIO-2 (inclusive). The lowest task priority specified by OS_LOWEST_PRIO is independent of OS_MAX_TASKS. For example, you can set OS_MAX_TASKS to 10 and OS_LOWEST_PRIO to 32 and have up to 10 application tasks, each of which can have a task priority value between 0 and 30 (inclusive). Note that each task must still have a different priority value. You must always set OS_LOWEST_PRIO to a value greater than the number of application tasks in your system. For example, if you set OS_MAX_TASKS to 20 and OS_LOWEST_PRIO to 10, you will not be able to create more than eight application tasks (0, ..., 7). You will simply be wasting RAM.

OS_TASK_IDLE_STK_SIZE

OS_TASK_IDLE_STK_SIZE specifies the size of the µC/OS-II idle task stack. The size is specified not in bytes, but in number of elements. This is because a stack must be declared to be of type OS_STK. The size of the idle task stack depends on the processor you are using and the deepest anticipated interrupt nesting level. Very little is being done in the idle task, but you should allow at least enough space to store all processor registers on the stack and enough storage to handle all nested interrupts.

OS_TASK_STAT_EN

OS_TASK_STAT_EN specifies whether or not you will enable the µC/OS-II statistic task, as well as its initialization function. When set to 1, the statistic task OSTaskStat() and the statistic task initialization function are enabled. OSTaskStat() computes the CPU usage of your application. When enabled, it executes every second and computes the 8-bit variable OSCPUUsage, which provides the percent CPU utilization of your application. OSTaskStat() calls OSTaskStatHook() every time it executes so that you can add your own statistics as needed. See OS_CORE.C for details on the statistic task. The priority of OSTaskStat() is always set to OS_LOWEST_PRIO-1.

The global variables OSCPUUsage, OSIdleCtrMax, OSIdleCtrRun, and OSStatRdy are not declared when OS_TASK_STAT_EN is set to 0. This reduces the amount of RAM needed by µC/OS-II if you don't intend to use the statistic task.

OS_TASK_STAT_STK_SIZE

OS_TASK_STAT_STK_SIZE specifies the size of the µC/OS-II statistic task stack. The size is specified not in bytes, but in number of elements. This is because a stack is declared as being of type OS_STK. The size of the statistic task stack depends on the processor you are using and the maximum of the following actions:

- The stack growth associated with performing 32-bit arithmetic
- The stack growth associated with calling OSTimeDly()
- The stack growth associated with calling OSTaskStatHook()
- The deepest anticipated interrupt nesting level

If you want to run stack checking on this task and determine its actual stack requirements, you must enable code generation for OSTaskCreateExt() by setting OS_TASK_CREATE_EXT_EN to 1. Again, the priority of OSTaskStat() is always set to OS_LOWEST_PRIO-1.

12

OS_CPU_HOOKS_EN

This configuration constant indicates whether OS_CPU_C.C declares the hook functions (when set to 1) or not (when set to 0). Recall that µC/OS-II expects the presence of five functions that can be defined either in the port (i.e., in OS_CPU_C.C) or by the application code. These functions are:

- OSTaskCreateHook()
- OSTaskDelHook()
- OSTaskStatHook()
- OSTaskSwHook()
- OSTimeTickHook()

OS_MBOX_EN

This constant enables (when set to 1) or disables (when set to 0) code generation of message mailbox services and data structures, which reduces the amount of code space when your application does not require the use of message mailboxes.

OS_MEM_EN

This constant enables (when set to 1) or disables (when set to 0) code generation of the µC/OS-II partition memory manager and its associated data structures. This reduces the amount of code and data space when your application does not require the use of memory partitions.

OS_Q_EN

This constant enables (when set to 1) or disables (when set to 0) code generation of the µC/OS-II message queue manager and its associated data structures, which reduces the amount of code and data space when your application does not require the use of message queues. Note that if OS_Q_EN is set to 0, the #define constant OS_MAX_QS is irrelevant.

OS_SEM_EN

This constant enables (when set to 1) or disables (when set to 0) code generation of the µC/OS-II semaphore manager and its associated data structures, which reduces the amount of code and data space when your application does not require the use of semaphores.

OS_TASK_CHANGE_PRIO_EN

This constant enables (when set to 1) or disables (when set to 0) code generation of the function OSTaskChangePrio(). If your application never changes task priorities once they are assigned, you can reduce the amount of code space used by µC/OS-II by setting OS_TASK_CHANGE_PRIO_EN to 0.

OS_TASK_CREATE_EN

This constant enables (when set to 1) or disables (when set to 0) code generation for the OSTaskCreate() function. Enabling this function makes μC/OS-II backward compatible with the μC/OS task creation function. If your application always uses OSTaskCreateExt() (recommended), you can reduce the amount of code space used by μC/OS-II by setting OS_TASK_CREATE_EN to 0. Note that you must set at least OS_TASK_CREATE_EN or OS_TASK_CREATE_EXT_EN to 1. If you wish, you can use both.

OS_TASK_CREATE_EXT_EN

This constant enables (when set to 1) or disables (when set to 0) code generation of the function OSTaskCreateExt(), which is the extended, more powerful version of the two task creation functions. If your application never uses OSTaskCreateExt(), you can reduce the amount of code space used by μC/OS-II by setting OS_TASK_CREATE_EXT_EN to 0. Note that you need the extended task create function to use the stack-checking function OSTaskStkChk().

OS_TASK_DEL_EN

This constant enables (when set to 1) or disables (when set to 0) code generation of the function OSTaskDel(), which deletes tasks. If your application never uses this function, you can reduce the amount of code space used by μC/OS-II by setting OS_TASK_DEL_EN to 0.

OS_TASK_SUSPEND_EN

This constant enables (when set to 1) or disables (when set to 0) code generation of the functions OSTaskSuspend() and OSTaskResume(), which allows you to explicitly suspend and resume tasks, respectively. If your application never uses these functions, you can reduce the amount of code space used by μC/OS-II by setting OS_TASK_SUSPEND_EN to 0.

OS_TICKS_PER_SEC

This constant specifies the rate at which you will call OSTimeTick(). It is up to your initialization code to ensure that OSTimeTick() is invoked at this rate. This constant is used by OSStatInit(), OSTaskStat(), and OSTimeDlyHMSM().

12

Example Source Code

A.00 Example 1

A.00.01 EX1L.C

```c
/*
*********************************************************************************************************
*                                              uC/OS-II
*                                        The Real-Time Kernel
*
*                        (c) Copyright 1992-1998, Jean J. Labrosse, Plantation, FL
*                                        All Rights Reserved
*
*                                              V2.00
*
*                                            EXAMPLE #1
*********************************************************************************************************
*/

#include "includes.h"

/*
*********************************************************************************************************
*                                             CONSTANTS
*********************************************************************************************************
*/

#define  TASK_STK_SIZE              512        /* Size of each task's stacks (# of WORDs)        */
#define  N_TASKS                     10        /* Number of identical tasks                      */

/*
*********************************************************************************************************
*                                             VARIABLES
*********************************************************************************************************
*/

OS_STK          TaskStk[N_TASKS][TASK_STK_SIZE];      /* Tasks stacks                            */
OS_STK          TaskStartStk[TASK_STK_SIZE];
char            TaskData[N_TASKS];                    /* Parameters to pass to each task         */
OS_EVENT        *RandomSem;

/*
*********************************************************************************************************
*                                         FUNCTION PROTOTYPES
*********************************************************************************************************
*/
void    Task(void *data);                             /* Function prototypes of tasks            */
void    TaskStart(void *data);                        /* Function prototypes of Startup task     */
```

```
/*
*********************************************************************************************
*                                           MAIN
*********************************************************************************************
*/

void main (void)
{
    PC_DispClrScr(DISP_FGND_WHITE + DISP_BGND_BLACK);      /* Clear the screen                   */
    OSInit();                                              /* Initialize uC/OS-II                */
    PC_DOSSaveReturn();                                    /* Save environment to return to DOS  */
    PC_VectSet(uCOS, OSCtxSw);                             /* Install uC/OS-II's context switch vector */
    RandomSem = OSSemCreate(1);                            /* Random number semaphore            */
    OSTaskCreate(TaskStart, (void *)0, (void *)&TaskStartStk[TASK_STK_SIZE - 1], 0);
    OSStart();                                             /* Start multitasking                 */
}
```

```
/*
*********************************************************************************************************
*                                          STARTUP TASK
*********************************************************************************************************
*/
void TaskStart (void *data)
{
    UBYTE  i;
    char   s[100];
    WORD   key;


    data = data;                                           /* Prevent compiler warning                 */

    PC_DispStr(26,  0, "uC/OS-II, The Real-Time Kernel", DISP_FGND_WHITE + DISP_BGND_RED + DISP_BLINK);
    PC_DispStr(33,  1, "Jean J. Labrosse", DISP_FGND_WHITE);
    PC_DispStr(36,  3, "EXAMPLE #1", DISP_FGND_WHITE);

    OS_ENTER_CRITICAL();
    PC_VectSet(0x08, OSTickISR);                           /* Install uC/OS-II's clock tick ISR        */
    PC_SetTickRate(OS_TICKS_PER_SEC);                      /* Reprogram tick rate                      */
    OS_EXIT_CRITICAL();

    PC_DispStr(0, 22, "Determining  CPU's capacity ...", DISP_FGND_WHITE);
    OSStatInit();                                          /* Initialize uC/OS-II's statistics         */
    PC_DispClrLine(22, DISP_FGND_WHITE + DISP_BGND_BLACK);

    for (i = 0; i < N_TASKS; i++) {                        /* Create N_TASKS identical tasks           */
        TaskData[i] = '0' + i;                             /* Each task will display its own letter    */
        OSTaskCreate(Task, (void *)&TaskData[i], (void *)&TaskStk[i][TASK_STK_SIZE - 1], i + 1);
    }
    PC_DispStr( 0, 22, "#Tasks        : xxxxx  CPU Usage: xxx %", DISP_FGND_WHITE);
    PC_DispStr( 0, 23, "#Task switch/sec: xxxxx", DISP_FGND_WHITE);
    PC_DispStr(28, 24, "<-PRESS 'ESC' TO QUIT->", DISP_FGND_WHITE + DISP_BLINK);
    for (;;) {
        sprintf(s, "%5d", OSTaskCtr);                      /* Display #tasks running                   */
        PC_DispStr(18, 22, s, DISP_FGND_BLUE + DISP_BGND_CYAN);
        sprintf(s, "%3d", OSCPUUsage);                     /* Display CPU usage in %                   */
        PC_DispStr(36, 22, s, DISP_FGND_BLUE + DISP_BGND_CYAN);
        sprintf(s, "%5d", OSCtxSwCtr);                     /* Display #context switches per second     */
        PC_DispStr(18, 23, s, DISP_FGND_BLUE + DISP_BGND_CYAN);
        OSCtxSwCtr = 0;

        sprintf(s, "V%3.2f", (float)OSVersion() * 0.01);   /* Display version number as Vx.yy          */
        PC_DispStr(75, 24, s, DISP_FGND_YELLOW + DISP_BGND_BLUE);
        PC_GetDateTime(s);                                 /* Get and display date and time            */
        PC_DispStr(0, 24, s, DISP_FGND_BLUE + DISP_BGND_CYAN);

        if (PC_GetKey(&key) == TRUE) {                     /* See if key has been pressed              */
            if (key == 0x1B) {                             /* Yes, see if it's the ESCAPE key          */
                PC_DOSReturn();                            /* Return to DOS                            */
            }
        }

        OSTimeDlyHMSM(0, 0, 1, 0);                         /* Wait one second                          */
    }
}
```

A

```
/*
*********************************************************************************************************
*                                               TASKS
*********************************************************************************************************
*/

void Task (void *data)
{
    UBYTE x;
    UBYTE y;
    UBYTE err;


    for (;;) {
        OSSemPend(RandomSem, 0, &err);          /* Acquire semaphore to perform random numbers    */
        x = random(80);                         /* Find X position where task number will appear  */
        y = random(16);                         /* Find Y position where task number will appear  */
        OSSemPost(RandomSem);                   /* Release semaphore                              */
                                                /* Display the task number on the screen          */
        PC_DispChar(x, y + 5, *(char *)data, DISP_FGND_LIGHT_GRAY);
        OSTimeDly(1);                           /* Delay 1 clock tick                             */
    }
}
```

EX1L.C

A.00.02   INCLUDES.H (Example 1)

```
/*
*********************************************************************************************
*                                        uC/OS-II
*                                    The Real-Time Kernel
*
*                     (c) Copyright 1992-1998, Jean J. Labrosse, Plantation, FL
*                                     All Rights Reserved
*
*                                    MASTER INCLUDE FILE
*********************************************************************************************
*/

#include      <stdio.h>
#include      <string.h>
#include      <ctype.h>
#include      <stdlib.h>
#include      <conio.h>
#include      <dos.h>
#include      <setjmp.h>

#include      "\software\ucos-ii\ix86l\os_cpu.h"
#include      "os_cfg.h"
#include      "\software\blocks\pc\source\pc.h"
#include      "\software\ucos-ii\source\ucos_ii.h"
```

A.00.03 OS_CFG.H (Example 1)

```
/*
*********************************************************************************************
*                                      uC/OS-II
*                                  The Real-Time Kernel
*
*                   (c) Copyright 1992-1998, Jean J. Labrosse, Plantation, FL
*                                   All Rights Reserved
*
*                              Configuration for Intel 80x86 (Large)
*
* File : OS_CFG.H
* By   : Jean J. Labrosse
*********************************************************************************************
*/


/*
*********************************************************************************************
*                                  uC/OS-II CONFIGURATION
*********************************************************************************************
*/

#define OS_MAX_EVENTS             2      /* Max. number of event control blocks in your application ... */
                                         /* ... MUST be >= 2                                            */
#define OS_MAX_MEM_PART           2      /* Max. number of memory partitions ...                        */
                                         /* ... MUST be >= 2                                            */
#define OS_MAX_QS                 2      /* Max. number of queue control blocks in your application ... */
                                         /* ... MUST be >= 2                                            */
#define OS_MAX_TASKS             11      /* Max. number of tasks in your application ...                */
                                         /* ... MUST be >= 2                                            */

#define OS_LOWEST_PRIO           12      /* Defines the lowest priority that can be assigned ...         */
                                         /* ... MUST NEVER be higher than 63!                           */

#define OS_TASK_IDLE_STK_SIZE   512      /* Idle task stack size (# of 16-bit wide entries)             */

#define OS_TASK_STAT_EN           1      /* Enable (1) or Disable(0) the statistics task                */
#define OS_TASK_STAT_STK_SIZE   512      /* Statistics task stack size (# of 16-bit wide entries)       */

#define OS_CPU_HOOKS_EN           1      /* uC/OS-II hooks are found in the processor port files        */
#define OS_MBOX_EN                0      /* Include code for MAILBOXES                                  */
#define OS_MEM_EN                 0      /* Include code for MEMORY MANAGER (fixed sized memory blocks) */
#define OS_Q_EN                   0      /* Include code for QUEUES                                     */
#define OS_SEM_EN                 1      /* Include code for SEMAPHORES                                 */
#define OS_TASK_CHANGE_PRIO_EN    0      /* Include code for OSTaskChangePrio()                         */
#define OS_TASK_CREATE_EN         1      /* Include code for OSTaskCreate()                             */
#define OS_TASK_CREATE_EXT_EN     0      /* Include code for OSTaskCreateExt()                          */
#define OS_TASK_DEL_EN            0      /* Include code for OSTaskDel()                                */
#define OS_TASK_SUSPEND_EN        0      /* Include code for OSTaskSuspend() and OSTaskResume()         */

#define OS_TICKS_PER_SEC        200      /* Set the number of ticks in one second                      */
```

A.01 Example 2

A.01.01 EX2L.C

```
/*
************************************************************************************************
*                                      uC/OS-II
*                                The Real-Time Kernel
*
*                 (c) Copyright 1992-1998, Jean J. Labrosse, Plantation, FL
*                                 All Rights Reserved
*
*                                       V2.00
*
*                                     EXAMPLE #2
************************************************************************************************
*/

#include "includes.h"

/*
************************************************************************************************
*                                      CONSTANTS
************************************************************************************************
*/

#define        TASK_STK_SIZE       512              /* Size of each task's stacks (# of WORDs)    */

#define        TASK_START_ID         0              /* Application tasks IDs                       */
#define        TASK_CLK_ID           1
#define        TASK_1_ID             2
#define        TASK_2_ID             3
#define        TASK_3_ID             4
#define        TASK_4_ID             5
#define        TASK_5_ID             6

#define        TASK_START_PRIO      10              /* Application tasks priorities               */
#define        TASK_CLK_PRIO        11
#define        TASK_1_PRIO          12
#define        TASK_2_PRIO          13
#define        TASK_3_PRIO          14
#define        TASK_4_PRIO          15
#define        TASK_5_PRIO          16

/*
************************************************************************************************
*                                      VARIABLES
************************************************************************************************
*/

OS_STK         TaskStartStk[TASK_STK_SIZE];         /* Startup    task stack                      */
OS_STK         TaskClkStk[TASK_STK_SIZE];           /* Clock      task stack                      */
OS_STK         Task1Stk[TASK_STK_SIZE];             /* Task #1    task stack                      */
OS_STK         Task2Stk[TASK_STK_SIZE];             /* Task #2    task stack                      */
OS_STK         Task3Stk[TASK_STK_SIZE];             /* Task #3    task stack                      */
OS_STK         Task4Stk[TASK_STK_SIZE];             /* Task #4    task stack                      */
OS_STK         Task5Stk[TASK_STK_SIZE];             /* Task #5    task stack                      */

OS_EVENT       *AckMbox;                            /* Message mailboxes for Tasks #4 and #5      */
OS_EVENT       *TxMbox;
```

```
/*
*************************************************************************************************
*                                    FUNCTION PROTOTYPES
*************************************************************************************************
*/

void            TaskStart(void *data);              /* Function prototypes of tasks            */
void            TaskClk(void *data);
void            Task1(void *data);
void            Task2(void *data);
void            Task3(void *data);
void            Task4(void *data);
void            Task5(void *data);


/*
*************************************************************************************************
*                                          MAIN
*************************************************************************************************
*/

void main (void)
{
    PC_DispClrScr(DISP_FGND_WHITE);                 /* Clear the screen                        */

    OSInit();                                       /* Initialize uC/OS-II                     */

    PC_DOSSaveReturn();                             /* Save environment to return to DOS       */

    PC_VectSet(uCOS, OSCtxSw);                      /* Install uC/OS-II's context switch vector */

    PC_ElapsedInit();                               /* Initialized elapsed time measurement    */

    OSTaskCreateExt(TaskStart, (void *)0, &TaskStartStk[TASK_STK_SIZE-1], TASK_START_PRIO,
                    TASK_START_ID, &TaskStartStk[0], TASK_STK_SIZE, (void *)0,
                    OS_TASK_OPT_STK_CHK | OS_TASK_OPT_STK_CLR);

    OSStart();                                      /* Start multitasking                      */
}
```

EX2L.C

A

```c
/*
*********************************************************************************************************
*                                           STARTUP TASK
*********************************************************************************************************
*/

void  TaskStart (void *data)
{
    char   s[80];
    INT16S key;


    data = data;                                        /* Prevent compiler warning                 */

    PC_DispStr(26,  0, "uC/OS-II, The Real-Time Kernel", DISP_FGND_WHITE + DISP_BGND_RED + DISP_BLINK);
    PC_DispStr(33,  1, "Jean J. Labrosse", DISP_FGND_WHITE);
    PC_DispStr(36,  3, "EXAMPLE #2", DISP_FGND_WHITE);
    PC_DispStr(0, 9,"Task            Total Stack  Free Stack   Used Stack   ExecTime (uS)", DISP_FGND_WHITE);
    PC_DispStr(0,10,"------------    ----------   ----------   ----------   -------------", DISP_FGND_WHITE);
    PC_DispStr( 0, 12, "TaskStart():", DISP_FGND_WHITE);
    PC_DispStr( 0, 13, "TaskClk() :", DISP_FGND_WHITE);
    PC_DispStr( 0, 14, "Task1()   :", DISP_FGND_WHITE);
    PC_DispStr( 0, 15, "Task2()   :", DISP_FGND_WHITE);
    PC_DispStr( 0, 16, "Task3()   :", DISP_FGND_WHITE);
    PC_DispStr( 0, 17, "Task4()   :", DISP_FGND_WHITE);
    PC_DispStr( 0, 18, "Task5()   :", DISP_FGND_WHITE);
    PC_DispStr(28, 24, "<-PRESS 'ESC' TO QUIT->", DISP_FGND_WHITE + DISP_BLINK);

    OS_ENTER_CRITICAL();                                /* Install uC/OS-II's clock tick ISR        */
    PC_VectSet(0x08, OSTickISR);
    PC_SetTickRate(OS_TICKS_PER_SEC);                   /* Reprogram tick rate                      */
    OS_EXIT_CRITICAL();

    PC_DispStr(0, 22, "Determining  CPU's capacity ...", DISP_FGND_WHITE);
    OSStatInit();                                       /* Initialize uC/OS-II's statistics         */
    PC_DispClrLine(22, DISP_FGND_WHITE + DISP_BGND_BLACK);

    AckMbox = OSMboxCreate((void *)0);                  /* Create 2 message mailboxes               */
    TxMbox  = OSMboxCreate((void *)0);

    OSTaskCreateExt(TaskClk, (void *)0, &TaskClkStk[TASK_STK_SIZE-1], TASK_CLK_PRIO,
                    TASK_CLK_ID, &TaskClkStk[0], TASK_STK_SIZE, (void *)0,
                    OS_TASK_OPT_STK_CHK | OS_TASK_OPT_STK_CLR);

    OSTaskCreateExt(Task1, (void *)0, &Task1Stk[TASK_STK_SIZE-1], TASK_1_PRIO,
                    TASK_1_ID, &Task1Stk[0], TASK_STK_SIZE, (void *)0,
                    OS_TASK_OPT_STK_CHK | OS_TASK_OPT_STK_CLR);

    OSTaskCreateExt(Task2, (void *)0, &Task2Stk[TASK_STK_SIZE-1], TASK_2_PRIO,
                    TASK_2_ID, &Task2Stk[0], TASK_STK_SIZE, (void *)0,
                    OS_TASK_OPT_STK_CHK | OS_TASK_OPT_STK_CLR);

    OSTaskCreateExt(Task3, (void *)0, &Task3Stk[TASK_STK_SIZE-1], TASK_3_PRIO,
                    TASK_3_ID, &Task3Stk[0], TASK_STK_SIZE, (void *)0,
                    OS_TASK_OPT_STK_CHK | OS_TASK_OPT_STK_CLR);

    OSTaskCreateExt(Task4, (void *)0, &Task4Stk[TASK_STK_SIZE-1], TASK_4_PRIO,
                    TASK_4_ID, &Task4Stk[0], TASK_STK_SIZE, (void *)0,
                    OS_TASK_OPT_STK_CHK | OS_TASK_OPT_STK_CLR);

    OSTaskCreateExt(Task5, (void *)0, &Task5Stk[TASK_STK_SIZE-1], TASK_5_PRIO,
                    TASK_5_ID, &Task5Stk[0], TASK_STK_SIZE, (void *)0,
                    OS_TASK_OPT_STK_CHK | OS_TASK_OPT_STK_CLR);

    PC_DispStr( 0, 22, "#Tasks          : xxxxx  CPU Usage: xxx %", DISP_FGND_WHITE);
    PC_DispStr( 0, 23, "#Task switch/sec: xxxxx", DISP_FGND_WHITE);
```

EX2L.C

```
    for (;;) {
        sprintf(s, "%5d", OSTaskCtr);                       /* Display #tasks running              */
        PC_DispStr(18, 22, s, DISP_FGND_BLUE + DISP_BGND_CYAN);
        sprintf(s, "%3d", OSCPUUsage);                      /* Display CPU usage in %               */
        PC_DispStr(36, 22, s, DISP_FGND_BLUE + DISP_BGND_CYAN);
        sprintf(s, "%5d", OSCtxSwCtr);                      /* Display #context switches per second */
        PC_DispStr(18, 23, s, DISP_FGND_BLUE + DISP_BGND_CYAN);

        OSCtxSwCtr = 0;                                     /* Clear context switch counter         */

        sprintf(s, "V%3.2f", (float)OSVersion() * 0.01);
        PC_DispStr(75, 24, s, DISP_FGND_YELLOW + DISP_BGND_BLUE);

        if (PC_GetKey(&key)) {                              /* See if key has been pressed          */
            if (key == 0x1B) {                              /* Yes, see if it's the ESCAPE key      */
                PC_DOSReturn();                             /* Yes, return to DOS                   */
            }
        }

        OSTimeDly(OS_TICKS_PER_SEC);                        /* Wait one second                      */
    }
}
```

EX2L.C

A

```
/*
*********************************************************************************************
*                                         TASK #1
*
* Description: This task executes every 100 mS and measures the time it task to perform stack checking
*              for each of the 5 application tasks.  Also, this task displays the statistics related to
*              each task's stack usage.
*********************************************************************************************
*/

void  Task1 (void *pdata)
{
    INT8U      err;
    OS_STK_DATA data;                          /* Storage for task stack data                */
    INT16U     time;                           /* Execution time (in uS)                     */
    INT8U      i;
    char       s[80];


    pdata = pdata;
    for (;;) {
        for (i = 0; i < 7; i++) {
            PC_ElapsedStart();
            err  = OSTaskStkChk(TASK_START_PRIO+i, &data);
            time = PC_ElapsedStop();
            if (err == OS_NO_ERR) {
                sprintf(s, "%31d          %31d          %31d          %5d",
                        data.OSFree + data.OSUsed,
                        data.OSFree,
                        data.OSUsed,
                        time);
                PC_DispStr(19, 12+i, s, DISP_FGND_YELLOW);
            }
        }
        OSTimeDlyHMSM(0, 0, 0, 100);                              /* Delay for 100 mS          */
    }
}


/*
*********************************************************************************************
*                                         TASK #2
*
* Description: This task displays a clockwise rotating wheel on the screen.
*********************************************************************************************
*/

void  Task2 (void *data)
{
    data = data;
    for (;;) {
        PC_DispChar(70, 15, '|',  DISP_FGND_WHITE + DISP_BGND_RED);
        OSTimeDly(10);
        PC_DispChar(70, 15, '/',  DISP_FGND_WHITE + DISP_BGND_RED);
        OSTimeDly(10);
        PC_DispChar(70, 15, '-',  DISP_FGND_WHITE + DISP_BGND_RED);
        OSTimeDly(10);
        PC_DispChar(70, 15, '\\', DISP_FGND_WHITE + DISP_BGND_RED);
        OSTimeDly(10);
    }
}
```

EX2L.C

```
/*
*************************************************************************************************
*                                          TASK #3
*
* Description: This task displays a counter-clockwise rotating wheel on the screen.
*
* Note(s)     : I allocated 100 bytes of storage on the stack to artificially 'eat' up stack space.
*************************************************************************************************
*/

void  Task3 (void *data)
{
    char    dummy[500];
    INT16U  i;


    data = data;
    for (i = 0; i < 499; i++) {          /* Use up the stack with 'junk'                          */
        dummy[i] = '?';
    }
    for (;;) {
        PC_DispChar(70, 16, '|',  DISP_FGND_WHITE + DISP_BGND_BLUE);
        OSTimeDly(20);
        PC_DispChar(70, 16, '\\', DISP_FGND_WHITE + DISP_BGND_BLUE);
        OSTimeDly(20);
        PC_DispChar(70, 16, '-',  DISP_FGND_WHITE + DISP_BGND_BLUE);
        OSTimeDly(20);
        PC_DispChar(70, 16, '/',  DISP_FGND_WHITE + DISP_BGND_BLUE);
        OSTimeDly(20);
    }
}


/*
*************************************************************************************************
*                                          TASK #4
*
* Description: This task sends a message to Task #5.  The message consist of a character that needs to
*              be displayed by Task #5.  This task then waits for an acknowledgement from Task #5
*              indicating that the message has been displayed.
*************************************************************************************************
*/

void  Task4 (void *data)
{
    char   txmsg;
    INT8U  err;


    data  = data;
    txmsg = 'A';
    for (;;) {
        while (txmsg <= 'Z') {
            OSMboxPost(TxMbox, (void *)&txmsg);   /* Send message to Task #5                      */
            OSMboxPend(AckMbox, 0, &err);         /* Wait for acknowledgement from Task #5        */
            txmsg++;                              /* Next message to send                         */
        }
        txmsg = 'A';                              /* Start new series of messages                 */
    }
}
```

EX2L.C

```
/*
***************************************************************************************************
*                                       TASK #5
*
* Description: This task displays messages sent by Task #4.  When the message is displayed, Task #5
*              acknowledges Task #4.
***************************************************************************************************
*/

void  Task5 (void *data)
{
    char  *rxmsg;
    INT8U  err;


    data = data;
    for (;;) {
        rxmsg = (char *)OSMboxPend(TxMbox, 0, &err);                /* Wait for message from Task #4 */
        PC_DispChar(70, 18, *rxmsg, DISP_FGND_YELLOW + DISP_BGND_RED);
        OSTimeDlyHMSM(0, 0, 1, 0);                                  /* Wait 1 second               */
        OSMboxPost(AckMbox, (void *)1);                             /* Acknowledge reception of msg */
    }
}


/*
***************************************************************************************************
*                                      CLOCK TASK
***************************************************************************************************
*/

void  TaskClk (void *data)
{
    struct time now;
    struct date today;
    char       s[40];


    data = data;
    for (;;) {
        PC_GetDateTime(s);
        PC_DispStr(0, 24, s, DISP_FGND_BLUE + DISP_BGND_CYAN);
        OSTimeDly(OS_TICKS_PER_SEC);
    }
}
```

A

EX2L.C

A.01.02 INCLUDES.H (Example 2)

```
/*
*********************************************************************************************
*                                          uC/OS-II
*                                     The Real-Time Kernel
*
*                      (c) Copyright 1992-1998, Jean J. Labrosse, Plantation, FL
*                                        All Rights Reserved
*
*                                      MASTER INCLUDE FILE
*********************************************************************************************
*/

#include     <stdio.h>
#include     <string.h>
#include     <ctype.h>
#include     <stdlib.h>
#include     <conio.h>
#include     <dos.h>
#include     <setjmp.h>

#include     "\software\ucos-ii\ix86l\os_cpu.h"
#include     "os_cfg.h"
#include     "\software\blocks\pc\source\pc.h"
#include     "\software\ucos-ii\source\ucos_ii.h"
```

A.01.03 OS_CFG.H (Example 2)

```
/*
********************************************************************************
*                                   uC/OS-II
*                              The Real-Time Kernel
*
*                (c) Copyright 1992-1998, Jean J. Labrosse, Plantation, FL
*                                 All Rights Reserved
*
*                          Configuration for Intel 80x86 (Large)
*
* File : OS_CFG.H
* By   : Jean J. Labrosse
********************************************************************************
*/

/*
********************************************************************************
*                               uC/OS CONFIGURATION
********************************************************************************
*/

#define OS_MAX_EVENTS          20    /* Max. number of event control blocks in your application ...   */
                                     /* ... MUST be >= 2                                              */
#define OS_MAX_MEM_PART        10    /* Max. number of memory partitions ...                          */
                                     /* ... MUST be >= 2                                              */
#define OS_MAX_QS               5    /* Max. number of queue control blocks in your application ...   */
                                     /* ... MUST be >= 2                                              */
#define OS_MAX_TASKS           32    /* Max. number of tasks in your application ...                  */
                                     /* ... MUST be >= 2                                              */

#define OS_LOWEST_PRIO         63    /* Defines the lowest priority that can be assigned ...          */
                                     /* ... MUST NEVER be higher than 63!                             */

#define OS_TASK_IDLE_STK_SIZE 512    /* Idle task stack size (# of 16-bit wide entries)               */

#define OS_TASK_STAT_EN         1    /* Enable (1) or Disable(0) the statistics task                  */
#define OS_TASK_STAT_STK_SIZE 512    /* Statistics task stack size (# of 16-bit wide entries)         */

#define OS_CPU_HOOKS_EN         1    /* uC/OS-II hooks are found in the processor port files          */
#define OS_MBOX_EN              1    /* Include code for MAILBOXES                                    */
#define OS_MEM_EN               0    /* Include code for MEMORY MANAGER (fixed sized memory blocks)   */
#define OS_Q_EN                 0    /* Include code for QUEUES                                       */
#define OS_SEM_EN               0    /* Include code for SEMAPHORES                                   */
#define OS_TASK_CHANGE_PRIO_EN  0    /* Include code for OSTaskChangePrio()                           */
#define OS_TASK_CREATE_EN       0    /* Include code for OSTaskCreate()                               */
#define OS_TASK_CREATE_EXT_EN   1    /* Include code for OSTaskCreateExt()                            */
#define OS_TASK_DEL_EN          0    /* Include code for OSTaskDel()                                  */
#define OS_TASK_SUSPEND_EN      0    /* Include code for OSTaskSuspend() and OSTaskResume()           */

#define OS_TICKS_PER_SEC      200    /* Set the number of ticks in one second                        */
```

A.02 Example 3

A.02.01 EX3L.C

```
/*
********************************************************************************************************
*                                            uC/OS-II
*                                        The Real-Time Kernel
*
*                         (c) Copyright 1992-1998, Jean J. Labrosse, Plantation, FL
*                                          All Rights Reserved
*
*                                              V2.00
*
*                                            EXAMPLE #3
********************************************************************************************************
*/

#define   EX3_GLOBALS
#include "includes.h"

/*
********************************************************************************************************
*                                            CONSTANTS
********************************************************************************************************
*/

#define        TASK_STK_SIZE     512              /* Size of each task's stacks (# of WORDs)      */

#define        TASK_START_ID     0                /* Application tasks                            */
#define        TASK_CLK_ID       1
#define        TASK_1_ID         2
#define        TASK_2_ID         3
#define        TASK_3_ID         4
#define        TASK_4_ID         5
#define        TASK_5_ID         6

#define        TASK_START_PRIO   10               /* Application tasks priorities                 */
#define        TASK_CLK_PRIO     11
#define        TASK_1_PRIO       12
#define        TASK_2_PRIO       13
#define        TASK_3_PRIO       14
#define        TASK_4_PRIO       15
#define        TASK_5_PRIO       16

#define        MSG_QUEUE_SIZE    20               /* Size of message queue used in example        */
```

```
/*
*******************************************************************************************************
*                                           VARIABLES
*******************************************************************************************************
*/

OS_STK          TaskStartStk[TASK_STK_SIZE];        /* Startup    task stack                   */
OS_STK          TaskClkStk[TASK_STK_SIZE];          /* Clock      task stack                   */
OS_STK          Task1Stk[TASK_STK_SIZE];            /* Task #1    task stack                   */
OS_STK          Task2Stk[TASK_STK_SIZE];            /* Task #2    task stack                   */
OS_STK          Task3Stk[TASK_STK_SIZE];            /* Task #3    task stack                   */
OS_STK          Task4Stk[TASK_STK_SIZE];            /* Task #4    task stack                   */
OS_STK          Task5Stk[TASK_STK_SIZE];            /* Task #5    task stack                   */

OS_EVENT        *MsgQueue;                          /* Message queue pointer                   */
void            *MsgQueueTbl[20];                   /* Storage for messages                    */

/*
*******************************************************************************************************
*                                       FUNCTION PROTOTYPES
*******************************************************************************************************
*/

void            TaskStart(void *data);              /* Function prototypes of tasks            */
void            TaskClk(void *data);
void            Task1(void *data);
void            Task2(void *data);
void            Task3(void *data);
void            Task4(void *data);
void            Task5(void *data);

/*
*******************************************************************************************************
*                                           MAIN
*******************************************************************************************************
*/

void main (void)
{
    PC_DispClrScr(DISP_BGND_BLACK);                 /* Clear the screen                        */

    OSInit();                                       /* Initialize uC/OS-II                     */

    PC_DOSSaveReturn();                             /* Save environment to return to DOS       */

    PC_VectSet(uCOS, OSCtxSw);                      /* Install uC/OS-II's context switch vector */

    PC_ElapsedInit();                               /* Initialized elapsed time measurement    */

    strcpy(TaskUserData[TASK_START_ID].TaskName, "StartTask");
    OSTaskCreateExt(TaskStart, (void *)0, &TaskStartStk[TASK_STK_SIZE-1], TASK_START_PRIO,
                TASK_START_ID, &TaskStartStk[0], TASK_STK_SIZE, &TaskUserData[TASK_START_ID], 0);
    OSStart();                                      /* Start multitasking                      */
}
```

EX3L.C

```
/*
*********************************************************************************************************
*                                          STARTUP TASK
*********************************************************************************************************
*/

void  TaskStart (void *data)
{
    char   s[80];
    INT16S key;

    data = data;                                          /* Prevent compiler warning               */
    PC_DispStr(26,  0, "uC/OS-II, The Real-Time Kernel", DISP_FGND_WHITE + DISP_BGND_RED + DISP_BLINK);
    PC_DispStr(33,  1, "Jean J. Labrosse", DISP_FGND_WHITE);
    PC_DispStr(36,  3, "EXAMPLE #3", DISP_FGND_WHITE);
    PC_DispStr(0,9,"Task Name           Counter  Exec.Time(uS)   Tot.Exec.Time(uS)  %Tot.", DISP_FGND_WHITE);
    PC_DispStr(0,10,"---------------- ------- ------------   ----------------- -----",DISP_FGND_WHITE);
    PC_DispStr(0, 22, "Determining  CPU's capacity ...", DISP_FGND_WHITE);
    PC_DispStr(28, 24, "<-PRESS 'ESC' TO QUIT->", DISP_FGND_WHITE + DISP_BLINK);

    OS_ENTER_CRITICAL();                                  /* Install uC/OS-II's clock tick ISR      */
    PC_VectSet(0x08, OSTickISR);
    PC_SetTickRate(OS_TICKS_PER_SEC);                     /* Reprogram tick rate                    */
    OS_EXIT_CRITICAL();

    OSStatInit();

    MsgQueue = OSQCreate(&MsgQueueTbl[0], MSG_QUEUE_SIZE); /* Create a message queue                 */

    strcpy(TaskUserData[TASK_CLK_ID].TaskName, "Clock Task");
    OSTaskCreateExt(TaskClk, (void *)0, &TaskClkStk[TASK_STK_SIZE-1], TASK_CLK_PRIO,
                    TASK_CLK_ID, &TaskClkStk[0], TASK_STK_SIZE, &TaskUserData[TASK_CLK_ID], 0);

    strcpy(TaskUserData[TASK_1_ID].TaskName, "MsgQ Tx Task");
    OSTaskCreateExt(Task1, (void *)0, &Task1Stk[TASK_STK_SIZE-1], TASK_1_PRIO,
                    TASK_1_ID, &Task1Stk[0], TASK_STK_SIZE, &TaskUserData[TASK_1_ID], 0);

    strcpy(TaskUserData[TASK_2_ID].TaskName, "MsgQ Rx Task #1");
    OSTaskCreateExt(Task2, (void *)0, &Task2Stk[TASK_STK_SIZE-1], TASK_2_PRIO,
                    TASK_2_ID, &Task2Stk[0], TASK_STK_SIZE, &TaskUserData[TASK_2_ID], 0);

    strcpy(TaskUserData[TASK_3_ID].TaskName, "MsgQ Rx Task #2");
    OSTaskCreateExt(Task3, (void *)0, &Task3Stk[TASK_STK_SIZE-1], TASK_3_PRIO,
                    TASK_3_ID, &Task3Stk[0], TASK_STK_SIZE, &TaskUserData[TASK_3_ID], 0);

    strcpy(TaskUserData[TASK_4_ID].TaskName, "MboxPostPendTask");
    OSTaskCreateExt(Task4, (void *)0, &Task4Stk[TASK_STK_SIZE-1], TASK_4_PRIO,
                    TASK_4_ID, &Task4Stk[0], TASK_STK_SIZE, &TaskUserData[TASK_4_ID], 0);

    strcpy(TaskUserData[TASK_5_ID].TaskName, "TimeDlyTask");
    OSTaskCreateExt(Task5, (void *)0, &Task5Stk[TASK_STK_SIZE-1], TASK_5_PRIO,
                    TASK_5_ID, &Task5Stk[0], TASK_STK_SIZE, &TaskUserData[TASK_5_ID], 0);

    PC_DispStr( 0, 22, "#Tasks          : xxxxx  CPU Usage: xxx %", DISP_FGND_WHITE);
    PC_DispStr( 0, 23, "#Task switch/sec: xxxxx", DISP_FGND_WHITE);
```

EX3L.C

```
    for (;;) {
        sprintf(s, "%5d", OSTaskCtr);                      /* Display #tasks running                   */
        PC_DispStr(18, 22, s, DISP_FGND_BLUE + DISP_BGND_CYAN);
        sprintf(s, "%3d", OSCPUUsage);                     /* Display CPU usage in %                   */
        PC_DispStr(36, 22, s, DISP_FGND_BLUE + DISP_BGND_CYAN);
        sprintf(s, "%5d", OSCtxSwCtr);                     /* Display #context switches per second     */
        PC_DispStr(18, 23, s, DISP_FGND_BLUE + DISP_BGND_CYAN);
        sprintf(s, "V%3.2f", (float)OSVersion() * 0.01);
        PC_DispStr(75, 24, s, DISP_FGND_YELLOW + DISP_BGND_BLUE);

        OSCtxSwCtr = 0;                                    /* Clear the context switch counter         */

        if (PC_GetKey(&key)) {                             /* See if key has been pressed              */
            if (key == 0x1B) {                             /* Yes, see if it's the ESCAPE key          */
                PC_DOSReturn();                            /* Yes, return to DOS                       */
            }
        }

        OSTimeDly(OS_TICKS_PER_SEC);                       /* Wait one second                          */
    }
}


/*
*********************************************************************************************************
*                                              TASK #1
*
* Description: This task executes 5 times per second but doesn't do anything.
*********************************************************************************************************
*/

void  Task1 (void *data)
{
    char one   = '1';
    char two   = '2';
    char three = '3';


    data = data;
    for (;;) {
        OSQPost(MsgQueue, (void *)&one);
        OSTimeDlyHMSM(0, 0, 1,   0);        /* Delay for 1 second                                      */
        OSQPost(MsgQueue, (void *)&two);
        OSTimeDlyHMSM(0, 0, 0, 500);        /* Delay for 500 mS                                        */
        OSQPost(MsgQueue, (void *)&three);
        OSTimeDlyHMSM(0, 0, 1,   0);        /* Delay for 1 second                                      */
    }
}
```

EX3L.C

```
/*
*********************************************************************************************
*                                          TASK #2
*
* Description: This task waits for messages sent by task #1.
*********************************************************************************************
*/

void  Task2 (void *data)
{
    INT8U *msg;
    INT8U  err;


    data = data;
    for (;;) {
        msg = (INT8U *)OSQPend(MsgQueue, 0, &err);     /* Wait forever for message              */
        PC_DispChar(70, 14, *msg, DISP_FGND_YELLOW + DISP_BGND_BLUE);
        OSTimeDlyHMSM(0, 0, 0, 500);                   /* Delay for 500 mS                      */
    }
}


/*
*********************************************************************************************
*                                          TASK #3
*
* Description: This task waits for up to 500 mS for a message sent by task #1.
*********************************************************************************************
*/

void  Task3 (void *data)
{
    INT8U *msg;
    INT8U  err;


    data = data;
    for (;;) {
        msg = (INT8U *)OSQPend(MsgQueue, OS_TICKS_PER_SEC / 4, &err);  /* Wait up to 250 mS for a msg  */
        if (err == OS_TIMEOUT) {
            PC_DispChar(70, 15, 'T',  DISP_FGND_YELLOW + DISP_BGND_RED);
        } else {
            PC_DispChar(70, 15, *msg, DISP_FGND_YELLOW + DISP_BGND_BLUE);
        }
    }
}
```

A

```
/*
*********************************************************************************************
*                                         TASK #4
*
* Description: This task posts a message to a mailbox and then immediately reads the message.
*********************************************************************************************
*/

void  Task4 (void *data)
{
    OS_EVENT *mbox;
    INT8U     err;


    data = data;
    mbox = OSMboxCreate((void *)0);
    for (;;) {
        OSMboxPost(mbox, (void *)1);            /* Send message to mailbox              */
        OSMboxPend(mbox, 0, &err);              /* Get message from mailbox             */
        OSTimeDlyHMSM(0, 0, 0, 10);             /* Delay 10 mS                          */
    }
}


/*
*********************************************************************************************
*                                         TASK #5
*
* Description: This task simply delays itself.  We basically want to determine how long OSTimeDly() takes
*              to execute.
*********************************************************************************************
*/

void  Task5 (void *data)
{
    data = data;
    for (;;) {
        OSTimeDly(1);
    }
}


/*
*********************************************************************************************
*                             DISPLAY TASK RELATED STATISTICS
*********************************************************************************************
*/

void DispTaskStat (INT8U id)
{
    char s[80];


    sprintf(s, "%-18s %05u       %5u            %101d",
            TaskUserData[id].TaskName,
            TaskUserData[id].TaskCtr,
            TaskUserData[id].TaskExecTime,
            TaskUserData[id].TaskTotExecTime);
    PC_DispStr(0, id + 11, s, DISP_FGND_LIGHT_GRAY);
}
```

EX3L.C

```
/*
*************************************************************************************************************
*                                          CLOCK TASK
*************************************************************************************************************
*/

void  TaskClk (void *data)
{
    char  s[40];


    data = data;
    for (;;) {
        PC_GetDateTime(s);
        PC_DispStr(0, 24, s, DISP_FGND_BLUE + DISP_BGND_CYAN);
        OSTimeDlyHMSM(0, 0, 0, 100);                    /* Execute every 100 mS                      */
    }
}


/*
*************************************************************************************************************
*                                       TASK CREATION HOOK
*
* Description: This function is called when a task is created.
*
* Arguments  : ptcb    is a pointer to the task being created.
*
* Note(s)    : 1) Interrupts are disabled during this call.
*************************************************************************************************************
*/
void OSTaskCreateHook (OS_TCB *ptcb)
{
    ptcb = ptcb;                       /* Prevent compiler warning                                   */
}


/*
*************************************************************************************************************
*                                       TASK DELETION HOOK
*
* Description: This function is called when a task is deleted.
*
* Arguments  : ptcb    is a pointer to the task being created.
*
* Note(s)    : 1) Interrupts are disabled during this call.
*************************************************************************************************************
*/
void OSTaskDelHook (OS_TCB *ptcb)
{
    ptcb = ptcb;                       /* Prevent compiler warning                                   */
}
```

EX3L.C

A

```c
/*
*********************************************************************************************************
*                                          TASK SWITCH HOOK
*
* Description: This function is called when a task switch is performed.  This allows you to perform other
*              operations during a context switch.
*
* Arguments  : none
*
* Note(s)    : 1) Interrupts are disabled during this call.
*              2) It is assumed that the global pointer 'OSTCBHighRdy' points to the TCB of the task that
*                 will be 'switched in' (i.e. the highest priority task) and, 'OSTCBCur' points to the task
*                 being switched out (i.e. the preempted task).
*********************************************************************************************************
*/
void OSTaskSwHook (void)
{
    INT16U          time;
    TASK_USER_DATA *puser;
    time  = PC_ElapsedStop();                     /* This task is done                               */
    PC_ElapsedStart();                            /* Start for next task                             */
    puser = OSTCBCur->OSTCBExtPtr;                 /* Point to used data                              */
    if (puser != (void *)0) {
        puser->TaskCtr++;                          /* Increment task counter                          */
        puser->TaskExecTime     = time;           /* Update the task's execution time                */
        puser->TaskTotExecTime += time;           /* Update the task's total execution time          */
    }
}


/*
*********************************************************************************************************
*                                         STATISTIC TASK HOOK
*
* Description: This function is called every second by uC/OS-II's statistics task.  This allows your
*              application to add functionality to the statistics task.
*
* Arguments  : none
*********************************************************************************************************
*/
void OSTaskStatHook (void)
{
    char   s[80];
    INT8U  i;
    INT32U total;
    INT8U  pct;
    total = 0L;                                   /* Totalize TOT. EXEC. TIME for each task */
    for (i = 0; i < 7; i++) {
        total += TaskUserData[i].TaskTotExecTime;
        DispTaskStat(i);                          /* Display task data                       */
    }
    if (total > 0) {
        for (i = 0; i < 7; i++) {                 /* Derive percentage of each task          */
            pct = 100 * TaskUserData[i].TaskTotExecTime / total;
            sprintf(s, "%3d %%", pct);
            PC_DispStr(62, i + 11, s, DISP_FGND_YELLOW);
        }
    }
    if (total > 1000000000L) {                    /* Reset total time counters at 1 billion */
        for (i = 0; i < 7; i++) {
            TaskUserData[i].TaskTotExecTime = 0L;
        }
    }
}
```

EX3L.C

```
/*
*********************************************************************************************
*                                      TICK HOOK
*
* Description: This function is called every tick.
*
* Arguments  : none
*
* Note(s)    : 1) Interrupts may or may not be are ENABLED during this call.
*********************************************************************************************
*/
void OSTimeTickHook (void)
{
}
```

A.02.02 INCLUDES.H (Example 3)

```
/*
*********************************************************************************************************
*                                          uC/OS-II
*                                     The Real-Time Kernel
*
*                        (c) Copyright 1992-1998, Jean J. Labrosse, Plantation, FL
*                                       All Rights Reserved
*
*                                      MASTER INCLUDE FILE
*********************************************************************************************************
*/

#include    <stdio.h>
#include    <string.h>
#include    <ctype.h>
#include    <stdlib.h>
#include    <conio.h>
#include    <dos.h>
#include    <setjmp.h>

#include    "\software\ucos-ii\ix86l\os_cpu.h"
#include    "os_cfg.h"
#include    "\software\blocks\pc\source\pc.h"
#include    "\software\ucos-ii\source\ucos_ii.h"

#ifdef      EX3_GLOBALS
#define     EX3_EXT
#else
#define     EX3_EXT   extern
#endif

/*
*********************************************************************************************************
*                                         DATA TYPES
*********************************************************************************************************
*/

typedef struct {
    char    TaskName[30];
    INT16U  TaskCtr;
    INT16U  TaskExecTime;
    INT32U  TaskTotExecTime;
} TASK_USER_DATA;

/*
*********************************************************************************************************
*                                          VARIABLES
*********************************************************************************************************
*/

EX3_EXT  TASK_USER_DATA  TaskUserData[10];

/*
*********************************************************************************************************
*                                      FUNCTION PROTOTYPES
*********************************************************************************************************
*/

void    DispTaskStat(INT8U id);
```

A.02.03 OS_CFG.H (Example 3)

```
/*
*********************************************************************************************
*                                        uC/OS-II
*                                  The Real-Time Kernel
*
*                      (c) Copyright 1992-1998, Jean J. Labrosse, Plantation, FL
*                                   All Rights Reserved
*
*                             Configuration for Intel 80x86 (Large)
*
* File : OS_CFG.H
* By   : Jean J. Labrosse
*********************************************************************************************
*/

/*
*********************************************************************************************
*                                  uC/OS-II CONFIGURATION
*********************************************************************************************
*/

#define OS_MAX_EVENTS           20      /* Max. number of event control blocks in your application ...  */
                                        /* ... MUST be >= 2                                            */
#define OS_MAX_MEM_PART         10      /* Max. number of memory partitions ...                        */
                                        /* ... MUST be >= 2                                            */
#define OS_MAX_QS                5      /* Max. number of queue control blocks in your application ...  */
                                        /* ... MUST be >= 2                                            */
#define OS_MAX_TASKS            32      /* Max. number of tasks in your application ...                 */
                                        /* ... MUST be >= 2                                            */

#define OS_LOWEST_PRIO          63      /* Defines the lowest priority that can be assigned ...         */
                                        /* ... MUST NEVER be higher than 63!                           */

#define OS_TASK_IDLE_STK_SIZE  512      /* Idle task stack size (# of 16-bit wide entries)             */

#define OS_TASK_STAT_EN          1      /* Enable (1) or Disable(0) the statistics task                */
#define OS_TASK_STAT_STK_SIZE  512      /* Statistics task stack size (# of 16-bit wide entries)       */

#define OS_CPU_HOOKS_EN          0      /* uC/OS-II hooks are NOT found in the processor port files    */
#define OS_MBOX_EN               1      /* Include code for MAILBOXES                                  */
#define OS_MEM_EN                0      /* Include code for MEMORY MANAGER (fixed sized memory blocks) */
#define OS_Q_EN                  1      /* Include code for QUEUES                                     */
#define OS_SEM_EN                0      /* Include code for SEMAPHORES                                 */
#define OS_TASK_CHANGE_PRIO_EN   0      /* Include code for OSTaskChangePrio()                         */
#define OS_TASK_CREATE_EN        0      /* Include code for OSTaskCreate()                             */
#define OS_TASK_CREATE_EXT_EN    1      /* Include code for OSTaskCreateExt()                          */
#define OS_TASK_DEL_EN           0      /* Include code for OSTaskDel()                                */
#define OS_TASK_SUSPEND_EN       0      /* Include code for OSTaskSuspend() and OSTaskResume()         */

#define OS_TICKS_PER_SEC       200      /* Set the number of ticks in one second                      */
```

A.03 PC Services

A.03.01 PC.C

```c
/*
*********************************************************************************************
*                                    PC SUPPORT FUNCTIONS
*
*                       (c) Copyright 1992-1998, Jean J. Labrosse, Plantation, FL
*                                     All Rights Reserved
*
* File : PC.C
* By   : Jean J. Labrosse
*********************************************************************************************
*/

#include "includes.h"

/*
*********************************************************************************************
*                                        CONSTANTS
*********************************************************************************************
*/
#define  DISP_BASE                 0xB800        /* Base segment of display (0xB800=VGA, 0xB000=Mono)  */
#define  DISP_MAX_X                   80          /* Maximum number of columns                          */
#define  DISP_MAX_Y                   25          /* Maximum number of rows                             */

#define  TICK_T0_8254_CWR          0x43          /* 8254 PIT Control Word Register address.            */
#define  TICK_T0_8254_CTR0         0x40          /* 8254 PIT Timer 0 Register address.                 */
#define  TICK_T0_8254_CTR1         0x41          /* 8254 PIT Timer 1 Register address.                 */
#define  TICK_T0_8254_CTR2         0x42          /* 8254 PIT Timer 2 Register address.                 */

#define  TICK_T0_8254_CTR0_MODE3   0x36          /* 8254 PIT Binary Mode 3 for Counter 0 control word. */
#define  TICK_T0_8254_CTR2_MODE0   0xB0          /* 8254 PIT Binary Mode 0 for Counter 2 control word. */
#define  TICK_T0_8254_CTR2_LATCH   0x80          /* 8254 PIT Latch command control word                */

#define  VECT_TICK                 0x08          /* Vector number for 82C54 timer tick                 */
#define  VECT_DOS_CHAIN            0x81          /* Vector number used to chain DOS                    */

/*
*********************************************************************************************
*                                  LOCAL GLOBAL VARIABLES
*********************************************************************************************
*/

static INT16U    PC_ElapsedOverhead;
static jmp_buf   PC_JumpBuf;
static BOOLEAN   PC_ExitFlag;
void             (*PC_TickISR)(void);
```

```
/*
*********************************************************************************************************
*                                         CLEAR SCREEN
*
* Description : This function clears the PC's screen by directly accessing video RAM instead of using
*               the BIOS.  It assumed that the video adapter is VGA compatible.  Video RAM starts at
*               absolute address 0x000B8000.  Each character on the screen is composed of two bytes:
*               the ASCII character to appear on the screen followed by a video attribute.  An attribute
*               of 0x07 displays the character in WHITE with a black background.
*
* Arguments   : color   specifies the foreground/background color combination to use
*                       (see PC.H for available choices)
*
* Returns     : None
*********************************************************************************************************
*/
void PC_DispClrScr (INT8U color)
{
    INT8U  far *pscr;
    INT16U     i;


    pscr = MK_FP(DISP_BASE, 0x0000);
    for (i = 0; i < (DISP_MAX_X * DISP_MAX_Y); i++) { /* PC display has 80 columns and 25 lines    */
        *pscr++ = ' ';                                /* Put ' ' character in video RAM            */
        *pscr++ = color;                              /* Put video attribute in video RAM          */
    }
}




/*
*********************************************************************************************************
*                                         CLEAR A LINE
*
* Description : This function clears one of the 25 lines on the PC's screen by directly accessing video
*               RAM instead of using the BIOS.  It assumed that the video adapter is VGA compatible.
*               Video RAM starts at absolute address 0x000B8000.  Each character on the screen is
*               composed of two bytes: the ASCII character to appear on the screen followed by a video
*               attribute.  An attribute of 0x07 displays the character in WHITE with a black background.
*
* Arguments   : y           corresponds to the desired line to clear.  Valid line numbers are from
*                           0 to 24.  Line 0 corresponds to the topmost line.
*
*               color       specifies the foreground/background color combination to use
*                           (see PC.H for available choices)
*
* Returns     : None
*********************************************************************************************************
*/
void PC_DispClrLine (INT8U y, INT8U color)
{
    INT8U far *pscr;
    INT8U     i;


    pscr = MK_FP(DISP_BASE, (INT16U)y * DISP_MAX_X * 2);
    for (i = 0; i < DISP_MAX_X; i++) {
        *pscr++ = ' ';                                /* Put ' ' character in video RAM            */
        *pscr++ = color;                              /* Put video attribute in video RAM          */
    }
}
```

PC.C

```
/*
********************************************************************************************************
*                           DISPLAY A SINGLE CHARACTER AT 'X' & 'Y' COORDINATE
*
* Description : This function writes a single character anywhere on the PC's screen.  This function
*               writes directly to video RAM instead of using the BIOS for speed reasons.  It assumed
*               that the video adapter is VGA compatible.  Video RAM starts at absolute address
*               0x000B8000.  Each character on the screen is composed of two bytes: the ASCII character
*               to appear on the screen followed by a video attribute.  An attribute of 0x07 displays
*               the character in WHITE with a black background.
*
* Arguments   : x       corresponds to the desired column on the screen.  Valid columns numbers are from
*                       0 to 79.  Column 0 corresponds to the leftmost column.
*               y       corresponds to the desired row on the screen.  Valid row numbers are from 0 to 24.
*                       Line 0 corresponds to the topmost row.
*               c       Is the ASCII character to display.  You can also specify a character with a
*                       numeric value higher than 128.  In this case, special character based graphics
*                       will be displayed.
*               color   specifies the foreground/background color to use (see PC.H for available choices)
*                       and whether the character will blink or not.
*
* Returns     : None
********************************************************************************************************
*/
void PC_DispChar (INT8U x, INT8U y, INT8U c, INT8U color)
{
    INT8U   far *pscr;
    INT16U      offset;


    offset  = (INT16U)y * DISP_MAX_X * 2 + (INT16U)x * 2;   /* Calculate position on the screen        */
    pscr    = MK_FP(DISP_BASE, offset);
    *pscr++ = c;                                            /* Put character in video RAM              */
    *pscr   = color;                                       /* Put video attribute in video RAM        */
}
```

A

PC.C

```
/*
*********************************************************************************************
*                         DISPLAY A STRING  AT 'X' & 'Y' COORDINATE
*
* Description : This function writes an ASCII string anywhere on the PC's screen.  This function writes
*               directly to video RAM instead of using the BIOS for speed reasons.  It assumed that the
*               video adapter is VGA compatible.  Video RAM starts at absolute address 0x000B8000.  Each
*               character on the screen is composed of two bytes: the ASCII character to appear on the
*               screen followed by a video attribute.  An attribute of 0x07 displays the character in
*               WHITE with a black background.
*
* Arguments   : x       corresponds to the desired column on the screen.  Valid columns numbers are from
*                       0 to 79.  Column 0 corresponds to the leftmost column.
*               y       corresponds to the desired row on the screen.  Valid row numbers are from 0 to 24.
*                       Line 0 corresponds to the topmost row.
*               s       Is the ASCII string to display.  You can also specify a string containing
*                       characters with numeric values higher than 128.  In this case, special character
*                       based graphics will be displayed.
*               color   specifies the foreground/background color to use (see PC.H for available choices)
*                       and whether the characters will blink or not.
*
* Returns     : None
*********************************************************************************************
*/
void PC_DispStr (INT8U x, INT8U y, INT8U *s, INT8U color)
{
    INT8U  far *pscr;
    INT16U      offset;


    offset = (INT16U)y * DISP_MAX_X * 2 + (INT16U)x * 2;   /* Calculate position of 1st character     */
    pscr   = MK_FP(DISP_BASE, offset);
    while (*s) {
        *pscr++ = *s++;                                    /* Put character in video RAM              */
        *pscr++ = color;                                   /* Put video attribute in video RAM        */
    }
}




/*
*********************************************************************************************
*                                      RETURN TO DOS
*
* Description : This functions returns control back to DOS by doing a 'long jump' back to the saved
*               location stored in 'PC_JumpBuf'.  The saved location was established by the function
*               'PC_DOSSaveReturn()'.  After execution of the long jump, execution will resume at the
*               line following the 'set jump' back in 'PC_DOSSaveReturn()'.  Setting the flag
*               'PC_ExitFlag' to TRUE ensures that the 'if' statement in 'PC_DOSSaveReturn()' executes.
*
* Arguments   : None
*
* Returns     : None
*********************************************************************************************
*/
void PC_DOSReturn (void)
{
    PC_ExitFlag = TRUE;                                    /* Indicate we are returning to DOS        */
    longjmp(PC_JumpBuf, 1);                                /* Jump back to saved environment          */
}
```

PC.C

```
/*
*********************************************************************************************************
*                                      SAVE DOS RETURN LOCATION
*
* Description : This function saves the location of where we are in DOS so that it can be recovered.
*               This allows us to abort multitasking under uC/OS-II and return back to DOS as if we had
*               never left.  When this function is called by 'main()', it sets 'PC_ExitFlag' to FALSE
*               so that we don't take the 'if' branch.  Instead, the CPU registers are saved in the
*               long jump buffer 'PC_JumpBuf' and we simply return to the caller.  If a 'long jump' is
*               performed using the jump buffer then, execution would resume at the 'if' statement and
*               this time, if 'PC_ExitFlag' is set to TRUE then we would execute the 'if' statements and
*               restore the DOS environment.
*
* Arguments   : None
*
* Returns     : None
*********************************************************************************************************
*/
void PC_DOSSaveReturn (void)
{
    PC_ExitFlag   = FALSE;                                 /* Indicate that we are not exiting yet!    */
    OSTickDOSCtr  =    1;                                  /* Initialize the DOS tick counter          */
    PC_TickISR    = PC_VectGet(VECT_TICK);                 /* Get MS-DOS's tick vector                 */

    OS_ENTER_CRITICAL();
    PC_VectSet(VECT_DOS_CHAIN, PC_TickISR);                /* Store MS-DOS's tick to chain             */
    OS_EXIT_CRITICAL();

    setjmp(PC_JumpBuf);                                    /* Capture where we are in DOS              */
    if (PC_ExitFlag == TRUE) {                             /* See if we are exiting back to DOS        */
        OS_ENTER_CRITICAL();
        PC_SetTickRate(18);                                /* Restore tick rate to 18.2 Hz             */
        PC_VectSet(VECT_TICK, PC_TickISR);                 /* Restore DOS's tick vector                */
        OS_EXIT_CRITICAL();
        PC_DispClrScr(DISP_FGND_WHITE + DISP_BGND_BLACK);  /* Clear the display                        */
        exit(0);                                           /* Return to DOS                            */
    }
}


/*
*********************************************************************************************************
*                                    ELAPSED TIME INITIALIZATION
*
* Description : This function initialize the elapsed time module by determining how long the START and
*               STOP functions take to execute.  In other words, this function calibrates this module
*               to account for the processing time of the START and STOP functions.
*
* Arguments   : None.
*
* Returns     : None.
*********************************************************************************************************
*/
void PC_ElapsedInit(void)
{
    PC_ElapsedOverhead = 0;
    PC_ElapsedStart();
    PC_ElapsedOverhead = PC_ElapsedStop();
}
```

A

PC.C

```
/*
*********************************************************************************************************
*                                      INITIALIZE PC'S TIMER #2
*
* Description : This function initialize the PC's Timer #2 to be used to measure the time between events.
*               Timer #2 will be running when the function returns.
*
* Arguments   : None.
*
* Returns     : None.
*********************************************************************************************************
*/
void PC_ElapsedStart(void)
{
    INT8U data;


    data  = (INT8U)inp(0x61);                            /* Disable timer #2                    */
    data &= 0xFE;
    outp(0x61, data);
    outp(TICK_T0_8254_CWR,  TICK_T0_8254_CTR2_MODE0);    /* Program timer #2 for Mode 0         */
    outp(TICK_T0_8254_CTR2, 0xFF);
    outp(TICK_T0_8254_CTR2, 0xFF);
    data |= 0x01;                                        /* Start the timer                     */
    outp(0x61, data);
}


/*
*********************************************************************************************************
*                         STOP THE PC'S TIMER #2 AND GET ELAPSED TIME
*
* Description : This function stops the PC's Timer #2, obtains the elapsed counts from when it was
*               started and converts the elapsed counts to micro-seconds.
*
* Arguments   : None.
*
* Returns     : The number of micro-seconds since the timer was last started.
*
* Notes       : - The returned time accounts for the processing time of the START and STOP functions.
*               - 54926 represents 54926S-16 or, 0.838097 which is used to convert timer counts to
*                 micro-seconds.  The clock source for the PC's timer #2 is 1.19318 MHz (or 0.838097 uS)
*********************************************************************************************************
*/
INT16U PC_ElapsedStop(void)
{
    INT8U  data;
    INT8U  low;
    INT8U  high;
    INT16U cnts;


    data  = inp(0x61);                                   /* Disable the timer                   */
    data &= 0xFE;
    outp(0x61, data);
    outp(TICK_T0_8254_CWR, TICK_T0_8254_CTR2_LATCH);     /* Latch the timer value               */
    low  = inp(TICK_T0_8254_CTR2);
    high = inp(TICK_T0_8254_CTR2);
    cnts = (INT16U)0xFFFF - (((INT16U)high << 8) + (INT16U)low); /* Compute time it took for operation */
    return ((INT16U)((ULONG)cnts * 54926L >> 16) - PC_ElapsedOverhead);
}
```

```
/*
*********************************************************************************************
*                          GET THE CURRENT DATE AND TIME
*
* Description: This function obtains the current date and time from the PC.
*
* Arguments  : s     is a pointer to where the ASCII string of the current date and time will be stored.
*                    You must allocate at least 19 bytes (includes the NUL) of storage in the return
*                    string.
*
* Returns    : none
*********************************************************************************************
*/
void PC_GetDateTime (char *s)
{
    struct time now;
    struct date today;


    gettime(&now);
    getdate(&today);
    sprintf(s, "%02d-%02d-%02d  %02d:%02d:%02d",
              today.da_mon,
              today.da_day,
              today.da_year,
              now.ti_hour,
              now.ti_min,
              now.ti_sec);
}


/*
*********************************************************************************************
*                          CHECK AND GET KEYBOARD KEY
*
* Description: This function checks to see if a key has been pressed at the keyboard and returns TRUE if
*              so.  Also, if a key is pressed, the key is read and copied where the argument is pointing
*              to.
*
* Arguments  : c     is a pointer to where the read key will be stored.
*
* Returns    : TRUE  if a key was pressed
*              FALSE otherwise
*********************************************************************************************
*/
BOOLEAN PC_GetKey (INT16S *c)
{
    if (kbhit()) {                              /* See if a key has been pressed         */
        *c = getch();                           /* Get key pressed                       */
        return (TRUE);
    } else {
        *c = 0x00;                              /* No key pressed                        */
        return (FALSE);
    }
}
```

```
/*
*********************************************************************************************
*                             SET THE PC'S TICK FREQUENCY
*
* Description: This function is called to change the tick rate of a PC.
*
* Arguments  : freq      is the desired frequency of the ticker (in Hz)
*
* Returns    : none
*
* Notes      : 1) The magic number 2386360 is actually twice the input frequency of the 8254 chip which
*                 is always 1.193180 MHz.
*              2) The equation computes the counts needed to load into the 8254.  The strange equation
*                 is actually used to round the number using integer arithmetic.  This is equivalent to
*                 the floating point equation:
*
*                         1193180.0 Hz
*                 count = ------------ + 0.5
*                             freq
*********************************************************************************************
*/
void PC_SetTickRate (INT16U freq)
{
    INT16U count;


    if (freq == 18) {                       /* See if we need to restore the DOS frequency       */
        count = 0;
    } else if (freq > 0) {
                                            /* Compute 8254 counts for desired frequency and ... */
                                            /* ... round to nearest count                        */
        count = (INT16U)(((INT32U)2386360L / freq + 1) >> 1);
    } else {
        count = 0;
    }
    outp(TICK_T0_8254_CWR,  TICK_T0_8254_CTR0_MODE3); /* Load the 8254 with desired frequency     */
    outp(TICK_T0_8254_CTR0, count & 0xFF);            /* Low  byte                                */
    outp(TICK_T0_8254_CTR0, (count >> 8) & 0xFF);     /* High byte                                */
}
```

PC.C

```
/*
*********************************************************************************************
*                               OBTAIN INTERRUPT VECTOR
*
* Description: This function reads the pointer stored at the specified vector.
*
* Arguments  : vect  is the desired interrupt vector number, a number between 0 and 255.
*
* Returns    : none
*********************************************************************************************
*/
void *PC_VectGet (INT8U vect)
{
    return (getvect(vect));
}


/*
*********************************************************************************************
*                               INSTALL INTERRUPT VECTOR
*
* Description: This function sets an interrupt vector in the interrupt vector table.
*
* Arguments  : vect  is the desired interrupt vector number, a number between 0 and 255.
*              isr   is a pointer to a function to execute when the interrupt or exception occurs.
*
* Returns    : none
*********************************************************************************************
*/
void PC_VectSet (INT8U vect, void (*isr)(void))
{
    setvect(vect, (void interrupt (*)(void))isr);
}
```

A

A.03.02 PC.H

```
/*
*********************************************************************************************
*                              PC SUPPORT FUNCTIONS
*
*                        (c) Copyright 1992-1998, Jean J. Labrosse, Plantation, FL
*                                      All Rights Reserved
*
* File : PC.H
* By   : Jean J. Labrosse
*********************************************************************************************
*/

/*
*********************************************************************************************
*                                       CONSTANTS
*                            COLOR ATTRIBUTES FOR VGA MONITOR
*
* Description: These #defines are used in the PC_Disp???() functions.  The 'color' argument in these
*              function MUST specify a 'foreground' color, a 'background' and whether the display will
*              blink or not.  If you don't specify a background color, BLACK is assumed.  You would
*              specify a color combination as follows:
*
*              PC_DispChar(0, 0, 'A', DISP_FGND_WHITE + DISP_BGND_BLUE + DISP_BLINK);
*
*              To have the ASCII character 'A' blink with a white letter on a blue background.
*********************************************************************************************
*/
#define DISP_FGND_BLACK          0x00
#define DISP_FGND_BLUE           0x01
#define DISP_FGND_GREEN          0x02
#define DISP_FGND_CYAN           0x03
#define DISP_FGND_RED            0x04
#define DISP_FGND_PURPLE         0x05
#define DISP_FGND_BROWN          0x06
#define DISP_FGND_LIGHT_GRAY     0x07
#define DISP_FGND_DARK_GRAY      0x08
#define DISP_FGND_LIGHT_BLUE     0x09
#define DISP_FGND_LIGHT_GREEN    0x0A
#define DISP_FGND_LIGHT_CYAN     0x0B
#define DISP_FGND_LIGHT_RED      0x0C
#define DISP_FGND_LIGHT_PURPLE   0x0D
#define DISP_FGND_YELLOW         0x0E
#define DISP_FGND_WHITE          0x0F

#define DISP_BGND_BLACK          0x00
#define DISP_BGND_BLUE           0x10
#define DISP_BGND_GREEN          0x20
#define DISP_BGND_CYAN           0x30
#define DISP_BGND_RED            0x40
#define DISP_BGND_PURPLE         0x50
#define DISP_BGND_BROWN          0x60
#define DISP_BGND_LIGHT_GRAY     0x70

#define DISP_BLINK               0x80
```

```
/*
**********************************************************************************************
*                                  FUNCTION PROTOTYPES
**********************************************************************************************
*/

void    PC_DispClrScr(INT8U bgnd_color);
void    PC_DispClrLine(INT8U y, INT8U bgnd_color);
void    PC_DispChar(INT8U x, INT8U y, INT8U c, INT8U color);
void    PC_DispStr(INT8U x, INT8U y, INT8U *s, INT8U color);

void    PC_DOSReturn(void);
void    PC_DOSSaveReturn(void);

void    PC_ElapsedInit(void);
void    PC_ElapsedStart(void);
INT16U  PC_ElapsedStop(void);

void    PC_GetDateTime(char *s);
BOOLEAN PC_GetKey(INT16S *c);

void    PC_SetTickRate(INT16U freq);

void    *PC_VectGet(INT8U vect);
void    PC_VectSet(INT8U vect, void (*isr)(void));
```

A

µC/OS-II Microprocessor-Independent Source Code

B.00 uCOS_II.C

```
/*
*********************************************************************************************************
*                                              uC/OS-II
*                                        The Real-Time Kernel
*
*                        (c) Copyright 1992-1998, Jean J. Labrosse, Plantation, FL
*                                           All Rights Reserved
*
*                                               V2.00
*
* File : uCOS_II.C
* By   : Jean J. Labrosse
*********************************************************************************************************
*/

#define  OS_GLOBALS                            /* Declare GLOBAL variables                            */
#include "includes.h"


#define  OS_MASTER_FILE                        /* Prevent the following files from including includes.h */
#include "\software\ucos-ii\source\os_core.c"
#include "\software\ucos-ii\source\os_mbox.c"
#include "\software\ucos-ii\source\os_mem.c"
#include "\software\ucos-ii\source\os_q.c"
#include "\software\ucos-ii\source\os_sem.c"
#include "\software\ucos-ii\source\os_task.c"
#include "\software\ucos-ii\source\os_time.c"
```

B.01 uCOS_II.H

```
/*
*********************************************************************************************************
*                                              uC/OS-II
*                                         The Real-Time Kernel
*
*                       (c) Copyright 1992-1998, Jean J. Labrosse, Plantation, FL
*                                         All Rights Reserved
*
*                                              V2.00
*
* File : uCOS_II.H
* By   : Jean J. Labrosse
*********************************************************************************************************
*/

/*
*********************************************************************************************************
*                                            MISCELLANEOUS
*********************************************************************************************************
*/

#define  OS_VERSION              200    /* Version of uC/OS-II (Vx.yy multiplied by 100)               */

#ifdef   OS_GLOBALS
#define  OS_EXT
#else
#define  OS_EXT   extern
#endif

#define  OS_PRIO_SELF            0xFF   /* Indicate SELF priority                                      */

#if      OS_TASK_STAT_EN
#define  OS_N_SYS_TASKS          2                        /* Number of system tasks                    */
#else
#define  OS_N_SYS_TASKS          1
#endif

#define  OS_STAT_PRIO          (OS_LOWEST_PRIO - 1)       /* Statistic task priority                   */
#define  OS_IDLE_PRIO          (OS_LOWEST_PRIO)           /* IDLE       task priority                  */

#define  OS_EVENT_TBL_SIZE  ((OS_LOWEST_PRIO) / 8 + 1)    /* Size of event table                       */
#define  OS_RDY_TBL_SIZE    ((OS_LOWEST_PRIO) / 8 + 1)    /* Size of ready table                       */

#define  OS_TASK_IDLE_ID       65535    /* I.D. numbers for Idle and Stat tasks                        */
#define  OS_TASK_STAT_ID       65534

                                        /* TASK STATUS (Bit definition for OSTCBStat)                  */
#define  OS_STAT_RDY           0x00     /* Ready to run                                                */
#define  OS_STAT_SEM           0x01     /* Pending on semaphore                                        */
#define  OS_STAT_MBOX          0x02     /* Pending on mailbox                                          */
#define  OS_STAT_Q             0x04     /* Pending on queue                                            */
#define  OS_STAT_SUSPEND       0x08     /* Task is suspended                                           */

#define  OS_EVENT_TYPE_MBOX      1
#define  OS_EVENT_TYPE_Q         2
#define  OS_EVENT_TYPE_SEM       3

                                        /* TASK OPTIONS (see OSTaskCreateExt())                        */
#define  OS_TASK_OPT_STK_CHK   0x0001   /* Enable stack checking for the task                          */
#define  OS_TASK_OPT_STK_CLR   0x0002   /* Clear the stack when the task is create                     */
#define  OS_TASK_OPT_SAVE_FP   0x0004   /* Save the contents of any floating-point registers           */
```

```
#ifndef  FALSE
#define  FALSE                    0
#endif

#ifndef  TRUE
#define  TRUE                     1
#endif

/*
*********************************************************************************************************
*                                         ERROR CODES
*********************************************************************************************************
*/

#define OS_NO_ERR                 0
#define OS_ERR_EVENT_TYPE         1
#define OS_ERR_PEND_ISR           2

#define OS_TIMEOUT                10
#define OS_TASK_NOT_EXIST         11

#define OS_MBOX_FULL              20

#define OS_Q_FULL                 30

#define OS_PRIO_EXIST             40
#define OS_PRIO_ERR               41
#define OS_PRIO_INVALID           42

#define OS_SEM_OVF                50

#define OS_TASK_DEL_ERR           60
#define OS_TASK_DEL_IDLE          61
#define OS_TASK_DEL_REQ           62
#define OS_TASK_DEL_ISR           63

#define OS_NO_MORE_TCB            70

#define OS_TIME_NOT_DLY           80
#define OS_TIME_INVALID_MINUTES   81
#define OS_TIME_INVALID_SECONDS   82
#define OS_TIME_INVALID_MILLI     83
#define OS_TIME_ZERO_DLY          84

#define OS_TASK_SUSPEND_PRIO      90
#define OS_TASK_SUSPEND_IDLE      91

#define OS_TASK_RESUME_PRIO       100
#define OS_TASK_NOT_SUSPENDED     101

#define OS_MEM_INVALID_PART       110
#define OS_MEM_INVALID_BLKS       111
#define OS_MEM_INVALID_SIZE       112
#define OS_MEM_NO_FREE_BLKS       113
#define OS_MEM_FULL               114

#define OS_TASK_OPT_ERR           130
```

B

uCOS_II.H

```
/*
*********************************************************************************************************
*                                        EVENT CONTROL BLOCK
*********************************************************************************************************
*/

#if (OS_MAX_EVENTS >= 2)
typedef struct {
    void    *OSEventPtr;                      /* Pointer to message or queue structure               */
    INT8U    OSEventTbl[OS_EVENT_TBL_SIZE];   /* List of tasks waiting for event to occur            */
    INT16U   OSEventCnt;                      /* Count of used when event is a semaphore             */
    INT8U    OSEventType;                     /* OS_EVENT_TYPE_MBOX, OS_EVENT_TYPE_Q or OS_EVENT_TYPE_SEM */
    INT8U    OSEventGrp;                      /* Group corresponding to tasks waiting for event to occur  */
} OS_EVENT;
#endif


/*
*********************************************************************************************************
*                                        MESSAGE MAILBOX DATA
*********************************************************************************************************
*/

#if OS_MBOX_EN
typedef struct {
    void    *OSMsg;                           /* Pointer to message in mailbox                       */
    INT8U    OSEventTbl[OS_EVENT_TBL_SIZE];   /* List of tasks waiting for event to occur            */
    INT8U    OSEventGrp;                      /* Group corresponding to tasks waiting for event to occur  */
} OS_MBOX_DATA;
#endif


/*
*********************************************************************************************************
*                                    MEMORY PARTITION DATA STRUCTURES
*********************************************************************************************************
*/

#if OS_MEM_EN && (OS_MAX_MEM_PART >= 2)
typedef struct {                             /* MEMORY CONTROL BLOCK                                 */
    void    *OSMemAddr;                       /* Pointer to beginning of memory partition            */
    void    *OSMemFreeList;                   /* Pointer to list of free memory blocks               */
    INT32U   OSMemBlkSize;                    /* Size (in bytes) of each block of memory             */
    INT32U   OSMemNBlks;                      /* Total number of blocks in this partition            */
    INT32U   OSMemNFree;                      /* Number of memory blocks remaining in this partition */
} OS_MEM;


typedef struct {
    void    *OSAddr;                          /* Pointer to the beginning address of the memory partition */
    void    *OSFreeList;                      /* Pointer to the beginning of the free list of memory blocks */
    INT32U   OSBlkSize;                       /* Size (in bytes) of each memory block                */
    INT32U   OSNBlks;                         /* Total number of blocks in the partition             */
    INT32U   OSNFree;                         /* Number of memory blocks free                        */
    INT32U   OSNUsed;                         /* Number of memory blocks used                        */
} OS_MEM_DATA;
#endif
```

uCOS_II.H

```
/*
********************************************************************************************************
*                                       MESSAGE QUEUE DATA
********************************************************************************************************
*/

#if OS_Q_EN
typedef struct {
    void    *OSMsg;                          /* Pointer to next message to be extracted from queue    */
    INT16U  OSNMsgs;                         /* Number of messages in message queue                   */
    INT16U  OSQSize;                         /* Size of message queue                                 */
    INT8U   OSEventTbl[OS_EVENT_TBL_SIZE];   /* List of tasks waiting for event to occur              */
    INT8U   OSEventGrp;                      /* Group corresponding to tasks waiting for event to occur */
} OS_Q_DATA;
#endif

/*
********************************************************************************************************
*                                        SEMAPHORE DATA
********************************************************************************************************
*/

#if OS_SEM_EN
typedef struct {
    INT16U  OSCnt;                           /* Semaphore count                                       */
    INT8U   OSEventTbl[OS_EVENT_TBL_SIZE];   /* List of tasks waiting for event to occur              */
    INT8U   OSEventGrp;                      /* Group corresponding to tasks waiting for event to occur */
} OS_SEM_DATA;
#endif

/*
********************************************************************************************************
*                                        TASK STACK DATA
********************************************************************************************************
*/

#if OS_TASK_CREATE_EXT_EN
typedef struct {
    INT32U  OSFree;                 /* Number of free bytes on the stack                              */
    INT32U  OSUsed;                 /* Number of bytes used on the stack                              */
} OS_STK_DATA;
#endif
```

B

```
/*
*********************************************************************************************
*                                    TASK CONTROL BLOCK
*********************************************************************************************
*/

typedef struct os_tcb {
    OS_STK          *OSTCBStkPtr;          /* Pointer to current top of stack                      */

#if OS_TASK_CREATE_EXT_EN
    void            *OSTCBExtPtr;          /* Pointer to user definable data for TCB extension     */
    OS_STK          *OSTCBStkBottom;       /* Pointer to bottom of stack                           */
    INT32U           OSTCBStkSize;         /* Size of task stack (in bytes)                        */
    INT16U           OSTCBOpt;             /* Task options as passed by OSTaskCreateExt()          */
    INT16U           OSTCBId;              /* Task ID (0..65535)                                   */
#endif

    struct os_tcb *OSTCBNext;              /* Pointer to next     TCB in the TCB list              */
    struct os_tcb *OSTCBPrev;              /* Pointer to previous TCB in the TCB list              */

#if (OS_Q_EN && (OS_MAX_QS >= 2)) || OS_MBOX_EN || OS_SEM_EN
    OS_EVENT        *OSTCBEventPtr;        /* Pointer to event control block                       */
#endif

#if (OS_Q_EN && (OS_MAX_QS >= 2)) || OS_MBOX_EN
    void            *OSTCBMsg;             /* Message received from OSMboxPost() or OSQPost()      */
#endif

    INT16U           OSTCBDly;             /* Nbr ticks to delay task or, timeout waiting for event */
    INT8U            OSTCBStat;            /* Task status                                          */
    INT8U            OSTCBPrio;            /* Task priority (0 == highest, 63 == lowest)           */

    INT8U            OSTCBX;               /* Bit position in group  corresponding to task priority (0..7) */
    INT8U            OSTCBY;               /* Index into ready table corresponding to task priority */
    INT8U            OSTCBBitX;            /* Bit mask to access bit position in ready table       */
    INT8U            OSTCBBitY;            /* Bit mask to access bit position in ready group       */

#if OS_TASK_DEL_EN
    BOOLEAN          OSTCBDelReq;          /* Indicates whether a task needs to delete itself      */
#endif
} OS_TCB;
```

```
/*
*****************************************************************************************************
*                                        GLOBAL VARIABLES
*****************************************************************************************************
*/

OS_EXT  INT32U      OSCtxSwCtr;                     /* Counter of number of context switches          */
#if     (OS_MAX_EVENTS >= 2)
OS_EXT  OS_EVENT     *OSEventFreeList;              /* Pointer to list of free EVENT control blocks   */
OS_EXT  OS_EVENT     OSEventTbl[OS_MAX_EVENTS];/* Table of EVENT control blocks                   */
#endif

OS_EXT  INT32U      OSIdleCtr;                      /* Idle counter                                   */

#if     OS_TASK_STAT_EN
OS_EXT  INT8S       OSCPUUsage;                     /* Percentage of CPU used                         */
OS_EXT  INT32U      OSIdleCtrMax;                   /* Maximum value that idle counter can take in 1 sec. */
OS_EXT  INT32U      OSIdleCtrRun;                   /* Value reached by idle counter at run time in 1 sec. */
OS_EXT  BOOLEAN     OSStatRdy;                      /* Flag indicating that the statistic task is ready */
#endif

OS_EXT  INT8U       OSIntNesting;                   /* Interrupt nesting level                        */

OS_EXT  INT8U       OSLockNesting;                  /* Multitasking lock nesting level                */

OS_EXT  INT8U       OSPrioCur;                      /* Priority of current task                       */
OS_EXT  INT8U       OSPrioHighRdy;                  /* Priority of highest priority task              */

OS_EXT  INT8U       OSRdyGrp;                       /* Ready list group                               */
OS_EXT  INT8U       OSRdyTbl[OS_RDY_TBL_SIZE];      /* Table of tasks which are ready to run          */

OS_EXT  BOOLEAN     OSRunning;                      /* Flag indicating that kernel is running         */

#if     OS_TASK_CREATE_EN  || OS_TASK_CREATE_EXT_EN ||  OS_TASK_DEL_EN
OS_EXT  INT8U       OSTaskCtr;                      /* Number of tasks created                        */
#endif

OS_EXT  OS_TCB      *OSTCBCur;                      /* Pointer to currently running TCB               */
OS_EXT  OS_TCB      *OSTCBFreeList;                 /* Pointer to list of free TCBs                   */
OS_EXT  OS_TCB      *OSTCBHighRdy;                  /* Pointer to highest priority TCB ready to run   */
OS_EXT  OS_TCB      *OSTCBList;                     /* Pointer to doubly linked list of TCBs          */
OS_EXT  OS_TCB      *OSTCBPrioTbl[OS_LOWEST_PRIO + 1];/* Table of pointers to created TCBs            */

OS_EXT  INT32U      OSTime;                         /* Current value of system time (in ticks)        */


extern  INT8U const  OSMapTbl[];                    /* Priority->Bit Mask lookup table                */
extern  INT8U const  OSUnMapTbl[];                  /* Priority->Index    lookup table                */
```

B

```
/*
*********************************************************************************************
*                                    FUNCTION PROTOTYPES
*                                 (Target Independant Functions)
*********************************************************************************************
*/

/*
*********************************************************************************************
*                                 MESSAGE MAILBOX MANAGEMENT
*********************************************************************************************
*/
#if        OS_MBOX_EN
void       *OSMboxAccept(OS_EVENT *pevent);
OS_EVENT   *OSMboxCreate(void *msg);
void       *OSMboxPend(OS_EVENT *pevent, INT16U timeout, INT8U *err);
INT8U       OSMboxPost(OS_EVENT *pevent, void *msg);
INT8U       OSMboxQuery(OS_EVENT *pevent, OS_MBOX_DATA *pdata);
#endif
/*
*********************************************************************************************
*                                     MEMORY MANAGEMENT
*********************************************************************************************
*/
#if        OS_MEM_EN && (OS_MAX_MEM_PART >= 2)
OS_MEM     *OSMemCreate(void *addr, INT32U nblks, INT32U blksize, INT8U *err);
void       *OSMemGet(OS_MEM *pmem, INT8U *err);
INT8U       OSMemPut(OS_MEM *pmem, void *pblk);
INT8U       OSMemQuery(OS_MEM *pmem, OS_MEM_DATA *pdata);
#endif
/*
*********************************************************************************************
*                                 MESSAGE QUEUE MANAGEMENT
*********************************************************************************************
*/
#if        OS_Q_EN && (OS_MAX_QS >= 2)
void       *OSQAccept(OS_EVENT *pevent);
OS_EVENT   *OSQCreate(void **start, INT16U size);
INT8U       OSQFlush(OS_EVENT *pevent);
void       *OSQPend(OS_EVENT *pevent, INT16U timeout, INT8U *err);
INT8U       OSQPost(OS_EVENT *pevent, void *msg);
INT8U       OSQPostFront(OS_EVENT *pevent, void *msg);
INT8U       OSQQuery(OS_EVENT *pevent, OS_Q_DATA *pdata);
#endif
```

```
/*
*********************************************************************************************
*                               SEMAPHORE MANAGEMENT
*********************************************************************************************
*/
#if         OS_SEM_EN
INT16U      OSSemAccept(OS_EVENT *pevent);
OS_EVENT    *OSSemCreate(INT16U value);
void        OSSemPend(OS_EVENT *pevent, INT16U timeout, INT8U *err);
INT8U       OSSemPost(OS_EVENT *pevent);
INT8U       OSSemQuery(OS_EVENT *pevent, OS_SEM_DATA *pdata);
#endif
/*
*********************************************************************************************
*                                 TASK MANAGEMENT
*********************************************************************************************
*/
#if         OS_TASK_CHANGE_PRIO_EN
INT8U       OSTaskChangePrio(INT8U oldprio, INT8U newprio);
#endif

INT8U       OSTaskCreate(void (*task)(void *pd), void *pdata, OS_STK *ptos, INT8U prio);

#if         OS_TASK_CREATE_EXT_EN
INT8U       OSTaskCreateExt(void   (*task)(void *pd),
                            void   *pdata,
                            OS_STK *ptos,
                            INT8U  prio,
                            INT16U id,
                            OS_STK *pbos,
                            INT32U stk_size,
                            void   *pext,
                            INT16U opt);
#endif

#if         OS_TASK_DEL_EN
INT8U       OSTaskDel(INT8U prio);
INT8U       OSTaskDelReq(INT8U prio);
#endif

#if         OS_TASK_SUSPEND_EN
INT8U       OSTaskResume(INT8U prio);
INT8U       OSTaskSuspend(INT8U prio);
#endif

#if         OS_TASK_CREATE_EXT_EN
INT8U       OSTaskStkChk(INT8U prio, OS_STK_DATA *pdata);
#endif

INT8U       OSTaskQuery(INT8U prio, OS_TCB *pdata);

/*
*********************************************************************************************
*                                 TIME MANAGEMENT
*********************************************************************************************
*/
void        OSTimeDly(INT16U ticks);
INT8U       OSTimeDlyHMSM(INT8U hours, INT8U minutes, INT8U seconds, INT16U milli);
INT8U       OSTimeDlyResume(INT8U prio);
INT32U      OSTimeGet(void);
void        OSTimeSet(INT32U ticks);
void        OSTimeTick(void);
```

B

```
/*
********************************************************************************************************
*                                          MISCELLANEOUS
********************************************************************************************************
*/

void        OSInit(void);

void        OSIntEnter(void);
void        OSIntExit(void);

void        OSSchedLock(void);
void        OSSchedUnlock(void);

void        OSStart(void);

void        OSStatInit(void);

INT16U      OSVersion(void);


/*
********************************************************************************************************
*                                  INTERNAL FUNCTION PROTOTYPES
*                          (Your application MUST NOT call these functions)
********************************************************************************************************
*/

#if         OS_MBOX_EN || OS_Q_EN || OS_SEM_EN
void        OSEventTaskRdy(OS_EVENT *pevent, void *msg, INT8U msk);
void        OSEventTaskWait(OS_EVENT *pevent);
void        OSEventTO(OS_EVENT *pevent);
void        OSEventWaitListInit(OS_EVENT *pevent);
#endif

#if         OS_MEM_EN && (OS_MAX_MEM_PART >= 2)
void        OSMemInit(void);
#endif

#if         OS_Q_EN
void        OSQInit(void);
#endif

void        OSSched(void);

void        OSTaskIdle(void *data);

#if         OS_TASK_STAT_EN
void        OSTaskStat(void *data);
#endif

INT8U       OSTCBInit(INT8U prio, OS_STK *ptos, OS_STK *pbos, INT16U id, INT16U stk_size,
                      void *pext, INT16U opt);
```

uCOS_II.H

```
/*
*********************************************************************************************
*                                    FUNCTION PROTOTYPES
*                                  (Target Specific Functions)
*********************************************************************************************
*/

void        OSCtxSw(void);

void        OSIntCtxSw(void);

void        OSStartHighRdy(void);

void        OSTaskCreateHook(OS_TCB *ptcb);
void        OSTaskDelHook(OS_TCB *ptcb);
void        OSTaskStatHook(void);
void        *OSTaskStkInit(void (*task)(void *pd), void *pdata, void *ptos, INT16U opt);
void        OSTaskSwHook(void);

void        OSTickISR(void);

void        OSTimeTickHook(void);
```

B

B.02 OS_CORE.C

```
/*
*********************************************************************************************************
*                                             uC/OS-II
*                                       The Real-Time Kernel
*                                          CORE FUNCTIONS
*
*                         (c) Copyright 1992-1998, Jean J. Labrosse, Plantation, FL
*                                          All Rights Reserved
*
*                                             V2.00
*
* File : OS_CORE.C
* By   : Jean J. Labrosse
*********************************************************************************************************
*/

#ifndef  OS_MASTER_FILE
#define  OS_GLOBALS
#include "includes.h"
#endif

/*
*********************************************************************************************************
*                                       LOCAL GLOBAL VARIABLES
*********************************************************************************************************
*/

static   INT8U       OSIntExitY;                   /* Variable used by 'OSIntExit' to prevent using locals */

static   OS_STK      OSTaskIdleStk[OS_TASK_IDLE_STK_SIZE];      /* Idle        task stack                */

#if      OS_TASK_STAT_EN
static   OS_STK      OSTaskStatStk[OS_TASK_STAT_STK_SIZE];      /* Statistics task stack                 */
#endif

static   OS_TCB      OSTCBTbl[OS_MAX_TASKS + OS_N_SYS_TASKS];   /* Table of TCBs                         */
```

```
/*
*********************************************************************************************************
*                           MAPPING TABLE TO MAP BIT POSITION TO BIT MASK
*
* Note: Index into table is desired bit position, 0..7
*       Indexed value corresponds to bit mask
*********************************************************************************************************
*/

INT8U  const  OSMapTbl[]    = {0x01, 0x02, 0x04, 0x08, 0x10, 0x20, 0x40, 0x80};

/*
*********************************************************************************************************
*                                    PRIORITY RESOLUTION TABLE
*
* Note: Index into table is bit pattern to resolve highest priority
*       Indexed value corresponds to highest priority bit position (i.e. 0..7)
*********************************************************************************************************
*/

INT8U  const  OSUnMapTbl[] = {
    0, 0, 1, 0, 2, 0, 1, 0, 3, 0, 1, 0, 2, 0, 1, 0,
    4, 0, 1, 0, 2, 0, 1, 0, 3, 0, 1, 0, 2, 0, 1, 0,
    5, 0, 1, 0, 2, 0, 1, 0, 3, 0, 1, 0, 2, 0, 1, 0,
    4, 0, 1, 0, 2, 0, 1, 0, 3, 0, 1, 0, 2, 0, 1, 0,
    6, 0, 1, 0, 2, 0, 1, 0, 3, 0, 1, 0, 2, 0, 1, 0,
    4, 0, 1, 0, 2, 0, 1, 0, 3, 0, 1, 0, 2, 0, 1, 0,
    5, 0, 1, 0, 2, 0, 1, 0, 3, 0, 1, 0, 2, 0, 1, 0,
    4, 0, 1, 0, 2, 0, 1, 0, 3, 0, 1, 0, 2, 0, 1, 0,
    7, 0, 1, 0, 2, 0, 1, 0, 3, 0, 1, 0, 2, 0, 1, 0,
    4, 0, 1, 0, 2, 0, 1, 0, 3, 0, 1, 0, 2, 0, 1, 0,
    5, 0, 1, 0, 2, 0, 1, 0, 3, 0, 1, 0, 2, 0, 1, 0,
    4, 0, 1, 0, 2, 0, 1, 0, 3, 0, 1, 0, 2, 0, 1, 0,
    6, 0, 1, 0, 2, 0, 1, 0, 3, 0, 1, 0, 2, 0, 1, 0,
    4, 0, 1, 0, 2, 0, 1, 0, 3, 0, 1, 0, 2, 0, 1, 0,
    5, 0, 1, 0, 2, 0, 1, 0, 3, 0, 1, 0, 2, 0, 1, 0,
    4, 0, 1, 0, 2, 0, 1, 0, 3, 0, 1, 0, 2, 0, 1, 0
};
```

B

OS_CORE.C

```
/*
*********************************************************************************************
*                      MAKE TASK READY TO RUN BASED ON EVENT OCCURING
*
* Description: This function is called by other uC/OS-II services and is used to ready a task that was
*              waiting for an event to occur.
*
* Arguments  : pevent    is a pointer to the event control block corresponding to the event.
*
*              msg       is a pointer to a message.  This pointer is used by message oriented services
*                        such as MAILBOXEs and QUEUEs.  The pointer is not used when called by other
*                        service functions.
*
*              msk       is a mask that is used to clear the status byte of the TCB.  For example,
*                        OSSemPost() will pass OS_STAT_SEM, OSMboxPost() will pass OS_STAT_MBOX etc.
*
* Returns    : none
*
* Note       : This function is INTERNAL to uC/OS-II and your application should not call it.
*********************************************************************************************
*/
#if   (OS_Q_EN && (OS_MAX_QS >= 2)) || OS_MBOX_EN || OS_SEM_EN
void  OSEventTaskRdy (OS_EVENT *pevent, void *msg, INT8U msk)
{
    OS_TCB *ptcb;
    INT8U   x;
    INT8U   y;
    INT8U   bitx;
    INT8U   bity;
    INT8U   prio;


    y    = OSUnMapTbl[pevent->OSEventGrp];            /* Find highest prio. task waiting for message  */
    bity = OSMapTbl[y];
    x    = OSUnMapTbl[pevent->OSEventTbl[y]];
    bitx = OSMapTbl[x];
    prio = (INT8U)((y << 3) + x);                     /* Find priority of task getting the msg        */
    if ((pevent->OSEventTbl[y] &= ~bitx) == 0) {      /* Remove this task from the waiting list       */
        pevent->OSEventGrp &= ~bity;
    }
    ptcb                 = OSTCBPrioTbl[prio];        /* Point to this task's OS_TCB                   */
    ptcb->OSTCBDly       = 0;                         /* Prevent OSTimeTick() from readying task       */
    ptcb->OSTCBEventPtr  = (OS_EVENT *)0;             /* Unlink ECB from this task                     */
#if (OS_Q_EN && (OS_MAX_QS >= 2)) || OS_MBOX_EN
    ptcb->OSTCBMsg       = msg;                       /* Send message directly to waiting task         */
#else
    msg                  = msg;                       /* Prevent compiler warning if not used          */
#endif
    ptcb->OSTCBStat     &= ~msk;                      /* Clear bit associated with event type          */
    if (ptcb->OSTCBStat == OS_STAT_RDY) {             /* See if task is ready (could be susp'd)        */
        OSRdyGrp        |= bity;                      /* Put task in the ready to run list             */
        OSRdyTbl[y]     |= bitx;
    }
}
#endif
```

```
/*
*********************************************************************************************
*                            MAKE TASK WAIT FOR EVENT TO OCCUR
*
* Description: This function is called by other uC/OS-II services to suspend a task because an event has
*              not occurred.
*
* Arguments  : pevent   is a pointer to the event control block for which the task will be waiting for.
*
* Returns    : none
*
* Note       : This function is INTERNAL to uC/OS-II and your application should not call it.
*********************************************************************************************
*/
#if (OS_Q_EN && (OS_MAX_QS >= 2)) || OS_MBOX_EN || OS_SEM_EN
void  OSEventTaskWait (OS_EVENT *pevent)
{
    OSTCBCur->OSTCBEventPtr = pevent;                       /* Store pointer to event control block in TCB    */
    if ((OSRdyTbl[OSTCBCur->OSTCBY] &= ~OSTCBCur->OSTCBBitX) == 0) {        /* Task no longer ready          */
        OSRdyGrp &= ~OSTCBCur->OSTCBBitY;
    }
    pevent->OSEventTbl[OSTCBCur->OSTCBY]  |= OSTCBCur->OSTCBBitX;           /* Put task in waiting list  */
    pevent->OSEventGrp                    |= OSTCBCur->OSTCBBitY;
}
#endif


/*
*********************************************************************************************
*                         MAKE TASK READY TO RUN BASED ON EVENT TIMEOUT
*
* Description: This function is called by other uC/OS-II services to make a task ready to run because a
*              timeout occurred.
*
* Arguments  : pevent   is a pointer to the event control block which is readying a task.
*
* Returns    : none
*
* Note       : This function is INTERNAL to uC/OS-II and your application should not call it.
*********************************************************************************************
*/
#if (OS_Q_EN && (OS_MAX_QS >= 2)) || OS_MBOX_EN || OS_SEM_EN
void  OSEventTO (OS_EVENT *pevent)
{
    if ((pevent->OSEventTbl[OSTCBCur->OSTCBY] &= ~OSTCBCur->OSTCBBitX) == 0) {
        pevent->OSEventGrp &= ~OSTCBCur->OSTCBBitY;
    }
    OSTCBCur->OSTCBStat     = OS_STAT_RDY;          /* Set status to ready                        */
    OSTCBCur->OSTCBEventPtr = (OS_EVENT *)0;        /* No longer waiting for event               */
}
#endif
```

B

```
/*
*********************************************************************************************
*                         INITIALIZE EVENT CONTROL BLOCK'S WAIT LIST
*
* Description: This function is called by other uC/OS-II services to initialize the event wait list.
*
* Arguments  : pevent    is a pointer to the event control block allocated to the event.
*
* Returns    : none
*
* Note       : This function is INTERNAL to uC/OS-II and your application should not call it.
*********************************************************************************************
*/
#if   (OS_Q_EN && (OS_MAX_QS >= 2)) || OS_MBOX_EN || OS_SEM_EN
void  OSEventWaitListInit (OS_EVENT *pevent)
{
    INT8U i;


    pevent->OSEventGrp = 0x00;                    /* No task waiting on event                    */
    for (i = 0; i < OS_EVENT_TBL_SIZE; i++) {
        pevent->OSEventTbl[i] = 0x00;
    }
}
#endif
```

```
/*
*********************************************************************************************
*                                    INITIALIZATION
*
* Description: This function is used to initialize the internals of uC/OS-II and MUST be called prior to
*              creating any uC/OS-II object and, prior to calling OSStart().
*
* Arguments  : none
*
* Returns    : none
*********************************************************************************************
*/
void OSInit (void)
{
    INT16U i;

    OSTime        = 0L;                              /* Clear the 32-bit system clock           */
    OSIntNesting  = 0;                               /* Clear the interrupt nesting counter     */
    OSLockNesting = 0;                               /* Clear the scheduling lock counter       */
#if OS_TASK_CREATE_EN  || OS_TASK_CREATE_EXT_EN || OS_TASK_DEL_EN
    OSTaskCtr     = 0;                               /* Clear the number of tasks               */
#endif
    OSRunning     = FALSE;                           /* Indicate that multitasking not started  */
    OSIdleCtr     = 0L;                              /* Clear the 32-bit idle counter           */
#if OS_TASK_STAT_EN && OS_TASK_CREATE_EXT_EN
    OSIdleCtrRun  = 0L;
    OSIdleCtrMax  = 0L;
    OSStatRdy     = FALSE;                           /* Statistic task is not ready             */
#endif
    OSCtxSwCtr    = 0;                               /* Clear the context switch counter        */
    OSRdyGrp      = 0;                               /* Clear the ready list                    */
    for (i = 0; i < OS_RDY_TBL_SIZE; i++) {
        OSRdyTbl[i] = 0;
    }
    OSPrioCur     = 0;
    OSPrioHighRdy = 0;
    OSTCBHighRdy  = (OS_TCB *)0;                      /* TCB Initialization                      */
    OSTCBCur      = (OS_TCB *)0;
    OSTCBList     = (OS_TCB *)0;
    for (i = 0; i < (OS_LOWEST_PRIO + 1); i++) {      /* Clear the priority table                */
        OSTCBPrioTbl[i] = (OS_TCB *)0;
    }
    for (i = 0; i < (OS_MAX_TASKS + OS_N_SYS_TASKS - 1); i++) {   /* Init. list of free TCBs      */
        OSTCBTbl[i].OSTCBNext = &OSTCBTbl[i + 1];
    }
    OSTCBTbl[OS_MAX_TASKS + OS_N_SYS_TASKS - 1].OSTCBNext = (OS_TCB *)0;    /* Last OS_TCB         */
    OSTCBFreeList                            = &OSTCBTbl[0];

#if OS_MAX_EVENTS >= 2
    for (i = 0; i < (OS_MAX_EVENTS - 1); i++) {       /* Init. list of free EVENT control blocks  */
        OSEventTbl[i].OSEventPtr = (OS_EVENT *)&OSEventTbl[i + 1];
    }
    OSEventTbl[OS_MAX_EVENTS - 1].OSEventPtr = (OS_EVENT *)0;
    OSEventFreeList                          = &OSEventTbl[0];
#endif

#if OS_Q_EN && (OS_MAX_QS >= 2)
    OSQInit();                                        /* Initialize the message queue structures  */
#endif

#if OS_MEM_EN && OS_MAX_MEM_PART >= 2
    OSMemInit();                                      /* Initialize the memory manager            */
#endif
```

OS_CORE.C

```
#if OS_STK_GROWTH == 1
    #if OS_TASK_CREATE_EXT_EN
    OSTaskCreateExt(OSTaskIdle,
                    (void *)0,                                  /* No arguments passed to OSTaskIdle() */
                    &OSTaskIdleStk[OS_TASK_IDLE_STK_SIZE - 1], /* Set Top-Of-Stack                     */
                    OS_IDLE_PRIO,                               /* Lowest priority level               */
                    OS_TASK_IDLE_ID,
                    &OSTaskIdleStk[0],                          /* Set Bottom-Of-Stack                 */
                    OS_TASK_IDLE_STK_SIZE,
                    (void *)0,                                  /* No TCB extension                    */
                    OS_TASK_OPT_STK_CHK | OS_TASK_OPT_STK_CLR);/* Enable stack checking + clear stack */
    #else
    OSTaskCreate(OSTaskIdle, (void *)0, &OSTaskIdleStk[OS_TASK_IDLE_STK_SIZE - 1], OS_IDLE_PRIO);
    #endif
#else
    #if OS_TASK_CREATE_EXT_EN
    OSTaskCreateExt(OSTaskIdle,
                    (void *)0,                                  /* No arguments passed to OSTaskIdle() */
                    &OSTaskIdleStk[0],                          /* Set Top-Of-Stack                     */
                    OS_IDLE_PRIO,                               /* Lowest priority level               */
                    OS_TASK_IDLE_ID,
                    &OSTaskIdleStk[OS_TASK_IDLE_STK_SIZE - 1], /* Set Bottom-Of-Stack                 */
                    OS_TASK_IDLE_STK_SIZE,
                    (void *)0,                                  /* No TCB extension                    */
                    OS_TASK_OPT_STK_CHK | OS_TASK_OPT_STK_CLR);/* Enable stack checking + clear stack */
    #else
    OSTaskCreate(OSTaskIdle, (void *)0, &OSTaskIdleStk[0], OS_IDLE_PRIO);
    #endif
#endif

#if OS_TASK_STAT_EN
    #if OS_TASK_CREATE_EXT_EN
        #if OS_STK_GROWTH == 1
        OSTaskCreateExt(OSTaskStat,
                        (void *)0,                                  /* No args passed to OSTaskStat()   */
                        &OSTaskStatStk[OS_TASK_STAT_STK_SIZE - 1],/* Set Top-Of-Stack                 */
                        OS_STAT_PRIO,                               /* One higher than the idle task    */
                        OS_TASK_STAT_ID,
                        &OSTaskStatStk[0],                          /* Set Bottom-Of-Stack              */
                        OS_TASK_STAT_STK_SIZE,
                        (void *)0,                                  /* No TCB extension                 */
                        OS_TASK_OPT_STK_CHK | OS_TASK_OPT_STK_CLR);  /* Enable stack checking + clear   */
        #else
        OSTaskCreateExt(OSTaskStat,
                        (void *)0,                                  /* No args passed to OSTaskStat()   */
                        &OSTaskStatStk[0],                          /* Set Top-Of-Stack                 */
                        OS_STAT_PRIO,                               /* One higher than the idle task    */
                        OS_TASK_STAT_ID,
                        &OSTaskStatStk[OS_TASK_STAT_STK_SIZE - 1],/* Set Bottom-Of-Stack              */
                        OS_TASK_STAT_STK_SIZE,
                        (void *)0,                                  /* No TCB extension                 */
                        OS_TASK_OPT_STK_CHK | OS_TASK_OPT_STK_CLR);  /* Enable stack checking + clear   */
        #endif
    #else
        #if OS_STK_GROWTH == 1
        OSTaskCreate(OSTaskStat,
                     (void *)0,                                  /* No args passed to OSTaskStat()   */
                     &OSTaskStatStk[OS_TASK_STAT_STK_SIZE - 1],    /* Set Top-Of-Stack                 */
                     OS_STAT_PRIO);                              /* One higher than the idle task    */
        #else
        OSTaskCreate(OSTaskStat,
                     (void *)0,                                  /* No args passed to OSTaskStat()   */
                     &OSTaskStatStk[0],                          /* Set Top-Of-Stack                 */
                     OS_STAT_PRIO);                              /* One higher than the idle task    */
        #endif
    #endif
#endif
}
```

OS_CORE.C

```
/*
*********************************************************************************************************
*                                              ENTER ISR
*
* Description: This function is used to notify uC/OS-II that you are about to service an interrupt
*              service routine (ISR).  This allows uC/OS-II to keep track of interrupt nesting and thus
*              only perform rescheduling at the last nested ISR.
*
* Arguments  : none
*
* Returns    : none
*
* Notes      : 1) Your ISR can directly increment OSIntNesting without calling this function because
*                 OSIntNesting has been declared 'global'.  You MUST, however, be sure that the increment
*                 is performed 'indivisibly' by your processor to ensure proper access to this critical
*                 resource.
*              2) You MUST still call OSIntExit() even though you increment OSIntNesting directly.
*              3) You MUST invoke OSIntEnter() and OSIntExit() in pair.  In other words, for every call
*                 to OSIntEnter() at the beginning of the ISR you MUST have a call to OSIntExit() at the
*                 end of the ISR.
*********************************************************************************************************
*/

void OSIntEnter (void)
{
    OS_ENTER_CRITICAL();
    OSIntNesting++;                              /* Increment ISR nesting level                       */
    OS_EXIT_CRITICAL();
}


/*
*********************************************************************************************************
*                                              EXIT ISR
*
* Description: This function is used to notify uC/OS-II that you have completed serviving an ISR.  When
*              the last nested ISR has completed, uC/OS-II will call the scheduler to determine whether
*              a new, high-priority task, is ready to run.
*
* Arguments  : none
*
* Returns    : none
*
* Notes      : 1) You MUST invoke OSIntEnter() and OSIntExit() in pair.  In other words, for every call
*                 to OSIntEnter() at the beginning of the ISR you MUST have a call to OSIntExit() at the
*                 end of the ISR.
*              2) Rescheduling is prevented when the scheduler is locked (see OSSchedLock())
*********************************************************************************************************
*/

void OSIntExit (void)
{
    OS_ENTER_CRITICAL();
    if ((--OSIntNesting | OSLockNesting) == 0) { /* Reschedule only if all ISRs completed & not locked */
        OSIntExitY    = OSUnMapTbl[OSRdyGrp];
        OSPrioHighRdy = (INT8U)((OSIntExitY << 3) + OSUnMapTbl[OSRdyTbl[OSIntExitY]]);
        if (OSPrioHighRdy != OSPrioCur) {        /* No context switch if current task is highest ready */
            OSTCBHighRdy  = OSTCBPrioTbl[OSPrioHighRdy];
            OSCtxSwCtr++;                         /* Keep track of the number of context switches       */
            OSIntCtxSw();                         /* Perform interrupt level context switch             */
        }
    }
    OS_EXIT_CRITICAL();
}
```

B

OS_CORE.C

```c
/*
*********************************************************************************************************
*                                            SCHEDULER
*
* Description: This function is called by other uC/OS-II services to determine whether a new, high
*              priority task has been made ready to run.  This function is invoked by TASK level code
*              and is not used to reschedule tasks from ISRs (see OSIntExit() for ISR rescheduling).
*
* Arguments  : none
*
* Returns    : none
*
* Notes      : 1) This function is INTERNAL to uC/OS-II and your application should not call it.
*              2) Rescheduling is prevented when the scheduler is locked (see OSSchedLock())
*********************************************************************************************************
*/

void OSSched (void)
{
    INT8U y;


    OS_ENTER_CRITICAL();
    if ((OSLockNesting | OSIntNesting) == 0) {    /* Task scheduling must be enabled and not ISR level  */
        y              = OSUnMapTbl[OSRdyGrp];     /* Get pointer to highest priority task ready to run  */
        OSPrioHighRdy = (INT8U)((y << 3) + OSUnMapTbl[OSRdyTbl[y]]);
        if (OSPrioHighRdy != OSPrioCur) {          /* No context switch if current task is highest ready */
            OSTCBHighRdy = OSTCBPrioTbl[OSPrioHighRdy];
            OSCtxSwCtr++;                          /* Increment context switch counter                   */
            OS_TASK_SW();                          /* Perform a context switch                           */
        }
    }
    OS_EXIT_CRITICAL();
}



/*
*********************************************************************************************************
*                                         PREVENT SCHEDULING
*
* Description: This function is used to prevent rescheduling to take place.  This allows your application
*              to prevent context switches until you are ready to permit context switching.
*
* Arguments  : none
*
* Returns    : none
*
* Notes      : 1) You MUST invoke OSSchedLock() and OSSchedUnlock() in pair.  In other words, for every
*                 call to OSSchedLock() you MUST have a call to OSSchedUnlock().
*********************************************************************************************************
*/

void OSSchedLock (void)
{
    if (OSRunning == TRUE) {                       /* Make sure multitasking is running                  */
        OS_ENTER_CRITICAL();
        OSLockNesting++;                           /* Increment lock nesting level                       */
        OS_EXIT_CRITICAL();
    }
}
```

OS_CORE.C

```
/*
*********************************************************************************************
*                                    ENABLE SCHEDULING
*
* Description: This function is used to re-allow rescheduling.
*
* Arguments   : none
*
* Returns     : none
*
* Notes       : 1) You MUST invoke OSSchedLock() and OSSchedUnlock() in pair.  In other words, for every
*                  call to OSSchedLock() you MUST have a call to OSSchedUnlock().
*********************************************************************************************
*/

void OSSchedUnlock (void)
{
    if (OSRunning == TRUE) {                             /* Make sure multitasking is running          */
        OS_ENTER_CRITICAL();
        if (OSLockNesting > 0) {                         /* Do not decrement if already 0              */
            OSLockNesting--;                             /* Decrement lock nesting level               */
            if ((OSLockNesting | OSIntNesting) == 0) {  /* See if scheduling re-enabled and not an ISR */
                OS_EXIT_CRITICAL();
                OSSched();                               /* See if a higher priority task is ready     */
            } else {
                OS_EXIT_CRITICAL();
            }
        } else {
            OS_EXIT_CRITICAL();
        }
    }
}


/*
*********************************************************************************************
*                                    START MULTITASKING
*
* Description: This function is used to start the multitasking process which lets uC/OS-II manages the
*              task that you have created.  Before you can call OSStart(), you MUST have called OSInit()
*              and you MUST have created at least one task.
*
* Arguments   : none
*
* Returns     : none
*
* Note        : OSStartHighRdy() MUST:
*                  a) Call OSTaskSwHook() then,
*                  b) Set OSRunning to TRUE.
*********************************************************************************************
*/

void OSStart (void)
{
    INT8U y;
    INT8U x;


    if (OSRunning == FALSE) {
        y            = OSUnMapTbl[OSRdyGrp];              /* Find highest priority's task priority number */
        x            = OSUnMapTbl[OSRdyTbl[y]];
        OSPrioHighRdy = (INT8U)((y << 3) + x);
        OSPrioCur    = OSPrioHighRdy;
        OSTCBHighRdy = OSTCBPrioTbl[OSPrioHighRdy];      /* Point to highest priority task ready to run  */
        OSTCBCur     = OSTCBHighRdy;
        OSStartHighRdy();                                /* Execute target specific code to start task   */
    }
}
```

```
/*
*********************************************************************************************
*                                 STATISTICS INITIALIZATION
*
* Description: This function is called by your application to establish CPU usage by first determining
*              how high a 32-bit counter would count to in 1 second if no other tasks were to execute
*              during that time.  CPU usage is then determined by a low priority task which keeps track
*              of this 32-bit counter every second but this time, with other tasks running.  CPU usage is
*              determined by:
*
*                                           OSIdleCtr
*                    CPU Usage (%) = 100 * (1 - ------------)
*                                           OSIdleCtrMax
*
* Arguments   : none
*
* Returns     : none
*********************************************************************************************
*/

#if OS_TASK_STAT_EN
void OSStatInit (void)
{
    OSTimeDly(2);                                /* Synchronize with clock tick                      */
    OS_ENTER_CRITICAL();
    OSIdleCtr    = 0L;                           /* Clear idle counter                               */
    OS_EXIT_CRITICAL();
    OSTimeDly(OS_TICKS_PER_SEC);                 /* Determine MAX. idle counter value for 1 second   */
    OS_ENTER_CRITICAL();
    OSIdleCtrMax = OSIdleCtr;                     /* Store maximum idle counter count in 1 second     */
    OSStatRdy    = TRUE;
    OS_EXIT_CRITICAL();
}
#endif


/*
*********************************************************************************************
*                                        IDLE TASK
*
* Description: This task is internal to uC/OS-II and executes whenever no other higher priority tasks
*              executes because they are waiting for event(s) to occur.
*
* Arguments   : none
*
* Returns     : none
*********************************************************************************************
*/

void OSTaskIdle (void *pdata)
{
    pdata = pdata;                               /* Prevent compiler warning for not using 'pdata'   */
    for (;;) {
        OS_ENTER_CRITICAL();
        OSIdleCtr++;
        OS_EXIT_CRITICAL();
    }
}
```

OS_CORE.C

```
/*
*********************************************************************************************************
*                                        STATISTICS TASK
*
* Description: This task is internal to uC/OS-II and is used to compute some statistics about the
*              multitasking environment.  Specifically, OSTaskStat() computes the CPU usage.
*              CPU usage is determined by:
*
*                                         OSIdleCtr
*                   OSCPUUsage = 100 * (1 - ------------)       (units are in %)
*                                         OSIdleCtrMax
*
* Arguments   : pdata      this pointer is not used at this time.
*
* Returns     : none
*
* Notes       : 1) This task runs at a priority level higher than the idle task.  In fact, it runs at the
*                  next higher priority, OS_IDLE_PRIO-1.
*               2) You can disable this task by setting the configuration #define OS_TASK_STAT_EN to 0.
*               3) We delay for 5 seconds in the beginning to allow the system to reach steady state and
*                  have all other tasks created before we do statistics.  You MUST have at least a delay
*                  of 2 seconds to allow for the system to establish the maximum value for the idle
*                  counter.
*********************************************************************************************************
*/

#if OS_TASK_STAT_EN
void OSTaskStat (void *pdata)
{
    INT32U run;
    INT8S  usage;


    pdata = pdata;                                  /* Prevent compiler warning for not using 'pdata'     */
    while (OSStatRdy == FALSE) {
        OSTimeDly(2 * OS_TICKS_PER_SEC);            /* Wait until statistic task is ready                 */
    }
    for (;;) {
        OS_ENTER_CRITICAL();
        OSIdleCtrRun = OSIdleCtr;                   /* Obtain the of the idle counter for the past second */
        run          = OSIdleCtr;
        OSIdleCtr    = 0L;                          /* Reset the idle counter for the next second         */
        OS_EXIT_CRITICAL();
        if (OSIdleCtrMax > 0L) {
            usage = (INT8S)(100L - 100L * run / OSIdleCtrMax);
            if (usage > 100) {
                OSCPUUsage = 100;
            } else if (usage < 0) {
                OSCPUUsage =   0;
            } else {
                OSCPUUsage = usage;
            }
        } else {
            OSCPUUsage = 0;
        }
        OSTaskStatHook();                           /* Invoke user definable hook                         */
        OSTimeDly(OS_TICKS_PER_SEC);                /* Accumulate OSIdleCtr for the next second           */
    }
}
#endif
```

B

OS_CORE.C

```
/*
*********************************************************************************************************
*                                          INITIALIZE TCB
*
* Description: This function is internal to uC/OS-II and is used to initialize a Task Control Block when
*              a task is created (see OSTaskCreate() and OSTaskCreateExt()).
*
* Arguments  : prio          is the priority of the task being created
*
*              ptos          is a pointer to the task's top-of-stack assuming that the CPU registers
*                            have been placed on the stack.  Note that the top-of-stack corresponds to a
*                            'high' memory location is OS_STK_GROWTH is set to 1 and a 'low' memory
*                            location if OS_STK_GROWTH is set to 0.  Note that stack growth is CPU
*                            specific.
*
*              pbos          is a pointer to the bottom of stack.  A NULL pointer is passed if called by
*                            'OSTaskCreate()'.
*
*              id            is the task's ID (0..65535)
*
*              stk_size      is the size of the stack (in 'stack units').  If the stack units are INT8Us
*                            then, 'stk_size' contains the number of bytes for the stack.  If the stack
*                            units are INT32Us then, the stack contains '4 * stk_size' bytes.  The stack
*                            units are established by the #define constant OS_STK which is CPU
*                            specific.  'stk_size' is 0 if called by 'OSTaskCreate()'.
*
*              pext          is a pointer to a user supplied memory area that is used to extend the task
*                            control block.  This allows you to store the contents of floating-point
*                            registers, MMU registers or anything else you could find useful during a
*                            context switch.  You can even assign a name to each task and store this name
*                            in this TCB extension.  A NULL pointer is passed if called by OSTaskCreate().
*
*              opt           options as passed to 'OSTaskCreateExt()' or,
*                            0 if called from 'OSTaskCreate()'.
*
* Returns    : OS_NO_ERR        if the call was successful
*              OS_NO_MORE_TCB   if there are no more free TCBs to be allocated and thus, the task cannot
*                               be created.
*
* Note       : This function is INTERNAL to uC/OS-II and your application should not call it.
*********************************************************************************************************
*/

INT8U OSTCBInit (INT8U prio, OS_STK *ptos, OS_STK *pbos, INT16U id, INT16U stk_size,
                 void *pext, INT16U opt)
{
    OS_TCB *ptcb;


    OS_ENTER_CRITICAL();
    ptcb = OSTCBFreeList;                                  /* Get a free TCB from the free TCB list   */
    if (ptcb != (OS_TCB *)0) {
        OSTCBFreeList      = ptcb->OSTCBNext;              /* Update pointer to free TCB list         */
        OS_EXIT_CRITICAL();
        ptcb->OSTCBStkPtr  = ptos;                         /* Load Stack pointer in TCB               */
        ptcb->OSTCBPrio    = (INT8U)prio;                  /* Load task priority into TCB             */
        ptcb->OSTCBStat    = OS_STAT_RDY;                  /* Task is ready to run                    */
        ptcb->OSTCBDly     = 0;                            /* Task is not delayed                     */
```

```
#if OS_TASK_CREATE_EXT_EN
        ptcb->OSTCBExtPtr     = pext;                    /* Store pointer to TCB extension        */
        ptcb->OSTCBStkSize    = stk_size;                /* Store stack size                      */
        ptcb->OSTCBStkBottom  = pbos;                    /* Store pointer to bottom of stack      */
        ptcb->OSTCBOpt        = opt;                     /* Store task options                    */
        ptcb->OSTCBId         = id;                      /* Store task ID                         */
#else
        pext                  = pext;                    /* Prevent compiler warning if not used  */
        stk_size              = stk_size;
        pbos                  = pbos;
        opt                   = opt;
        id                    = id;
#endif

#if OS_TASK_DEL_EN
        ptcb->OSTCBDelReq     = OS_NO_ERR;
#endif

        ptcb->OSTCBY          = prio >> 3;               /* Pre-compute X, Y, BitX and BitY       */
        ptcb->OSTCBBitY       = OSMapTbl[ptcb->OSTCBY];
        ptcb->OSTCBX          = prio & 0x07;
        ptcb->OSTCBBitX       = OSMapTbl[ptcb->OSTCBX];

#if     OS_MBOX_EN || (OS_Q_EN && (OS_MAX_QS >= 2)) || OS_SEM_EN
        ptcb->OSTCBEventPtr   = (OS_EVENT *)0;           /* Task is not pending on an event       */
#endif

#if     OS_MBOX_EN || (OS_Q_EN && (OS_MAX_QS >= 2))
        ptcb->OSTCBMsg        = (void *)0;               /* No message received                   */
#endif

        OS_ENTER_CRITICAL();
        OSTCBPrioTbl[prio]    = ptcb;
        ptcb->OSTCBNext       = OSTCBList;               /* Link into TCB chain                   */
        ptcb->OSTCBPrev       = (OS_TCB *)0;
        if (OSTCBList != (OS_TCB *)0) {
            OSTCBList->OSTCBPrev = ptcb;
        }
        OSTCBList                 = ptcb;
        OSRdyGrp                 |= ptcb->OSTCBBitY;     /* Make task ready to run                */
        OSRdyTbl[ptcb->OSTCBY]   |= ptcb->OSTCBBitX;
        OS_EXIT_CRITICAL();
        return (OS_NO_ERR);
    } else {
        OS_EXIT_CRITICAL();
        return (OS_NO_MORE_TCB);
    }
}
```

B

```
/*
*********************************************************************************************
*                                   PROCESS SYSTEM TICK
*
* Description: This function is used to signal to uC/OS-II the occurrence of a 'system tick' (also known
*              as a 'clock tick').  This function should be called by the ticker ISR but, can also be
*              called by a high priority task.
*
* Arguments   : none
*
* Returns     : none
*********************************************************************************************
*/

void OSTimeTick (void)
{
    OS_TCB *ptcb;


    OSTimeTickHook();                                     /* Call user definable hook                 */
    ptcb = OSTCBList;                                     /* Point at first TCB in TCB list           */
    while (ptcb->OSTCBPrio != OS_IDLE_PRIO) {             /* Go through all TCBs in TCB list          */
        OS_ENTER_CRITICAL();
        if (ptcb->OSTCBDly != 0) {                        /* Delayed or waiting for event with TO     */
            if (--ptcb->OSTCBDly == 0) {                  /* Decrement nbr of ticks to end of delay   */
                if (!(ptcb->OSTCBStat & OS_STAT_SUSPEND)) {   /* Is task suspended?                   */
                    OSRdyGrp                |= ptcb->OSTCBBitY; /* No,  Make task Rdy to Run (timed out)*/
                    OSRdyTbl[ptcb->OSTCBY]  |= ptcb->OSTCBBitX;
                } else {                                  /* Yes, Leave 1 tick to prevent ...         */
                    ptcb->OSTCBDly = 1;                   /* ... loosing the task when the ...        */
                }                                         /* ... suspension is removed.               */
            }
        }
        ptcb = ptcb->OSTCBNext;                           /* Point at next TCB in TCB list            */
        OS_EXIT_CRITICAL();
    }
    OS_ENTER_CRITICAL();                                  /* Update the 32-bit tick counter           */
    OSTime++;
    OS_EXIT_CRITICAL();
}



/*
*********************************************************************************************
*                                      GET VERSION
*
* Description: This function is used to return the version number of uC/OS-II.  The returned value
*              corresponds to uC/OS-II's version number multiplied by 100.  In other words, version 2.00
*              would be returned as 200.
*
* Arguments   : none
*
* Returns     : the version number of uC/OS-II multiplied by 100.
*********************************************************************************************
*/

INT16U OSVersion (void)
{
    return (OS_VERSION);
}
```

OS_CORE.C

B.03 OS_MBOX.C

```
/*
********************************************************************************************
*                                        uC/OS-II
*                                    The Real-Time Kernel
*                                  MESSAGE MAILBOX MANAGEMENT
*
*                     (c) Copyright 1992-1998, Jean J. Labrosse, Plantation, FL
*                                      All Rights Reserved
*
*                                           V2.00
*
* File : OS_MBOX.C
* By   : Jean J. Labrosse
********************************************************************************************
*/

#ifndef  OS_MASTER_FILE
#include "includes.h"
#endif

#if OS_MBOX_EN
/*
********************************************************************************************
*                               ACCEPT MESSAGE FROM MAILBOX
*
* Description: This function checks the mailbox to see if a message is available.  Unlike OSMboxPend(),
*             OSMboxAccept() does not suspend the calling task if a message is not available.
*
* Arguments  : pevent        is a pointer to the event control block
*
* Returns    : != (void *)0  is the message in the mailbox if one is available.  The mailbox is cleared
*                            so the next time OSMboxAccept() is called, the mailbox will be empty.
*              == (void *)0  if the mailbox is empty or if you didn't pass the proper event pointer.
********************************************************************************************
*/

void *OSMboxAccept (OS_EVENT *pevent)
{
    void  *msg;


    OS_ENTER_CRITICAL();
    if (pevent->OSEventType != OS_EVENT_TYPE_MBOX) {        /* Validate event block type              */
        OS_EXIT_CRITICAL();
        return ((void *)0);
    }
    msg = pevent->OSEventPtr;
    if (msg != (void *)0) {                                 /* See if there is already a message      */
        pevent->OSEventPtr = (void *)0;                     /* Clear the mailbox                      */
    }
    OS_EXIT_CRITICAL();
    return (msg);                                           /* Return the message received (or NULL)  */
}
```

OS_MBOX.C

```
/*
*********************************************************************************************
*                             CREATE A MESSAGE MAILBOX
*
* Description: This function creates a message mailbox if free event control blocks are available.
*
* Arguments  : msg          is a pointer to a message that you wish to deposit in the mailbox.  If
*                           you set this value to the NULL pointer (i.e. (void *)0) then the mailbox
*                           will be considered empty.
*
* Returns    : != (void *)0 is a pointer to the event control clock (OS_EVENT) associated with the
*                           created mailbox
*              == (void *)0 if no event control blocks were available
*********************************************************************************************
*/

OS_EVENT *OSMboxCreate (void *msg)
{
    OS_EVENT *pevent;


    OS_ENTER_CRITICAL();
    pevent = OSEventFreeList;                    /* Get next free event control block          */
    if (OSEventFreeList != (OS_EVENT *)0) {      /* See if pool of free ECB pool was empty     */
        OSEventFreeList = (OS_EVENT *)OSEventFreeList->OSEventPtr;
    }
    OS_EXIT_CRITICAL();
    if (pevent != (OS_EVENT *)0) {
        pevent->OSEventType = OS_EVENT_TYPE_MBOX;
        pevent->OSEventPtr  = msg;               /* Deposit message in event control block     */
        OSEventWaitListInit(pevent);
    }
    return (pevent);                             /* Return pointer to event control block      */
}
```

```
/*
*********************************************************************************************
*                              PEND ON MAILBOX FOR A MESSAGE
*
* Description: This function waits for a message to be sent to a mailbox
*
* Arguments  : pevent           is a pointer to the event control block associated with the desired mailbox
*
*              timeout          is an optional timeout period (in clock ticks).  If non-zero, your task will
*                               wait for a message to arrive at the mailbox up to the amount of time
*                               specified by this argument.  If you specify 0, however, your task will wait
*                               forever at the specified mailbox or, until a message arrives.
*
*              err              is a pointer to where an error message will be deposited.  Possible error
*                               messages are:
*
*                               OS_NO_ERR         The call was successful and your task received a message.
*                               OS_TIMEOUT        A message was not received within the specified timeout
*                               OS_ERR_EVENT_TYPE Invalid event type
*                               OS_ERR_PEND_ISR   If you called this function from an ISR and the result
*                                                 would lead to a suspension.
*
* Returns    : != (void *)0  is a pointer to the message received
*              == (void *)0  if no message was received or you didn't pass the proper pointer to the
*                            event control block.
*********************************************************************************************
*/
```

B

```c
void *OSMboxPend (OS_EVENT *pevent, INT16U timeout, INT8U *err)
{
    void  *msg;


    OS_ENTER_CRITICAL();
    if (pevent->OSEventType != OS_EVENT_TYPE_MBOX) {  /* Validate event block type            */
        OS_EXIT_CRITICAL();
        *err = OS_ERR_EVENT_TYPE;
        return ((void *)0);
    }
    msg = pevent->OSEventPtr;
    if (msg != (void *)0) {                           /* See if there is already a message     */
        pevent->OSEventPtr = (void *)0;               /* Clear the mailbox                     */
        OS_EXIT_CRITICAL();
        *err = OS_NO_ERR;
    } else if (OSIntNesting > 0) {                    /* See if called from ISR ...            */
        OS_EXIT_CRITICAL();                           /* ... can't PEND from an ISR            */
        *err = OS_ERR_PEND_ISR;
    } else {
        OSTCBCur->OSTCBStat |= OS_STAT_MBOX;          /* Message not available, task will pend */
        OSTCBCur->OSTCBDly  = timeout;                /* Load timeout in TCB                   */
        OSEventTaskWait(pevent);                      /* Suspend task until event or timeout occurs */
        OS_EXIT_CRITICAL();
        OSSched();                                    /* Find next highest priority task ready to run */
        OS_ENTER_CRITICAL();
        if ((msg = OSTCBCur->OSTCBMsg) != (void *)0) {    /* See if we were given the message  */
            OSTCBCur->OSTCBMsg      = (void *)0;           /* Yes, clear message received       */
            OSTCBCur->OSTCBStat     = OS_STAT_RDY;
            OSTCBCur->OSTCBEventPtr = (OS_EVENT *)0;       /* No longer waiting for event       */
            OS_EXIT_CRITICAL();
            *err                    = OS_NO_ERR;
        } else if (OSTCBCur->OSTCBStat & OS_STAT_MBOX) {   /* If status is not OS_STAT_RDY, timed out */
            OSEventTO(pevent);                             /* Make task ready                   */
            OS_EXIT_CRITICAL();
            msg                     = (void *)0;           /* Set message contents to NULL      */
            *err                    = OS_TIMEOUT;          /* Indicate that a timeout occured   */
        } else {
            msg                     = pevent->OSEventPtr;  /* Message received                  */
            pevent->OSEventPtr      = (void *)0;           /* Clear the mailbox                 */
            OSTCBCur->OSTCBEventPtr = (OS_EVENT *)0;
            OS_EXIT_CRITICAL();
            *err                    = OS_NO_ERR;
        }
    }
    return (msg);                                     /* Return the message received (or NULL) */
}
```

OS_MBOX.C

```
/*
*********************************************************************************************
*                              POST MESSAGE TO A MAILBOX
*
* Description: This function sends a message to a mailbox
*
* Arguments  : pevent          is a pointer to the event control block associated with the desired mailbox
*
*              msg             is a pointer to the message to send.  You MUST NOT send a NULL pointer.
*
* Returns    : OS_NO_ERR        The call was successful and the message was sent
*              OS_MBOX_FULL     If the mailbox already contains a message.  You can can only send one
*                               message at a time and thus, the message MUST be consumed before you are
*                               allowed to send another one.
*              OS_ERR_EVENT_TYPE  If you are attempting to post to a non mailbox.
*********************************************************************************************
*/

INT8U OSMboxPost (OS_EVENT *pevent, void *msg)
{
    OS_ENTER_CRITICAL();
    if (pevent->OSEventType != OS_EVENT_TYPE_MBOX) {  /* Validate event block type              */
        OS_EXIT_CRITICAL();
        return (OS_ERR_EVENT_TYPE);
    }
    if (pevent->OSEventGrp) {                         /* See if any task pending on mailbox     */
        OSEventTaskRdy(pevent, msg, OS_STAT_MBOX);    /* Ready highest priority task waiting on event */
        OS_EXIT_CRITICAL();
        OSSched();                                    /* Find highest priority task ready to run */
        return (OS_NO_ERR);
    } else {
        if (pevent->OSEventPtr != (void *)0) {        /* Make sure mailbox doesn't already have a msg */
            OS_EXIT_CRITICAL();
            return (OS_MBOX_FULL);
        } else {
            pevent->OSEventPtr = msg;                 /* Place message in mailbox               */
            OS_EXIT_CRITICAL();
            return (OS_NO_ERR);
        }
    }
}
```

B

OS_MBOX.C

```
/*
*********************************************************************************************
*                                    QUERY A MESSAGE MAILBOX
*
* Description: This function obtains information about a message mailbox.
*
* Arguments  : pevent         is a pointer to the event control block associated with the desired mailbox
*
*              pdata          is a pointer to a structure that will contain information about the message
*                             mailbox.
*
* Returns    : OS_NO_ERR        The call was successful and the message was sent
*              OS_ERR_EVENT_TYPE If you are attempting to obtain data from a non mailbox.
*********************************************************************************************
*/

INT8U OSMboxQuery (OS_EVENT *pevent, OS_MBOX_DATA *pdata)
{
    INT8U  i;
    INT8U *psrc;
    INT8U *pdest;


    OS_ENTER_CRITICAL();
    if (pevent->OSEventType != OS_EVENT_TYPE_MBOX) {        /* Validate event block type           */
        OS_EXIT_CRITICAL();
        return (OS_ERR_EVENT_TYPE);
    }
    pdata->OSEventGrp = pevent->OSEventGrp;                 /* Copy message mailbox wait list      */
    psrc              = &pevent->OSEventTbl[0];
    pdest             = &pdata->OSEventTbl[0];
    for (i = 0; i < OS_EVENT_TBL_SIZE; i++) {
        *pdest++ = *psrc++;
    }
    pdata->OSMsg = pevent->OSEventPtr;                      /* Get message from mailbox            */
    OS_EXIT_CRITICAL();
    return (OS_NO_ERR);
}
#endif
```

OS_MBOX.C

B.04 OS_MEM.C

```
/*
*********************************************************************************************
*                                        uC/OS-II
*                                   The Real-Time Kernel
*                                   MEMORY MANAGEMENT
*
*                         (c) Copyright 1992-1998, Jean J. Labrosse, Plantation, FL
*                                      All Rights Reserved
*
*                                          V2.00
*
* File : OS_MEM.C
* By   : Jean J. Labrosse
*********************************************************************************************
*/

#ifndef  OS_MASTER_FILE
#include "includes.h"
#endif

#if OS_MEM_EN && OS_MAX_MEM_PART >= 2
/*
*********************************************************************************************
*                                   LOCAL GLOBAL VARIABLES
*********************************************************************************************
*/

static  OS_MEM      *OSMemFreeList;              /* Pointer to free list of memory partitions    */
static  OS_MEM       OSMemTbl[OS_MAX_MEM_PART];  /* Storage for memory partition manager          */
```

B

```
/*
*********************************************************************************************************
*                                    CREATE A MEMORY PARTITION
*
* Description : Create a fixed-sized memory partition that will be managed by uC/OS-II.
* Arguments   : addr     is the starting address of the memory partition
*
*               nblks    is the number of memory blocks to create from the partition.
*
*               blksize  is the size (in bytes) of each block in the memory partition.
*
*               err      is a pointer to a variable containing an error message which will be set by
*                        this function to either:
*                        OS_NO_ERR           if the memory partition has been created correctly.
*                        OS_MEM_INVALID_PART no free partitions available
*                        OS_MEM_INVALID_BLKS user specified an invalid number of blocks (must be >= 2)
*                        OS_MEM_INVALID_SIZE user specified an invalid block size
*                                            (must be greater than the size of a pointer)
* Returns     : != (OS_MEM *)0  is the partition was created
*               == (OS_MEM *)0  if the partition was not created because of invalid arguments or, no
*                               free partition is available.
*********************************************************************************************************
*/
OS_MEM *OSMemCreate (void *addr, INT32U nblks, INT32U blksize, INT8U *err)
{
    OS_MEM  *pmem;
    INT8U   *pblk;
    void    **plink;
    INT32U  i;


    if (nblks < 2) {                                /* Must have at least 2 blocks per partition   */
        *err = OS_MEM_INVALID_BLKS;
        return ((OS_MEM *)0);
    }
    if (blksize < sizeof(void *)) {                 /* Must contain space for at least a pointer   */
        *err = OS_MEM_INVALID_SIZE;
        return ((OS_MEM *)0);
    }
    OS_ENTER_CRITICAL();
    pmem = OSMemFreeList;                            /* Get next free memory partition              */
    if (OSMemFreeList != (OS_MEM *)0) {             /* See if pool of free partitions was empty    */
        OSMemFreeList = (OS_MEM *)OSMemFreeList->OSMemFreeList;
    }
    OS_EXIT_CRITICAL();
    if (pmem == (OS_MEM *)0) {                       /* See if we have a memory partition           */
        *err = OS_MEM_INVALID_PART;
        return ((OS_MEM *)0);
    }
    plink = (void **)addr;                           /* Create linked list of free memory blocks    */
    pblk  = (INT8U *)addr + blksize;
    for (i = 0; i < (nblks - 1); i++) {
        *plink = (void *)pblk;
        plink  = (void **)pblk;
        pblk   = pblk + blksize;
    }
    *plink = (void *)0;                              /* Last memory block points to NULL            */
    OS_ENTER_CRITICAL();
    pmem->OSMemAddr     = addr;                      /* Store start address of memory partition     */
    pmem->OSMemFreeList = addr;                      /* Initialize pointer to pool of free blocks   */
    pmem->OSMemNFree    = nblks;                     /* Store number of free blocks in MCB          */
    pmem->OSMemNBlks    = nblks;
    pmem->OSMemBlkSize  = blksize;                   /* Store block size of each memory blocks      */
    OS_EXIT_CRITICAL();
    *err    = OS_NO_ERR;
    return (pmem);
}
```

OS_MEM.C

```
/*
*********************************************************************************************
*                                    GET A MEMORY BLOCK
*
* Description : Get a memory block from a partition
*
* Arguments   : pmem    is a pointer to the memory partition control block
*
*               err     is a pointer to a variable containing an error message which will be set by this
*                       function to either:
*
*                       OS_NO_ERR          if the memory partition has been created correctly.
*                       OS_MEM_NO_FREE_BLKS if there are no more free memory blocks to allocate to caller
*
* Returns     : A pointer to a memory block if no error is detected
*               A pointer to NULL if an error is detected
*********************************************************************************************
*/

void *OSMemGet (OS_MEM *pmem, INT8U *err)
{
    void    *pblk;


    OS_ENTER_CRITICAL();
    if (pmem->OSMemNFree > 0) {                     /* See if there are any free memory blocks      */
        pblk            = pmem->OSMemFreeList;       /* Yes, point to next free memory block         */
        pmem->OSMemFreeList = *(void **)pblk;        /*      Adjust pointer to new free list         */
        pmem->OSMemNFree--;                          /*      One less memory block in this partition  */
        OS_EXIT_CRITICAL();
        *err = OS_NO_ERR;                            /*      No error                                */
        return (pblk);                               /*      Return memory block to caller           */
    } else {
        OS_EXIT_CRITICAL();
        *err = OS_MEM_NO_FREE_BLKS;                  /* No,  Notify caller of empty memory partition */
        return ((void *)0);                          /*      Return NULL pointer to caller           */
    }
}
```

B

```
/*
*********************************************************************************************
*                               INITIALIZE MEMORY PARTITION MANAGER
*
* Description : This function is called by uC/OS-II to initialize the memory partition manager.  Your
*               application MUST NOT call this function.
*
* Arguments   : none
*
* Returns     : none
*********************************************************************************************
*/

void OSMemInit (void)
{
    OS_MEM   *pmem;
    INT16U   i;


    pmem = (OS_MEM *)&OSMemTbl[0];                       /* Point to memory control block (MCB)        */
    for (i = 0; i < (OS_MAX_MEM_PART - 1); i++) {        /* Init. list of free memory partitions       */
        pmem->OSMemFreeList = (void *)&OSMemTbl[i+1];    /* Chain list of free partitions              */
        pmem->OSMemAddr     = (void *)0;                 /* Store start address of memory partition    */
        pmem->OSMemNFree    = 0;                         /* No free blocks                             */
        pmem->OSMemNBlks    = 0;                         /* No blocks                                  */
        pmem->OSMemBlkSize  = 0;                         /* Zero size                                  */
        pmem++;
    }
    OSMemTbl[OS_MAX_MEM_PART - 1].OSMemFreeList = (void *)0;
    OSMemFreeList                               = (OS_MEM *)&OSMemTbl[0];
}
```

```
/*
*********************************************************************************************************
*                                       RELEASE A MEMORY BLOCK
*
* Description : Returns a memory block to a partition
*
* Arguments   : pmem    is a pointer to the memory partition control block
*
*               pblk    is a pointer to the memory block being released.
*
* Returns     : OS_NO_ERR       if the memory block was inserted into the partition
*               OS_MEM_FULL     if you are returning a memory block to an already FULL memory partition
*                               (You freed more blocks than you allocated!)
*********************************************************************************************************
*/

INT8U OSMemPut (OS_MEM  *pmem, void *pblk)
{
    OS_ENTER_CRITICAL();
    if (pmem->OSMemNFree >= pmem->OSMemNBlks) {  /* Make sure all blocks not already returned     */
        OS_EXIT_CRITICAL();
        return (OS_MEM_FULL);
    }
    *(void **)pblk       = pmem->OSMemFreeList;  /* Insert released block into free block list     */
    pmem->OSMemFreeList = pblk;
    pmem->OSMemNFree++;                          /* One more memory block in this partition        */
    OS_EXIT_CRITICAL();
    return (OS_NO_ERR);                          /* Notify caller that memory block was released   */
}


/*
*********************************************************************************************************
*                                       QUERY MEMORY PARTITION
*
* Description : This function is used to determine the number of free memory blocks and the number of
*               used memory blocks from a memory partition.
*
* Arguments   : pmem    is a pointer to the memory partition control block
*
*               pdata   is a pointer to a structure that will contain information about the memory
*                       partition.
*
* Returns     : OS_NO_ERR       Always returns no error.
*********************************************************************************************************
*/

INT8U OSMemQuery (OS_MEM *pmem, OS_MEM_DATA *pdata)
{
    OS_ENTER_CRITICAL();
    pdata->OSAddr     = pmem->OSMemAddr;
    pdata->OSFreeList = pmem->OSMemFreeList;
    pdata->OSBlkSize  = pmem->OSMemBlkSize;
    pdata->OSNBlks    = pmem->OSMemNBlks;
    pdata->OSNFree    = pmem->OSMemNFree;
    OS_EXIT_CRITICAL();
    pdata->OSNUsed    = pdata->OSNBlks - pdata->OSNFree;
    return (OS_NO_ERR);
}
#endif
```

B

B.05 OS_Q.C

```
/*
*********************************************************************************************************
*                                            uC/OS-II
*                                      The Real-Time Kernel
*                                    MESSAGE QUEUE MANAGEMENT
*
*                        (c) Copyright 1992-1998, Jean J. Labrosse, Plantation, FL
*                                        All Rights Reserved
*
*                                            V2.00
*
* File : OS_Q.C
* By   : Jean J. Labrosse
*********************************************************************************************************
*/

#ifndef  OS_MASTER_FILE
#include "includes.h"
#endif

#if OS_Q_EN && (OS_MAX_QS >= 2)
/*
*********************************************************************************************************
*                                        LOCAL DATA TYPES
*********************************************************************************************************
*/

typedef struct os_q {                    /* QUEUE CONTROL BLOCK                                       */
    struct os_q   *OSQPtr;               /* Link to next queue control block in list of free blocks   */
    void        **OSQStart;              /* Pointer to start of queue data                            */
    void        **OSQEnd;                /* Pointer to end   of queue data                            */
    void        **OSQIn;                 /* Pointer to where next message will be inserted  in   the Q */
    void        **OSQOut;                /* Pointer to where next message will be extracted from the Q */
    INT16U        OSQSize;               /* Size of queue (maximum number of entries)                 */
    INT16U        OSQEntries;            /* Current number of entries in the queue                    */
} OS_Q;

/*
*********************************************************************************************************
*                                      LOCAL GLOBAL VARIABLES
*********************************************************************************************************
*/

static  OS_Q        *OSQFreeList;        /* Pointer to list of free QUEUE control blocks              */
static  OS_Q         OSQTbl[OS_MAX_QS];  /* Table of QUEUE control blocks                             */
```

```
/*
*********************************************************************************************
*                                  ACCEPT MESSAGE FROM QUEUE
*
* Description: This function checks the queue to see if a message is available.  Unlike OSQPend(),
*              OSQAccept() does not suspend the calling task if a message is not available.
*
* Arguments  : pevent          is a pointer to the event control block
*
* Returns    : != (void *)0    is the message in the queue if one is available.  The message is removed
*                              from the so the next time OSQAccept() is called, the queue will contain
*                              one less entry.
*              == (void *)0    if the queue is empty
*                              if you passed an invalid event type
*********************************************************************************************
*/

void *OSQAccept (OS_EVENT *pevent)
{
    void   *msg;
    OS_Q   *pq;


    OS_ENTER_CRITICAL();
    if (pevent->OSEventType != OS_EVENT_TYPE_Q) {        /* Validate event block type                  */
        OS_EXIT_CRITICAL();
        return ((void *)0);
    }
    pq = pevent->OSEventPtr;                             /* Point at queue control block               */
    if (pq->OSQEntries != 0) {                           /* See if any messages in the queue           */
        msg = *pq->OSQOut++;                             /* Yes, extract oldest message from the queue */
        pq->OSQEntries--;                                /* Update the number of entries in the queue  */
        if (pq->OSQOut == pq->OSQEnd) {                  /* Wrap OUT pointer if we are at the end of the queue */
            pq->OSQOut = pq->OSQStart;
        }
    } else {
        msg = (void *)0;                                 /* Queue is empty                             */
    }
    OS_EXIT_CRITICAL();
    return (msg);                                        /* Return message received (or NULL)          */
}
```

```
/*
*********************************************************************************************************
*                                    CREATE A MESSAGE QUEUE
*
* Description: This function creates a message queue if free event control blocks are available.
*
* Arguments  : start           is a pointer to the base address of the message queue storage area.  The
*                              storage area MUST be declared as an array of pointers to 'void' as follows
*
*                              void *MessageStorage[size]
*
*              size            is the number of elements in the storage area
*
* Returns    : != (void *)0  is a pointer to the event control clock (OS_EVENT) associated with the
*                              created queue
*              == (void *)0  if no event control blocks were available
*********************************************************************************************************
*/

OS_EVENT *OSQCreate (void **start, INT16U size)
{
    OS_EVENT *pevent;
    OS_Q     *pq;


    OS_ENTER_CRITICAL();
    pevent = OSEventFreeList;                        /* Get next free event control block             */
    if (OSEventFreeList != (OS_EVENT *)0) {          /* See if pool of free ECB pool was empty        */
        OSEventFreeList = (OS_EVENT *)OSEventFreeList->OSEventPtr;
    }
    OS_EXIT_CRITICAL();
    if (pevent != (OS_EVENT *)0) {                   /* See if we have an event control block         */
        OS_ENTER_CRITICAL();                         /* Get a free queue control block                */
        pq = OSQFreeList;
        if (OSQFreeList != (OS_Q *)0) {
            OSQFreeList = OSQFreeList->OSQPtr;
        }
        OS_EXIT_CRITICAL();
        if (pq != (OS_Q *)0) {                       /* See if we were able to get a queue control block */
            pq->OSQStart      = start;               /* Yes, initialize the queue                     */
            pq->OSQEnd        = &start[size];
            pq->OSQIn         = start;
            pq->OSQOut        = start;
            pq->OSQSize       = size;
            pq->OSQEntries    = 0;
            pevent->OSEventType = OS_EVENT_TYPE_Q;
            pevent->OSEventPtr  = pq;
            OSEventWaitListInit(pevent);
        } else {                                     /* No,  since we couldn't get a queue control block */
            OS_ENTER_CRITICAL();                     /* Return event control block on error           */
            pevent->OSEventPtr = (void *)OSEventFreeList;
            OSEventFreeList    = pevent;
            OS_EXIT_CRITICAL();
            pevent = (OS_EVENT *)0;
        }
    }
    return (pevent);
}
```

OS_Q.C

```
/*
*********************************************************************************************
*                                    FLUSH QUEUE
*
* Description : This function is used to flush the contents of the message queue.
*
* Arguments   : none
*
* Returns     : OS_NO_ERR          upon success
*               OS_ERR_EVENT_TYPE  If you didn't pass a pointer to a queue
*********************************************************************************************
*/

INT8U OSQFlush (OS_EVENT *pevent)
{
    OS_Q   *pq;


    OS_ENTER_CRITICAL();
    if (pevent->OSEventType != OS_EVENT_TYPE_Q) {      /* Validate event block type          */
        OS_EXIT_CRITICAL();
        return (OS_ERR_EVENT_TYPE);
    }
    pq              = pevent->OSEventPtr;              /* Point to queue storage structure   */
    pq->OSQIn       = pq->OSQStart;
    pq->OSQOut      = pq->OSQStart;
    pq->OSQEntries = 0;
    OS_EXIT_CRITICAL();
    return (OS_NO_ERR);
}


/*
*********************************************************************************************
*                                QUEUE MODULE INITIALIZATION
*
* Description : This function is called by uC/OS-II to initialize the message queue module.  Your
*               application MUST NOT call this function.
*
* Arguments   : none
*
* Returns     : none
*********************************************************************************************
*/

void OSQInit (void)
{
    INT16U i;


    for (i = 0; i < (OS_MAX_QS - 1); i++) {       /* Init. list of free QUEUE control blocks     */
        OSQTbl[i].OSQPtr = &OSQTbl[i+1];
    }
    OSQTbl[OS_MAX_QS - 1].OSQPtr = (OS_Q *)0;
    OSQFreeList                  = &OSQTbl[0];
}
```

B

OS_Q.C

```
/*
*********************************************************************************************
*                            PEND ON A QUEUE FOR A MESSAGE
*
* Description: This function waits for a message to be sent to a queue
*
* Arguments  : pevent       is a pointer to the event control block associated with the desired queue
*
*              timeout      is an optional timeout period (in clock ticks).  If non-zero, your task will
*                           wait for a message to arrive at the queue up to the amount of time
*                           specified by this argument.  If you specify 0, however, your task will wait
*                           forever at the specified queue or, until a message arrives.
*
*              err          is a pointer to where an error message will be deposited.  Possible error
*                           messages are:
*
*                           OS_NO_ERR         The call was successful and your task received a message.
*                           OS_TIMEOUT        A message was not received within the specified timeout
*                           OS_ERR_EVENT_TYPE You didn't pass a pointer to a queue
*                           OS_ERR_PEND_ISR   If you called this function from an ISR and the result
*                                             would lead to a suspension.
*
* Returns    : != (void *)0  is a pointer to the message received
*              == (void *)0  if no message was received or you didn't pass a pointer to a queue.
*********************************************************************************************
*/
```

OS_Q.C

```
void *OSQPend (OS_EVENT *pevent, INT16U timeout, INT8U *err)
{
    void   *msg;
    OS_Q   *pq;


    OS_ENTER_CRITICAL();
    if (pevent->OSEventType != OS_EVENT_TYPE_Q) {/* Validate event block type                */
        OS_EXIT_CRITICAL();
        *err = OS_ERR_EVENT_TYPE;
        return ((void *)0);
    }
    pq = pevent->OSEventPtr;                      /* Point at queue control block             */
    if (pq->OSQEntries != 0) {                    /* See if any messages in the queue         */
        msg = *pq->OSQOut++;                       /* Yes, extract oldest message from the queue */
        pq->OSQEntries--;                         /* Update the number of entries in the queue */
        if (pq->OSQOut == pq->OSQEnd) {           /* Wrap OUT pointer if we are at the end of the queue */
            pq->OSQOut = pq->OSQStart;
        }
        OS_EXIT_CRITICAL();
        *err = OS_NO_ERR;
    } else if (OSIntNesting > 0) {                /* See if called from ISR ...               */
        OS_EXIT_CRITICAL();                       /* ... can't PEND from an ISR               */
        *err = OS_ERR_PEND_ISR;
    } else {
        OSTCBCur->OSTCBStat    |= OS_STAT_Q;      /* Task will have to pend for a message to be posted */
        OSTCBCur->OSTCBDly     = timeout;         /* Load timeout into TCB                     */
        OSEventTaskWait(pevent);                  /* Suspend task until event or timeout occurs */
        OS_EXIT_CRITICAL();
        OSSched();                                /* Find next highest priority task ready to run */
        OS_ENTER_CRITICAL();
        if ((msg = OSTCBCur->OSTCBMsg) != (void *)0) {/* Did we get a message?                */
            OSTCBCur->OSTCBMsg     = (void *)0;       /* Extract message from TCB (Put there by QPost) */
            OSTCBCur->OSTCBStat    = OS_STAT_RDY;
            OSTCBCur->OSTCBEventPtr = (OS_EVENT *)0;  /* No longer waiting for event          */
            OS_EXIT_CRITICAL();
            *err                   = OS_NO_ERR;
        } else if (OSTCBCur->OSTCBStat & OS_STAT_Q) { /* Timed out if status indicates pending on Q */
            OSEventTO(pevent);
            OS_EXIT_CRITICAL();
            msg                    = (void *)0;       /* No message received                  */
            *err                   = OS_TIMEOUT;      /* Indicate a timeout occured           */
        } else {
            msg = *pq->OSQOut++;                      /* Extract message from queue           */
            pq->OSQEntries--;                         /* Update the number of entries in the queue */
            if (pq->OSQOut == pq->OSQEnd) {           /* Wrap OUT pointer if we are at the end of Q */
                pq->OSQOut = pq->OSQStart;
            }
            OSTCBCur->OSTCBEventPtr = (OS_EVENT *)0;
            OS_EXIT_CRITICAL();
            *err = OS_NO_ERR;
        }
    }
    return (msg);                                 /* Return message received (or NULL)        */
}
```

B

OS_Q.C

```
/*
*********************************************************************************************
*                                  POST MESSAGE TO A QUEUE
*
* Description: This function sends a message to a queue
*
* Arguments   : pevent       is a pointer to the event control block associated with the desired queue
*
*               msg          is a pointer to the message to send.  You MUST NOT send a NULL pointer.
*
* Returns     : OS_NO_ERR          The call was successful and the message was sent
*               OS_Q_FULL          If the queue cannot accept any more messages because it is full.
*               OS_ERR_EVENT_TYPE  If you didn't pass a pointer to a queue.
*********************************************************************************************
*/

INT8U OSQPost (OS_EVENT *pevent, void *msg)
{
    OS_Q    *pq;


    OS_ENTER_CRITICAL();
    if (pevent->OSEventType != OS_EVENT_TYPE_Q) {   /* Validate event block type              */
        OS_EXIT_CRITICAL();
        return (OS_ERR_EVENT_TYPE);
    }
    if (pevent->OSEventGrp) {                        /* See if any task pending on queue       */
        OSEventTaskRdy(pevent, msg, OS_STAT_Q);     /* Ready highest priority task waiting on event */
        OS_EXIT_CRITICAL();
        OSSched();                                  /* Find highest priority task ready to run */
        return (OS_NO_ERR);
    } else {
        pq = pevent->OSEventPtr;                     /* Point to queue control block           */
        if (pq->OSQEntries >= pq->OSQSize) {         /* Make sure queue is not full            */
            OS_EXIT_CRITICAL();
            return (OS_Q_FULL);
        } else {
            *pq->OSQIn++ = msg;                      /* Insert message into queue              */
            pq->OSQEntries++;                        /* Update the nbr of entries in the queue */
            if (pq->OSQIn == pq->OSQEnd) {           /* Wrap IN ptr if we are at end of queue  */
                pq->OSQIn = pq->OSQStart;
            }
            OS_EXIT_CRITICAL();
        }
        return (OS_NO_ERR);
    }
}
```

```
/*
*********************************************************************************************
*                            POST MESSAGE TO THE FRONT OF A QUEUE
*
* Description: This function sends a message to a queue but unlike OSQPost(), the message is posted at
*              the front instead of the end of the queue.  Using OSQPostFront() allows you to send
*              'priority' messages.
*
* Arguments   : pevent         is a pointer to the event control block associated with the desired queue
*
*               msg            is a pointer to the message to send.  You MUST NOT send a NULL pointer.
*
* Returns     : OS_NO_ERR         The call was successful and the message was sent
*               OS_Q_FULL         If the queue cannot accept any more messages because it is full.
*               OS_ERR_EVENT_TYPE If you didn't pass a pointer to a queue.
*********************************************************************************************
*/

INT8U OSQPostFront (OS_EVENT *pevent, void *msg)
{
    OS_Q    *pq;


    OS_ENTER_CRITICAL();
    if (pevent->OSEventType != OS_EVENT_TYPE_Q) {       /* Validate event block type                 */
        OS_EXIT_CRITICAL();
        return (OS_ERR_EVENT_TYPE);
    }
    if (pevent->OSEventGrp) {                            /* See if any task pending on queue          */
        OSEventTaskRdy(pevent, msg, OS_STAT_Q);         /* Ready highest priority task waiting on event */
        OS_EXIT_CRITICAL();
        OSSched();                                       /* Find highest priority task ready to run   */
        return (OS_NO_ERR);
    } else {
        pq = pevent->OSEventPtr;                         /* Point to queue control block              */
        if (pq->OSQEntries >= pq->OSQSize) {            /* Make sure queue is not full               */
            OS_EXIT_CRITICAL();
            return (OS_Q_FULL);
        } else {
            if (pq->OSQOut == pq->OSQStart) {           /* Wrap OUT ptr if we are at the 1st queue entry */
                pq->OSQOut = pq->OSQEnd;
            }
            pq->OSQOut--;
            *pq->OSQOut = msg;                           /* Insert message into queue                 */
            pq->OSQEntries++;                            /* Update the nbr of entries in the queue    */
            OS_EXIT_CRITICAL();
        }
        return (OS_NO_ERR);
    }
}
```

B

```
/*
*********************************************************************************************
*                                   QUERY A MESSAGE QUEUE
*
* Description: This function obtains information about a message queue.
*
* Arguments  : pevent        is a pointer to the event control block associated with the desired mailbox
*
*              pdata         is a pointer to a structure that will contain information about the message
*                            queue.
*
* Returns    : OS_NO_ERR        The call was successful and the message was sent
*              OS_ERR_EVENT_TYPE  If you are attempting to obtain data from a non queue.
*********************************************************************************************
*/

INT8U OSQQuery (OS_EVENT *pevent, OS_Q_DATA *pdata)
{
    OS_Q    *pq;
    INT8U   i;
    INT8U   *psrc;
    INT8U   *pdest;


    OS_ENTER_CRITICAL();
    if (pevent->OSEventType != OS_EVENT_TYPE_Q) {        /* Validate event block type            */
        OS_EXIT_CRITICAL();
        return (OS_ERR_EVENT_TYPE);
    }
    pdata->OSEventGrp = pevent->OSEventGrp;              /* Copy message mailbox wait list       */
    psrc            = &pevent->OSEventTbl[0];
    pdest           = &pdata->OSEventTbl[0];
    for (i = 0; i < OS_EVENT_TBL_SIZE; i++) {
        *pdest++ = *psrc++;
    }
    pq = (OS_Q *)pevent->OSEventPtr;
    if (pq->OSQEntries > 0) {
        pdata->OSMsg = pq->OSQOut;                       /* Get next message to return if available  */
    } else {
        pdata->OSMsg = (void *)0;
    }
    pdata->OSNMsgs = pq->OSQEntries;
    pdata->OSQSize = pq->OSQSize;
    OS_EXIT_CRITICAL();
    return (OS_NO_ERR);
}
#endif
```

B.06 OS_SEM.C

```
/*
*********************************************************************************************
*                                        uC/OS-II
*                                   The Real-Time Kernel
*                                   SEMAPHORE MANAGEMENT
*
*                     (c) Copyright 1992-1998, Jean J. Labrosse, Plantation, FL
*                                      All Rights Reserved
*
*                                          V2.00
*
* File : OS_SEM.C
* By   : Jean J. Labrosse
*********************************************************************************************
*/

#ifndef  OS_MASTER_FILE
#include "includes.h"
#endif

#if OS_SEM_EN
/*
*********************************************************************************************
*                                     ACCEPT SEMAPHORE
*
* Description: This function checks the semaphore to see if a resource is available or, if an event
*              occurred.  Unlike OSSemPend(), OSSemAccept() does not suspend the calling task if the
*              resource is not available or the event did not occur.
*
* Arguments  : pevent      is a pointer to the event control block
*
* Returns    : >  0        if the resource is available or the event did not occur the semaphore is
*                          decremented to obtain the resource.
*              == 0        if the resource is not available or the event did not occur or,
*                          you didn't pass a pointer to a semaphore
*********************************************************************************************
*/

INT16U OSSemAccept (OS_EVENT *pevent)
{
    INT16U cnt;


    OS_ENTER_CRITICAL();
    if (pevent->OSEventType != OS_EVENT_TYPE_SEM) {    /* Validate event block type              */
        OS_EXIT_CRITICAL();
        return (0);
    }
    cnt = pevent->OSEventCnt;
    if (cnt > 0) {                                     /* See if resource is available           */
        pevent->OSEventCnt--;                          /* Yes, decrement semaphore and notify caller  */
    }
    OS_EXIT_CRITICAL();
    return (cnt);                                      /* Return semaphore count                 */
}
```

```
/*
*********************************************************************************************
*                                   CREATE A SEMAPHORE
*
* Description: This function creates a semaphore.
*
* Arguments  : cnt           is the initial value for the semaphore.  If the value is 0, no resource is
*                            available (or no event has occurred).  You initialize the semaphore to a
*                            non-zero value to specify how many resources are available (e.g. if you have
*                            10 resources, you would initialize the semaphore to 10).
*
* Returns    : != (void *)0  is a pointer to the event control clock (OS_EVENT) associated with the
*                            created semaphore
*             == (void *)0   if no event control blocks were available
*********************************************************************************************
*/

OS_EVENT *OSSemCreate (INT16U cnt)
{
    OS_EVENT *pevent;


    OS_ENTER_CRITICAL();
    pevent = OSEventFreeList;                               /* Get next free event control block        */
    if (OSEventFreeList != (OS_EVENT *)0) {                 /* See if pool of free ECB pool was empty   */
        OSEventFreeList = (OS_EVENT *)OSEventFreeList->OSEventPtr;
    }
    OS_EXIT_CRITICAL();
    if (pevent != (OS_EVENT *)0) {                          /* Get an event control block               */
        pevent->OSEventType = OS_EVENT_TYPE_SEM;
        pevent->OSEventCnt  = cnt;                          /* Set semaphore value                      */
        OSEventWaitListInit(pevent);
    }
    return (pevent);
}
```

```
/*
*********************************************************************************************
*                                  PEND ON SEMAPHORE
*
* Description: This function waits for a semaphore.
*
* Arguments  : pevent        is a pointer to the event control block associated with the desired
*                            semaphore.
*
*              timeout       is an optional timeout period (in clock ticks).  If non-zero, your task will
*                            wait for the resource up to the amount of time specified by this argument.
*                            If you specify 0, however, your task will wait forever at the specified
*                            semaphore or, until the resource becomes available (or the event occurs).
*
*              err           is a pointer to where an error message will be deposited.  Possible error
*                            messages are:
*
*                            OS_NO_ERR          The call was successful and your task owns the resource
*                                               or, the event you are waiting for occurred.
*                            OS_TIMEOUT         The semaphore was not received within the specified
*                                               timeout.
*                            OS_ERR_EVENT_TYPE  If you didn't pass a pointer to a semaphore.
*                            OS_ERR_PEND_ISR    If you called this function from an ISR and the result
*                                               would lead to a suspension.
*
* Returns    : none
*********************************************************************************************
*/

void OSSemPend (OS_EVENT *pevent, INT16U timeout, INT8U *err)
{
    OS_ENTER_CRITICAL();
    if (pevent->OSEventType != OS_EVENT_TYPE_SEM) {   /* Validate event block type                 */
        OS_EXIT_CRITICAL();
        *err = OS_ERR_EVENT_TYPE;
    }
    if (pevent->OSEventCnt > 0) {                     /* If sem. is positive, resource available ... */
        pevent->OSEventCnt--;                         /* ... decrement semaphore only if positive.   */
        OS_EXIT_CRITICAL();
        *err = OS_NO_ERR;
    } else if (OSIntNesting > 0) {                    /* See if called from ISR ...                */
        OS_EXIT_CRITICAL();                           /* ... can't PEND from an ISR                */
        *err = OS_ERR_PEND_ISR;
    } else {                                          /* Otherwise, must wait until event occurs   */
        OSTCBCur->OSTCBStat   |= OS_STAT_SEM;         /* Resource not available, pend on semaphore */
        OSTCBCur->OSTCBDly    = timeout;              /* Store pend timeout in TCB                 */
        OSEventTaskWait(pevent);                      /* Suspend task until event or timeout occurs */
        OS_EXIT_CRITICAL();
        OSSched();                                    /* Find next highest priority task ready     */
        OS_ENTER_CRITICAL();
        if (OSTCBCur->OSTCBStat & OS_STAT_SEM) {      /* Must have timed out if still waiting for event*/
            OSEventTO(pevent);
            OS_EXIT_CRITICAL();
            *err = OS_TIMEOUT;                        /* Indicate that didn't get event within TO  */
        } else {
            OSTCBCur->OSTCBEventPtr = (OS_EVENT *)0;
            OS_EXIT_CRITICAL();
            *err = OS_NO_ERR;
        }
    }
}
```

B

```
/*
*********************************************************************************************
*                                   POST TO A SEMAPHORE
*
* Description: This function signals a semaphore
*
* Arguments   : pevent        is a pointer to the event control block associated with the desired
*                             semaphore.
*
* Returns     : OS_NO_ERR       The call was successful and the semaphore was signaled.
*               OS_SEM_OVF      If the semaphore count exceeded its limit.  In other words, you have
*                               signalled the semaphore more often than you waited on it with either
*                               OSSemAccept() or OSSemPend().
*               OS_ERR_EVENT_TYPE If you didn't pass a pointer to a semaphore
*********************************************************************************************
*/

INT8U OSSemPost (OS_EVENT *pevent)
{
    OS_ENTER_CRITICAL();
    if (pevent->OSEventType != OS_EVENT_TYPE_SEM) {          /* Validate event block type         */
        OS_EXIT_CRITICAL();
        return (OS_ERR_EVENT_TYPE);
    }
    if (pevent->OSEventGrp) {                                /* See if any task waiting for semaphore */
        OSEventTaskRdy(pevent, (void *)0, OS_STAT_SEM);      /* Ready highest prio task waiting on event */
        OS_EXIT_CRITICAL();
        OSSched();                                           /* Find highest priority task ready to run */
        return (OS_NO_ERR);
    } else {
        if (pevent->OSEventCnt < 65535) {                    /* Make sure semaphore will not overflow */
            pevent->OSEventCnt++;                            /* Increment semaphore count to register event */
            OS_EXIT_CRITICAL();
            return (OS_NO_ERR);
        } else {                                             /* Semaphore value has reached its maximum */
            OS_EXIT_CRITICAL();
            return (OS_SEM_OVF);
        }
    }
}
```

```
/*
*********************************************************************************************
*                                  QUERY A SEMAPHORE
*
* Description: This function obtains information about a semaphore
*
* Arguments  : pevent        is a pointer to the event control block associated with the desired
*                            semaphore
*
*              pdata         is a pointer to a structure that will contain information about the
*                            semaphore.
*
* Returns    : OS_NO_ERR         The call was successful and the message was sent
*              OS_ERR_EVENT_TYPE If you are attempting to obtain data from a non semaphore.
*********************************************************************************************
*/

INT8U OSSemQuery (OS_EVENT *pevent, OS_SEM_DATA *pdata)
{
    INT8U  i;
    INT8U *psrc;
    INT8U *pdest;


    OS_ENTER_CRITICAL();
    if (pevent->OSEventType != OS_EVENT_TYPE_SEM) {           /* Validate event block type        */
        OS_EXIT_CRITICAL();
        return (OS_ERR_EVENT_TYPE);
    }
    pdata->OSEventGrp = pevent->OSEventGrp;                   /* Copy message mailbox wait list   */
    psrc              = &pevent->OSEventTbl[0];
    pdest             = &pdata->OSEventTbl[0];
    for (i = 0; i < OS_EVENT_TBL_SIZE; i++) {
        *pdest++ = *psrc++;
    }
    pdata->OSCnt      = pevent->OSEventCnt;                   /* Get semaphore count              */
    OS_EXIT_CRITICAL();
    return (OS_NO_ERR);
}
#endif
```

B

B.07 OS_TASK.C

```
/*
*********************************************************************************************************
*                                           uC/OS-II
*                                      The Real-Time Kernel
*                                      TASK MANAGEMENT
*
*                          (c) Copyright 1992-1998, Jean J. Labrosse, Plantation, FL
*                                       All Rights Reserved
*
*                                           V2.00
*
* File : OS_TASK.C
* By   : Jean J. Labrosse
*********************************************************************************************************
*/

#ifndef  OS_MASTER_FILE
#include "includes.h"
#endif

/*
*********************************************************************************************************
*                                    LOCAL FUNCTION PROTOTYPES
*********************************************************************************************************
*/


static  void  OSDummy(void);

/*
*********************************************************************************************************
*                                       DUMMY FUNCTION
*
* Description: This function doesn't do anything.  It is called by OSTaskDel() to ensure that interrupts
*              are disabled immediately after they are enabled.
*
* Arguments  : none
*
* Returns    : none
*********************************************************************************************************
*/

static void  OSDummy (void)
{
}
```

```
/*
*********************************************************************************************
*                             CHANGE PRIORITY OF A TASK
*
* Description: This function allows you to change the priority of a task dynamically.  Note that the new
*              priority MUST be available.
*
* Arguments  : oldp      is the old priority
*
*              newp      is the new priority
*
* Returns    : OS_NO_ERR       is the call was successful
*              OS_PRIO_INVALID if the priority you specify is higher that the maximum allowed
*                              (i.e. >= OS_LOWEST_PRIO)
*              OS_PRIO_EXIST   if the new priority already exist.
*              OS_PRIO_ERR     there is no task with the specified OLD priority (i.e. the OLD task does
*                              not exist.
*********************************************************************************************
*/
```

B

```
#if OS_TASK_CHANGE_PRIO_EN
INT8U OSTaskChangePrio (INT8U oldprio, INT8U newprio)
{
    OS_TCB   *ptcb;
    OS_EVENT *pevent;
    INT8U    x;
    INT8U    y;
    INT8U    bitx;
    INT8U    bity;


    if ((oldprio >= OS_LOWEST_PRIO && oldprio != OS_PRIO_SELF)  ||
         newprio >= OS_LOWEST_PRIO) {
        return (OS_PRIO_INVALID);
    }
    OS_ENTER_CRITICAL();
    if (OSTCBPrioTbl[newprio] != (OS_TCB *)0) {                 /* New priority must not already exist */
        OS_EXIT_CRITICAL();
        return (OS_PRIO_EXIST);
    } else {
        OSTCBPrioTbl[newprio] = (OS_TCB *)1;                   /* Reserve the entry to prevent others */
        OS_EXIT_CRITICAL();
        y    = newprio >> 3;                                   /* Precompute to reduce INT. latency   */
        bity = OSMapTbl[y];
        x    = newprio & 0x07;
        bitx = OSMapTbl[x];
        OS_ENTER_CRITICAL();
        if (oldprio == OS_PRIO_SELF) {                         /* See if changing self               */
            oldprio = OSTCBCur->OSTCBPrio;                     /* Yes, get priority                  */
        }
        if ((ptcb = OSTCBPrioTbl[oldprio]) != (OS_TCB *)0) {   /* Task to change must exist          */
            OSTCBPrioTbl[oldprio] = (OS_TCB *)0;               /* Remove TCB from old priority       */
            if (OSRdyTbl[ptcb->OSTCBY] & ptcb->OSTCBBitX) {    /* If task is ready make it not ready */
                if ((OSRdyTbl[ptcb->OSTCBY] &= ~ptcb->OSTCBBitX) == 0) {
                    OSRdyGrp &= ~ptcb->OSTCBBitY;
                }
                OSRdyGrp    |= bity;                           /* Make new priority ready to run     */
                OSRdyTbl[y] |= bitx;
            } else {
                if ((pevent = ptcb->OSTCBEventPtr) != (OS_EVENT *)0) { /* Remove from event wait list */
                    if ((pevent->OSEventTbl[ptcb->OSTCBY] &= ~ptcb->OSTCBBitX) == 0) {
                        pevent->OSEventGrp &= ~ptcb->OSTCBBitY;
                    }
                    pevent->OSEventGrp    |= bity;             /* Add new priority to wait list      */
                    pevent->OSEventTbl[y] |= bitx;
                }
            }
            OSTCBPrioTbl[newprio] = ptcb;                      /* Place pointer to TCB @ new priority */
            ptcb->OSTCBPrio       = newprio;                   /* Set new task priority              */
            ptcb->OSTCBY          = y;
            ptcb->OSTCBX          = x;
            ptcb->OSTCBBitY       = bity;
            ptcb->OSTCBBitX       = bitx;
            OS_EXIT_CRITICAL();
            OSSched();                                         /* Run highest priority task ready    */
            return (OS_NO_ERR);
        } else {
            OSTCBPrioTbl[newprio] = (OS_TCB *)0;               /* Reserve Release the reserved prio. */
            OS_EXIT_CRITICAL();
            return (OS_PRIO_ERR);                              /* Task to change didn't exist        */
        }
    }
}
#endif
```

OS_TASK.C

```
/*
*********************************************************************************************
*                                    CREATE A TASK
*
* Description: This function is used to have uC/OS-II manage the execution of a task.  Tasks can either
*              be created prior to the start of multitasking or by a running task.  A task cannot be
*              created by an ISR.
*
* Arguments  : task      is a pointer to the task's code
*
*              pdata     is a pointer to an optional data area which can be used to pass parameters to
*                        the task when the task first executes.  Where the task is concerned it thinks
*                        it was invoked and passed the argument 'pdata' as follows:
*
*                            void Task (void *pdata)
*                            {
*                                for (;;) {
*                                    Task code;
*                                }
*                            }
*
*              ptos      is a pointer to the task's top of stack.  If the configuration constant
*                        OS_STK_GROWTH is set to 1, the stack is assumed to grow downward (i.e. from high
*                        memory to low memory).  'pstk' will thus point to the highest (valid) memory
*                        location of the stack.  If OS_STK_GROWTH is set to 0, 'pstk' will point to the
*                        lowest memory location of the stack and the stack will grow with increasing
*                        memory locations.
*
*              prio      is the task's priority.  A unique priority MUST be assigned to each task and the
*                        lower the number, the higher the priority.
*
* Returns    : OS_NO_ERR       if the function was successful.
*              OS_PRIO_EXIT    if the task priority already exist
*                              (each task MUST have a unique priority).
*              OS_PRIO_INVALID if the priority you specify is higher that the maximum allowed
*                              (i.e. >= OS_LOWEST_PRIO)
*********************************************************************************************
*/
```

B

```
#if OS_TASK_CREATE_EN
INT8U OSTaskCreate (void (*task)(void *pd), void *pdata, OS_STK *ptos, INT8U prio)
{
    void    *psp;
    INT8U   err;


    if (prio > OS_LOWEST_PRIO) {                   /* Make sure priority is within allowable range        */
        return (OS_PRIO_INVALID);
    }
    OS_ENTER_CRITICAL();
    if (OSTCBPrioTbl[prio] == (OS_TCB *)0) { /* Make sure task doesn't already exist at this priority */
        OSTCBPrioTbl[prio] = (OS_TCB *)1;     /* Reserve the priority to prevent others from doing ... */
                                               /* ... the same thing until task is created.            */
        OS_EXIT_CRITICAL();
        psp = (void *)OSTaskStkInit(task, pdata, ptos, 0); /* Initialize the task's stack              */
        err = OSTCBInit(prio, psp, (void *)0, 0, 0, (void *)0, 0);
        if (err == OS_NO_ERR) {
            OS_ENTER_CRITICAL();
            OSTaskCtr++;                                   /* Increment the #tasks counter             */
            OSTaskCreateHook(OSTCBPrioTbl[prio]);          /* Call user defined hook                   */
            OS_EXIT_CRITICAL();
            if (OSRunning) {                    /* Find highest priority task if multitasking has started */
                OSSched();
            }
        } else {
            OS_ENTER_CRITICAL();
            OSTCBPrioTbl[prio] = (OS_TCB *)0;/* Make this priority available to others              */
            OS_EXIT_CRITICAL();
        }
        return (err);
    } else {
        OS_EXIT_CRITICAL();
        return (OS_PRIO_EXIST);
    }
}
#endif
```

OS_TASK.C

```
/*
*********************************************************************************************
*                              CREATE A TASK (Extended Version)
*
* Description: This function is used to have uC/OS-II manage the execution of a task.  Tasks can either
*              be created prior to the start of multitasking or by a running task.  A task cannot be
*              created by an ISR.  This function is similar to OSTaskCreate() except that it allows
*              additional information about a task to be specified.
*
* Arguments  : task       is a pointer to the task's code
*
*              pdata      is a pointer to an optional data area which can be used to pass parameters to
*                         the task when the task first executes.  Where the task is concerned it thinks
*                         it was invoked and passed the argument 'pdata' as follows:
*
*                             void Task (void *pdata)
*                             {
*                                 for (;;) {
*                                     Task code;
*                                 }
*                             }
*
*              ptos       is a pointer to the task's top of stack.  If the configuration constant
*                         OS_STK_GROWTH is set to 1, the stack is assumed to grow downward (i.e. from high
*                         memory to low memory).  'pstk' will thus point to the highest (valid) memory
*                         location of the stack.  If OS_STK_GROWTH is set to 0, 'pstk' will point to the
*                         lowest memory location of the stack and the stack will grow with increasing
*                         memory locations.  'pstk' MUST point to a valid 'free' data item.
*
*              prio       is the task's priority.  A unique priority MUST be assigned to each task and the
*                         lower the number, the higher the priority.
*
*              id         is the task's ID (0..65535)
*
*              pbos       is a pointer to the task's bottom of stack.  If the configuration constant
*                         OS_STK_GROWTH is set to 1, the stack is assumed to grow downward (i.e. from high
*                         memory to low memory).  'pbos' will thus point to the LOWEST (valid) memory
*                         location of the stack.  If OS_STK_GROWTH is set to 0, 'pbos' will point to the
*                         HIGHEST memory location of the stack and the stack will grow with increasing
*                         memory locations.  'pbos' MUST point to a valid 'free' data item.
*
*              stk_size   is the size of the stack in number of elements.  If OS_STK is set to INT8U,
*                         'stk_size' corresponds to the number of bytes available.  If OS_STK is set to
*                         INT16U, 'stk_size' contains the number of 16-bit entries available.  Finally, if
*                         OS_STK is set to INT32U, 'stk_size' contains the number of 32-bit entries
*                         available on the stack.
*
*              pext       is a pointer to a user supplied memory location which is used as a TCB extension.
*                         For example, this user memory can hold the contents of floating-point registers
*                         during a context switch, the time each task takes to execute, the number of times
*                         the task has been switched-in, etc.
*
*              opt        contains additional information (or options) about the behavior of the task.  The
*                         LOWER 8-bits are reserved by uC/OS-II while the upper 8 bits can be application
*                         specific.  See OS_TASK_OPT_??? in uCOS-II.H.
*
* Returns    : OS_NO_ERR       if the function was successful.
*              OS_PRIO_EXIT    if the task priority already exist
*                              (each task MUST have a unique priority).
*              OS_PRIO_INVALID if the priority you specify is higher that the maximum allowed
*                              (i.e. > OS_LOWEST_PRIO)
*********************************************************************************************
*/
```

B

OS_TASK.C

```c
#if   OS_TASK_CREATE_EXT_EN
INT8U OSTaskCreateExt (void    (*task)(void *pd),
                       void    *pdata,
                       OS_STK  *ptos,
                       INT8U   prio,
                       INT16U  id,
                       OS_STK  *pbos,
                       INT32U  stk_size,
                       void    *pext,
                       INT16U  opt)
{
    void    *psp;
    INT8U   err;
    INT16U  i;
    OS_STK  *pfill;


    if (prio > OS_LOWEST_PRIO) {                /* Make sure priority is within allowable range    */
        return (OS_PRIO_INVALID);
    }
    OS_ENTER_CRITICAL();
    if (OSTCBPrioTbl[prio] == (OS_TCB *)0) { /* Make sure task doesn't already exist at this priority */
        OSTCBPrioTbl[prio] = (OS_TCB *)1;    /* Reserve the priority to prevent others from doing ... */
                                             /* ... the same thing until task is created.        */
        OS_EXIT_CRITICAL();

        if (opt & OS_TASK_OPT_STK_CHK) {     /* See if stack checking has been enabled           */
            if (opt & OS_TASK_OPT_STK_CLR) { /* See if stack needs to be cleared                 */
                pfill = pbos;                /* Yes, fill the stack with zeros                   */
                for (i = 0; i < stk_size; i++) {
                    #if OS_STK_GROWTH == 1
                    *pfill++ = (OS_STK)0;
                    #else
                    *pfill-- = (OS_STK)0;
                    #endif
                }
            }
        }

        psp = (void *)OSTaskStkInit(task, pdata, ptos, opt); /* Initialize the task's stack      */
        err = OSTCBInit(prio, psp, pbos, id, stk_size, pext, opt);
        if (err == OS_NO_ERR) {
            OS_ENTER_CRITICAL();
            OSTaskCtr++;                                /* Increment the #tasks counter          */
            OSTaskCreateHook(OSTCBPrioTbl[prio]);       /* Call user defined hook                */
            OS_EXIT_CRITICAL();
            if (OSRunning) {                /* Find highest priority task if multitasking has started */
                OSSched();
            }
        } else {
            OS_ENTER_CRITICAL();
            OSTCBPrioTbl[prio] = (OS_TCB *)0;/* Make this priority available to others            */
            OS_EXIT_CRITICAL();
        }
        return (err);
    } else {
        OS_EXIT_CRITICAL();
        return (OS_PRIO_EXIST);
    }
}
#endif
```

OS_TASK.C

B

```
/*
*********************************************************************************************
*                                   DELETE A TASK
*
* Description: This function allows you to delete a task.  The calling task can delete itself by
*              its own priority number.  The deleted task is returned to the dormant state and can be
*              re-activated by creating the deleted task again.
*
* Arguments  : prio    is the priority of the task to delete.  Note that you can explicitly delete
*                      the current task without knowing its priority level by setting 'prio' to
*                      OS_PRIO_SELF.
*
* Returns    : OS_NO_ERR           if the call is successful
*              OS_TASK_DEL_IDLE    if you attempted to delete uC/OS-II's idle task
*              OS_PRIO_INVALID     if the priority you specify is higher that the maximum allowed
*                                  (i.e. >= OS_LOWEST_PRIO) or, you have not specified OS_PRIO_SELF.
*              OS_TASK_DEL_ERR     if the task you want to delete does not exist
*              OS_TASK_DEL_ISR     if you tried to delete a task from an ISR
*
* Notes      : 1) To reduce interrupt latency, OSTaskDel() 'disables' the task:
*                    a) by making it not ready
*                    b) by removing it from any wait lists
*                    c) by preventing OSTimeTick() from making the task ready to run.
*                 The task can then be 'unlinked' from the miscellaneous structures in uC/OS-II.
*              2) The function OSDummy() is called after OS_EXIT_CRITICAL() because, on most processors,
*                 the next instruction following the enable interrupt instruction is ignored.  You can
*                 replace OSDummy() with a macro that basically executes a NO OP (i.e. OS_NOP()).  The
*                 NO OP macro would avoid the execution time of the function call and return.
*              3) An ISR cannot delete a task.
*              4) The lock nesting counter is incremented because, for a brief instant, if the current
*                 task is being deleted, the current task would not be able to be rescheduled because it
*                 is removed from the ready list.  Incrementing the nesting counter prevents another task
*                 from being schedule.  This means that the ISR would return to the current task which is
*                 being deleted.  The rest of the deletion would thus be able to be completed.
*********************************************************************************************
*/
```

OS_TASK.C

```
#if OS_TASK_DEL_EN
INT8U OSTaskDel (INT8U prio)
{
    OS_TCB   *ptcb;
    OS_EVENT *pevent;


    if (prio == OS_IDLE_PRIO) {                              /* Not allowed to delete idle task    */
        return (OS_TASK_DEL_IDLE);
    }
    if (prio >= OS_LOWEST_PRIO && prio != OS_PRIO_SELF) {    /* Task priority valid ?              */
        return (OS_PRIO_INVALID);
    }
    OS_ENTER_CRITICAL();
    if (OSIntNesting > 0) {                                  /* See if trying to delete from ISR   */
        OS_EXIT_CRITICAL();
        return (OS_TASK_DEL_ISR);
    }
    if (prio == OS_PRIO_SELF) {                              /* See if requesting to delete self   */
        prio = OSTCBCur->OSTCBPrio;                          /* Set priority to delete to current  */
    }
    if ((ptcb = OSTCBPrioTbl[prio]) != (OS_TCB *)0) {        /* Task to delete must exist          */
        if ((OSRdyTbl[ptcb->OSTCBY] &= ~ptcb->OSTCBBitX) == 0) {/* Make task not ready            */
            OSRdyGrp &= ~ptcb->OSTCBBitY;
        }
        if ((pevent = ptcb->OSTCBEventPtr) != (OS_EVENT *)0) {  /* If task is waiting on event     */
            if ((pevent->OSEventTbl[ptcb->OSTCBY] &= ~ptcb->OSTCBBitX) == 0) { /* ... remove task from */
                pevent->OSEventGrp &= ~ptcb->OSTCBBitY;                        /* ... event ctrl block */
            }
        }
        ptcb->OSTCBDly  = 0;                                 /* Prevent OSTimeTick() from updating */
        ptcb->OSTCBStat = OS_STAT_RDY;                       /* Prevent task from being resumed    */
        OSLockNesting++;
        OS_EXIT_CRITICAL();                                 /* Enabling INT. ignores next instruc. */
        OSDummy();                                          /* ... Dummy ensures that INTs will be */
        OS_ENTER_CRITICAL();                                /* ... disabled HERE!                 */
        OSLockNesting--;
        OSTaskDelHook(ptcb);                                /* Call user defined hook             */
        OSTaskCtr--;                                        /* One less task being managed        */
        OSTCBPrioTbl[prio] = (OS_TCB *)0;                   /* Clear old priority entry           */
        if (ptcb->OSTCBPrev == (OS_TCB *)0) {               /* Remove from TCB chain              */
            ptcb->OSTCBNext->OSTCBPrev = (OS_TCB *)0;
            OSTCBList                  = ptcb->OSTCBNext;
        } else {
            ptcb->OSTCBPrev->OSTCBNext = ptcb->OSTCBNext;
            ptcb->OSTCBNext->OSTCBPrev = ptcb->OSTCBPrev;
        }
        ptcb->OSTCBNext = OSTCBFreeList;                    /* Return TCB to free TCB list        */
        OSTCBFreeList   = ptcb;
        OS_EXIT_CRITICAL();
        OSSched();                                          /* Find new highest priority task     */
        return (OS_NO_ERR);
    } else {
        OS_EXIT_CRITICAL();
        return (OS_TASK_DEL_ERR);
    }
}
#endif
```

OS_TASK.C

```
/*
*********************************************************************************************
*                           REQUEST THAT A TASK DELETE ITSELF
*
* Description: This function is used to:
*                 a) notify a task to delete itself.
*                 b) to see if a task requested that the current task delete itself.
*              This function is a little tricky to understand.  Basically, you have a task that needs
*              to be deleted however, this task has resources that it has allocated (memory buffers,
*              semaphores, mailboxes, queues etc.).  The task cannot be deleted otherwise these
*              resources would not be freed.  The requesting task calls OSTaskDelReq() to indicate that
*              the task needs to be deleted.  Deleting of the task is however, deferred to the task to
*              be deleted.  For example, suppose that task #10 needs to be deleted.  The requesting task
*              example, task #5, would call OSTaskDelReq(10).  When task #10 gets to execute, it calls
*              this function by specifying OS_PRIO_SELF and monitors the returned value.  If the return
*              value is OS_TASK_DEL_REQ, another task requested a task delete.  Task #10 would look like
*              this:
*
*                 void Task(void *data)
*                 {
*                         .
*                         .
*                     while (1) {
*                         OSTimeDly(1);
*                         if (OSTaskDelReq(OS_PRIO_SELF) == OS_TASK_DEL_REQ) {
*                             Release any owned resources;
*                             De-allocate any dynamic memory;
*                             OSTaskDel(OS_PRIO_SELF);
*                         }
*                     }
*                 }
*
* Arguments  : prio    is the priority of the task to request the delete from
*
* Returns    : OS_NO_ERR          if the task exist and the request has been registered
*              OS_TASK_NOT_EXIST  if the task has been deleted.  This allows the caller to know whether
*                                 the request has been executed.
*              OS_TASK_DEL_IDLE   if you requested to delete uC/OS-II's idle task
*              OS_PRIO_INVALID    if the priority you specify is higher that the maximum allowed
*                                 (i.e. >= OS_LOWEST_PRIO) or, you have not specified OS_PRIO_SELF.
*              OS_TASK_DEL_REQ    if a task (possibly another task) requested that the running task be
*                                 deleted.
*********************************************************************************************
*/
```

```
#if OS_TASK_DEL_EN
INT8U OSTaskDelReq (INT8U prio)
{
    BOOLEAN   stat;
    INT8U     err;
    OS_TCB    *ptcb;


    if (prio == OS_IDLE_PRIO) {                              /* Not allowed to delete idle task     */
        return (OS_TASK_DEL_IDLE);
    }
    if (prio >= OS_LOWEST_PRIO && prio != OS_PRIO_SELF) {    /* Task priority valid ?               */
        return (OS_PRIO_INVALID);
    }
    if (prio == OS_PRIO_SELF) {                              /* See if a task is requesting to ...  */
        OS_ENTER_CRITICAL();                                 /* ... this task to delete itself      */
        stat = OSTCBCur->OSTCBDelReq;                        /* Return request status to caller     */
        OS_EXIT_CRITICAL();
        return (stat);
    } else {
        OS_ENTER_CRITICAL();
        if ((ptcb = OSTCBPrioTbl[prio]) != (OS_TCB *)0) {    /* Task to delete must exist           */
            ptcb->OSTCBDelReq = OS_TASK_DEL_REQ;             /* Set flag indicating task to be DEL. */
            err               = OS_NO_ERR;
        } else {
            err               = OS_TASK_NOT_EXIST;           /* Task must be deleted                 */
        }
        OS_EXIT_CRITICAL();
        return (err);
    }
}
#endif
```

B

```
/*
*********************************************************************************************************
*                                       RESUME A SUSPENDED TASK
*
* Description: This function is called to resume a previously suspended task.  This is the only call that
*              will remove an explicit task suspension.
*
* Arguments  : prio      is the priority of the task to resume.
*
* Returns    : OS_NO_ERR                if the requested task is resumed
*              OS_PRIO_INVALID          if the priority you specify is higher that the maximum allowed
*                                       (i.e. >= OS_LOWEST_PRIO)
*              OS_TASK_RESUME_PRIO      if the task to resume does not exist
*              OS_TASK_NOT_SUSPENDED    if the task to resume has not been suspended
*********************************************************************************************************
*/

#if OS_TASK_SUSPEND_EN
INT8U OSTaskResume (INT8U prio)
{
    OS_TCB    *ptcb;


    if (prio >= OS_LOWEST_PRIO) {                              /* Make sure task priority is valid    */
        return (OS_PRIO_INVALID);
    }
    OS_ENTER_CRITICAL();
    if ((ptcb = OSTCBPrioTbl[prio]) == (OS_TCB *)0) {          /* Task to suspend must exist          */
        OS_EXIT_CRITICAL();
        return (OS_TASK_RESUME_PRIO);
    } else {
        if (ptcb->OSTCBStat & OS_STAT_SUSPEND) {                       /* Task must be suspended      */
            if (((ptcb->OSTCBStat &= ~OS_STAT_SUSPEND) == OS_STAT_RDY) &&  /* Remove suspension       */
                (ptcb->OSTCBDly  == 0)) {                              /* Must not be delayed         */
                OSRdyGrp              |= ptcb->OSTCBBitY;              /* Make task ready to run       */
                OSRdyTbl[ptcb->OSTCBY] |= ptcb->OSTCBBitX;
                OS_EXIT_CRITICAL();
                OSSched();
            } else {
                OS_EXIT_CRITICAL();
            }
            return (OS_NO_ERR);
        } else {
            OS_EXIT_CRITICAL();
            return (OS_TASK_NOT_SUSPENDED);
        }
    }
}
#endif
```

OS_TASK.C

```
/*
*********************************************************************************************************
*                                          STACK CHECKING
*
* Description: This function is called to check the amount of free memory left on the specified task's
*              stack.
*
* Arguments  : prio       is the task priority
*
*              pdata      is a pointer to a data structure of type OS_STK_DATA.
*
* Returns    : OS_NO_ERR            upon success
*              OS_PRIO_INVALID      if the priority you specify is higher that the maximum allowed
*                                   (i.e. > OS_LOWEST_PRIO) or, you have not specified OS_PRIO_SELF.
*              OS_TASK_NOT_EXIST    if the desired task has not been created
*              OS_TASK_OPT_ERR      if you did NOT specified OS_TASK_OPT_STK_CHK when the task was created
*********************************************************************************************************
*/
#if    OS_TASK_CREATE_EXT_EN
INT8U OSTaskStkChk (INT8U prio, OS_STK_DATA *pdata)
{
    OS_TCB   *ptcb;
    OS_STK   *pchk;
    INT32U   free;
    INT32U   size;


    pdata->OSFree = 0;                                          /* Assume failure, set to 0 size        */
    pdata->OSUsed = 0;
    if (prio > OS_LOWEST_PRIO && prio != OS_PRIO_SELF) {        /* Make sure task priority is valid     */
        return (OS_PRIO_INVALID);
    }
    OS_ENTER_CRITICAL();
    if (prio == OS_PRIO_SELF) {                                 /* See if check for SELF                */
        prio = OSTCBCur->OSTCBPrio;
    }
    ptcb = OSTCBPrioTbl[prio];
    if (ptcb == (OS_TCB *)0) {                                  /* Make sure task exist                 */
        OS_EXIT_CRITICAL();
        return (OS_TASK_NOT_EXIST);
    }
    if ((ptcb->OSTCBOpt & OS_TASK_OPT_STK_CHK) == 0) { /* Make sure stack checking option is set        */
        OS_EXIT_CRITICAL();
        return (OS_TASK_OPT_ERR);
    }
    free = 0;
    size = ptcb->OSTCBStkSize;
    pchk = ptcb->OSTCBStkBottom;
    OS_EXIT_CRITICAL();
#if OS_STK_GROWTH == 1
    while (*pchk++ == 0) {                                      /* Compute the number of zero entries on the stk */
        free++;
    }
#else
    while (*pchk-- == 0) {
        free++;
    }
#endif
    pdata->OSFree = free * sizeof(OS_STK);                      /* Compute number of free bytes on the stack    */
    pdata->OSUsed = (size - free) * sizeof(OS_STK);  /* Compute number of bytes used on the stack    */
    return (OS_NO_ERR);
}
#endif
```

B

```
/*
*********************************************************************************************************
*                                         SUSPEND A TASK
*
* Description: This function is called to suspend a task.  The task can be the calling task if the
*              priority passed to OSTaskSuspend() is the priority of the calling task or OS_PRIO_SELF.
*
* Arguments  : prio     is the priority of the task to suspend.  If you specify OS_PRIO_SELF, the
*                       calling task will suspend itself and rescheduling will occur.
*
* Returns    : OS_NO_ERR               if the requested task is suspended
*              OS_TASK_SUSPEND_IDLE     if you attempted to suspend the idle task which is not allowed.
*              OS_PRIO_INVALID          if the priority you specify is higher that the maximum allowed
*                                       (i.e. >= OS_LOWEST_PRIO) or, you have not specified OS_PRIO_SELF.
*              OS_TASK_SUSPEND_PRIO     if the task to suspend does not exist
*
* Note       : You should use this function with great care.  If you suspend a task that is waiting for
*              an event (i.e. a message, a semaphore, a queue ...) you will prevent this task from
*              running when the event arrives.
*********************************************************************************************************
*/

#if OS_TASK_SUSPEND_EN
INT8U OSTaskSuspend (INT8U prio)
{
    BOOLEAN   self;
    OS_TCB    *ptcb;


    if (prio == OS_IDLE_PRIO) {                                /* Not allowed to suspend idle task    */
        return (OS_TASK_SUSPEND_IDLE);
    }
    if (prio >= OS_LOWEST_PRIO && prio != OS_PRIO_SELF) {      /* Task priority valid ?               */
        return (OS_PRIO_INVALID);
    }
    OS_ENTER_CRITICAL();
    if (prio == OS_PRIO_SELF) {                                /* See if suspend SELF                 */
        prio = OSTCBCur->OSTCBPrio;
        self = TRUE;
    } else if (prio == OSTCBCur->OSTCBPrio) {                  /* See if suspending self              */
        self = TRUE;
    } else {
        self = FALSE;                                          /* No suspending another task          */
    }
    if ((ptcb = OSTCBPrioTbl[prio]) == (OS_TCB *)0) {          /* Task to suspend must exist          */
        OS_EXIT_CRITICAL();
        return (OS_TASK_SUSPEND_PRIO);
    } else {
        if ((OSRdyTbl[ptcb->OSTCBY] &= ~ptcb->OSTCBBitX) == 0) {  /* Make task not ready              */
            OSRdyGrp &= ~ptcb->OSTCBBitY;
        }
        ptcb->OSTCBStat |= OS_STAT_SUSPEND;                    /* Status of task is 'SUSPENDED'       */
        OS_EXIT_CRITICAL();
        if (self == TRUE) {                                    /* Context switch only if SELF         */
            OSSched();
        }
        return (OS_NO_ERR);
    }
}
#endif
```

OS_TASK.C

```
/*
*********************************************************************************************************
*                                            QUERY A TASK
*
* Description: This function is called to obtain a copy of the desired task's TCB.
*
* Arguments  : prio     is the priority of the task to obtain information from.
*
* Returns    : OS_NO_ERR       if the requested task is suspended
*              OS_PRIO_INVALID if the priority you specify is higher that the maximum allowed
*                              (i.e. > OS_LOWEST_PRIO) or, you have not specified OS_PRIO_SELF.
*              OS_PRIO_ERR     if the desired task has not been created
*********************************************************************************************************
*/

INT8U OSTaskQuery (INT8U prio, OS_TCB *pdata)
{
    OS_TCB *ptcb;


    if (prio > OS_LOWEST_PRIO && prio != OS_PRIO_SELF) {   /* Task priority valid ?               */
        return (OS_PRIO_INVALID);
    }
    OS_ENTER_CRITICAL();
    if (prio == OS_PRIO_SELF) {                            /* See if suspend SELF                 */
        prio = OSTCBCur->OSTCBPrio;
    }
    if ((ptcb = OSTCBPrioTbl[prio]) == (OS_TCB *)0) {      /* Task to query must exist            */
        OS_EXIT_CRITICAL();
        return (OS_PRIO_ERR);
    }
    *pdata = *ptcb;                                        /* Copy TCB into user storage area     */
    OS_EXIT_CRITICAL();
    return (OS_NO_ERR);
}
```

B

B.08 OS_TIME.C

```
/*
*********************************************************************************************************
*                                               uC/OS-II
*                                         The Real-Time Kernel
*                                           TIME MANAGEMENT
*
*                            (c) Copyright 1992-1998, Jean J. Labrosse, Plantation, FL
*                                           All Rights Reserved
*
*                                                V2.00
*
* File : OS_TIME.C
* By   : Jean J. Labrosse
*********************************************************************************************************
*/

#ifndef  OS_MASTER_FILE
#include "includes.h"
#endif

/*
*********************************************************************************************************
*                            DELAY TASK 'n' TICKS    (n from 0 to 65535)
*
* Description: This function is called to delay execution of the currently running task until the
*              specified number of system ticks expires.  This, of course, directly equates to delaying
*              the current task for some time to expire.  No delay will result If the specified delay is
*              0.  If the specified delay is greater than 0 then, a context switch will result.
*
* Arguments  : ticks     is the time delay that the task will be suspended in number of clock 'ticks'.
*              Note that by specifying 0, the task will not be delayed.
*
* Returns    : none
*********************************************************************************************************
*/

void OSTimeDly (INT16U ticks)
{
    if (ticks > 0) {                                            /* 0 means no delay!        */
        OS_ENTER_CRITICAL();
        if ((OSRdyTbl[OSTCBCur->OSTCBY] &= ~OSTCBCur->OSTCBBitX) == 0) {  /* Delay current task       */
            OSRdyGrp &= ~OSTCBCur->OSTCBBitY;
        }
        OSTCBCur->OSTCBDly = ticks;                             /* Load ticks in TCB        */
        OS_EXIT_CRITICAL();
        OSSched();                                             /* Find next task to run!   */
    }
}
```

OS_TIME.C

```
/*
*********************************************************************************************
*                                DELAY TASK FOR SPECIFIED TIME
*
* Description: This function is called to delay execution of the currently running task until some time
*              expires.  This call allows you to specify the delay time in HOURS, MINUTES, SECONDS and
*              MILLISECONDS instead of ticks.
*
* Arguments  : hours     specifies the number of hours that the task will be delayed (max. is 255)
*              minutes   specifies the number of minutes (max. 59)
*              seconds   specifies the number of seconds (max. 59)
*              milli     specifies the number of milliseconds (max. 999)
*
* Returns    : OS_NO_ERR
*              OS_TIME_INVALID_MINUTES
*              OS_TIME_INVALID_SECONDS
*              OS_TIME_INVALID_MS
*              OS_TIME_ZERO_DLY
*
* Note(s)    : The resolution on the milliseconds depends on the tick rate.  For example, you can't do
*              a 10 mS delay if the ticker interrupts every 100 mS.  In this case, the delay would be
*              set to 0.  The actual delay is rounded to the nearest tick.
*********************************************************************************************
*/

INT8U OSTimeDlyHMSM (INT8U hours, INT8U minutes, INT8U seconds, INT16U milli)
{
    INT32U ticks;
    INT16U loops;


    if (hours > 0 || minutes > 0 || seconds > 0 || milli > 0) {
        if (minutes > 59) {
            return (OS_TIME_INVALID_MINUTES);    /* Validate arguments to be within range            */
        }
        if (seconds > 59) {
            return (OS_TIME_INVALID_SECONDS);
        }
        if (milli > 999) {
            return (OS_TIME_INVALID_MILLI);
        }
                                                 /* Compute the total number of clock ticks required.. */
                                                 /* .. (rounded to the nearest tick)                   */
        ticks = ((INT32U)hours * 3600L + (INT32U)minutes * 60L + (INT32U)seconds) * OS_TICKS_PER_SEC
              + OS_TICKS_PER_SEC * ((INT32U)milli + 500L / OS_TICKS_PER_SEC) / 1000L;
        loops = ticks / 65536L;                  /* Compute the integral number of 65536 tick delays  */
        ticks = ticks % 65536L;                  /* Obtain  the fractional number of ticks            */
        OSTimeDly(ticks);
        while (loops > 0) {
            OSTimeDly(32768);
            OSTimeDly(32768);
            loops--;
        }
        return (OS_NO_ERR);
    } else {
        return (OS_TIME_ZERO_DLY);
    }
}
```

B

```
/*
*********************************************************************************************************
*                                    RESUME A DELAYED TASK
*
* Description: This function is used resume a task that has been delayed through a call to either
*              OSTimeDly() or OSTimeDlyHMSM().  Note that you MUST NOT call this function to resume a
*              task that is waiting for an event with timeout.  This situation would make the task look
*              like a timeout occurred (unless you desire this effect).  Also, you cannot resume a task
*              that has called OSTimeDlyHMSM() with a combined time that exceeds 65535 clock ticks.  In
*              other words, if the clock tick runs at 100 Hz then, you will not be able to resume a
*              delayed task that called OSTimeDlyHMSM(0, 10, 55, 350) or higher.
*
*                      (10 Minutes * 60 + 55 Seconds + 0.35) * 100 ticks/second.
*
* Arguments  : prio      specifies the priority of the task to resume
*
* Returns    : OS_NO_ERR            Task has been resumed
*              OS_PRIO_INVALID      if the priority you specify is higher that the maximum allowed
*                                   (i.e. >= OS_LOWEST_PRIO)
*              OS_TIME_NOT_DLY      Task is not waiting for time to expire
*              OS_TASK_NOT_EXIST    The desired task has not been created
*********************************************************************************************************
*/

INT8U OSTimeDlyResume (INT8U prio)
{
    OS_TCB *ptcb;


    if (prio >= OS_LOWEST_PRIO) {
        return (OS_PRIO_INVALID);
    }
    OS_ENTER_CRITICAL();
    ptcb = (OS_TCB *)OSTCBPrioTbl[prio];                        /* Make sure that task exist          */
    if (ptcb != (OS_TCB *)0) {
        if (ptcb->OSTCBDly != 0) {                             /* See if task is delayed             */
            ptcb->OSTCBDly  = 0;                               /* Clear the time delay               */
            if (!(ptcb->OSTCBStat & OS_STAT_SUSPEND)) {        /* See if task is ready to run        */
                OSRdyGrp             |= ptcb->OSTCBBitY;       /* Make task ready to run             */
                OSRdyTbl[ptcb->OSTCBY] |= ptcb->OSTCBBitX;
                OS_EXIT_CRITICAL();
                OSSched();                                     /* See if this is new highest priority */
            } else {
                OS_EXIT_CRITICAL();                            /* Task may be suspended              */
            }
            return (OS_NO_ERR);
        } else {
            OS_EXIT_CRITICAL();
            return (OS_TIME_NOT_DLY);                          /* Indicate that task was not delayed  */
        }
    } else {
        OS_EXIT_CRITICAL();
        return (OS_TASK_NOT_EXIST);                            /* The task does not exist            */
    }
}
```

OS_TIME.C

```
/*
*********************************************************************************************
*                                  GET CURRENT SYSTEM TIME
*
* Description: This function is used by your application to obtain the current value of the 32-bit
*              counter which keeps track of the number of clock ticks.
*
* Arguments  : none
*
* Returns    : The current value of OSTime
*********************************************************************************************
*/

INT32U OSTimeGet (void)
{
    INT32U ticks;


    OS_ENTER_CRITICAL();
    ticks = OSTime;
    OS_EXIT_CRITICAL();
    return (ticks);
}

/*
*********************************************************************************************
*                                    SET SYSTEM CLOCK
*
* Description: This function sets the 32-bit counter which keeps track of the number of clock ticks.
*
* Arguments  : ticks      specifies the new value that OSTime needs to take.
*
* Returns    : none
*********************************************************************************************
*/

void OSTimeSet (INT32U ticks)
{
    OS_ENTER_CRITICAL();
    OSTime = ticks;
    OS_EXIT_CRITICAL();
}
```

B

80x86 Real Mode, Large Model Source Code

C.00 *OS_CPU_A.ASM*

```
;********************************************************************************************************
;                                              uC/OS-II
;                                         The Real-Time Kernel
;
;                         (c) Copyright 1992-1998, Jean J. Labrosse, Plantation, FL
;                                         All Rights Reserved
;
;
;                                      80x86/80x88 Specific code
;                                         LARGE MEMORY MODEL
;
;                                      IBM/PC Compatible Target
;
; File : OS_CPU_A.ASM
; By   : Jean J. Labrosse
;********************************************************************************************************

          PUBLIC  _OSTickISR
          PUBLIC  _OSStartHighRdy
          PUBLIC  _OSCtxSw
          PUBLIC  _OSIntCtxSw

          EXTRN   _OSIntExit:FAR
          EXTRN   _OSTimeTick:FAR
          EXTRN   _OSTaskSwHook:FAR

          EXTRN   _OSIntNesting:BYTE
          EXTRN   _OSTickDOSCtr:BYTE
          EXTRN   _OSPrioHighRdy:BYTE
          EXTRN   _OSPrioCur:BYTE
          EXTRN   _OSRunning:BYTE
          EXTRN   _OSTCBCur:DWORD
          EXTRN   _OSTCBHighRdy:DWORD

.MODEL    LARGE
.CODE
.186
```

```
;************************************************************************************************
;                                        START MULTITASKING
;                                      void OSStartHighRdy(void)
;
; The stack frame is assumed to look as follows:
;
; OSTCBHighRdy->OSTCBStkPtr --> DS                                        (Low memory)
;                               ES
;                               DI
;                               SI
;                               BP
;                               SP
;                               BX
;                               DX
;                               CX
;                               AX
;                               OFFSET  of task code address
;                               SEGMENT of task code address
;                               Flags to load in PSW
;                               OFFSET  of task code address
;                               SEGMENT of task code address
;                               OFFSET  of 'pdata'
;                               SEGMENT of 'pdata'                        (High memory)
;
; Note : OSStartHighRdy() MUST:
;          a) Call OSTaskSwHook() then,
;          b) Set OSRunning to TRUE,
;          c) Switch to the highest priority task.
;************************************************************************************************

_OSStartHighRdy  PROC FAR

          MOV    AX, SEG _OSTCBHighRdy       ; Reload DS
          MOV    DS, AX                      ;
;
          CALL   FAR PTR _OSTaskSwHook       ; Call user defined task switch hook
;
          INC    BYTE PTR DS:_OSRunning      ; Indicate that multitasking has started
;
          LES    BX, DWORD PTR DS:_OSTCBHighRdy ; SS:SP = OSTCBHighRdy->OSTCBStkPtr
          MOV    SS, ES:[BX+2]               ;
          MOV    SP, ES:[BX+0]               ;
;
          POP    DS                          ; Load task's context
          POP    ES                          ;
          POPA                               ;
;
          IRET                               ; Run task

_OSStartHighRdy  ENDP
```

OS_CPU_A.ASM

```
;*********************************************************************************************
;                        PERFORM A CONTEXT SWITCH (From task level)
;                                  void OSCtxSw(void)
;
; Note(s): 1) Upon entry,
;             OSTCBCur     points to the OS_TCB of the task to suspend
;             OSTCBHighRdy points to the OS_TCB of the task to resume
;
;          2) The stack frame of the task to suspend looks as follows:
;
;                 SP -> OFFSET  of task to suspend    (Low memory)
;                       SEGMENT of task to suspend
;                       PSW     of task to suspend    (High memory)
;
;          3) The stack frame of the task to resume looks as follows:
;
;                 OSTCBHighRdy->OSTCBStkPtr --> DS                          (Low memory)
;                                               ES
;                                               DI
;                                               SI
;                                               BP
;                                               SP
;                                               BX
;                                               DX
;                                               CX
;                                               AX
;                                               OFFSET  of task code address
;                                               SEGMENT of task code address
;                                               Flags to load in PSW        (High memory)
;*********************************************************************************************

_OSCtxSw    PROC    FAR
;
            PUSHA                                   ; Save current task's context
            PUSH    ES                              ;
            PUSH    DS                              ;
;
            MOV     AX, SEG _OSTCBCur               ; Reload DS in case it was altered
            MOV     DS, AX                          ;
;
            LES     BX, DWORD PTR DS:_OSTCBCur      ; OSTCBCur->OSTCBStkPtr = SS:SP
            MOV     ES:[BX+2], SS                   ;
            MOV     ES:[BX+0], SP                   ;
;
            CALL    FAR PTR _OSTaskSwHook           ; Call user defined task switch hook
;
            MOV     AX, WORD PTR DS:_OSTCBHighRdy+2 ; OSTCBCur = OSTCBHighRdy
            MOV     DX, WORD PTR DS:_OSTCBHighRdy   ;
            MOV     WORD PTR DS:_OSTCBCur+2, AX     ;
            MOV     WORD PTR DS:_OSTCBCur, DX       ;
;
            MOV     AL, BYTE PTR DS:_OSPrioHighRdy  ; OSPrioCur = OSPrioHighRdy
            MOV     BYTE PTR DS:_OSPrioCur, AL      ;
;
            LES     BX, DWORD PTR DS:_OSTCBHighRdy  ; SS:SP = OSTCBHighRdy->OSTCBStkPtr
            MOV     SS, ES:[BX+2]                   ;
            MOV     SP, ES:[BX]                     ;
;
            POP     DS                              ; Load new task's context
            POP     ES                              ;
            POPA                                    ;
;
            IRET                                    ; Return to new task
;
_OSCtxSw    ENDP
```

OS_CPU_A.ASM

```
;*****************************************************************************************************
;                          PERFORM A CONTEXT SWITCH (From an ISR)
;                                    void OSIntCtxSw(void)
;
; Note(s): 1) Upon entry,
;             OSTCBCur     points to the OS_TCB of the task to suspend
;             OSTCBHighRdy points to the OS_TCB of the task to resume
;
;          2) The stack frame of the task to suspend looks as follows:
;
;                              SP+0 --> OFFSET  of return address of OSIntCtxSw()  (Low memory)
;                                +2     SEGMENT of return address of OSIntCtxSw()
;                                +4     PSW saved by OS_ENTER_CRITICAL() in OSIntExit()
;                                +6     OFFSET  of return address of OSIntExit()
;                                +8     SEGMENT of return address of OSIntExit()
;                                +10    DS
;                                       ES
;                                       DI
;                                       SI
;                                       BP
;                                       SP
;                                       BX
;                                       DX
;                                       CX
;                                       AX
;                                       OFFSET  of task code address
;                                       SEGMENT of task code address
;                                       Flags to load in PSW                      (High memory)
;
;          3) The stack frame of the task to resume looks as follows:
;
;             OSTCBHighRdy->OSTCBStkPtr --> DS                                    (Low memory)
;                                           ES
;                                           DI
;                                           SI
;                                           BP
;                                           SP
;                                           BX
;                                           DX
;                                           CX
;                                           AX
;                                           OFFSET  of task code address
;                                           SEGMENT of task code address
;                                           Flags to load in PSW       (High memory)
;*****************************************************************************************************
```

OS_CPU_A.ASM

```
_OSIntCtxSw PROC    FAR
;                                               ;  Ignore calls to OSIntExit and OSIntCtxSw
;           ADD     SP,8                        ; (Uncomment if OS_CRITICAL_METHOD is 1, see OS_CPU.H)
            ADD     SP,10                       ; (Uncomment if OS_CRITICAL_METHOD is 2, see OS_CPU.H)
;
            MOV     AX, SEG _OSTCBCur           ; Reload DS in case it was altered
            MOV     DS, AX                      ;
;
            LES     BX, DWORD PTR DS:_OSTCBCur  ; OSTCBCur->OSTCBStkPtr = SS:SP
            MOV     ES:[BX+2], SS               ;
            MOV     ES:[BX+0], SP               ;
;
            CALL    FAR PTR _OSTaskSwHook       ; Call user defined task switch hook
;
            MOV     AX, WORD PTR DS:_OSTCBHighRdy+2 ; OSTCBCur = OSTCBHighRdy
            MOV     DX, WORD PTR DS:_OSTCBHighRdy   ;
            MOV     WORD PTR DS:_OSTCBCur+2, AX  ;
            MOV     WORD PTR DS:_OSTCBCur, DX    ;
;
            MOV     AL, BYTE PTR DS:_OSPrioHighRdy ; OSPrioCur = OSPrioHighRdy
            MOV     BYTE PTR DS:_OSPrioCur, AL   ;
;
            LES     BX, DWORD PTR DS:_OSTCBHighRdy ; SS:SP = OSTCBHighRdy->OSTCBStkPtr
            MOV     SS, ES:[BX+2]               ;
            MOV     SP, ES:[BX]                ;
;
            POP     DS                          ; Load new task's context
            POP     ES                          ;
            POPA                                ;
;
            IRET                                ; Return to new task
;
_OSIntCtxSw ENDP
```

C

```
;**********************************************************************************************
;                                        HANDLE TICK ISR
;
; Description: This function is called 199.99 times per second or, 11 times faster than the normal DOS
;              tick rate of 18.20648 Hz.  Thus every 11th time, the normal DOS tick handler is called.
;              This is called chaining.  10 times out of 11, however, the interrupt controller on the PC
;              must be cleared to allow for the next interrupt.
;
; Arguments  : none
;
; Returns    : none
;
; Note(s)    : The following C-like pseudo-code describe the operation being performed in the code below.
;
;              Save all registers on the current task's stack;
;              OSIntNesting++;
;              OSTickDOSCtr--;
;              if (OSTickDOSCtr == 0) {
;                  INT 81H;              Chain into DOS every 54.925 mS
;                                        (Interrupt will be cleared by DOS)
;              } else {
;                  Send EOI to PIC;      Clear tick interrupt by sending an End-Of-Interrupt to the 8259
;                                        PIC (Priority Interrupt Controller)
;              }
;              OSTimeTick();             Notify uC/OS-II that a tick has occured
;              OSIntExit();              Notify uC/OS-II about end of ISR
;              Restore all registers that were save on the current task's stack;
;              Return from Interrupt;
;**********************************************************************************************
;
_OSTickISR  PROC    FAR
            PUSHA                                   ; Save interrupted task's context
            PUSH    ES
            PUSH    DS
;
            MOV     AX, SEG _OSTickDOSCtr           ; Reload DS
            MOV     DS, AX
;
            INC     BYTE PTR _OSIntNesting          ; Notify uC/OS-II of ISR
;
            DEC     BYTE PTR DS:_OSTickDOSCtr
            CMP     BYTE PTR DS:_OSTickDOSCtr, 0
            JNE     SHORT _OSTickISR1               ; Every 11 ticks (~199.99 Hz), chain into DOS
;
            MOV     BYTE PTR DS:_OSTickDOSCtr, 11
            INT     081H                            ; Chain into DOS's tick ISR
            JMP     SHORT _OSTickISR2

_OSTickISR1:
            MOV     AL, 20H                         ; Move EOI code into AL.
            MOV     DX, 20H                         ; Address of 8259 PIC in DX.
            OUT     DX, AL                          ; Send EOI to PIC if not processing DOS timer.
;
_OSTickISR2:
            CALL    FAR PTR _OSTimeTick             ; Process system tick
;
            CALL    FAR PTR _OSIntExit              ; Notify uC/OS-II of end of ISR
;
            POP     DS                              ; Restore interrupted task's context
            POP     ES
            POPA
;
            IRET                                    ; Return to interrupted task
;
_OSTickISR  ENDP
;
            END
```

OS_CPU_A.ASM

C.01 *OS_CPU_C.C*

```
/*
*********************************************************************************************************
*                                             uC/OS-II
*                                       The Real-Time Kernel
*
*                       (c) Copyright 1992-1998, Jean J. Labrosse, Plantation, FL
*                                        All Rights Reserved
*
*
*                                       80x86/80x88 Specific code
*                                       LARGE MEMORY MODEL
*
* File : OS_CPU_C.C
* By   : Jean J. Labrosse
*********************************************************************************************************
*/

#define  OS_CPU_GLOBALS
#include "includes.h"

/*
*********************************************************************************************************
*                                     INITIALIZE A TASK'S STACK
*
* Description: This function is called by either OSTaskCreate() or OSTaskCreateExt() to initialize the
*              stack frame of the task being created.  This function is highly processor specific.
*
* Arguments  : task        is a pointer to the task code
*
*              pdata       is a pointer to a user supplied data area that will be passed to the task
*                          when the task first executes.
*
*              ptos        is a pointer to the top of stack.  It is assumed that 'ptos' points to
*                          a 'free' entry on the task stack.  If OS_STK_GROWTH is set to 1 then
*                          'ptos' will contain the HIGHEST valid address of the stack.  Similarly, if
*                          OS_STK_GROWTH is set to 0, the 'ptos' will contains the LOWEST valid address
*                          of the stack.
*
*              opt         specifies options that can be used to alter the behavior of OSTaskStkInit().
*                          (see uCOS_II.H for OS_TASK_OPT_???).
*
* Returns    : Always returns the location of the new top-of-stack' once the processor registers have
*              been placed on the stack in the proper order.
*
* Note(s)    : Interrupts are enabled when your task starts executing. You can change this by setting the
*              PSW to 0x0002 instead.  In this case, interrupts would be disabled upon task startup.  The
*              application code would be responsible for enabling interrupts at the beginning of the task
*              code.  You will need to modify OSTaskIdle() and OSTaskStat() so that they enable
*              interrupts.  Failure to do this will make your system crash!
*********************************************************************************************************
*/
```

C

```
void *OSTaskStkInit (void (*task)(void *pd), void *pdata, void *ptos, INT16U opt)
{
    INT16U *stk;

    opt    = opt;                        /* 'opt' is not used, prevent warning          */
    stk    = (INT16U *)ptos;             /* Load stack pointer                          */
    *stk-- = (INT16U)FP_SEG(pdata);      /* Simulate call to function with argument     */
    *stk-- = (INT16U)FP_OFF(pdata);
    *stk-- = (INT16U)FP_SEG(task);
    *stk-- = (INT16U)FP_OFF(task);
    *stk-- = (INT16U)0x0202;             /* SW = Interrupts enabled                     */
    *stk-- = (INT16U)FP_SEG(task);       /* Put pointer to task   on top of stack       */
    *stk-- = (INT16U)FP_OFF(task);
    *stk-- = (INT16U)0xAAAA;             /* AX = 0xAAAA                                 */
    *stk-- = (INT16U)0xCCCC;             /* CX = 0xCCCC                                 */
    *stk-- = (INT16U)0xDDDD;             /* DX = 0xDDDD                                 */
    *stk-- = (INT16U)0xBBBB;             /* BX = 0xBBBB                                 */
    *stk-- = (INT16U)0x0000;             /* SP = 0x0000                                 */
    *stk-- = (INT16U)0x1111;             /* BP = 0x1111                                 */
    *stk-- = (INT16U)0x2222;             /* SI = 0x2222                                 */
    *stk-- = (INT16U)0x3333;             /* DI = 0x3333                                 */
    *stk-- = (INT16U)0x4444;             /* ES = 0x4444                                 */
    *stk    = _DS;                       /* DS = Current value of DS                    */
    return ((void *)stk);
}
```

OS_CPU_C.C

```c
#if OS_CPU_HOOKS_EN
/*
*********************************************************************************************************
*                                         TASK CREATION HOOK
*
* Description: This function is called when a task is created.
*
* Arguments  : ptcb   is a pointer to the task control block of the task being created.
*
* Note(s)    : 1) Interrupts are disabled during this call.
*********************************************************************************************************
*/
void OSTaskCreateHook (OS_TCB *ptcb)
{
    ptcb = ptcb;                    /* Prevent compiler warning                                   */
}


/*
*********************************************************************************************************
*                                         TASK DELETION HOOK
*
* Description: This function is called when a task is deleted.
*
* Arguments  : ptcb   is a pointer to the task control block of the task being deleted.
*
* Note(s)    : 1) Interrupts are disabled during this call.
*********************************************************************************************************
*/
void OSTaskDelHook (OS_TCB *ptcb)
{
    ptcb = ptcb;                    /* Prevent compiler warning                                   */
}

/*
*********************************************************************************************************
*                                          TASK SWITCH HOOK
*
* Description: This function is called when a task switch is performed.  This allows you to perform other
*              operations during a context switch.
*
* Arguments  : none
*
* Note(s)    : 1) Interrupts are disabled during this call.
*              2) It is assumed that the global pointer 'OSTCBHighRdy' points to the TCB of the task that
*                 will be 'switched in' (i.e. the highest priority task) and, 'OSTCBCur' points to the
*                 task being switched out (i.e. the preempted task).
*********************************************************************************************************
*/
void OSTaskSwHook (void)
{
}

/*
*********************************************************************************************************
*                                         STATISTIC TASK HOOK
*
* Description: This function is called every second by uC/OS-II's statistics task.  This allows your
*              application to add functionality to the statistics task.
*
* Arguments  : none
*********************************************************************************************************
*/
void OSTaskStatHook (void)
{
}
```

C

OS_CPU_C.C

```
/*
*********************************************************************************************************
*                                            TICK HOOK
*
* Description: This function is called every tick.
*
* Arguments  : none
*
* Note(s)    : 1) Interrupts may or may not be ENABLED during this call.
*********************************************************************************************************
*/
void OSTimeTickHook (void)
{
}
#endif
```

C.02 OS_CPU.H

```
/*
*********************************************************************************************************
*                                             uC/OS-II
*                                         The Real-Time Kernel
*
*                         (c) Copyright 1992-1998, Jean J. Labrosse, Plantation, FL
*                                         All Rights Reserved
*
*                                        80x86/80x88 Specific code
*                                        LARGE MEMORY MODEL
*
* File : OS_CPU.H
* By   : Jean J. Labrosse
*********************************************************************************************************
*/

#ifdef  OS_CPU_GLOBALS
#define OS_CPU_EXT
#else
#define OS_CPU_EXT  extern
#endif

/*
*********************************************************************************************************
*                                             DATA TYPES
*                                          (Compiler Specific)
*********************************************************************************************************
*/

typedef unsigned char  BOOLEAN;
typedef unsigned char  INT8U;            /* Unsigned  8 bit quantity                    */
typedef signed   char  INT8S;            /* Signed    8 bit quantity                    */
typedef unsigned int   INT16U;           /* Unsigned 16 bit quantity                    */
typedef signed   int   INT16S;           /* Signed   16 bit quantity                    */
typedef unsigned long  INT32U;           /* Unsigned 32 bit quantity                    */
typedef signed   long  INT32S;           /* Signed   32 bit quantity                    */
typedef float          FP32;             /* Single precision floating point             */
typedef double         FP64;             /* Double precision floating point             */

typedef unsigned int   OS_STK;           /* Each stack entry is 16-bit wide             */

#define BYTE           INT8S             /* Define data types for backward compatibility ... */
#define UBYTE          INT8U             /* ... to uC/OS V1.xx.  Not actually needed for ... */
#define WORD           INT16S            /* ... uC/OS-II.                               */
#define UWORD          INT16U
#define LONG           INT32S
#define ULONG          INT32U
```

C

```
/*
*********************************************************************************************************
*                           Intel 80x86 (Real-Mode, Large Model)
*
* Method #1:  Disable/Enable interrupts using simple instructions.  After critical section, interrupts
*             will be enabled even if they were disabled before entering the critical section.  You MUST
*             change the constant in OS_CPU_A.ASM, function OSIntCtxSw() from 10 to 8.
*
* Method #2:  Disable/Enable interrupts by preserving the state of interrupts.  In other words, if
*             interrupts were disabled before entering the critical section, they will be disabled when
*             leaving the critical section.  You MUST change the constant in OS_CPU_A.ASM, function
*             OSIntCtxSw() from 8 to 10.
*********************************************************************************************************
*/
#define  OS_CRITICAL_METHOD    2

#if      OS_CRITICAL_METHOD == 1
#define  OS_ENTER_CRITICAL()   asm  CLI              /* Disable interrupts                          */
#define  OS_EXIT_CRITICAL()    asm  STI              /* Enable  interrupts                          */
#endif

#if      OS_CRITICAL_METHOD == 2
#define  OS_ENTER_CRITICAL()   asm {PUSHF; CLI}      /* Disable interrupts                          */
#define  OS_EXIT_CRITICAL()    asm  POPF             /* Enable  interrupts                          */
#endif

/*
*********************************************************************************************************
*                           Intel 80x86 (Real-Mode, Large Model) Miscellaneous
*********************************************************************************************************
*/

#define  OS_STK_GROWTH         1                     /* Stack grows from HIGH to LOW memory on 80x86 */

#define  uCOS                  0x80                  /* Interrupt vector # used for context switch  */

#define  OS_TASK_SW()          asm  INT  uCOS

/*
*********************************************************************************************************
*                                       GLOBAL VARIABLES
*********************************************************************************************************
*/

OS_CPU_EXT  INT8U  OSTickDOSCtr;        /* Counter used to invoke DOS's tick handler every 'n' ticks   */
```

OS_CPU.H

HPLISTC and TO

HPLISTC and TO are DOS utilities provided in both executable and source form for your convenience.

D.00 HPLISTC

HPLISTC prints C source files on an HP Laserjet in compressed mode: 17 characters per inch (CPI). An 8 1/2- by 11-inch page (*portrait*) accommodates up to 132 characters. An 11- by 8$^1/_2$-inch page (*landscape*) accommodates up to 175 characters. Once the source code is printed, HPLISTC returns the printer to its default print mode.

The DOS executable is in \SOFTWARE\HPLISTC\EXE\HPLISTC.EXE, and the source code is in \SOFT-WARE\HPLISTC\SOURCE\HPLISTC.C.

HPLISTC prints the current date and time, the filename, its extension, and the page number at the top of each page. An optional title can also be printed at the top of each page. As HPLISTC prints the source code, it looks for two special comments: /*$TITLE=*/ (or /*$title=*/) and /*$PAGE*/ (or /*$page*/).

The /*$TITLE=*/ comment specifies the title to be printed on the second line of each page. Define a new to begin printing at the top of the next page as follows:

```
/*$TITLE=Matrix Keyboard Driver*/
```

This sets the title for the next page and each subsequent page of your source code until the title is changed again to *Matrix Keyboard Driver.*

The /*$PAGE*/ comment forces a page break in your source code listing. HPLISTC does not force a page break unless you specify the /*$PAGE*/ comment. Otherwise, the printer controls page breaks when it reaches its maximum number of lines per page and may print a short listing on two pages. The page number on the top of each page indicates the number of occurrences of the /*$PAGE*/ comment encountered by HPLISTC.

Before each line is printed, HPLISTC prints a line count that can be used for reference. HPLISTC also allows you to print source code in *landscape* mode. The program is invoked as follows:

```
HPLISTC filename.ext [L | l] [destination]
```

where *filename*.ext is the name of the file to print and *destination* is the destination of the printout. Since HPLISTC sends the output to stdout, the printout can be redirected to a file, a printer (PRN, LPT1, LPT2), or a COM port (COM1, COM2) by using the DOS redirector >. By default, HPLISTC outputs to the monitor.

[L/l] (L or l) means to print the file in *landscape* mode, which allows you to print about 175 columns wide!

D.01 TO

TO is a DOS utility that allows you to go to a directory without typing

    CD *path*

or

    CD ..*path*

TO is probably the DOS utility I use most because it allows me to move between directories very quickly. At the DOS prompt, simply type TO followed by the name you associated with a directory, then press Enter:

    TO *name*

where *name* is a name you associated with a path. The names and paths are placed in an ASCII file called TO.TBL, which resides in the root directory of the current drive. TO scans TO.TBL for the name you specified on the command line. If the name exists in TO.TBL, the directory is changed to the path specified with the name. If *name* is not found in TO.TBL, the message Invalid *NAME*. is displayed.

The DOS executable is in \SOFTWARE\TO\EXE\TO.EXE, an example of the names and paths is in \SOFT-WARE\TO\EXE\TO.TBL, and the source code is in \SOFTWARE\TO\SOURCE\TO.C.

An example of TO.TBL and its format is shown in Listing D.1. Note that the name must be separated from the path by a comma.

Listing D.1 Example of TO.TBL

```
A,          ..\SOURCE
C,          ..\SOURCE
D,          ..\DOC
L,          ..\LST
O,          ..\OBJ
P,          ..\PROD
W,          ..\WORK
EX1L,       \SOFTWARE\uCOS-II\EX1_x86L                    (1)
EX2L,       \SOFTWARE\uCOS-II\EX2_x86L
EX3L,       \SOFTWARE\uCOS-II\EX3_x86L
Ix86L,      \SOFTWARE\uCOS-II\Ix86L
HPLISTC,    \SOFTWARE\HPLISTC\SOURCE                      (2)
TO,         \SOFTWARE\TO\SOURCE
uCOS-II,    \SOFTWARE\uCOS-II\SOURCE
```

You can add an entry to TO.TBL by typing the path associated with a name on the command line as follows:

TO *name path*

TO appends this new entry to the end of TO.TBL. This avoids having to use a text editor to add a new entry. If you type

TO EX1L

TO changes directory to \SOFTWARE\uCOS-II\EX1_x86L [LD.1(1)]. Similarly, if you type

TO hplistc

TO changes directory to \SOFTWARE\HPLISTC\SOURCE [LD.1(2)]. TO.TBL can be as long as needed, but each name must be unique. Note that two names can be associated with the same directory. If you add entries in TO.TBL using a text editor, all entries must be entered in uppercase. When you invoke TO at the DOS prompt, the name you specify is converted to uppercase before the program searches through the table. TO searches TO.TBL linearly from the first entry to the last. For faster response, you may want to place your most frequently used directories at the beginning of the file.

D

Appendix E

Bibliography

Allworth, Steve T. 1981. *Introduction To Real-Time Software Design.* New York: Springer-Verlag. ISBN 0-387-91175-8.

Bal Sathe, Dhananjay. 1988. Fast Algorithm Determines Priority. *EDN* (India), September, p. 237.

Comer, Douglas. 1984.*Operating System Design, The XINU Approach.* Englewood Cliffs, New Jersey: Prentice-Hall. ISBN 0-13-637539-1.

Deitel, Harvey M. and Michael S. Kogan. 1992. *The Design Of OS/2.* Reading, Massachusetts: Addison-Wesley. ISBN 0-201-54889-5.

Ganssle, Jack G. 1992. *The Art of Programming Embedded Systems.* San Diego: Academic Press. ISBN 0-122-748808.

Gareau, Jean L. 1998. Embedded x86 Programming: Protected Mode. *Embedded Systems Programming*, April, p. 80–93.

Halang, Wolfgang A. and Alexander D. Stoyenko. 1991. *Constructing Predictable Real Time Systems.* Norwell, Massachusetts: Kluwer Academic Publishers Group. ISBN 0-7923-9202-7.

Hunter & Ready. 1986. *VRTX Technical Tips.* Palo Alto, California: Hunter & Ready.

Hunter & Ready. 1983. *Dijkstra Semaphores, Application Note.* Palo Alto, California: Hunter & Ready.

Hunter & Ready. 1986. *VRTX and Event Flags.* Palo Alto, California: Hunter & Ready.

Intel Corporation. 1986. *iAPX 86/88, 186/188 User's Manual: Programmer's Reference.* Santa Clara, California: Intel Corporation.

Kernighan, Brian W. and Dennis M. Ritchie. 1988. *The C Programming Language,* 2nd edition. Englewood Cliffs, New Jersey: Prentice Hall. ISBN 0-13-110362-8.

E

Klein, Mark H., Thomas Ralya, Bill Pollak, Ray Harbour Obenza, and Michael Gonzlez. 1993. *A Practioner's Handbook for Real-Time Analysis: Guide to Rate Monotonic Analysis for Real-Time Systems.* Norwell, Massachusetts: Kluwer Academic Publishers Group. ISBN 0-7923-9361-9.

Labrosse, Jean J. 1992. µ*C/OS, The Real-Time Kernel.* Lawrence, Kansas: R&D Publications. ISBN 0-87930-444-8.

Laplante, Phillip A. 1992. *Real-Time Systems Design and Analysis, An Engineer's Handbook.* Piscataway, New Jersey: IEEE Computer Society Press. ISBN 0-780-334000.

Lehoczky, John, Lui Sha, and Ye Ding. 1989. The Rate Monotonic Scheduling Algorithm: Exact Characterization and Average Case Behavior. In: *Proceedings of the IEEE Real-Time Systems Symposium.,* Los Alamitos, California. Piscataway, New Jersey: IEEE Computer Society, p. 166–171.

Madnick, E. Stuart and John J. Donovan. 1974. *Operating Systems.* New York: McGraw-Hill. ISBN 0-07-039455-5.

Ripps, David L. 1989. *An Implementation Guide To Real-Time Programming.* Englewood Cliffs, New Jersey: Yourdon Press. ISBN 0-13-451873-X.

Savitzky, Stephen R. 1985. *Real-Time Microprocessor Systems.* New York: Van Nostrand Reinhold. ISBN 0-442-28048-3.

Wood, Mike and Tom Barrett . 1990. A Real-Time Primer. *Embedded Systems Programming*, February, p. 20–28.

Licensing & the µC/OS-II Web Site

µC/OS-II source and object code can be freely distributed (to students) by accredited colleges and universities without requiring a license, as long as there is no commercial application involved. In other words, no licensing is required if µC/OS-II is used for educational use.

You must obtain an Object Code Distribution License to embed µC/OS-II in a commercial product. This is a license to put µC/OS-II in a product that is sold with the intent to make a profit. There will be a license fee for such situations, and you need to contact me (see below) for pricing.

You must obtain a Source Code Distribution License to distribute µC/OS-II source code. Again, there is a fee for such a license, and you need to contact me for pricing.

You can contact me at:

`Jean.Labrosse@uCOS-II.com`

or

Jean J. Labrosse
9540 NW 9th Court
Plantation, FL 33324
U.S.A.

1-954-472-5094 (Phone)
1-954-472-7779 (Fax)

F

The μC/OS-II Web site (www.uCOS-II.com) contains

- news on μC/OS and μC/OS-II,
- bug fixes,
- availability of ports,
- answers to frequently asked questions (FAQs),
- application notes,
- information about embedded and real-time books,
- information about upcoming classes,
- links to other Web sites, and more.

Index

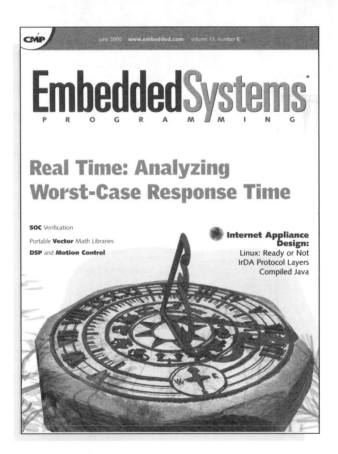

RD2736   **$49.95**

Math Toolkit for Real-Time Programming

by Jack W. Crenshaw

Develop a solid understanding of the math behind common functions — and learn how to make your programs run faster and more efficiently! You get a solid course in applied math from the renowned columnist of *Embedded Systems Programming Magazine* — and a versatile set of algorithms to use in your own projects. CD-ROM included, 466pp, ISBN 1-929629-09-5

Microcontroller Projects with Basic Stamps

by Al Williams

Cut your time to market by prototyping microcontrollers with basic stamps! — This book has it all; from fundamental design principles, to the more advanced analog I/O, serial communications, and LCDs. Includes a Basic Stamp emulator and a PIC programmer based on the Basic Stamp. CD-ROM included, 432pp, ISBN 0-87930-587-8

RD3246   **$44.95**

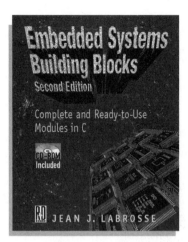

What's on the Disk?

The companion diskette for μC/OS-II, The Real-Time Kernel, contains V2.00 of the source code which matches the contents and explanations of the book. V2.00 was compiled with, and assumes, the Borland C++ compiler V3.1.

As a bonus, the floppy also contains V2.04 which assumes the Borland C++ compiler V4.51 and is provided with 'makefiles.' To install V2.04, simply execute uCOSV204.EXE from the floppy and follow the directions from this self-extracting executable.

You can use a Microsoft C/C++ compiler to compile μC/OS-II but you will most likely need to adjust the constant added to the SP in the function OSIntCtxSw(). You may also refer to FAQ #6 on www.Micrium.com/faqs.htm#FAQ-06 for an alternate method.

- There are a large number of ports available for μC/OS-II (μC/OS-II is actually easier to port than μC/OS!). Ports are posted on www.Micrium.com as they become available.

For up-to-date information about μC/OS-II including new versions, bug-fixes, application notes and much more, visit the official μC/OS-II web site at www.Micrium.com

---

Seelling & typo's
196
145